2·50

D1598195

THE MARXIST PHILOSOPHY OF ERNST BLOCH

THE MARXIST PHILOSOPHY OF ERNST BLOCH

Wayne Hudson

St. Martin's Press   New York

ISBN 0-312-51860-9

Library of Congress Cataloging in Publication Data

Hudson, Wayne.
  The Marxist philosophy of Ernst Bloch.

  Bibliography: p.
  Includes index.
  1. Bloch, Ernst, 1885-1977. I. Title.
B3209.B78H82   1982   193   80-20438
ISBN 0-312-51860-9

For Da

Contents

Acknowledgements

First and foremost, I wish to thank the late Ernst Bloch, who granted me two lengthy interviews and approved the plan of the book, and his widow Karola Bloch, who read and criticised the manuscript and made many helpful suggestions. I also wish to thank Leszek Kołakowski, Martin Jay, Steven Lukes, David McLellan, Burghart Schmidt, Herminio Martins, Gillian Rose, Hiram Caton and Catherine Hudson, who read the manuscript at various stages and were unsparing with encouragement and criticisms. My thanks are also due to the Council of Griffith University, Brisbane, Australia, who gave me leave and financial assistance to work in German and Hungarian archives, and to the Governing Body of Linacre College, Oxford, who provided me with a fellowship and ideal working conditions. My special thanks to Eva Wagner of Linacre College, who tirelessly guided me through the darker waters of Bloch's texts, and to John Raffan.

I am also grateful to Suhrkamp Verlag for permission to quote from Ernst Bloch's *Das Prinzip Hoffnung.*

1 *Incipit vita nova*

I am. But I do not possess myself.
That is why we are only beginning
to become.

Traces

Ernst Bloch: political philosopher of the irrational, hermetic
Marxist, utopian, encyclopaedist, process philosopher of our
immanence in an unfinished world; a densely timed man who
cannot be sifted quickly. This study attempts to introduce
Bloch at a time when his thought is little known in the English
speaking world and when there is no satisfactory account of his
Marxism as a whole in any language. Hitherto, Bloch has often
suffered at the hands of his interpreters. In Eastern Europe and
the Soviet Union he has been labelled 'an idealist', 'a religious
mystic', 'a pantheist', while in the West a large and rapidly
growing literature has only recently shown signs of emergence
from misrepresentation and caricature.[1] Even thoughtful readers
have concluded that Bloch is (1) a notoriously unsystematic
poetic thinker, best understood through his literary works; (2) a
Marxist philosopher of man, who restores an anthropological,
voluntaristic perspective to Marxism; (3) a Marxist philosopher of
hope, of utopia, of the future; (4) a Marxist mystic; (5) a Marxist Messianist, Thomas Münzer *redivivus*: an atheist theologian
who unites the moral fervour of an Old Testament prophet
with the utopian eschatology of chiliasm; (6) a Marxist Schelling, an anachronistic neo-Romantic who combines a form of
identity metaphysics with a materialist world soul.[2] These
characterisations are not entirely mistaken, but they fail to do
justice to Bloch's achievement or to the significance of his work
in the context of Marxism.

In fairness, it must be said that almost any attempt to interpret
Bloch encounters formidable difficulties. Bloch is a literary
original, and his style is justly famous for its sublime passages,
its gnomic utterances, its luminous aphorisms set amidst pages
of Expressionist prose. 'Great Bloch music' (Adorno),[3] however,

does not make for easy reading or admit of univocal exegesis, especially since Bloch expresses his meaning in a wealth of metaphors, which remain ambiguous and esoteric, and employs a technique of recursive modernism, whereby well known quotations, cultural allusions and philosophical terminology are used with transformed (*umfunktioniert*) meanings. This technique poses special problems for the English reader, for whom neither the reference back nor the transformation may be immediately apparent. Again, Bloch uses cabbalistical and non-discursive techniques to refer indirectly (*Umweg*) to levels of experience under-represented or repressed by positivist epistemology. Like Benjamin, he regards such literary techniques as a form of materialist cognition, and his indirect communication, allegory, symbolism and 'colourful speech' are designed to reveal traces of world contents not given in the abstract appearance of capitalist society. Riddles, ciphers, magic sayings, little narratives and literary forms, however, do not yield propositions which can be readily translated into formal terms.

Similarly, the mixed form of Bloch's discourse, with its quasi-musical techniques of counterpoint and coda, makes it difficult to isolate ideas and phrases without distortion, or to convey the holistic aspects of themes which in context have a place in a symphonic arrangement. Moreover, Bloch's books are constructed on unusual principles. Themes are announced and reappear in open textures which resemble loosely grouped essays; books begin with Expressionist sketches and develop according to apocalyptical principles. By the end of a volume Bloch's argument has emerged, but indirectly, and with more emotional colouring than in almost any other modern German writer. Bloch's books are not only intrinsically dramatic; they are also unfinished by design, and the unity of a volume is often rhetorical or maieutic, with the reader left to supply the missing unities with arguments which could fulfil the foreboding of significance conjured up by the title and the style. Then there is the problem of length and range. Bloch has written over 10,000 pages of sparsely paragraphed, at times almost untranslatable German, dealing with an astonishing range of subjects: from quantum physics, music, jurisprudence, psychology, logic and art criticism to political developments, advertising, fashion, industrial design, occultism and the women's movement. No reader can be equally proficient in all these areas, and it is not always easy to appreciate the subtler implications of Bloch's arguments, especially since he assumes an unreasonable amount of background knowledge. Finally there is the problem of Bloch's pattern of publication. Bloch did not publish his books as they were conceived, nor does he explain in them the whole of his thought on a subject, or even the real meaning of fundamental terms. His books in isolation are tips of icebergs, which assume a vast network of philosophical concepts not adequately explained in their texts. Many of Bloch's most important ideas were formulated between 1902 and 1918. Bloch, however, never provides a clear guide to his early thought, which remains behind his texts as a key which is held back. In his works, the ideas stemming from his early period appear in overpacked words and phrases, explained, if at all, only in scattered passages far from the primary discussions, which without them tend to be misleading. As a result, Bloch's thought cannot be grasped selectively or by reading only one or two books. A single constellation of concerns and even phrases informs his works, no one of which provides a satisfactory guide to his thought as a whole.

The difficulty of Bloch is not extrinsic, but part of the phenomenon to be explained. Bloch's work is non-contemporaneous, and the history of the reception of his interventions is a history of impact delayed, not unsuitable to the kind of thinking involved. His books have been deliberately unprecedented, over-full of new and dialectically aimed ideas, which only slowly emerge from esoteric opacity as contemporary thought develops towards their reception. There is also something not wholly conscious about the thinking in Bloch's books, as if he thought beneath the level of readily socialisable intelligibility, and then attempted to convey his insights to a readership increasingly encapsulated in articulated meanings. Bloch intends a critique of habits of thought which lack the 'long breath' necessary for philosophy which goes beyond the self guaranteed; his choice of half light as light enough is grounded in an interpretation of the obstacles to philosophical consciousness in his time. As a result, like Heidegger, he is open to dismissal and critique at the very point where his work may be important.

These difficulties mean that it is not possible to offer an interpretation of Bloch's thought which is free from ambiguity, or which will not be subject to correction as more specialised studies appear. The aim of this study is therefore both an ambitious and a limited one. It is to introduce Bloch in a way which throws light on his highly esoteric texts and draws attention to the significance of his thought in the context of Marxism. It is limited in the sense that compared with the number of technical issues involved, it is only a beginning. The strategy of the study is both historical and analytical. Chapter 1 provides an account of Bloch's life and writings and draws attention to the function of Bloch's difficult operator 'not yet'. Chapter 2 introduces some of the main themes of Bloch's early utopian philosophy and outlines his development as a Marxist, his rehabilitation of utopia as a critique of the Marxist tradition, and some of the main features of his controversial interpretation of Marx. The discussion then proceeds, at a more advanced level, to an analysis of Bloch's 'Open System' or Marxist metaphysics in chapters 3 and 4. This makes it possible to consider Bloch's developments of Marxism in chapter 5. Chapter 6 provides an assessment of Bloch's work as a whole.

BLOCH'S LIFE AND WRITINGS

Bloch's life illustrates the complex relationship between the future and the past which is central to all his work. Bloch was born in 1885 in Ludwigshafen, an industrial city on the Rhine, the son of a Bavarian railway official. Although his family were assimilated Jews, he received some religious training and celebrated his *Bar Mizvah*.[4] There is no evidence that his homelife was in anyway intellectual. Nonetheless, Bloch was an intellectual prodigy. By the age of thirteen he was an atheist and set out his views about the meaning of life in a manuscript entitled *The World-All in the Light of Atheism (Das Weltall im Lichte des Atheismus)*. There was no immaterial essence; matter was the mother of all things; the world was a machine.[5] This early disillusionment was soon transformed into a search for enchantment. Like other young Germans of the *fin de siècle* period, Bloch revolted against the nihilism, philistinism and materialism of industrial civilisation. He was influenced by the general turn against intellectualism and in another early manuscript he called for a renaissance of 'sensuousness'.[6] In 1902–3 Bloch corresponded while still at school with Theodor Lipps, Wilhelm Wundt, Eduard von Hartmann, Wilhelm Windelband and Ernst Mach.[7]

His main preoccupations were already clear: philosophy, music, psychology, physics. Moreover, he was already immersed in two authors who were to influence profoundly his whole development: Hegel and Karl May, the writer of popular adventure stories. At the age of seventeen, he wrote another early manuscript entitled *On Force and Its Essence (Über die Kraft und ihr Wesen)*, in which many of the themes of his later philosophy were present: the essence of the world was an energetic driving to higher forms in an attempt to find the secret of life; the thing in itself was the objective imagination (*Phantasie*).[8] The fact that Bloch was trying to formulate a new philosophical outlook while he was still an adolescent means that his philosophical sympathies were shaped, at least in part, in an intellectual climate far removed from the technological world of the later twentieth century.

Bloch's subsequent development was influenced by the double existence which he led as a boy: in the workers' city of Ludwigshafen, where from an early age he was in contact with the industrial proletariat and the ugliest features of capitalism, and in Mannheim, a cultural treasure house on the other side of the Rhine, with its theatre, concerts, castle and library. In the library of Mannheim castle, Bloch had access to the mine of classical German philosophy and literature, and he immersed himself not only in Hegel and his school, but in the works of Kant, Fichte, and, above all, Schelling, whose *Philosophy of Mythology and Revelation* made a particular impression on him.[9] As a result, he confronted his century as a leftist, familiar from his youth with the writings of Marx, Engels, Bebel and Rosa Luxemburg,[10] more in love with the world of classical German philosophy and literature than with the world of industrial civilisation. When he entered the German university system, Bloch already 'a philosopher in his own house', who believed that the thinkers from whom he could learn most were long since dead.

The first phase of Bloch's life (until 1918) can be seen as a period of formation, in which he passed through various phases (including an anti-metaphysical psychological phase)[11] and attempted to combine a number of different ideas in a new utopian philosophy. Bloch began his university studies with Theodor Lipps at Munich in 1905. Lipps was the leading exponent of empathy psychology, and through him Bloch was introduced to a neo-Romantic phenomenology and a psychology based on self observation.[12] Through Lipps, Bloch came into contact with Scheler and Husserl. In 1907 Bloch studied philosophy, physics and music at Würzburg, where he worked for six semesters with Oswald Külpe. Külpe was one of the leading experimental psychologists and epistemologists of his generation, and Bloch was influenced by his critical realism. In Würzburg, Bloch became interested through a Zionist friend in the Cabbala and in Jewish mysticism.[13] The fundamental breakthrough came when at the age of 22 he wrote a manuscript entitled *On the Category Not-Yet (Über die Kategorie Noch-Nicht)*.[14] Henceforth, Bloch had one fundamental idea important enough to set him apart from other thinkers, which he developed for the rest of his life: the idea that man possessed an anticipatory consciousness which gave him not-yet-conscious knowledge of future possibilities. Bloch wrote his doctoral dissertation under Külpe on the neo-Kantian philosopher, Heinrich Rickert. In it he attacked Rickert's dualistic oscillation between positivism and apriorism, and tried to show how a critique of neo-Kantianism could lead to a new utopian philosophy.[15]

From 1908–11 Bloch studied in Berlin with the philosopher and sociologist, Georg Simmel, who admitted him to his private colloquium and took him on a holiday to Italy. Bloch rejected Simmel's formalism and lack of system; but he was influenced by his doctrine of perspective with its stress on the invisibility of the immediate, by his emphasis on 'the lived moment', by his project of a universal hermeneutics of soul, and by his doctrine of 'perhaps'.[16] Bloch was critical of *Lebensphilosophie,* but he shared Simmel's polymath interests and his concern that philosophy should involve itself with real life. In Berlin Bloch also met the young Hungarian philosopher Georg Lukács. It was to be a crucial friendship. For a time Bloch had a decisive influence on his new friend. It was Bloch who convinced Lukács that classical German philosophy was still possible, and in 1912 he visited Lukács in Florence and persuaded him to come to Heidelberg.[17] In 1913–14 Lukács and Bloch were often in contact daily, and later they kept in touch by a stream of postcards and letters, and by means of weekend meetings.[18] In Heidelberg the two friends moved in a pacifist circle which included Jaspers and Radbruch, and in the circle of Max Weber. Bloch, however, remained apart from academic orthodoxy, and Weber, who disliked his prophetic manner, distanced himself from him as a syncretist and a mystic.[19] In 1913 Bloch married his first wife, Else von Stritzky, a wealthy sculptress from Riga. She was deeply religious and influenced him towards a positive evaluation of Christianity.[20] From 1914-17 they lived in Grünwald in the Isar valley, where Bloch began work on his first book *Spirit of Utopia (Geist der Utopie)*.

Bloch left Germany in 1917 and joined the German opposition in Switzerland. He was already a socialist, steeped in Marx, and a sharp critic of German militarism, and in Switzerland he became a friend of Hugo Ball and Emmy Hennings. Bloch may have been influenced by Ball's religious anarchism, while Ball's *Zur Kritik der deutschen Intelligenz* (1919) contained material on Franz von Baader and Thomas Münzer, as well as a reassertion of Weitling's religious socialism. Surrounded by painters, poets, and alienated intellectuals full of Messianic hopes, Bloch completed *Spirit of Utopia* and wrote an essay on political programmes and utopias in Switzerland for the *Archiv für Sozialwissenschaft*, which was then edited by Max Weber.

Spirit of Utopia appeared in Munich in 1918. It was Bloch's first attempt at a utopian fusion and combined Expressionist culture criticism directed against the cold external world of capitalism, with a philosophical renewal of utopianism and revolutionary Messianism. *Spirit of Utopia*, however, was not only an Expressionist outburst. As the influential Jewish intellectual Margarete Susman recognised, it also contained the elements of a new German metaphysics.[21] Nonetheless, it did not provide an easy access to Bloch's philosophy, on which he had already been working for over ten years, especially since Bloch's recursive modernism made it possible to mistake his quotations from Gnostic, Biblical, Romantic and other sources for pastiche. Nor was the book a favourable omen for his later orthodoxy as a Marxist. In 1918 Bloch appeared to be a neo-Marxist syncretist who proposed to combine the sobriety of Marx's economics with 'political mysticism'; both his call for a new 'Alexander relation' to 'oriental light', and his identification of the Bolsheviks with the rule of 'Christ as Caesar' seemed closer to Communist mysticism than to Marxism.[22]

In the second phase of his life (1919-33), Bloch developed into a major political and cultural essayist, and a hard-line, if unorthodox, Marxist. In 1919 he returned to Berlin, and then to Munich, where he moved in Expressionist circles. He had already written a major work on philosophical logic (later lost in the Nazi period), and his views were becoming more systematic. In 1921 he published *Thomas Münzer as Theologian of Revolution (Thomas Münzer als Theologe der Revolution)*, a brilliant study of Münzer's theology from a half Communist, half chiliastic point of view. Bloch himself later described it as a work of 'revolutionary romanticism' and as a coda to *Spirit of Utopia*.[23] *Thomas Münzer* showed that Bloch's unorthodox sympathies could lead to original orientations in Marxism, in this case a sharp break with the over-simplifications of Engels and Kautsky, and an anticipation of a possible Marxist inheritance of the political theology and subject-laden Christianity of the heretical sects. Shortly afterwards Bloch's first wife died, and in 1922 he married Linda Oppenheimer, a painter from Frankfurt. It was not a lasting relationship and Bloch felt the loss of his first wife deeply. In 1923 a second, heavily rewritten edition of *Spirit of Utopia* appeared, giving a more systematic introduction to Bloch's utopian philosophy, including his theory of the not-yet-conscious. Bloch was now close to a fully fledged Marxism, and an important review of Lukács'*History and Class Consciousness* (1923) suggests that he was attempting a systematic fusion of his utopian philosophy with Marxism.[24] Characteristically, Bloch delayed publication of essential aspects of this fusion for many decades.

In the 1920s Bloch wrote political and cultural essays in which he criticised the abstraction of life under late capitalism, while attacking the Weimar Republic and calling for a new German orientation to the East. He extended the 'essayistic thinking' of *Spirit of Utopia* and made the essay the vehicle for a new kind of philosophical commentary, in which politics, metaphysics and aesthetics were fused in an exploitation of the unfinished nature of the form. A collection of his early critical essays, *Through the Desert (Durch die Wüste)*, appeared in 1923. In 1924, 1925 and 1926 Bloch travelled outside Germany, and lived at Positano in Italy, and in Paris and Sanary in France, before returning to Berlin. During these years Bloch was friendly with Benjamin, Kracauer, and Adorno, and their interaction generated examples of common stylistic devices and language, which took on a different meaning in the hands of each author. With Benjamin, Bloch achieved a symbiosis which can only be compared with his early friendship with Lukács. Bloch first met

Benjamin in Switzerland in 1919 and their friendship lasted 20 years. Benjamin recognised Bloch's genius and wrote a review of *Spirit of Utopia*. Although he reacted unfavourably to *Thomas Münzer,* he was one of the first to grasp the importance of Bloch's review of *History and Class Consciousness.* [25] Bloch stayed in the same hotel in Paris with Benjamin in 1926 while Benjamin was working on his book on Baudelaire, and despite differences of temperament, a remarkable inter-change developed out of their endless discussion and conversations.[26] Like Bloch, Benjamin was fascinated by Messianism, eschatology and the Cabbala, and attempted to rethink religious, utopian and eschatological themes in a Marxist context; while Bloch shared Benjamin's sensitivity for detail, for little things passed over by a concentration on great events, and found him a welcome counter to Lukács in this respect. Bloch took part in some of Benjamin's experiments with hashish, and in 1924 they went on a holiday together to Capri, where they discussed literary questions with Lukács.[27] This meeting made it clear to Bloch that it was Benjamin rather than Lukács who understood the need for a Marxist appropriation of fantasy. Subsequently, Bloch wrote a perceptive review of Benjamin's *One-Way Street,*[28] while Benjamin ranked Bloch with Kafka and Brecht: as the writer who perfected the German essay.[29]

Bloch's relationship with Kracauer was more testy. It began with a sharp polemic which Bloch launched against Kracauer's review of his Münzer book in *Through the Desert* (1923). Bloch complained that Kracauer had failed to understand his work and had wrongly compared him with Martin Buber.[30] Then in June 1925 they met in Paris and became friends. Bloch was amazed by the quality of Kracauer's journalism and admired his contributions to the delineation of social and cultural change.[31] Later in *Heritage of this Time* he reviewed his work on the emergence of a class of office employees.[32] Bloch maintained a correspondence with Kracauer and attempted to influence his Marxism. He defended Lukács against Kracauer's charges that he had fallen behind Marx into idealism and concealed Marx's scientific concepts in Hegelianism.[33] Later, he attacked Kracauer for a critical review of Brecht and accused him of losing his militancy. There were no classless intellectuals, Bloch insisted.[34] Despite considerable contention their friendship survived, and Kracauer was among the first to emphasise the importance of Bloch's attempt to develop a Marxist philosophy of time.³⁵ Bloch's relationship with Adorno was also stormy. As a young man Adorno was impressed by *Spirit of Utopia* and came to see Bloch in Berlin.³⁶ For some years they were good friends. Bloch contributed essays on music to the Viennese *avant-garde* journal *Anbruch* and praised Adorno's work on contemporary musical trends. Later their relations became strained, especially in America, but Adorno did not deny his debt to Bloch and in their last years there was a certain *rapprochement* even in their views.³⁷ Like Lukács, Adorno acknowledged Bloch's greatness and could never entirely escape from the magic of Bloch's style, even when he suspected that Bloch used it to advance an out-of-date identity metaphysics.

In Berlin Bloch wrote for leading magazines and newspapers such as *Die Weltbühne* and the *Vossische Zeitung,* and some of his stories appeared in the *Berliner Tageblatt.* He was close to Berlin Dada and artistic circles generally, and was friendly with Otto Klemperer, Hanns Eisler, and Kurt Weill as well as Bertolt Brecht. Bloch first met Brecht in Berlin in 1921 and their friendship, based on a common struggle against dogmatism in Marxist aesthetics, continued until Brecht's death. Bloch championed Brecht against his vulgar Marxist detractors and wrote perceptive early essays interpreting Brecht's *Threepenny Opera* and *Mahagonny.*³⁸ Moreover, Bloch's enthusiasm and critical praise extended to all of Brecht's phases, despite marked differences between them on theoretical questions. Nonetheless, it was Klemperer rather than Brecht who appreciated Bloch's greatness as a philosopher concerned to uncover the ontological significance of music.³⁹

In 1930 Bloch published a major literary work, *Traces (Spuren),* in which he offered a new kind of fabulation literature in the spirit of Hebel's *Schatzkästlein,* based on a hermeneutic of strange experiences, little fables, legends and details from everyday life. Originally planned around 1917, *Traces* provided access to Bloch the *raconteur* and lover of Hassidic stories. Like Adorno's *Minima Moralia* and Benjamin's *One-Way Street,* it reflected a belief that literary indirection could break through a world of reified relationships. Despite the Romantic terminology, the theosophical allegory and the theme of a 'world secret' which left 'traces' everywhere, Bloch managed to evoke a world full of not-yet-conscious meanings, and to explore the fantasies through which men relate to life in a way which grounded the metaphysical in ordinary life. By the early 1930s Bloch was emerging as the leading Marxist defender of modernism and the *avant-garde*, and the parallels between his philosophical modernism and the literary, artistic and musical varieties attracted attention.

In the third phase of his life, the exile years (1933–49), Bloch was a leading anti-fascist writer and critic of the Nazis, working on vastly ambitious but mostly unpublished manuscripts. In 1933 Bloch left Germany for Zürich to avoid arrest, and in 1934 he married his third wife, Karola Piotrkowska, a Polish architect from Łodz, who was to be his loyal co-worker and unfailing support until his death. In Zürich in 1935 Bloch published *Heritage of this Time (Erbschaft dieser Zeit),* an outstanding work of social and cultural analysis, in which he reviewed the 'Golden Twenties' with bitter irony and outlined an original analysis of the nature of fascism. Once again his range was enormous and, as Hermann Hesse noted in a highly favourable review, he provided a critique which ranged over the whole of capitalist culture.[40] In *Heritage of this Time* Bloch dealt with new developments in poetry, drama, art, film, architecture, philosophy, music, popular entertainment and physics as well as politics.

Bloch was now an important, if independent, Marxist philosopher, fully committed to the proletariat and to dialectical materialism. His philosophical and cultural sophistication, however, combined with the esoteric presentation of his ideas, distanced him from Marxist orthodoxy.[41] Bloch attacked the orthodox Marxists for taking over the abstraction, nihilism and positivism of late capitalism, and argued for a different theory of the nature of bourgeois decadence, and for a more dialectical conception of the Marxist inheritance of great culture. His defence of modernism and of authors such as Joyce and Brecht, together with his refutation of Lukács' attacks on Expressionism, brought him into conflict not only with Lukács, but with Stalinist literary henchmen such as Kurella and Becher.[42] Likewise, his stress on the need for imagination and ideals in Marxism, and his attempt to widen historical materialism to include a theory of the dialectics of non-contemporaneity (*Ungleichzeitigkeit*), were subversive and the orthodox Marxists denounced him as a mystical irrationalist, who tried to equate Marxism with 'subjective idealism' and backward-looking 'conservative revolution'.

The issue was not straightforward. Bloch was influenced by the widespread revolt against *Zivilisation* and capitalism among German youth before 1918. He shared the general hostility to positivism, abstract rationalism, and egoistic materialism; the enthusiasm for Eckhart, Boehme, Dostoevsky and Nietzsche; the demand for absolute values; the hatred of *Technik*; the Volkish cult of landscapes and little towns; the cult of neo-Romantic organicism; as well as the widespread antipathy to Western liberalism. Both his anti-capitalism and his cult of 'the mystical East', in which the Bolsheviks were seen as the successors to Dostoevsky, were shared by conservative revolutionary ideologists such as Möller van den Bruck. Again, some conservative revolutionaries believed in utopian socialism and a modern realisation of Joachim of Flora's third kingdom (*Reich*); and the central European political mysticism which flourished both before 1918 and after 1930 also influenced the basically right-wing intellectuals known as the National Bolsheviks, who were sometimes linked with the KPD.[43] Bloch's position, however, was more complex than these parallels suggest, and the charges against him were partly the result of his delay in publishing his own system, and of his tendency to use language which, in light of his system, bore a highly qualified sense.

In practice Bloch stood apart from conservative revolutionary thought, while seeking critically to inherit its insights. As a Jew, he was isolated from its more objectionable Volkish and later racist aspects, and as a rationalist he opposed its irrationalist dimensions. Again, Bloch always recognised the need for a genuine break with the past. For Bloch, 'inheritance' meant taking over and using with a transformed functionality (*Umfunktionierung*), not revival or imitation. As he stressed in his essay on Thomas Mann's political manifesto, it was necessary to be first revolutionary, and only then to think of inheriting the past in a way which activated its good contents.[44] Moreover, although Bloch accepted parts of the conservative revolutionaries' critique of capitalism, he equated socialism with democracy and with the abolition of the state, not with the corporate state favoured by many conservative revolutionaries or with utopian Caesarism.[45]

Nor, however, was Bloch an orthodox Communist. He did not join the KPD and he implied that the party's barren objectivism and failure to provide alternative ideals was partly responsible for the rise of Hitler. In the 1930s he criticised cold 'Roman' Communism and its tragic separation of 'bread' and 'violin', and claimed that the Communists were mechanical materialists, followers of Büchner and Moleschott rather than Marx or Engels.[46] Similarly, he drew a sharp distinction between the Bolshevik revolution, which had occurred in the primitive conditions of Russia (which he never visited), and the German revolution which would set classical German philosophy and culture 'on their feet'. Bloch's theoretical position was an implicit critique of orthodox Marxism and its inadequate theory and propaganda, to which he opposed the 'warm stream' in Marxism, friendly to poetry, ideals and imagination (*Phantasie*), and a conception of Marxism as the true salvation of morality and culture.[47] Politically, however, he leant towards Stalinism as the most realistic commitment in a difficult time. In his essays he continued to denounce the Nazi corruption of German culture and to support the anti-fascist front.[48] His interpretation of the tendencies of capitalism alienated him from the West and he reduced contemporary politics to a stark option: Hitler or Stalin? The view from Vienna (1934), Paris (1935) and Prague (1936-38) only confirmed him in his hatred of capitalism and, as in 1918, he placed his hope in 'oriental light'. He continued to be loyal to Stalin even during the Moscow trials and attacked those who wavered as 'renegades'.[49]

From 1938-49 Bloch lived in exile in the United States, in New York City (1938-40), Marlborough, New Hampshire (1940-1), and Cambridge, Massachusetts (1942-9). At first his attitude to American society was friendly, but he remained an outsider speaking little English and deeply concerned with German affairs. Apart from publishing essays in *Freies Deutschland,* an anti-fascist journal published in Mexico, he worked on a series of important manuscripts. Part of his book on hope appeared in New York in 1946, and in East Berlin in 1947, under the title *Freedom and Order, A Digest of Social Utopias (Freiheit und Ordnung, Abriss der Sozialutopien),* and his controversial study of Hegel was first published in Spanish in Mexico and Buenos Aires in 1949 under the title *Il pensamiento de Hegel.* In America Bloch kept in touch with other emigré intellectuals, such as Bertolt Brecht, Kurt Weill, Hanns Eisler, George Grosz, Thomas Mann, Paul Tillich and Hermann Broch. He remained firmly oriented to the East, and to a historiosophical programme which required a break with the moral compromises of class society. With Brecht, he was associated with the Comintern-sponsored National Committee for a Free Germany, and when peace came he accepted a chair as Ordinarius for Philosophy at Leipzig. Bloch's decision to return to East Germany was entirely consistent with the pattern of his political career. Ever since 1918 he had hoped for a new Germany, based on an orientation to 'oriental light', in which it might be possible to realise the inheritance of classical Germany philosophy and culture in a rectified Marxist form. Whereas West Germany offered only the prospect of a renewal of capitalism, the East offered the hope that humane socialism could be built 'in a new land'.[50]

Bloch's return to the East in 1949 marked the beginning of the fourth phase of his career: the phase in which he was a semi-institutionalised Marxist philosopher in a 'socialist' country. Bloch was already in his mid-60s when he arried in Leipzig to take up his first academic appointment. His early years in the DDR were full of hope. He filled the chair at Leipzig with distinction, and used his lectures to initiate a renaissance of philosophical Marxism. He had a group of brilliant students, including Wolfgang Harich, and it seemed possible that he might be able to influence party policy through Kurt Hager, the party's chief ideologist. Moreover, at first he seemed an almost exemplary apologist for the regime, who denounced 'American imperialism' as a new form of fascism, while lauding 'the German Army of Peace' and 'the salvation of culture and morals' becoming possible in the East.[51] If the DDR had its defects, it was 'a new world', firmly set on the only meaningful historical journey: *zu Haus*. Like other members of the old German élite who returned to the East (Hans Mayer, Alfred Kantorowicz), Bloch was allowed a certain latitude as long as he supported 'socialist construction' and lent his name to cold war propaganda. He did not join the party, although his wife Karola was a party member, but he made an attempt to observe 'party discipline'. The German version of Bloch's Hegel study was published in Berlin in 1951, under the title *Subject-Object, Commentaries on Hegel (Subjekt-Objekt, Erläuterungen zu Hegel)*. It challenged the standard Stalinist dismissal of Hegel as a 'reactionary idealist', and was widely attacked.[52] In 1952 Bloch published a monograph on Avicenna, entitled *Avicenna and the Aristotelian Left (Avicenna und die Aristotelische Linke)*, designed to introduce his new

Marxist concept of matter; and a monograph on the seventeenth century German jurist Christian Thomasius, entitled *Christian Thomasius: A German Scholar without Misery (Christian Thomasius: Ein deutscher Gelehrter ohne Misere)*, designed to introduce his Marxist inheritance of natural law. In the same year Bloch became joint editor with Harich of the *Deutsche Zeitschrift für Philosophie*. In 1954 and 1955 the first two volumes of his 1800 page masterpiece *The Principle of Hope (Das Prinzip Hoffnung)*[53] appeared in East Berlin. Bloch was now recognised as an outstanding East German philosopher, and was awarded the National Prize of the DDR and made a member of the German Academy of Sciences.

Nonetheless, there was resistance to Bloch's claim to be a Marxist from the spokesmen for vulgar Marxist orthodoxy led by Rugard Gropp. Bloch's interpretation of Hegel continued to be attacked, and there were criticisms of his attempt to turn the *Deutsche Zeitschrift für Philosophie* into the organ of a philosophical Marxism at odds with vulgar orthodoxy.[54] Again, his outline of a new Marxist philosophy of history, *Differentiations in the Concept of Progress (Differenzierungen im Begriff Fortschritt)* (1955), and his lecture delineating a more voluntaristic and contingent account of the relationship between freedom and determinism aroused opposition. As in the 1930s he was accused of conflating Marxism with idealism and mysticism.

There can be little doubt that Bloch's reassertion of philosophical Marxism was heretical by East German standards. He was ruthless in his attacks on 'narrow gauge' Marxism, and in his rejection of 'objectivism', 'schematicism', and 'mechanical materialism'. Marxism, he insisted, descended from the wide culture of Marx and the polyhistorian Engels, and was not a sectarian proletarian ideology. Similarly, he identified partisanship in cognition with objectivity, and made the proletariat the class whose interest coincided with the truth.[55] He attacked any 'pogrom against artists', and called for Marxist-Christian dialogue. He also characterised Marxism as the philosophy of historical-dialectical materialism, and argued that there could be no genuine theory-praxis without the 'total view' called philosophy.[56] Indeed, he seemed to give philosophy the right to set the goals of praxis, and defined it as the universal science which offered a view of the whole and its tendencies in contrast to the specialised sciences.[57] Inevitably there were widespread suspicions that Bloch was using his base in Leipzig to develop a humanist alternative to the orthodox Stalinism emanating from Berlin. If Bloch's Marxism was too humanistic and universalistic for the orthodox, at least he was loyal. After Khrushchev's exposure of Stalin in 1956, however, Bloch's heresy took on a new character.

In the context of revisionist stirrings in Eastern Europe, Bloch's students, especially Harich, began to equate socialism with democratic humanism, and Bloch came to be seen as the theorist of a possible 'Hungary' in the DDR. Belatedly, Bloch at last recognised the moral horror of Stalinism and the truth of reports which he had dismissed for years as 'capitalist lies'. In response to the Twentieth Congress of the Soviet Communist Party, he argued that the Soviet Union was not the sole model of socialism, and called for different national forms of socialism, for an end to dogmatism, and to dictatorship over the proletariat, and for a return to democratic centralism.[58] In a lecture at Humboldt University in November 1956, he called for a radical 'development' of Marxism, based on a materialist rectification of Hegel's system.[59]

Bloch was now openly calling for both a political and a philosophical transformation of East German socialism, and his views were immediately attacked. In December Ulbricht himself wrote an article in *Neues Deutschland,* and in January 1957 he accused Bloch of trying to promote a Maoist 'Hundred Flowers' in the DDR.[60] A campaign against 'revisionism' in philosophy, politics and economics followed. Harich was sentenced to ten years imprisonment, and Bloch's other students, Zehm, Hertwig, Lorenz and Zwerenz, were either jailed or forced to flee to the West. The *Deutsche Zeitschrift für Philosophie* was placed under Stalinist control, and all references to Bloch and Harich were purged from the index. An order for Bloch's own arrest was issued but then withdrawn. He was forbidden to publish or to associate with his former students, and a conference on his philosophy was held at Leipzig, at which he was denounced as an irrationalist whose mystical *Hoffnungsphilosophie* was closer to pantheism than to Marxism. Articles denouncing his ideas appeared in party journals, and conferences designed to combat 'revisionism' were held on socialist morality, the Marxist theory of the state, and dialectical materialism.[61]

Misrepresented and accused of corrupting the young, Bloch

nonetheless chose to remain to criticise on East German soil. Subsequently, the campaign against him was dropped. In 1959 a small edition of the third volume of *The Principle of Hope* appeared in East Berlin, without the alterations demanded by the SED, and in 1960 his book on Münzer was reissued. Nonetheless, he was increasingly subject to restrictions. In 1961 he was in West Germany when the Berlin Wall began to be built. His disillusionment was now complete and he applied for political asylum.

Bloch's life now entered its fifth and final phase: the period in which he received recognition in the West as an outstanding thinker. Given a guest professorship at Tübingen, the old university town of Hegel, Schelling and Hölderlin, Bloch became a national figure as a philosopher-prophet prepared to speak out with moral fervour on internal and international affairs. As one of the last of the pre-1918 generation, and perhaps the last representative of the speculative side of classical German philosophy, he commanded widespread respect. When aspects of his thought were taken up by Jürgen Moltmann and other German theologians, his reputation reached a world-wide audience. With Heidegger and Bultmann, Bloch was now recognised as one of the most important theological thinkers of the twentieth century. The subsequent 'theologising' of Bloch harmed his reputation in Marxist circles, but it also gave his thought a practical importance in the context of the new Christian Marxist dialogue, especially in Latin America, which previously it had not possessed. During the German student unrest, Bloch emerged as a cult figure like Marcuse in the United States. His long experience, violent anti-capitalism and hostility to the state made him a hero to young radicals such as Rudi Dutschke. He was now bitterly anti-Soviet and a champion of humane socialism in opposition to the 'red Tsarism' of the East.[62] He supported the Prague Spring and defended Israel's right to existence as a state. He was equally critical of 'American imperialism' and the Vietnam War, and called for a renewal of the 'creative socialism' of Lenin and the October Revolution. His commitment to 'socialism with a human face' made him attractive to Czech philosophers and to the Yugoslav Praxis group. In 1968 he took part with Marcuse in a Summer School at Korčula, and in 1969 he received an honorary doctorate from the University of Zagreb. Nonetheless, although he now conceded that Soviet experience showed that there was a lack of emphasis on safeguards, and even a certain lack of enlightenment in Marx, he remained in other respects a hard-line Marxist, who accepted the whole of Marx's economics and a form of dialectical materialism.[63]

Canonised as the 'Magus of Tübingen', Bloch now published many of the manuscripts on which he had been working for decades, in some cases since before 1918. The result was a stream of books providing a key to his attitudes and development over the previous 50 years. Apart from revised editions of *Thomas Münzer as Theologian of Revolution* (1962), *Subject-Object* (1962), *Heritage of this Time* (1962), *Avicenna and the Aristotelian Left* (1963), *Through the Desert* (1964) and *Spirit of Utopia* (1964, 1923 edition), and over a dozen paperbacks (mainly selections or reprints), Bloch now published a Marxist study of natural law, *Natural Right and Human Dignity (Naturrecht und menschliche Würde)* (1961); two introductions to metaphysics, *Fundamental Questions in Philosophy (Philosophische Grundfragen)* (1961), and *Tübingen Introduction to Philosophy (Tübinger Einleitung in die Philosophie)* (1963, 1964); a volume of essays containing his contributions to aesthetics, *Literary Essays (Literarische Aufsätze)* (1965); a major work on Marxism and Christianity, *Atheism in Christianity (Atheismus im Christentum)* (1968); a volume of philosophical essays, including hitherto unpublished material from his early manuscripts, *Philosophical Essays on Objective Imagination (Philosophische Aufsätze zur objektiven Phantasie)* (1969); a volume of political essays, *Political Assessments, The Plague Period, Before the Revolution (Politische Messungen, Pestzeit, Vormärz)* (1970); a seminal work on Marxist materialism, including a Marxist history of philosophical concepts of matter, *The Problem of Materialism (Das Materialismusproblem)* (1972); a new Marxist theory of categories, *Experimentum Mundi* (1975); and a volume of selections from his 3000 page unpublished work on the Marxist inheritance of the history of philosophy, *Leipzig Lectures on the History of Philosophy (Leipziger Vorlesungen zur Geschichte der Philosophie)*, entitled *Between Worlds in the History of Philosophy (Zwischenwelten in der Philosophiegeschichte)* (1977).

Bloch at last began to receive the recognition he deserved. His books were translated into many languages, including Persian, Arabic and Japanese, and in 1975 he was given an honorary doctorate from the Sorbonne. Praised by the German press, he continued working despite his blindness. When he died in Tübingen in August 1977 at the age of 92, he was a world figure, whose passing marked not only the end of a great world of German Jewish hope, but a break with a range and intensity of knowledge which may not be achieved again in our century.[64]

Bloch's life, with its pattern of delayed publication and recognition, illustrates the time paradox which is central to his achievement. All his life Bloch tried to be futuristic, to elaborate ideas and to anticipate developments which it would fall to others to execute in detail. At the same time, he involved himself with the past, especially those aspects of the past which were neglected, or which escaped contemporary notice. As a result, there is a tension in his work between the attempt to be futuristic and the attempt to make the past live again in a new 'corrected' form. Again, by writing so much and so obscurely, Bloch ensured that many of his own ideas would be neglected, despite the fact that it was these ideas which were important for his claim to be futuristic. Throughout his life Bloch remained doubly anachronistic: both non- and over-contemporaneous in his relation to a present in which both the renewal of the neglected past and the future which would make such a renewal possible were 'not yet'.

NOT YET

Bloch belongs to the class of thinkers who employ one central operator in many different contexts, as though it embodied some new and crucial insight. Bloch's central operator is the operator 'not yet' (*noch nicht*). Like Vaihinger's 'as if', Bloch's 'not yet' functions as a radical operator which transforms traditional concepts and ideas when it is applied to them. Bloch's 'not yet', however, is not an operator in the sense of an operator in logic, because he does not use the term 'not yet' in an unambiguous or always identical sense.

Bloch's 'not yet' is complex because he fails to distinguish the different meanings of 'not yet', and the temporal reference relevant to each. 'Not yet' may refer to something not actual now, but it may also apply to a future determination of something that is partially actual now: the child is not yet a man, the dam is not yet full. Again, 'not yet' may mean 'not so far', in which case it refers to the past as well as the present. Then 'not yet' may mean 'still not', implying that something expected or envisaged in the past has failed to eventuate. Here the stress falls on the past non-occurrence, and in some cases this failure to eventuate in the past increases the likelihood of a future realisation. This ambiguity is even stronger in German since *noch nicht* means both 'still not' and 'not yet'. Or 'not yet' may mean not so far, but 'expected in the future'. Here the stress falls on the future even more than the past, and the 'yet' implies an expectation that the event will occur. In addition, among many other uses of 'not yet', there are two more literary uses: the utopian 'not yet', which implies that something is 'conceivable now, but not yet possible'; and the eschatological 'now and not yet', which implies that the end is 'present now in a problematic manner, but still to come in its actual realisation'. Bloch uses all these senses of 'not yet'; hence there is a tension in his thought between 'not yet' in the sense of 'not actual now'; 'not yet' in the sense of 'actual, but not yet having reached a future determination'; 'not yet' in the sense of 'not so far'. 'not yet' in the sense of 'still not'; 'not yet' in the sense of 'not yet, but expected in the future'; 'not yet' in the sense of 'conceivable now, but not yet possible'; and 'not yet' in the sense of 'present now in a problematic manner, but still to come in its actual realisation'.

The fact that Bloch's fundamental operator is syncretic is consistent with his recursive modernism. It also warns against simplistic interpretations. Hitherto, Bloch's 'not yet' has often been interpreted as univocal or as purely rhetorical, with the result that Bloch's positions have been confused with traditional doctrines, which in Bloch are radicalised and given projective meaning.

2 Marxism and Utopia

Marxism therefore is not a non-utopia,
but the genuine, concretely mediated
and processually open one.

Freedom and Order

BLOCH'S EARLY UTOPIAN PHILOSOPHY

Bloch's early utopian philosophy has received little critical attention, although it throws light on the problem of his development
and on the meaning of some of his most difficult concepts. Bloch
tries to present his work as a unified whole; hence, the non-
chronological listing of works in the *Gesamtausgabe* and the replacement of the original texts by revised editions. Nonetheless,
it is important to note that Bloch formulated many of his fundamental ideas either before he became a Marxist or before
Marxism became as central to his thought as it would later become.

Bloch's early utopian philosophy was an *avant-garde* philosophical modernism. In it he attempted to refunction terminology
from philosophical, literary, mythological, mystical and religious
sources in an activist philosophy, inspired by Nietzsche's summons to 'embark' and an imperative of *incipit vita nova*.[1] Under
the cover of wild but often very beautiful language, Bloch made
radical moves designed to re-pose traditional philosophical problems in the context of an unfinished world. If he seemed a philosophical *provocateur* with a surplus of allegedly new ideas, he
also developed a utopian system which anticipated both his own
mature thought and some of the central concerns of European
philosophy for the next half century.

As part of his early utopian philosophy Bloch developed a
philosophical anthropology based on the idea that man was still
'within', an *incognito*, 'not yet'. He was influenced in his doctoral dissertation by Weidenbach's doctrine that the soul was an
enigma or secret, full of latent possibilities;[2] and in *Spirit of*

Utopia he spoke of the 'utopian subject', 'the soul', 'the moral mystical Paracletic I'. The 'am' of 'I am' was still 'under', 'not yet out', and our secret name remained to be discovered.[3] This philosophical anthropology was essentially speculative and not clearly integrated with a social perspective, other than that provided by the degree to which the 'hidden secret man' could not manifest himself in a humanly inadequate world.

Similarly, in the early years of the twentieth century Bloch was at work on a utopian psychology, based on the idea that man possessed an anticipatory consciousness which gave him not-yet-conscious knowledge.[4] The idea that the 'not yet' was partially accessible through the informed futurity of human consciousness meant that psychological manifestations could be interrogated for future content, and provided a new perspective on the hermeneutical indirection of human culture. It also gave Bloch the basis for a refunctioning of Romantic psychology as a positive alternative to Freud. Bloch was not insensitive to Freud's achievements and he wrote a number of very early articles on psychoanalysis and on adult and child psychology.[5] From 1907 onwards however his stress fell on the directedness of consciousness to objects and its intentionality to future possibilities.

Bloch also proposed in his early writings to develop a new utopian epistemology and logic. He attacked the abstract, staticist character of contemporary rationalism and called instead for a wider rationalism, able to take account of particulars and singularities, and to grasp the integral moral experience of the subject.[6] Following Schelling and von Hartmann, Bloch rejected the equation of thought and being and castigated contemporary rationalism for its over-preoccupation with thought and its internal logic, as if the world was given to man in concepts. He argued for a greater representation of the world in philosophy, and emphasised the limits of all human rationalisms.[7] The world was not at hand as something given, finished and solved, which fell neatly into human concepts without a remainder. It was temporal and in process: essentially unfinished, unsolved, objectively problematic. Hence, it could not be ontologised on the basis of appearance or current predicates which had not been thought through to the end. The world at hand was essentially modal, and a true rationalism had to be based on knowledge of what it could become. Appearance was not yet essence, and existence itself stood in the relation of an objective genitive to creative thought.[8]

For Bloch, this assertion of the open, unsolved, unfinished character of the world led to a Messianic conception of human cognition and to an imperative of world completion. The fact that the world was unfinished meant that the problem of ontology needed to be understood as a journey problem,[9] and that human cognition had an active constitutive role to play in determining what the world could become. Bloch saw that such a perspective involved a break with the classical doctrine of identity, and he emphasised the need to rethink traditional epistemological problems in the light of man's not-yet-conscious knowledge.[10] He rejected the reduction of thinking to its most economical forms, 'subjectless empiricism' and the pretence that thinking could be value-free. Instead, he called for a new motoristic epistemology based on the constitutive role of imagination.[11] If the cognition of the subject was causal, then it was important to develop a theory of knowledge which kept close to the deep experiences of the subject. Hence he called for *Eingedenken* or the internalisation and bearing in mind of intensive experiences, and spoke of 'a rationalism of the heart', and of a 'mystical empiricism' of the self encounters, ciphers and symbols of the 'absolute subject'.[12]

Bloch saw, however, that an empiricism of the depth experiences of the subject would be ineffective unless the counterfactual yearning of the subject could be grounded in the possibility structure of the world. He therefore combined a hermeneutical analysis of the apparently 'irrational' experiences of the subject with a utopian realism, based on a revival of elements of scholastic realism[13] and an attempt to turn von Hartmann's Transcendental Realism in a utopian direction. Like von Hartmann, Bloch claimed that the thing in itself was accessible to human consciousness and that men possessed participatory knowledge (*Mitwissenheit*) of the external world.[14] In addition, he developed a critique of Oswald Külpe's Critical Realism, which emphasised that there was no need to regard reality as concluded, and that there was no need to confine the reality reflected in consciousness to the reality at hand.[15] In this way, Bloch aimed at a realism which extended to the 'not yet' (an extension made possible by man's possession of not-yet-consciousness),[16] while admitting the refinements of Transcendental and Critical Realism.

Similarly, Bloch criticised contemporary rationalism's reliance on a 'reflexive', 'fact logic', and called for a 'productive', 'constitutive' logic which would help men to invent the world which was not yet.[17] Under the influence of Brentano (whom he heard lecture at Munich) and Meinong, he extended Brentano's doctrine that all thought acts were directed to objects to cover intentionality towards objects which were 'not yet'. Meinong's *Gegenstandstheorie* provided Bloch with a model for a theory of directedness towards non-existent objects, and with the doctrine that the objects of judgements and suppositions were objectives, not things. Under Meinong's influence, Bloch proposed to develop a new logic of objects, based on research into objects which could become actual and were related to the unfinished objects at hand.[18] The objects at hand, he emphasised, were not fixed and concluded, but qualitative modal forms, which were 'in suspense' and full of immanent reference to their future development.[19] Bloch also proposed to widen Kant's theory of judgement to allow for a productive synthetic judgement which extended to contents which were 'not yet'. Moreover, he already envisaged a transcendence of identity logic,[20] and saw that a utopian epistemology and logic implied the need for a new theory of categories for an unfinished world.[21]

To assist men to shape an unfinished world, Bloch proposed to develop an ethical metaphysics of tasks: of *desiderata* for the world of 'the second truth'. He saw that the Heidelberg neo-Kantians' (1) attempt to apply Kant's ideas to history, (2) treatment of values as non-factuals, and (3) doctrine that history realised goals set by practical reason, could all be pressed into the service of a new utopian philosophy. In this context, he made a detailed study of the work of Heinrich Rickert and of value theory generally, although he attacked Rickert's dualistic oscillation between positivism and apriorism, reliance on an over-mathematical identity logic, and inability to assimilate the utopian demands of history.[22] He also learnt from Windelband's insistence that man was not a natural being and from his emphasis on an emergent teleology of *a priori*s developing in the course of history.[23] Similarly, he studied the works of Hermann Cohen, although he rejected Cohen's mathematical formalism.[24] Again, like Lukács, he was influenced by the Heidelberg neo-Kantian Emil Lask, some of whose lectures he attended, and took up his insistence on the primacy of practical reason in philosophy and logic.[25] It was Hans Vaihinger, however, in his *The Philosophy of As-If* (1911) who provided him with the most radical model for an extension of Kant. Bloch was sympathetic to Vaihinger's Nietzschean activism and to his emphasis on the need for fact-transcendent postulates which had to be accepted 'as if' they were true. He saw that it would be possible to vary Vaihinger's position and to interpret Kant's fact-transcendent postulates as 'not yet'.[26]

Against this neo-Kantian background, Bloch discovered the foundation for a metaphysics of hope in the Kant who admitted in *Dreams of a Spirit-Seer* that all human thinking was biased towards hope in the future.[27] He proposed to overcome Kant's prohibition against metaphysics by uncovering the ethical metaphysics implicit in Kant himself. According to Bloch, Kant provided a possible foundation for a meta-empirical philosophy when he admitted a supersensuous realm of values and insisted on the need for postulates of practical reasons such as God, freedom, immortality and the other world.[28] Kant however confined his postulates of practical reason to purely regulative *a prioris*; he made his realm of values a 'bad infinite' (Hegel) and failed to relate his ethics to the world.[29] In contrast, under the influence of Franz von Baader, Bloch proposed to widen Kant's postulates of practical reason to include existential moral postulates based on the lived experience of the subject, and to take account of the finality which such postulates involved.[30] He proposed to relate these wider postulates of practical reason to the real world (as Kant had not) and to interpret them as tasks.

To make this ethical metaphysics of tasks historically effective, Bloch attempted to combine Kant's openness to new contents with the comprehensiveness and power of Hegel's system. The movement back to Hegel was characteristic of much contemporary neo-Kantianism, and Brunstäd had already argued that Hegel's philosophy of history could serve as the basis for a fulfilment system (*Erfüllungssystem*) based on the postulates of practical reason.[31] Bloch's admiration for Hegel was not uncritical. On the contrary, he criticised Hegel's concluded system, including his panlogism, conceptual realism, excessive objectivism, and inadequate ethics. He also agreed with Kierkegaard that Hegel's system was too abstract, and that his dialectic was too symmetrical and purely logical to apply to the real world.[32] Nonetheless, Bloch held that there was another Hegel: the Hegel who developed a system of fulfilment for the whole world, and provided a model of the world as a subject-object process in which 'subject' became 'substance'.[33] In a bold move, Bloch proposed to combine this Hegel with Kant: to inherit Hegel's model of the process in a new fulfilment system based on the *a prioris* of the utopian subject. Thus, Bloch's early utopian philosophy involved an activist historical programme, according to which the subject needed to cast itself out into the external world and to overcome the objectifications which were inadequate to it, until the within (*Innen*) became the without (*Aussen*) and vice versa, and the whole world became a world of 'soul'.[34]

Bloch's historical activism, however, required an ontological correlate for its utopian excess. In an original fusion of Kierkegaard's emphasis on the need to understand oneself in existence (*sich in Existenz zu verstehen*) and Schelling, Bloch developed an esoteric philosophy of immanence for which the nowhere actualised 'world secret' could be identified with our 'uncovered countenance' (Eckhart).[35] Bloch envisaged a new utopian metaphysics based on the darkness of the moment (which he believed had never received adequate categorial representation in any philosophy, despite the fact that it was the most concrete region of existence which coloured all experience)[36] in his doctoral dissertation; and in his subsequent writings he related the problem of the darkness of the moment to his theory of the not-yet-conscious. Bloch introduced this philosophy of immanence in the 1918 edition of *Spirit of Utopia* in a section entitled 'On the Metaphysics of Inwardness', which he expanded in the 1923 edition and retitled 'On the Metaphysics of Our Darkness'. Following Schelling, Bloch implied that human existence took its character from the fact that we were only self present in the blind spot of the moment, which remained invisible because it was 'too near', 'lived in' (*gelebt*) but not experienced (*erlebt*). We ourselves were the starting point, but we lay in self darkness, and the problem of our self cognition was the world problem itself.[37] In this sense, the problem of the Self (*Selbst*) and We (*Wir*) was the fundamental problem of utopian philosophy.[38] According to Bloch, a philosophy which remained true to our experience of metaphysical wonder (*Staunen*), and to the unconstruable metaphysical question implicit to it, could proceed from the darkness of the lived moment, in which men experienced an anticipatory transcendence of the interval between subject and object. The alpha and omega of our self comprehension was present in the moment, and the symbolic intention to utopia given in the moment provided a foundation for an attempt to elaborate a world adequate to us.[39]

Bloch did not elucidate this immanentist-transcendentalist turn in *Spirit of Utopia*, but he illustrated its hermeneutical foundations. An identity of subject and object pre-appeared in the intensive experiences of the subject, and manifested a symbolic intention to the realisation of such an identity in the world. Over half of *Spirit of Utopia* was devoted to illustrating this thesis from different standpoints. Bloch's utopian hermeneutics was designed to uncover *Evidenz* of utopia or *Ich* content throughout the world. It combined a neo-Romantic phenomenology of fulfilment, an Expressionist emphasis on the presence of *Innen* in the outer world, borrowings from Simmel's hermeneutics of soul and the self observation psychology of Carl Stumpf and Theodor Lipps, with recast phenomenology. Bloch was critical of Husserl's staticism, contemplative idealism, and quasimystical concept of intuition, but he was influenced by his doctrine of *Evidenz* and his theory of intentionality,[40] especially as it had been developed by Max Scheler. Like Scheler, Bloch relied on a phenomenology of material (i.e. contentful) *a priori*s which could be known to belong to 'essence'; and in *Spirit of Utopia* he called for Luciferic in-sight (*Anschauung*) into 'essence', as if a phenomenology of utopian contents could yield knowledge of the 'not yet'.[41] Bloch also borrowed freely from Schopenhauer. He rejected Schopenhauer's blind will, hostile to reason and ethics, but he refunctioned Schopenhauer's thelism in a hermeneutical phenomenology for which the thing in itself could be defined as 'the will to our countenance and finally as the countenance of our will'.[42]

Despite these diverse sources, Bloch's utopian hermeneutics pointed beyond any psychologistic expressivism to the problem of a future correlation of subject and object, to which the 'subjective metaphysical evidence' of 'self encounter' bore witness. Thus, although Bloch devoted a section of *Spirit of Utopia* to an essay on 'The Production of Ornament', the expression of the subject had consequences for the world. Similarly, despite his flirtation with the tone mysticism fashionable in occultist as well as Expressionist circles,[43] Bloch's lengthy exposition of his philosophy of music was not a manifesto for subjectivism. For Bloch, music was a revelation of *Innen*, subject theurgy which contained the 'We' (*Wir*) or 'essence', the content which would be 'the Last' or the 'apocalypse': the futuristic appearing of an intensity which could become a world of the second truth.[44] In this sense, music provided privileged access to the 'world secret' or 'thing in itself'.[45] Moreover, Bloch expounded the 'metaphysical' meaning of the history of art and architecture, the significance of the comic hero and a utopian approach to drama from a related standpoint.[46]

Given the range and syncretic character of these innovations, the question arises whether Bloch really wanted his early utopian philosophy to be understood. Where an analytical philosopher would be bound to demand more detailed argumentation, Bloch relied on brilliant language and rhetorical effect to show a new apprehension of existence in operation, without bothering to secure each step. His aim was to develop a philosophical modernism with a theurgic effect: a modernism directed against the 'occlusion of the subject' under capitalism. In this he succeeded, as contemporary reactions reveal; but his success involved the difficulty that the precise meaning of 'utopian' in his 'utopian philosophy' was not really clear.

In his early utopian philosophy Bloch made syncretism a principle of utopianism which had become philosophical. He did not detail the historical manifestations of utopianism, but he refunctioned them, in a way which combined (1) the need to mobilise utopian images which remained powerful; with (2) the insight that the decision to affirm utopian perspectives when they are still utopian is basic to utopianism as a method. In *Spirit of Utopia* Bloch's emphasis seemed to fall on a subject utopianism for which utopia was to be identified with a world adequate to 'the soul' or the utopian subject. He spoke of the 'archetypal' mystical function of the soul, of the 'canonical', 'moral', 'Paracletic' I, and emphasised that the subject alone provided the yardstick of utopia, not the external world.[47] The soul was the genuine cosmos and contained the elements of a new creation within itself,[48] and the fulfilment of the value theoretical subject was the final criterion of truth in utopian philosophy.[49] In the language of Expressionist utopianism with its dualism between the 'warm' of *Innen* and the 'cold' of *Aussen*, utopia could be equated with a 'paradise of the heart' (Comenius).[50] The central utopian problem was not to imagine an ideal or rational society, but to express *Innen* in the outer world. Similarly, the possibility of utopia depended on a form of voluntarism which proceeded outwards from the subject. An 'internal concrescence' was necessary before the subject cast itself into the external world, but the outer world could only be raised to 'the star of its utopian destiny' by human activity and will.[51] Because everything had to be determined from the 'I', and not from the 'bad empiricism' of the world at hand, the subject had to take a path of constitutive imagination (*Phantasie*) and seek the truth 'where the facts disappeared'.[52]

Bloch also made use, however, of the language and doctrines of other traditions of utopian thought. Like Reinhold Schneider, Benjamin and Tillich, he saw the need to combine utopia and eschatology in order to correct the over-immanence of utopia and the other-worldly estrangement of eschatology.[53] He emphasised the opening up function of eschatological images, and, in a fusion of Jewish apocalyptic, gnosticism, and the cabbalistical eschatology of Franz von Baader, he spoke of 'universal eschatology or self encounter' and of an apocalypse which would be the fulfilment of all revolutionary gnosis.[54] In Bloch's early utopian philosophy subject utopianism, Messianism and eschatology were combined.[55] Thus *Spirit of Utopia* had earlier been called *The Eschatological Man*, and although Bloch was outlining a new utopian philosophy, he also referred to it, possibly under the influence of Hermann Cohen, as a 'System of Theoretical Messianism'.[56]

Similarly, as part of his strategy of reactivating materials with a utopian surplus wherever they were to be found, Bloch made use of the language of Goethe, Jean Paul and Novalis,[57] as well as of terminology and doctrines derived from theosophy, which he interpreted as intentional acts (Husserl). Thus, he spoke of a possible humanisation of nature (*Makanthropos*), and developed an intentional interpretation of the doctrine of metempsychosis, which he argued could serve as the basis for a new cultural ideology.[58] Bloch's knowledge of theosophical and occult doctrines derived from the Zohar and the Cabbala, and from the Austrian occultist Rudolf Steiner, whose republication of the occultist heritage attracted international attention. Bloch met Steiner and he returned many times to the criticism of his ideas.[59]

In the same way, Bloch made use of the fact-transcendent imagery of religion and included in his utopian philosophy a form of 'religious atheism'. Bloch learnt from Nietzsche that 'the death of God' required a new positive value system, not merely the recognition that God did not exist, and that atheism made it necessary to rethink the central categories of philosophy, which were often implicitly theistic.[60] In language influenced by Dostoevsky, he attempted to uncover the utopian meaning of ciphers such as 'Jesus', 'the soul' and 'the Messiah',[61] and envisaged an 'heroic mystical atheism', based on 'a new piety', for which God was 'not yet': not a fact, but an objective (Meinong) to be called into being. In this sense, he spoke of his early utopian philosophy as 'a God-conjuring philosophy' and of 'truth as prayer'.[62]

Finally, Bloch's early utopian philosophy contained a process philosophy dimension which has often been overlooked. Even in his doctoral dissertation Bloch was convinced that it was possible to renovate metaphysics by a treatment of the problem of temporality which related the subject's internal experience of time to a model of the world process, and that the whole process was present in each moment.[63] In other early writings he spoke of the world as an articulation process (*Drehungsprozess, Objektivierungsprozess*), whose 'core' or 'kernel' was 'not yet': as a process with an unidentified 'subject' which drove 'below' in us and in all things.[64] This process philosophy dimension added to the obscurity of Bloch's utopian philosophy as an esoteric system and to the paradox of a cabbalistical philosophy with revolutionary intentions. But it also meant that Bloch came to Marxism as a modernist metaphysician who had already developed technical positions over a wide area.

Despite its obscurity, Bloch's early utopian philosophy is a mine of seminal ideas. It also reveals the extent to which he developed a complex syncretist outlook, including a web of interpenetrating doctrines, before 1923. For the rest of his life Bloch reformulated this outlook in ever more complex terms. This raises the possibility that Bloch fused his early utopian philosophy with Marxism without the radical modification and recasting which such a project would seem to require.

BLOCH'S DEVELOPMENT AS A MARXIST

It is not uncommon in the history of philosophical revisionism for men who were originally attracted by doctrines in tension with Marx's assumptions to allow those doctrines to colour their later Marxism. Bloch began reading Marx and Engels as a boy in Ludwigshafen,[65] but a detour into process philosophy was necessary before he could reconcile Marxism with his own maximalist qualitative perspectives. Even in his youth, however, he was especially interested in Engels' *Anti-Dühring*,[66] and the link between Engels' dialectical materialism and process philosophy was to be crucial for his development.

As a young man, Bloch was a radical democrat and a sharp critic of the philistinism and authoritarianism of Wilhelmine Germany. He analysed Germany's social and economic problems along Marxist lines in terms of the logic of finance capital, the aspirations of the proletariat and the bourgeoisie, and the underlying economic drive behind imperialism and the military industrial complex.[67] When war came, his pacifism was related to the rejection of an 'imperialist' war, and he identified with the anti-Kaiser 'southern German' opposition in Switzerland. By the time he wrote *Spirit of Utopia* Bloch recognised that Marx's achievements were crucial to any further development of socialism. In 1918, however, Bloch was at most a neo-Marxist. He idealised the Bolshevik revolution in the language of Dostoevsky and Communist mysticism, but his fusion of moralism, *Kulturpolitik*, and revolutionary theology, in the tradition of Münzer, Lamennais and Weitling, seemed to make Marxism the means of implementing a meta-political vision derived from other sources. Moreover, his historiosophical programme, based on an alliance of Marx's scientific socialism, classical German philosophy, Jewish Messianism and Bolshevik politics was highly voluntarist.[68] Bloch moved closer to Marx as a result of his work for the *Archiv für Sozialwissenschaft*.[69] In Switzerland he contributed to the *Freie Zeitung* and surveyed the various strands of socialist thought. He was influenced by Gustav Landauer's romantic socialism and by Hugo Ball's social anarchist ideas, but he also increasingly emphasised the movement beyond 'economy' and the state present in Marx himself.[70]

When he returned to Germany Bloch was an active Communist sympathiser. Unlike Ernst Toller, he took no active part in the Bavarian Soviet but he was in touch with Paul Levi and Communist circles. Despite his enthusiasm for Russia, he was already critical of the Marxist bureaucrats who forgot that Marxism remained 'theology' after it became economics.[71] He made no comment on the March uprising of 1921 and remained

Moscow-oriented, despite the mass arrests which followed. Bloch's critical engagement with the Marxist tradition and his acceptance of historical materialism were more evident in *Thomas Münzer as Theologian of Revolution* (1921), in which he interpreted Münzer as a political theologian and anticipated a future Christian-Marxist convergence. Nonetheless, his call for an alliance of revolutionary politics and 'political mysticism', and his stress on the apocalypse as the meta-political, meta-religious principle of all revolution were hardly orthodox.[72] Indeed, his emphasis on an inheritance of 'theology', and on the need for meta-political perspectives, implied that Marxism alone was inadequate, and that it was necessary to take account of the secret transcendental elements in socialism which Marx had overlooked.[73]

It is possible that Bloch was closer to a fully developed Marxist position when he wrote *Spirit of Utopia* (1923), although he himself later emphasised the continuity of the editions and the purely artistic nature of the changes. In the heavily revised second edition (1923), Bloch eliminated much of the looseness and excess of the 1918 version and gave the impression that his views had become more systematic.[74] Even in 1923, however, Bloch was a heretic with scant respect for what passed for Marxist theory in Russia. He spoke in religious anarchist terms of the state as a Satanic institution, and envisaged the classless society in non-collectivist terms: as a liberation of the individual from the state, society and economics.[75] Similarly, he spoke of the emergence of real privacy and of a time for Dostoevsky's 'ultimate questions', when Baal Shem's dream was fulfilled and all the guests were seated at the banquet.[76] As in 1918, in a final section entitled 'Karl Marx, Death and Apocalypse', he assigned Marxism to the 'order of works', and stressed the need to supplement a purely socio-economic Marxism with 'the external cosmic function of utopia'.[77]

Despite his difficult language, Bloch, the pupil of Simmel, Weber and Sorel, was already attempting to go back to the deeper roots of human thought and action in order to understand why the socialist tradition was inadequate, and why the irrational features of modern capitalism were so difficult to displace. Bloch was convinced that the problem of human subjectivity had not been correctly resolved, and that a premature disillusionment had led to a crude realism which left fundamental alienations untouched. He was conscious that the capitalist occlusion of the subject tended to result in a subject conformed to a false reality, who was then unable to rise to the self encounter, will and decision needed for change. He was also conscious that a superficial epistemology had led to a premature rejection of irrealism in general, as if there were no problems about the ontologisation of 'the single sciences', and as if disillusioned thinking could build an adequate human reality without the images and sources of energy which had appeared in history in the great manifestations of supra-empirical optimism. Rightly or not, Bloch was convinced that there could be no way forward without Marx, but that Marxism needed to be supplemented with a meta-factual, utopian perspective.

By 1923, despite his commitment to the 'organising *ratio*' of Marxism,[78] Bloch had formulated a critique of Marxism based on the insight that there was a problem about the historical conditioning of Marx's own thought, the adequacy of his development, and the extent to which the development of socialism had been distorted by the identity of its opponent. Marx confronted capitalism in its own purely economic terms; but in the process, Bloch hinted, the detective of capitalism had become conformed to the criminal. Marx's economic analyses had added a much needed element of sobriety to the socialist movement; but then the man who had expelled every fetish from the economy had gone on to treat the forces of production in a panlogical, pantheistic and mystifying way. He had placed 'externals' over man, despite the fact that people, not things, made history.[79] Marx, Bloch argued, had placed too much emphasis on economic determining factors to the neglect of the secret transcendental elements in socialism, with the result that Marxism was near to being a Critique of Pure Reason for which no Critique of Practical Reason had yet been written.[80] Marx had only aimed his attack at a young and derivative cancer, and not at the age old core of all enslavement: the supremacist world at large. He had not seen a problem in the claim that the self interest of a particular class coincided with the realisation of maximalist ethical goals, including the abolition of all classes.[81] Again, Marx had not been wholly free of automaticism, of the idea (derived from Hegel) of an objective irony in history, whereas history was a difficult journey and there could be no guarantee that the attempt to create a good society would be successful.[82] Moreover, Marx-

ism, as Marx and Engels left it, was one-sided and lacked many
of the elements necessary for the implementation of its project.
Morality and love had not been given their proper place in the
revolutionary struggle; and Engels' conception of the classless
society as a restoration of primitive Communism, fell short of
the constructive cultural and ideal counterpart which was necessary to supplement the social effort.[83] Similarly, the Marxist
concentration on a heaven on earth was inadequate. Instead,
it was necessary to take account of man's primal religious
desire and to formulate a concept adequate to its intention.[84]
There had been too great a progress from utopia to science in
Marxism, Bloch implied. Marx had been right to reject abstract
utopianism, but he had failed to take account of 'the inherent
utopian tendency' in history and in human psychology.[85]

Granted this critique, Bloch proposed to supplement Marxism with the secret transcendental elements in socialism, to
return to the utopian superiority of the love communism of
Weitling, Baader and Tolstoy, to add to the purely economic
analyses of Marxism the soul and the faith which were missing.[86]
He called for a Marxist inheritance of the heretical subject-
laden Christianity of Thomas Münzer and for an alliance of
Marxism and religion in 'a will to the kingdom'.[87]

Bloch's plans to supplement Marxism with voluntarist, ideal,
ethical and religious perspectives had parallels in the thought of
the Austro-Marxists and in the ideas of Russian Legal Marxists
such as Struve and Berdyaev. From 1923 on however, Bloch began to fuse his early utopian philosophy and Marxism in a single
syncretist system, in which his process philosophy interests and
dialectical materialism increasingly converged.

Bloch's development into a fully fledged Marxist philosopher
was accelerated by the publication of Lukács' *History and Class
Consciousness* (1923). Bloch first met Lukács at one of Simmel's
private seminars in Berlin in 1910,[88] at which Simmel asked his
opinion of the young Hungarian philosopher. It was indifferent
rather than favourable, but Bloch got to know Lukács better
later in 1910 when he went to Budapest to visit Emma Ritoók.
Bloch had a profound influence on Lukács' development. Indeed, Lukács wrote later that Bloch influenced him as no other
contemporary:[89]

The experience of meeting Bloch (1910) convinced me that
philosophy in the classical sense was nevertheless possible. I

spent the winter of 1911-12 in Florence under the influence of this experience . . . In the spring of 1912 Bloch came to Florence and persuaded me to go to Heidelberg with him where the environment was favourable to our work.[90]

In Heidelberg, Bloch and Lukács were together 'day and night' discussing the major contemporary questions in philosophy and politics. Lukács was Bloch's 'Professor for Kierkegaard and Dostovesky' and introduced him to the German mystics; while Bloch was Lukács' 'Professor for Hegel' whom Lukács then 'did not know well'.[91] The intense symbiosis which resulted was to have major consequences for both men. Lukács was overwhelmed to meet a modern German who spoke the *Muttersprache* of classical German philosophy, and awed by Bloch's genius for evocative language; while Bloch found an equal who shared his essentially metaphysical rejection of capitalism and yearning for a renewal of totality. For a time at least, there was a measure of agreement between them. Later Bloch claimed that they were in agreement 'from Eckhart to Hegel', that one could continue where the other left off, that it was necessary for them to invent differences in order to maintain a dialectic, and that when they separated and met again some months later, they found that they had developed in the same direction.[92] Clearly there was an exchange of countenance at the level of language and to some extent theme, although, as the example of the German mystics shows, it is by no means obvious who originated material for which the other later became famous.

This exchange of language reflected the fact that they were working on divergent solutions to similar problems and agreed on many of the key variables, though not on their ranking. During these years, both Bloch and Lukács cultivated a conscious esoterism in an attempt to break through the false immediacy of capitalism and speak of contents condemned to silence by the agnosticism of contemporary epistemology. As late as 1914, Lukács was rumoured to be working on a philosophy of Messianism. Like Bloch, he used allegorical theosophy as a way of developing new concepts, and spoke of the soul as the only 'metaphysical' reality.[93] He was also in the habit of using Bloch's turns of phrase to illustrate his meaning, for example, Bloch's 'beautiful metaphor' of the 'eternal *a priori* objectification of the soul'.[94]

Some aspects of the intellectual interchange between Lukács

and Bloch can be documented from Bloch's letters to Lukács, which reveal their common involvement with theosophy, mysticism, theoretical Messianism and the need to inherit the history of philosophy from Aristotle to Hegel.[95] Both men were concerned to develop a utopian apriorism based on the utopian demands of the soul as the source of 'essence'. Lukács' form of subject utopianism can be documented from his correspondence, and from *The Theory of the Novel*, in which (in parallel language to Bloch) he referred to the 'utopian aim of every philosophy', to 'heroic atheism', to the *incognito* of the soul, to the 'concretely immanent utopia of the historical hour', to the way in which in certain artistic forms the pure interiority of the soul became substance.[96] The main point is not that Lukács achieved a fusion of 'right epistemology' and 'left ethics' before Bloch's *Spirit of Utopia*, or that Lukács may have pioneered the Kierkegaardisation of Hegel and the turn to Tolstoy and Dostoevsky, but that even during the height of their symbiosis Bloch and Lukács interpreted the significance of utopia differently. Unlike Bloch, Lukács was inherently pessimistic and emphasised that reality could never be forced up to the level demanded by the *a priori*s of the soul:

> This utopian demand of the soul is directed at something unattainable from the start — at an outside world which might be adequate to a highly differentiated, refined soul that has become an interiority.[97]

Moreover, the non-realisability, at least for present man, of utopia was essential to its ethical superiority:

> The utopian longing of the soul is a legitimate desire, worthy of being the centre of a world, only if it is absolutely incapable of being satisfied in the present intellectual state of man, that is to say incapable of being satisfied in any world that can be imagined and given form, whether past, present or mythical.[98]

For Lukács, unlike Bloch, utopia was an ethical problem and questions, such as whether the inner reality of the soul was superior to outer reality or vice versa, or whether man's ability to imagine a better world could serve as the basis for an integrated life, were problematic.[99]

An exchange between Bloch and Lukács was also evident in *Spirit of Utopia*. Bloch discussed the main themes of the book with Lukács before publication, including the problem of Don Quixote and the comic hero, and in *Spirit of Utopia* he made use of Lukács' terminology and dubbed Lukács 'the genius of morality'.[100] Like Lukács, he spoke of the need for 'essayistic thinking'; he also accepted Lukács' doctrine of metaphysical castes, including the concept of a spiritual aristocracy, and cited Lukács on the interpretation of Marx.[101] Bloch, however, already differed with Lukács' treatment of aesthetic questions. He argued against Lukács' essay 'The Metaphysics of Tragedy' that there was a paradox of optimistic tragedy: that great tragedy needed to be understood in terms of an open and not a closed conception of reality, as something which spurred men on to self invention and self completion.[102] Similarly, he criticised the formalism of Lukács' *The Theory of the Novel* and emphasised the ontological radicalism of great works rather than their form.[103] *Spirit of Utopia* also witnessed to a common engagement with Hegel. If Bloch decisively influenced Lukács' Hegel studies, the Kierkegaardisation of Hegel appeared in *The Theory of the Novel* before Bloch advanced it in *Spirit of Utopia*, and the evidence suggests that it was Lukács rather than Bloch who first appreciated the full importance of Hegel for Marx. On the other hand, for Lukács the understanding of the Hegel-Marx relation within a historico-philosophical problematic clearly belonged to the period of his symbiosis with Bloch, when he discussed with him the relationship between Marx and Nietzsche as well as Hegel. During this period, both Lukács and Bloch were 'right-wing' leftists imbued with Romantic anti-capitalism, who yearned for a moral revolution against the nihilism, secularism and moral compromises of bourgeois civilisation.[104] Both combined meta-politics with meta-mystical tendencies; both were pessimistic about the machine world, in which men were dominated by 'externals', and *Geist* had become so poor.

Bloch and Lukács kept in touch after Lukács' return to Hungary, and as late as 1918 Lukács proposed that they work together on a common philosophy.[105] The break between them emerged when Lukács became a fully committed Communist who believed that he had transcended the immature utopianism of his pre-Marxist period. In 1918 Lukács joined the newly formed Hungarian Communist party and in 1919 he became

Deputy Minister for Education in the Hungarian Soviet. Lukács was now a self-conscious political realist with experience of an actual revolution and of personal danger. Bloch recognised that the question of the correct handling of utopia was the central question between them, and in 1920 he proposed that they hold an exchange on the question of whether there had been too great a progress from utopia to science in socialism.[106] But Lukács, the young revolutionary about to meet Lenin, had outgrown Bloch's Messianic utopian tendencies. When Bloch and Lukács met again in 1921 their basic disagreement emerged in a dispute over Schopenhauer, whom Bloch praised for introducing a valuative element into truth with his doctrine that the existing world was 'untrue'. Where Bloch was concerned to deny that the world at hand was the criterion of truth, Lukács was concerned to stress the need to keep close to the real world in the sense of what had become actual.[107] For Lukács, the extent of the gulf was underlined by the appearance of Bloch's *Thomas Münzer as Theologian of Revolution* (1921), which seemed to embody the voluntarism, subjectivism and lack of mediation at the heart of Bloch's position.

The appearance of *History and Class Consciousness* in 1923 provided a negative verdict from Lukács on the question of a return to utopia in Marxism. Nonetheless, the break was not as sharp as might appear. Indeed, Bloch later claimed:

> There are parts and ideas in *History and Class Consciousness* which are expressions of a common point of view and which really came from me, just as parts of *Spirit of Utopia* and aspects of its contents originated with Lukács, to the point that both of us found it hard to say 'This is my idea, this is yours'.[108]

In *History and Class Consciousness* Bloch's influence was visible in the section on 'Reification and the Consciousness of the Proletariat', especially in Lukács' discussion of the problem of how to sublate classical German philosophy and also perhaps in the chapter on Rosa Luxemburg.[109] Lukács followed Bloch's analysis of how to surmount the 'pernicious chasm' of the present in order to make the present moment the moment of active mediation and the birth of the new. Moreover, he made a class's capacity to achieve a concrete relation to the now fundamental to

Marxist politics. He still made use of phrases from Bloch and specifically referred his readers to Bloch's work on 'the moment' and theory of not-yet-conscious knowledge.[110] In *History and Class Consciousness*, however, Lukács was convinced that a post-utopian approach to politics was necessary. He emphasised the methodological inadequacy of the utopian tendency to confront a bad reality with a truth imported from some other region; he also contrasted Marx's insistence that consciousness was a practical, social reality, with the utopian's attempt to derive a normative judgement on society from subjectivity, separation of politics and economics, and failure to provide concrete proposals for action.[111]

Moreover, *History and Class Consciousness* contained an explicit polemic against Bloch. Lukács was critical of the strategy implicit in Bloch's Münzer book and rejected the idea that social reality could be changed by awakening man's inwardness. He also implied that Bloch had not come to terms with Hegel's notion of mediation and failed to go beyond immediacy. Bloch failed to see, Lukács charged, that religious utopianism merely projected the problem of immediacy on to a higher plane, and could only end in mysticism and conceptual mythology.[112] Again, Lukács applied to Münzer (and so to Bloch) Bloch's own critique of those who set up a chasm between theory and practice.[113] He also raised implicitly the problem of whether Bloch had sublated the materials which he professed to activate, the problem of whether his utopian philosophy could ever serve as a foundation for a concrete social practice, and the problem of whether his emphasis on revolutionary subjectivism did not evade the primacy of the social in Marxism. Lukács was now convinced that Bloch's thought was pre-Marxist, and he implied that Bloch failed to understand Marx's materialism when he suggested that an alliance of revolution and religion could be used to deepen the 'merely economic' outlook of historical materialism.[114]

Bloch replied to Lukács in a warm review. He shared Lukács' conviction that Hegel's subject-object process provided the model for an advance over the bourgeois incapacity to grasp the present, and he emphasised that the treatment of the problem of history in *History and Class Consciousness* was different from, but conformable to, his own treatment in *Spirit of Utopia*.[115] Bloch, however, was critical of what he saw as the one-sided, reductionist aspect of Lukács' position. He felt that Lukács destroyed the possibility of an adequate Marxist ontology by reducing Marxist materialism to social materialism, and he accused Lukács of lapsing into mechanical homogeneity and sociologism.[116] According to Bloch, Lukács reduced history to a one-dimensional linear structure and failed to do justice to the depth dimension of being, whereas history was a polyrhythmical process with many levels which was open not only to the emergence of the still concealed 'social man', but to the emergence of the artistic, the religious, the 'secret transcendental man'.[117]

Bloch also saw that Lukács' concept of totality, with the closed conception of the world which it implied, was potentially oppressive. Lukács postulated a purely social totality, which was inadequate to the contents which needed to find adequation in a humanly successful world. Bloch, in contrast, envisaged a totality open to a praxis of the 'eccentric' contents which appeared in human consciousness, and to their possible fulfilment in a world transformed by adequate human action. Many of the 'eccentric' contents in the world, such as religion, could never be fulfilled socially, Bloch argued. Moreover, nature had not yet entered the historical process, and its activating agent or 'subject' had not yet been found.[118] Therefore, in place of Lukács' finished world, which could only be varied under socialism, a more open concept of totality was necessary, which took account of the fact that such 'eccentric' contents could eventually find their adequation. Totality, Bloch argued, needed to be 'weighted down' with the concept of 'the dianoetic sphere' in which such eccentric contents could find a place before they reached the stage when they could be made goals for praxis.[119] This was also Bloch's implicit answer to Lukács' one-sided rejection of 'subjectivity'. Such eccentric contents, he argued, could only be 'subjective' at first, since they had no correlation in the external world and denoted goals for praxis still to be achieved. Finally, Bloch rejected Lukács' treatment of the relationship between Marxism and utopia as dualistic. Utopia, Bloch argued, was not opposed to actuality, but present in the now of the moment:

> Actuality and utopia are not opposites, but 'the now' is finally the sole concern of utopia, whether one understands it as the constant demand to throw off masks, ideologies, and transit mythologies, or as premonition of the adequation of the process which recognises both the driving tendency and the hidden genuine reality in the now.[120]

In other words, Lukács' treatment of the problem was too simple. The drive to an unrealisable perfection was more fundamental to the critical forward motion of human history than Lukács suggested, just as there was a mysterious premonition of that perfection in the experience of the moment.

Bloch's reply made it clear that two very different versions of Marxist philosophy could be developed from Marx's alleged 'materialist rectification' of Hegel. Whereas Lukács' version provided an Enlightenment-type Marxist rationalism in which Hegel's excesses were either eliminated or glossed as secret sense, Bloch's version continued Hegel's excess on new utopian premises. Where Lukács conformed himself to the agnosticism of the capitalist *ratio*, Bloch reasserted the scandal of 'a world secret' present in the darkness of the moment. The 'We' was 'not yet', and our task was to realise its alpha and omega as they were pre-illumined in the moment.[121] Whereas Lukács secularised Hegel, Bloch held that Hegel's model of a process in which subject became substance could be taken as regulative; and that Marxism needed to be supplemented with a hermeneutics of the 'eccentric' contents of the dianoetic sphere which would yield additional goals for theory-praxis.

The issue of the relationship between Marxism and utopia was to grow in importance with the years. To Lukács, the issue seemed settled. Indeed, Lukács later criticised even his position in *History and Class Consciousness* as still too utopian.[122] He looked back on *The Theory of the Novel* as a work based on 'a highly naïve and totally unfounded utopianism', and attributed the connection between *The Theory of the Novel* and Bloch's *Spirit of Utopia* and *Thomas Münzer*, to the fact that all three were attempts to combine 'left-wing ethics' with 'right-wing epistemology', or a conventional exegesis of reality.[123] Bloch's position, Lukács was convinced, was outdated, and the only real question was why Bloch remained steadfastly 'left' when so many others wavered. He did not doubt Bloch's greatness, but he emphasised that the fundamental conception of Bloch's philosophy was a utopian one.[124]

Bloch's subsequent development was determined by what he took to be the realities of class struggle in his lifetime. Like Lukács, he identified with the Communist cause to a point where he related his historic utterances to their likely effects, and presented his views in a way designed not to separate him entirely from the only forces which he believed could give social and economic reality to his vision. Granted that Bloch proposed to reassert a utopian perspective in Marxism, this still left open the means to be used in realising utopia. As early as *Spirit of Utopia* Bloch held that it was necessary for the categorical imperative to carry a gun,[125] and his acceptance of revolutionary violence was unequivocal in *Thomas Münzer*. To the extent that he accepted an element of guilt as part of his endorsement of such violence, Bloch subscribed to the view that utopia could only be realised as an end if there was a temporary and partial renunciation of utopian means. Where Bloch differed from the orthodox Marxists was in holding that such renunciation should be partial.

In the 1920s Bloch emerged as a fierce critic of capitalism who called for the destruction of the structures which maintained oppression. He attacked the Weimar Republic, with its rentier culture and naked orientation to economics, and represented Russia as the 'absolute tonic', whose 'ferment of genuineness' was to be contrasted with the nihilism of the petty bourgeoisie and the trader morals of the West.[126] He was also one of the first to appreciate the reasons for Hitler's appeal, and the danger of the appropriation by the Right of 'rootedness in the soil' as well as such traditional images as 'order' and 'kingdom' (*Reich*).[127] He saw the political potential of Romantic anti-capitalism and its critique of urbanism, and emphasised that a new relation to nature was fundamental to Marxism.[128] Nonetheless, Bloch did not join the KPD. Instead he emerged as a non-party Communist philosopher in touch with party circles but distant from the prevailing orthodoxy. Sadly perhaps, he did not meet Karl Korsch, although he shared his opposition to the mechanistic doctrines of the Second International, his emphasis on 'philosophy' in Marxism, and his stress on the political significance of struggle on the cultural and ideological fronts.

In the 1930s Bloch emerged as the philosopher of an alternative Marxism, who claimed that there was 'a warm stream', or concrete utopian perspective, within Marxism itself. In his political essays, and, above all, in *Heritage of this Time* (1935), he developed a critique of Marxist orthodoxy of outstanding depth and penetration. Even allowing for his Aesopian expression, he raised fundamental issues for the future of Marxism. Bloch criticised the KPD for its failure to counter the Nazis' appeal. He rejected its exclusivist sectarian outlook, its patriarchal and philistine tendencies, its neglect of people's real needs and of the fantasy of the masses, as well as its crude anti-religion, its hostility to sexual radicalism (for example, Sex-Pol and the women's movement), its mishandling of the intelligentsia and the artistic *avant-garde*.[129] Similarly, Bloch railed at the 'malnutrition of the socialist imagination' and at the orthodox Marxist hostility to fantasy, enthusiasm and ideals.[130] In the face of orthodox Marxist sterility, Bloch offered a counter-analysis of the German social formation and of the nature of late capitalism, based on his own sensitive and concrete situation analysis (*Zeitkritik*), which, in its faithfulness to detail and local colourings, contrasted sharply with the official Marxist faith in abstractions.

As in *Spirit of Utopia* and *Through the Desert*, he started from the potentialities immanently developing within the present, and not from theoreticist grammar or 'party Chinese'. Bloch argued that Germany was the classical land of non-contemporaneity (*Ungleichzeitigkeit*) and that the key to the structuration of contradictions in Germany lay in the non-contemporaneous contradictions which existed side by side with the contemporaneous contradiction between the proletariat and the bourgeoisie.[131] Bloch's theory of non-contemporaneity allowed him to analyse the different social strata in German society in terms of their relation to the now, and to the capitalist mode of production developing in it; to distinguish the false non-contemporaneity of the immiserated middle class, who yearned for pre-war conditions and retreated from the now, from the contemporaneity of the proletariat, who were directly involved in capitalist production. It also enabled him to analyse the retreat of middle class youth into Romantic anti-capitalism, the changing structure of the middle class, and the emergence of a new strata of office workers (*Angestellte*) whose interests did not necessarily coincide with those of the bourgeoisie.[132] He also drew attention to the authentic non-contemporaneity of the peasantry, whose consciousness and mode of life were still tied to older modes of production. Bloch's achievement was to replace crude paper models of class structure with differentiations and an analysis of the discontinuities in and between different classes, to allow for genuine regional differences, and for the effectivity of the perceptions and aspirations of different strata.

Bloch used these concrete analyses to offer an alternative analysis of the nature of German fascism. He rejected the official

analysis of fascism as a product of the decadence of the Imperialist bourgeoisie, and argued that fascism had to be taken
seriously as (1) a cultural synthesis; (2) a mass movement; and (3)
a distorted revolution, 'a swindle of fulfilment', which mobilised
the non-contemporaneous contradictions in German society,
and the widespread rebellion against the nihilism and relativism
of the bourgeoisie, because it 'stopped up' the 'hollow space' of
capitalism.[133] Bloch's emphasis on capitalist-activated non-contemporaneity as the key to fascism allowed him to decode its
propaganda and appeal. Where the orthodox Marxists dismissed
the upsurge of Romanticism and occultism in Germany as
'irrationalism', Bloch argued that the fascists succeeded by
appealing to the dreams, fantasies and motivations of non-
contemporaneous strata. By detailed analyses of fascist images
and slogans, he showed that fascism was 'an insanity of non-
contemporaneity' in which images from the past reappeared and
were given a reactionary functionality, including images such as
'the third *Reich*' which descended from the medieval chiliasts
and originally belonged to the revolution.[134]

In effect, Bloch was outlining an alternative understanding of
historical materialism: as a philosophy of revolution, and not
simply a proto-science which came too late. In this understanding, the lessons of Thomas Münzer and the Peasant Wars were
crucial. Bloch held that Marxism needed to replace its one-sided
theoreticist quest for correct theory and ideological purity with
involvement in the actual development of society and its imminent trajectories. This involved a new relation to effective tradition
and a will to bring the old to success (*Erbe*), as well as a new understanding of the materiality of ideas when they were grasped by
the masses. It meant a critique of rationalist reformism and
practicist spontaneity, in favour of an analysis of 'the living
yesterday' which needed to be baptised by Marxism, and careful
attention to the felt needs and operative motivations of each
strata of society.[135] Above all, it involved the insight that Marxism must bring all the potentially progressive elements within
its organising *ratio*, and accept the engagement with ideology
and enthusiasm involved in its becoming man's rational hope,
including the need for 'theology' in the sense of an imaginative,
dream-laden occupation of the irrational.[136]

Here Bloch's position involved a critique of the whole tradition of left rationalism, and the pathology of its cultural and

psychological style. From within Marxism, Bloch brought a
Burkean perspective to bear on the official Marxist inheritance
of the abstract rationalism and nihilism of the late bourgeoisie.
Bloch's point was not only that the Communists fetishised an
abstract reason (*Verstand*), and failed to develop a political economy of rationalism, but that their abstract rationalism was omissive and operationally irrationalist.[137] More clearly than any
other Communist critic, Bloch saw that the mechanistic intellectualism and abstract rationalism of the Left were having catas-
trophic consequences, that because Marxists feared to go where
angels dared to tread, the upsurge of protest against the hollow
space of capitalism was being channelled by reaction.

For Bloch, there was no question of a rejection of the Enlightenment, although he queried its schematic opposition between
'enthusiasm' and 'rationality', and dismissed an uncritical perpet-
uation of its polemics and battle lines as anachronistic.[138] Bloch
called for a Marxism which combined Enlightenment with dialectical wisdom: for a Marxism based on (1) concrete materialist
reason, which uncovered the rational in the irrational; and (2) a
concrete utopian praxis of the potentially revolutionary elements
developing within the present.[139] Marxism had to counter and
not repeat the hollow space of capitalism, Bloch argued. It needed
to occupy all the dream areas of the imagination, which otherwise would be given a politically harmful functionality: to com-
pile an inventory of all the illusory pre-appearances of happiness
and to dialectically activate those contents which necessarily
appeared in class society in an irrationalist form.[140] Instead of a
jargon ridden theoreticist propaganda addressed to only the most
contemporaneous elements in German society, Marxism needed
to speak to people about their situation in language they could
understand: to develop a propaganda which related to the ideology inside their heads, instead of superstitiously relying on correct theoretical analyses to win a path for truth in the world.[141]
In this context, Bloch called for a socialist propaganda addressed
to other strata as well as the proletariat, which stressed the
morality of the socialist cause, and the positive ideals which
socialism sought to realise.[142]

Bloch also implied that orthodox Marxism was wrong on both
the fundamental questions concerning the inheritance of capitalism: that it wrongly condemned advanced late capitalist culture,
while uncritically inheriting capitalist technology.[143] Instead,

Bloch called for a new Marxist *Kulturpolitik*, and a critical attitude to capitalist technology, based on the positive goal of a new relation of man to nature. Similarly, he rejected orthodox Marxist anti-religion as anachronistic, and called for an alliance with anti-fascist Christians, and for a renewed depth dimension in Marxism, based on 'belief without lies'.[144] Finally, Bloch rejected both the mechanical materialism of Marxist orthodoxy, which uncritically inherited the materialism of Büchner, Moleschott and Haeckel, and Lukács' doctrine of totality. According to Bloch, Marxism needed to develop a more differentiated, multi-temporal, multi-spaced dialectics which reflected the heterogeneous contents, disparities, discontinuities and interruptions in the world, instead of forcing them within the rubrics of an idealist materialism, or subjecting them to a panlogical closed totality, and the *a priori* labels and fixed evaluations which followed from it.[145] Thus, Bloch's differences with Marxist orthodoxy culminated in the project of a more encompassing Marxism based on a more sophisticated dialectical materialism: a Marxism which would not be hostile to revolutionary imagination or to a concrete utopian conception of praxis.[146]

These differences did not affect Bloch's commitment to Moscow or to the Communist cause. He accepted the historical necessity of Stalinism and defended the need for a proletarian dictatorship in Russia. Indeed, he prided himself on his ability to accept a degree of moral evil and the 'unmistakable smell of blood' as evidence of his political maturity, in contrast to those leftward-leaning intellectuals who abandoned the Red Flag when it came to the test.[147] He idealised the reality of Stalinist murder, and avoided the moral dilemma by accepting violence and 'red terror' in a context in which the fundamental good intentions of the revolutionary forces and their commitment to moral values as teleological ends could not be doubted. It is true that he favoured a greater emphasis on utopian means in the industrialised West than was possible in 'backward' and 'primitive' Russia, but the moralist pathos of his public statements should not conceal his even more eloquent silences.

Bloch's relationship to Marxist orthodoxy remained ambiguous during his years in the DDR when he was a Marxist philosopher *intra muros*, more concerned with the construction of socialism than with the critique of capitalism. On the one hand, Bloch was a loyal oppositional figure: a critic of Marxist orthodoxy with an alternative Marxism. On the other, his position was defined *vis-à-vis* a body of ideas which were functional in terms of political power. As a semi-institutionalised Marxist philosopher, Bloch found it necessary to make compromises in order to have the chance of influencing the development of 'socialism' in Eastern Europe. Unlike many Marxists, he had no quarrel with the idea of an ontological dialectical materialism, and his process philosophy interests enabled him to interpret the works of Engels, Lenin and Stalin as elementary treatments of essentially correct principles. He was conscious of Engels' philosophical shortcomings, but he could hardly be hostile to an admirer of Hegel who claimed that the universe was a process and applied the dialectic to all material being.[148] Similarly, he found unsuspected philosophical depths in Lenin and Stalin. He lionised the Lenin of *Materialism and Empirio-Criticism* and the *Philosophical Notebooks*, who seemed so ready to give full credit to great idealist philosophy, and praised Stalin 'the theoretician', whose views on the dialectic, on the creative role of the superstructure, on the presence of a cosmological dimension in Marxism, could sometimes be made to appear consonant with his own.[149] If Bloch no longer spoke of 'false emphases' in Marx, or of 'the need to raise Marx to a higher level', his theoretical work during these years constitutes an immense legacy which has never received the attention it deserves. Apart from his savage criticisms of 'objectivism', 'sociologism', 'automatism' and 'mechanical materialism', Bloch attempted to formulate the elements of a positive socialist programme which covered human rights, education and religion, as well as cultural and philosophical questions.

Nonetheless, the pattern of Bloch's political development was not reassuring. If Marxism was to have a utopian perspective, then it was crucial to show that it was possible to have a utopian perspective without utopian illusions. Bloch's own record as a judge of Communist parties in power, however, was hardly impressive. Despite private reservations, he did not respond publicly to the 1953 riots in East Berlin, to the use of forced labour, or to countless other examples of cruelty and injustice. Nor did he provide any systematic analysis of social or political conditions in the DDR, just as later he would offer no adequate explanation of the distortions of socialism which he alleged had taken place in the Soviet Union. For as long as possible, he chose silence, and explained the inadequacies of socialist reality as the proneness to illness of a young child who would later outgrow such complaints.[150] Moreover, despite his personal goodness, even nobility of character, Bloch failed to illumine the relation between means and ends in Marxism, despite the fact that this was a problem which no amount of moralistic rhetoric could dislodge, or even to work out the exact relationship between a philosophical outlook and an operative political ideology. On the contrary, he seemed to confuse the one with the other by accommodating his own views to Marxist-Leninist ideology, and to theoretical statements by Marx, Engels, Lenin and Stalin, which were strictly of political rather than philosophical importance.

Part of the problem was that Bloch was divorced from the detail of organisational problems. He did not descend to political or economic technicalities in his early utopian philosophy, and he showed little flair for them in his later Marxism. But this meant that a crucial nexus was missing, and that he could only consort with Caesarist Bolsheviks, while advocating loftier principles, or oppose the distortionary nature of actual 'socialist' regimes in the name of political ideals for which no administrative machinery was available, at least in his own writings. Even after 1956, when he emerged as an advocate of a radical development of Marxism, and of humane socialism, national paths to Communism and genuine socialist democracy,[151] Bloch still failed to explain how the good society would be organised, or how phenomena such as bureaucracy and the emergence of new élites were to be prevented in the future.

This was the problem which Bloch brought with him to the West. In the safety of West Germany, Bloch abandoned some of his Marxist-Leninist trappings and made common front with other advocates of humane socialism such as the Yugoslav praxis philosophers and the theorists of the Prague Spring. He now conceded that Marx had been wrong to think that no kind of utopia was necessary, and that there were genuine problems of the revision of Marx.[152] As in 1918, he was prepared to admit in conversation that Marx was not enough.[153] The problem was that Bloch's own Marxism was not enough either, because it provided no coherent political or social theory which could explain the detail of the history of capitalism since 1923, or indicate how an alternative society could be organised and maintained in purity over an extended period.

Similarly, at the end of Bloch's life the problem of his intellectual development also emerged as unsolved. When Bloch's manuscripts were published in the West, each confirmed his importance as a Marxist philosopher, but also provided fresh evidence of the non-Marxist sources of many of his insights. Moreover, Bloch's late works contained evidence that he had made less than a complete break with the monist speculations of his adolescence, including the claim that matter was the mother of all being, the anti-dualist identification of morality with sensuousness, the stress on an energeticism based on the will-like character of reality, and the notion of a subject-object correlation which undercut the positivism and the agnosticism of modern epistemology.[154] To this extent, Lukács may have been right to argue that there were problems about the nature of Bloch's assimilation of historical materialism and about the utopian orientation which he brought to it. Bloch was not 'the German philosopher of the October Revolution', but a consistent heretic, whose evasive coherence and inability to win his contemporaries to his insights was the price he paid for his originality.

UTOPIA AND THE CRITIQUE OF THE MARXIST TRADITION

Bloch's Marxism is best understood as a critique of the Marxist tradition which attempts to overcome the failures and distortions it uncovers via a radical rehabilition of utopia. According to Bloch, after Marx a fundamental distortion of Marxism took place, characterised by an undernourishment of revolutionary imagination, and a schematic, practistic foreshortening of totality, or the object and goal of revolutionary activity. At times there was too great a progress from utopia to science,[155] and Marxism degenerated into a dogma, as Marx's integralist outlook was replaced by half-enlightenment and a naturalistic scientism of the 'laws of history'. The goals of Marxism were reduced to narrowly conceived social and ecomonic changes, and a profound devaluation of man himself occurred, of which the vulgar anti-religion and cultural popery of the Marxist tradition were symptomatic. The countermove against capitalism became conformed to the criminal as 'the occlusion of the subject' under capitalism distorted socialist thought as well, and Marxism hardened into economism and an automaticist objectivism.

Bloch attempts to reverse this fundamental distortion of Marxism: to challenge the Marxist inheritance of the nihilism and
abstraction of capitalism by rehabilitating utopia as a fundamental political and philosophical category. The modern rehabilitation of utopia dates from Landauer's *Die Revolution* (1907)
and from Mannheim's *Ideology and Utopia* (German edition,
1929), which was indebted to Bloch's *Spirit of Utopia* (1918).[156]
Landauer's contribution was to emphasise the revolutionary
function of utopias as elements which broke up stable existing
orders.[157] Mannheim, in a modified version of the same argument, drew a famous distinction between *utopian orientations*
which transcended the world at hand in a way which, when they
passed into conduct, tended to shatter the existing order of
things, and *ideology*, which was also incongruent with the world
at hand, but which contained projects which could never be realised and tended to maintain the existing order.[158] Bloch's rehabilitation of utopia however goes beyond Landauer and Mannheim.

The standard critique of utopia rests on the ontological claim
that the nature of things is given, on the regional claim that
utopia is not grounded in the world at hand, and on the psychological claim that men depart from reality when they dream of
perfection beyond the limitations which the reality at hand
imposes.[159] It maintains that utopia is not only unrealistic and
impractical, but potentially dangerous; since it encourages men
to give vent to totalistic, adolescent psychological states, and
provides an illusory basis for human action. According to this
critique, utopia is a form of unbridled subjectivism which ignores
the fact that man cannot re-shape the objective world in his own
image, make it conform to abstract plans and schemata, or base
his practical activities on maximally preferred values. It is
irrational in its refusal to acknowledge the authority of objective reality, *immature* in its inability to realise the limited nature
of the possible, and *irresponsible* in its failure to understand the
role of fallibilism in the realisation of the good. The standard
critique, summed up in the smart phrase 'That's rather utopian', recognises that there are different kinds of utopians and
that utopianism can adopt a scientific as well as a Messianic guise;
but it maintains that all utopians err in preferring the fulfilment
of ideal representations to the more mundane improvements
which are possible in their time.

Bloch rehabilitates utopia by denying the ontological, regional and psychological claims on which this critique is based. He denies that the nature of things is given, and argues that utopia is fundamental to the nature of reality as something unfinished. For Bloch, utopia is the philosophical concept of the century, in the sense of the concept which is adequate to the task of setting a goal for humanity, at a time when traditional absolutes have collapsed.[160] It is an operative alternative to nihilism, a concept which functions motoristically to help men shape the world in a humanistic direction, and that can do so because it has a basis in the world.[161] Bloch emphasises the productivity of utopia: its *cognitive function* as a mode of operation of constructive reason, its *educative function* as a mythography which instructs men to will and desire more and better, its *anticipatory function* as a futurology of possibilities which later become actual, and its *causal function* as an agent of historical change. Utopia has a 'work character' as a form of research into as yet unrealised possibilities, and a normative goal setting function as an anticipatory transcendence of the interval between subject and object.[162] Again, a correct evaluation of utopia is crucial for the question of whether we understand our own humanity and our part in the humanisation of the world. Humanism has developed in utopia, Bloch declares, and rightly understood, utopia is revolutionary and constitutive in human history.[163]

Moreover, utopia is not only fundamental to any adequate philosophical anthropology and critical *vis-à-vis* all conditions which are still humanly inadequate. According to Bloch, it has a centrality in the world as men experience it, which Landauer and Mannheim with their political and social orientation ignored. Utopia not only instructs men about what they want and informs them about what may one day be possible. It is not only a region for research, full of models and *topoi* for a prospectivism which is historically active. Utopia is fundamental to the ontology of a world open to new developments, to a world which is not pre-given or pre-formed *ante rem*, but *a process*, in which new contents emerge as a result of human intervention and labour:

Utopia extends so far and imparts itself so powerfully to all human activities that every account of man and the world must essentially contain it. *There is no realism, worthy of the name, which abstracts from this strongest element in reality as something which is unfinished.*[164]

In this sense, utopia extends not only to the problem of the best social philosophy, but to the potentiality which may be released in the world as a whole.[165]

Similarly, Bloch denies that utopia is 'no place' and has no basis in the world at hand. Bloch argues that utopia has 'a place' in the 'nearest near' of human experience, and is already present in the world at hand in a proleptic manner. The far is present in the near, and the problem of the identification and realisation of what is needed is not only a problem of our relationship to the external world and its possibility content, but a problem of our relationship to the now of the lived moment.[166] Here Bloch may seem simply to revive chiliastic utopianism, to be Thomas Münzer *redivivus*. Unlike the rational utopian, the chiliast bases his belief in a perfect future not on external possibilities, but on his inner experience of an eschatological presence in the now of the moment. Unlike the rational utopian, the chiliast is not discouraged by the poverty of external possibilities. On the contrary, the worse things get the more hopeful he becomes. The chiliast believes in an *eschaton* which will sweep away the present world, because he experiences 'the end' now:

> The Chiliast expects a union with the immediate present . . . He is not actually concerned with the millennium that is to come; what is important for him is that it happened here and now, and that it arose from mundane existence, as a sudden swing over into another kind of existence. The promise of the future which is to come is not for him a reason for postponement, but merely a point of orientation . . . [167]

The world after the *eschaton* will be new, and cannot be detailed now except by metaphors, intensives, and negations. This has a subtle consequence. As Mannheim observed: 'The essential feature of Chiliasm is its tendency always to dissociate itself from its own images and symbols'.[168] Like the chiliast, Bloch makes the moment central to his utopianism, and relies on subject theurgy as well as rational argument. Similarly, the tendency to dissociate or at least distance himself from his symbols may be a key to Bloch's all-pervasive syncretism, which tends to deprive any particular borrowing of precise ontological reference. Nonetheless, despite the resemblance which Mannheim detected between Bloch and Münzer, Bloch does not simply restate chiliasm.

Bloch locates utopia in regard to the present and the future via his operator 'not yet'. Utopia is 'now', in the sense that the intensive content which men search for under the name of utopia is present in the lived moment. In place of the traditional problem of an abstract extrapolation of an ideal order, Bloch makes the problem of utopia the problem of an authentic relation to the now of the moment: the problem of a depth relation to our own immanence and that of the world, in which utopia occurs. Utopia, however, is also 'not yet' in at least three senses. It is 'not yet', in the sense that it has never come to be and functions normatively against the inadequate which has become actual. Hence the failure of utopia is a reason for its survival. Man the utopian errs:

> But the main thing persists and, persisting, holds more importance than the plan of journey, which is not decisive in principle. The main thing is that the utopian conscience-and-knowledge grows wise through the damage which it suffers from facts, yet does not grow to full wisdom. It is *rectified* — but never *refuted* by the mere power of that which, at any particular time, *is*. On the contrary, it confronts and judges the latter if it is failing and failing inhumanly; indeed, first and foremost it provides the *standard* to measure such facticity precisely as departure from the right; and, above all, to measure it immanently: that is, by the ideas which have resounded and been inculcated from time immemorial before such a departure, and which are still displayed and proposed in the face of it.[169]

Utopia is also 'not yet' in the sense that it is something which men have envisaged in different forms through the centuries. It has not eventuated, except in isolated moments and fragmentary experiences, but the fact that it has been anticipated and foreshadowed (as a result of the operation of not-yet-conscious knowledge)[170] adds to its power, and increases the intuitive conviction that it is not wholly ungrounded. Moreover, its pre-appearances are themselves potentially productive, and can be thematised and mobilised as a programme for human action. Finally, utopia is 'not yet' in the sense that it is still not fully possible, and looks ahead to new contents and developments beyond the limitations of the present world. It has a critical, meta-eschatological function against the foreclosures and premature disenchantments of current conceptions of possibility.

Bloch also denies the claim that men depart from reality when they dream of perfection beyond the limitations of the world at hand, not because he denies that utopia is adolescent, totalistic and naïve, but because he regards such a claim as undialectical and one-sided. Utopia is bound up with illusory expectations and wish-fulfilment, but its naïvety has a heuristic function and belongs to the logic of discovery. The totalism of utopia is not wise, but it can lead to wisdom. It is often the method of delivery of new ideas and its initial immaturity and enthusiasm often relates to the discovery of the new. In this sense, utopia may be necessary if men are continually to re-relate to their own uncovered countenance and to the future new; and the need to control and correct it should not lead to an elision of the creative moment in which the potential productivity of utopia first appears.

Bloch's rehabilitation of utopia has major consequences for the Marxist tradition, in so far as an understanding of utopia implies a non-naturalistic understanding of history and an indefeasible productive function for 'active hope' and 'dreaming ahead' (Lenin). According to Bloch, Marxism has need of the utopianism of utopia even after Marx:

> A merely empirically aimed Marxism eliminates two kinds of materials with utopian connotations which are actually inspirational in the end: firstly, *ideals* and secondly, the *finale utopica* in general . . . It is precisely these two elements which belong to Marxism, both today and tomorrow.[171]

Nonetheless, Marxism cannot adopt a passive or uncritical attitude to utopia, even if, as Bloch suggests, it should respect the enchantment of the utopian moment and not eliminate it with a criticism after which it never recurs. Bloch emphasises that a radical critique of utopia is necessary: to exclude ideology and illusion and to relate utopian projections to developing historical tendencies. He rejects Mannheim's oversharp separation of utopia and ideology,[172] and stresses that all the products of the imagination have ideological aspects as long as the social constituents of ideology operate.[173] Hence there is ideology in utopian projections, just as reactionary ideological productions are not without their utopian moments. For Bloch, however, Marxism provides such a critique of utopia, just as utopia potentially provides a critique of the Marxist tradition in which it was eliminated or suppressed. But this raises the question of whether Marxism already understands utopia, or whether it does not understand it, and needs to be recast in the light of such an understanding.

Bloch's response reflects the problem of his development and the identification with the Marxist tradition which remained the elusive goal of his maturity. Bloch implies that Marxism already understands utopia and that his own contribution is simply to draw out what was always implicit.[174] He argues that Marxism understands utopia and sets it 'on its feet' as something 'concrete', just as it discovers the rational kernel in the idealist dialectic.[175] It overcomes all 'abstract' utopianism, and exposes the illusion and class interest in utopias of every kind. Nonetheless, the Marxist critique of utopia is a positive one. Marxism does not break with the utopian intention. Instead, it discovers the 'concrete utopia' developing in the dialectics of the society at hand.[176] According to Bloch:

> Processual concrete utopia is present in both the fundamental elements of reality as known by Marxism: in its *tendency*, as the tension of obstructed capabilities, in its *latency*, as the correlate of the not yet actual objective real possibilities in the world.[177]

As subsequent chapters will make clear, this is a more complex claim than it first appears, despite the fact that Bloch relates the 'concrete utopia' of Marxism to the 'dream of a thing' which the young Marx suggested the world had long possessed and needed only to become conscious of for it to be realised in reality.[178] Granted that his rhetoric serves to obscure the distinction between the utopia already implicit in Marxism and the utopia which would be implicit in a Marxism which understood utopia as he rehabilitates it, Bloch's argument is important because it implies that utopia is a neglected, but fundamental,

Marxist category. This is a claim with decisive implications for the interpretation of Marx.

BLOCH'S INTERPRETATION OF MARX

Bloch's interpretation of Marx is controversial, but serves to draw attention to latent dimensions in Marx's thought and to under-emphasised texts. First, whereas in *Spirit of Utopia* Bloch proposed to add a utopian dimension to Marx, in his mature writings he argues that a form of concrete utopianism is implicit in Marx himself. Bloch concedes that Marx rejected all abstract utopianism and confined most of his attention to the next step, but he did so, Bloch argues, for the sake of the immanent goal.[179] Marx fought against both mechanical empiricism and over-reaching utopianism. He sublated the dualism between the empirical and utopia by grounding utopia in tendencies developing in and out of the economy at hand:

> Marx . . . explains the dialectics of history which leads to tensions, utopias and revolutions, in a materialistic way for the first time. He grounds and corrects the anticipations of utopia through economics, through immanent revolutions of production and exchange.[180]

The relative lack of depictions of the future in Marx did not follow from a lack of interest in the future, but from the nature of Marx's method:

> Marx's critique shows no folds of the heart, as Hegel would say, but for that reason it shows all the more strongly the folds, fissures, tensions and oppositions in the economy which is objectively at hand . . . The abstract utopias devoted nine tenths of their space to painting the future and only one tenth to critical, often purely negative analysis of the present. . . . Marx devoted more than nine tenths of his writings to the critical analysis of the present, and a relatively small space to designations of the future . . . Genuine *designations* of the future are lacking . . . because Marx's whole work serves the future, and indeed can only be understood and carried out in the horizon of the future, not indeed as one that is depicted

in an abstract utopian way, but as one that takes effect in and out of the past as well as the present.[181]

Bloch's argument here, as Alfred Schmidt has emphasised, is of considerable interest. Schmidt accepts Bloch's thesis that Marx's contribution was to replace abstract projections and metaphysical declarations with the analysis of concrete tendencies, but insists that Marx's utopia is strictly qualified, and is basically a social and human one.[182] He denies that the exuberance of the young Marx can be attributed to the mature Marx, whom, he claims, recognised that any utopia would be limited by the finite possibilities of men and nature, and that there would be a permanent non-identity between subject and object.

The issue is a complex one. Bloch is almost certainly right to emphasise that there is a form of utopianism in Marx, and that Marx continued an older tradition of utopianism on new foundations. Such a conclusion does not pre-judge the question of Marx's methodology, or imply any denigration of Marx. Indeed, part of Bloch's contribution is to show that certain charges levelled against Marx by hostile critics are true, but in a sense which adds to rather than detracts from Marx's achievement. The difficulty is that Bloch does not analyse the nature of Marx's utopianism in detail, or in the context of his total development; nor does he give full weight to the zigzags and ambiguities of Marx's position in each work. Clearly, neither Marx nor Engels was hostile to utopian socialism or utopian communism *per se*. On the contrary, they recognised the critical element in the utopias of Saint-Simon, Fourier and Owen. 'They attack every principle of existing society. Hence, they are full of the most valuable materials for the enlightenment of the working class', they wrote in *The Communist Manifesto*.[183] Granted that they also made the local judgement that such fantastic attacks on the existing order would lose their practical value and theoretical justification as the proletariat developed, Marx and Engels accepted that fantastic manifestations of the imagination could: (1) educate and inspire later actors in the historical drama; and (2) stand in an anticipatory relationship to the future maturity of political forces and historical conditions. Indeed, in a letter to Kugelmann on 9 October 1866, Marx defended the utopias of 'a Fourier, an Owen etc.,' against Proudhon's criticisms, and declared that in such utopias there was 'the anticipation and imaginative expression of a new world'.[184] Moreover, in his classical treatment of the problem of utopian socialism, *Social-ism: Utopian and Scientific* (1880) Engels was, if anything, even more sympathetic to utopianisn than Marx. Referring to the 'great utopians' Saint-Simon, Fourier and Owen, he declared: 'we delight in these stupendously grand thoughts and germs of thought that everywhere break out of their phantastic covering . . . '[185] Again, Engels recognised that the utopians possessed a superiority over their contemporaries, despite their failure to grasp the realities of class struggle.[186] When he claimed that socialism developed from utopia to science with Marx's discovery of 'the materialistic conception of history' and 'the secret of capitalist production', he may have implied that the moment for such abstract utopias was over, but he did not claim that anticipatory imagination could never again make a positive con-tribution to socialism.[187]

It is also clear that there is a form of utopianism in the writings of the young Marx, up to and including the Paris Manuscripts (1844). In the Paris Manuscripts Marx spoke of communism as a state in which man's natural existence would have become his human existence and nature would have become human for him:

> This communism as completed naturalism is humanism, as completed humanism it is naturalism. It is the *genuine* res-olution of the antagonism between man and nature and be-tween man and man; it is the true resolution of the conflict between existence and essence, objectification and self-affirm-ation, freedom and necessity, individual and species. It is the riddle of history solved and knows itself as this solution.[188]

Even the utopianism of the early Marx, however, was not of one kind. Some of Marx's maximalist projections are 'utopian' in the sense of too ideal to be realisable, for example, the young Marx's projections of the *full* development of an individual's social powers and the development of *all* sides of human nature. Others, however, are 'utopian' in the sense of unrealisable now, and dependent on distant and still undecided developments for their possibility, such as his projections of a classless society and an end to the division of labour. Here, Bloch's lack of analytical differentiation weakens his position, since it is not the existence of the evidence, but its interpretation which is in issue.

Similarly, it is clear that a form of utopianism was also present in the works of the mature Marx. The mature Marx envisaged *inter alia*: (1) the abolition of social classes; (2) the abolition of the division of labour; (3) the humanisation of the labour process; (4) a society free of commodity fetishism, in which the relations of production had become intelligible, and ideology had either disappeared or lost its distortionary character; (5) a society in which each would receive according to his needs; (6) the further development of men's labour powers, the emergence of more and more 'free time' in which men could develop their latent powers, as well as increasingly high levels of technology which would enable the narrow specialist to become the totally developed individual, to whom his different social functions are but so many modes of giving free scope to his natural and acquired powers; (7) the emergence of free associations of men who would cooperate according to a settled plan; and (8) the end of alienation, in the sense of the end of man's self estrangement from his own essential powers and from the products of his life activity.[189] He envisaged a stage in history when the social process of production would be brought under rational control, and men would begin to produce history consciously in a just society of rich social individuals.

The objection that some or all of these projections may turn out to be possible, and, in any event, are compatible with a hard headed, even pessimistic conception of reality, loses its force as soon as the term 'utopian' is not equated with 'permanently impossible' or 'unrealistic'. Indeed, to claim that the mature Marx's utopianism was realistic is to cede part of Bloch's point; and it is not very persuasive to locate Marx in the tradition of European pessimism on the grounds that for Marx the realm of necessity continues (although it declines in importance *vis-à-vis* the social sphere) and man always stands in relation of domination to nature.[190] The problem is not that Marx was rather optimistic at crucial points. What needs to be clarified is the question of the relationship between means and ends: the question of whether Marx was, as many commentators have claimed, an anti-utopian utopian, who trusted to objective economic forces and tough political action to realise the good, and maintained that a move away from the psychology and tactics of utopianism was necessary for its realisation.

Finally, it seems clear that Marx did ground his expectation of a future communist society in tendencies currently at work in the economy, and what could be implicated from them. The difficulty is that, even on the strongest construction, only a formal adequation of Marx's projections can be derived from what is currently at hand, not the utopian character which he assumed such adequation would have. Thus, for example, even if we assume that the inner logic of capitalism will lead to revolution and the establishment of a socialist society in which exploitation and commodity production will cease, there is no way to ground the supposition that the new conditions then prevailing will be utopian from the conditions which allow us now to project the occurrence of those conditions. This may not be a problem for Marx, but it suggests a problem for Bloch: that Marx did not ground utopia in the tendencies of the economy at hand, but in the future development of conditions which would be the adequation of language which seemed utopian when it was advanced.

Second, Bloch claims that there is a 'warm' as well as a 'cold' stream in Marxism, not only detectivistic economic analysis but also anticipatory prospective.[191] This follows from Bloch's account of Marx's analysis of tendencies, but it involves a major reassessment of the psychological and cultural style of Marxism. Bloch rejects the Marxist tradition's presentation of Marx and Engels as tough-minded revolutionaries who discovered the science of historical materialism, after which concern with imagination, ideals, wishes and hopes belonged to the past. Instead, Bloch tries to show that Marxism rests on a dialectical unity of sobriety and enthusiasm, and that it is precisely this dialectical unity which gives it its practical power and its ability to grasp historical trends:

> . . . Marxism . . . overcomes the rigid antithesis of sobriety versus enthusiasm by bringing them both to a new state, and enabling them to work together for exact anticipation, concrete utopia . . . The real . . . is encountered only through the permanent oscillation of both aspects united in a responsibly educated perspective.[192]

For Bloch, Marx himself provides the paradigm of the cold and warm stream working together, as a passage from the *Critique of the Gotha Program* in which Marx is at once coldly detectivistic and warmly prospective shows:

Right can never be higher than the economic structure of society and its cultural development conditioned thereby.

In a higher phase of communist society, after the enslaving subordination of the individual to the division of labour, and therewith also the antithesis between mental and physical labour, has vanished; after labour has become not only a means of life but life's prime want; after the productive forces have also increased with the all-round development of the individual, and all the springs of co-operative wealth flow more abundantly — only then can the narrow horizon of bourgeois right be crossed in its entirety and society inscribe on its banners: From each according to his ability, to each according to his needs![193]

Bloch also emphasises the integralist character of Marx's epistemology, for which the ability to understand the world was not wholly independent of the will to change it.[194] Moreover, he finds the same integralist dimension in Engels, who spoke of the vocation of socialists to become the Templars of the Holy Grail and to risk their lives in a 'last holy war that will be followed by the millennium of freedom', envisaged 'the reconciliation of mankind with nature and with itself', and dreamt of a time when men would escape from natural history and the alien rule of their own social forces.[195] Here Bloch's point is not only that the 'warm stream' was basic to Marx's and Engels' commitment as revolutionaries and to their emancipatory intention, but that it was an essential ingredient of their immanent method.

Third, Bloch claims that Marx pioneered a science of historical tendencies which discovered the future in the present. To show that the young Marx conceived of the future as to some degree immanent in the present, Bloch cites a passage from Marx's letter to his father in 1837:

. . . for every metamorphosis is partly a swan song, partly the overture to a great new poem, which strives to achieve form in still blurred but brilliant colours.[196]

and another passage from the same letter, in which Marx declared:

. . . in the concrete expression of a living world of ideas, as in law, the state, . . . philosophy as a whole, the object itself must be studied in its development; arbitrary divisions must not be introduced, the reason of the thing itself must develop as something imbued with contradictions in itself and find its unity in itself.[197]

Similarly, Bloch cites a passage from Marx's letter to Ruge in September, 1843 in which he argued that the true reality could be inferred from the reality at hand:

> The critic, therefore, can . . . develop the true actuality out of the forms *inherent* in existing actuality as its ought-to-be and goal.[198]

In his mature writings, Bloch claims, Marx discovered the immanence of the future in the present in the form of tendency. Marx showed that it was possible to go beyond the things at hand without leaping into empty air or abstract imagining: by analysing and then activating the concrete historical tendency.[199] Here Bloch finds an important link between Marx and Leibniz. Leibniz held that the present was pregnant with the future in the form of active tendencies, which only needed the impediments to their realisation to be removed for them to become actual. In this sense, for Leibniz the future was only the greater dimension of the present. Bloch argues that a similar conception lies at the heart of Marx's discovery. He cites Marx's doctrine that time is only the greater space of production and his claim that the present society is pregnant with the productive forces of the next, to show that Marx conceived of the future as in no way abstractly separate from the present, but as something already developing in the present as tendency.[200]

According to Bloch, Marxism makes it possible to become conscious of the concrete 'over-stepping' within the world at hand.[201] It is the dialectical historical tendency science which makes the horizon of the future knowable; and which relates this horizon to the past, as the corridor to it.[202] In this sense, Marxism is a science which is wholly concerned with the goal of action. It does not understand the future naturalistically, but it understands the new as something developing in what is at hand, which requires men to know and activate the tendency to it if it is to become actual. The difficulty is that although Bloch reasserts the idea of tendency in Marx against crude determinism and the claim that there are mechanistic laws in history, he does not explain in sufficient detail which tendencies Marx analysed or show that such analyses were in fact accurate. He leaves the crucial question of the criteria for assessing the extent and nature of the scientificity of Marxism vague, and so leaves open the objection that Marx's thought is an inadequate guide to the future, in that its selection of tendencies operates to repress the tendencies which it omits.

Fourth, Bloch implies that Marx had an immanentist conception of method and a 'realisationist' conception of revolution. In support of this claim, Bloch cites a passage from Marx's letter to Ruge in 1843 in which Marx wrote:

> It will . . . become evident that the world has long possessed the dream of a thing, of which it needs only to become conscious in order to possess it in reality. It will become evident that it is not a question of drawing a great mental line between past and future, but of *realising* the thoughts of the past.[203]

Bloch takes Marx's approach in 1843 as an indication of his immanentist method. This avoids the question of how far Marx's views in 1843 can be attributed to the author of *Capital*, but Bloch does not mean that Marx proposed to realise the ideas of the past without subjecting them to a thorough criticism and transformation. The Marxist method is to rectify good contents from the past: to set them 'on their feet'. 'Marxism never renounces its heritage, and least of all the primal intention: the Golden Age. In all its *analyses* Marxism plays the part of a sober detective, yet takes the *legend* seriously . . .',[204] Bloch argues. Rectification does not imply devaluation, and Bloch criticises the claim that Marx's ideas are 'secularisations' of Romantic, mystical, theosophical or Judaeo-Christian ideas. A good content is not 'secularised' when it is set upright and put into effect, he insists.[205] Instead, the presence of such good contents must be understood as a concrete utopian heritage, which remains to be realised. Here, Bloch makes his own conservative redemptionist tendencies basic to the method of Marxism, including a certain nostalgia for what has still not become actual. Applying the method to Marx himself, Bloch emphasises that Marxism did not begin with Marx, that Marx can be seen as raising the whole Western tradition to a higher level. For Bloch, Marx carries on the tradition of the Hebrew prophets, Joachim of

Flora, Thomas Münzer and the heretical sects, just as he inherits and corrects the best thoughts of the Enlightenment.

Bloch also implies that Marx preserved the anti-mundane, maximalist, qualitative dimension in what he inherited, and gave it a basis in reality for the first time. Marx was not a 'cut rate merchant'; he did not squander 'the temple treasure'.[206] Here, Bloch shows insight into an important aspect of Marx's character. He describes the young Marx as 'a young Faust',[207] and emphasises the extent to which Marx always retained a partiality for maximalist qualitative perspectives. This dimension of the young Marx is well known. The Romanticism of the early poems, the theme of the divinisation of man in Marx's attempt at a novel, the sympathy for Goethe, are not, however, often attributed to the mature Marx; and it is usual to regard the exuberance of the young Marx with some reservations. Bloch's originality is to stress the extent to which Marx always remained the man prone to these attractions: the man who read Aeschylus in Greek each year, respected Hegel, admired Kepler, and regarded Prometheus as his favourite saint.

Bloch confronts the Marxist tradition with an immensely learned and cultured Marx,[208] whose whole style of thinking challenges the emaciated image of Marx as a left wing Enlightenment ideologue who had the sense to abandon 'philosophy' when he became a revolutionary. Moreover, Bloch uses this perspective to evoke, if not 'a right wing Marx', then a Marx who drew more heavily on 'the philosophical right' (in the sense of thinkers who maintained that the world was objectively enchanted, anti-mundane and hierarchical) than is always realised. Thus, Bloch draws attention to Marx's use at crucial points of mystical terminology taken from the works of Boehme, Paracelsus and Agrippa.[209] Again, in contrast to most other interpreters, Bloch highlights Marx's debt to Schelling. Bloch notes that Marx praised Schelling's 'sincere youthful philosophy' in a letter to Feuerbach in 1843, and claims that Marx's analysis of the fetishism of commodities in his *Contribution to the Critique of Political Economy* echoes Schelling's famous injunction 'not to forget the producer in the product'. Here Bloch's position suggests a new reading of Marx in the context of a positive inheritance of Schelling and the subject-object problematic of German idealism.[210]

Fifth, Bloch interprets Marx as an active humanist who corrects and realises the class humanisms of the past. Marx combined passion and conscience with objective insight. He was motivated by moral indignation in the face of oppression, and by love of man. Bloch admits that Marx rejected the abstract love of man of the 'true socialists', however he emphasises that Marx's humanism was not sentimental, but an active humanism, which included hatred of the oppressors and action designed to bring oppression to an end. Bloch asserts that humanism was at the centre of Marx's critique of alienation, and of his criticism of civil society, and he denies that this humanism diminished when Marx's 'real humanism' became 'the materialist philosophy of history'.[211] Indeed, Marx wrote in the *Theses on Feuerbach* that the standpoint of the new materialism was 'socialised humanity'. According to Bloch, Marx inherited the progressive *humanum* of the revolutionary bourgeoisie, and the *humanum* remained the guide and critical standard in all his works, including *Capital*.[212] Clearly there is a distinction between the claim that Marx was motivated by concern for man, and the claim that Marx was committed to methodological humanism. For Bloch, however, Marx's method is precisely to show that 'the root of all things' in the human world is man, and to generate from that insight an immanent standard of criticism.[213] Bloch does not mean that the structure of a social formation or a mode of production can be explained solely in terms of the actions and motives of individuals, but that Marx criticises commodity production precisely because it separates the product from the producer and sets up heteronomous relationships which rob individuals of their humanity. For Marx, this was a false independence, something to be criticised in the name of the ontology of the individual producer which it deformed and distorted.

Finally, Bloch interprets Marx as a follower of Hegel, the greatest philosopher of the bourgeois period who sometimes did not need much 'inverting' to show red.[214] This is conventional enough; but Bloch does not adopt the standard schematic interpretation. Bloch interprets Hegel as a process philosopher, and then reads Marx through process philosophy lenses. According to Bloch, Marx set Hegel's subject-object process 'upright'. He dropped Hegel's false subject (the World Spirit), his doubly spiritualised account of the process, his inverted world, and his illusory abolition of the object. Marx made the process an earthly process, not a process of the production of absolute knowledge in the mind of the philosopher or a process of the World Spirit.[215] He and Engels identified the real 'subject' in history as the working man, and applied the lawfulness of Hegel's dialectic to the materialistic interpretation of nature and history.[216] But Marx, Bloch claims, retained Hegel's stress on 'process' in contrast to isolated 'facts'. He made the process a material process:[217] the process of dialectically developing matter.[218] Here, Bloch comes close to Soviet style dialectical materialism, for which Marx and Engels are materialist philosophers who found dialectical processuality at work in all material being.[219] This pattern of interpretation is discussed in more detail in chapter 3. It means, however, that when Bloch argues that Marxism is an outgrowth of Hegel's philosophy inverted so that it stands right way up,[220] he means something which no other Marxist has envisaged.

As an interpreter of Marx, Bloch is original but idiosyncratic. Bloch highlights neglected aspects of Marx's *corpus*, including aspects which Marx regarded as essential, but subsequently underemphasised. He also casts new light on Marx's epistemology, ethics, critique of religion and materialism. On the other hand, he eschews detailed scholarship and confuses crucial distinctions in a way which assimilates Marx's views to his own. He also gives a central place to statements (such as that history only sets itself tasks which it can solve or that reality presses towards thought as much as thought presses towards reality[221]) which are not as focal in Marx as many better known *dicta* which he never treats at all. Again, he concentrates to an unjustifiable extent on texts from 1839–45, and fails to deal adequately with Marx's later development. Nonetheless, Bloch does not ignore the 'mature' Marx. Rather, he argues for a continuationist thesis, for which the same Marx wrote the letters of 1843 and *Grundrisse*. This is a more defensible view than some of the English and French literature suggests. Bloch realises that Marx's early pronouncements are admixed with idealism; but he sees that the young Marx already possessed a revolutionary method, and that the problem is to interpret the mature Marx in a way which does not involve attributing to him positions which he had already rejected by 1845. His achievement is to restore to Marxism a Marx who is a more complex and sophisticated thinker than most of the Marxist tradition tends to suggest. But this achievement may not be sufficient for Bloch's purposes. Bloch claims that

Marx was a materialist from 1843 on, and interprets Marx's later views as consistent with his *Theses on Feuerbach*.[222] But even apart from the objections to such an interpretation, he does not show that Marx's critique of abstract utopianism was adequate or complete, nor that Marx's own work is free from bad utopianism. As a result, he vitiates the critical force of his critique of the Marxist tradition by appealing to a critique of utopia which is never subjected to rigorous analysis, and by invoking a rehabilitation of utopia which may suffer from the same defects which he has failed to observe in Marx.

MARXISM TRANSFORMED

Granted Bloch's critique of the Marxist tradition and his interpretation of Marx, it follows that Marxism needs to be further developed and expanded, in both range and depth. For Bloch, Marxism can only be continued if it is developed, and such development is not to be judged against Marx's texts as scriptures, but by its adequacy as a response to the failures of Marxism in theory and practice since Marx's death. Marxism beyond Marx must not abandon Marx's insights, but it must break with out of date and inhibiting premises, and expand its constricted horizons.

In this context Bloch attempts to supplement Marxism with a series of radical developments designed to counter the main *lacunae* of the Marxist tradition. To overcome the practicist foreshortening of the goal which has occurred in the Marxist tradition, Bloch attempts to supplement Marxism with a new conception of reality or Marxist metaphysics. The analysis will now turn to this Marxist metaphysics or 'Open System'.

3 Open System: Marxist Metaphysics I

M. Terentius Varro is supposed to
have forgotten the future tense in
his first attempt at a Latin grammar,
but in philosophy it has not been
adequately recognised even today.
The Principle of Hope

Open System: Marxist metaphysics — the conception is so unfamiliar in the Marxist tradition that there is a danger that
Bloch's achievement will be read down to the sources which
were his starting points. Bloch, however, is not a metaphysician
manqué, but a Marxist philosopher of unusual originality. In
this and the following chapter, an attempt is made to give an
account of Open System which remains faithful to the radicalism
of the design. Hitherto, many commentators have trivialised
Bloch's stress on process, and then complained of his 'lack of
system'. They have domesticated his central concepts, and then
found the pseudo-radicalism of the neo-classical metaphysics
which ensued incompatible with Marxism. In contrast, these
chapters attempt to explain Bloch's central concepts and categories without making them clearer than they actually are. It is
argued that Open System is not reducible to earlier systems but
belongs, like Heidegger's attempt to overcome the history of
being as metaphysics or Adorno's critique of identity thinking,
to the rim of twentieth century philosophical speculation: to
the region in which a limitation is perceived in the inherited
pattern of thinking at a time when no alternative is available,
except the alternative of making this inherited pattern of thinking think against itself. Stress is placed on the fact that Bloch
was influenced by several forms of process philosophy, and it is
argued that Open System resembles some forms of modern process philosophy in important respects. It is necessary, however, to
see how Bloch uses his process philosophy model in an attempt

to bring Marxism into a theory-praxis relationship with the future as something which can be shaped by men. No attempt is made to discount Bloch's metaphysical radicalism, but emphasis is placed: (1) on the initiatory character of his thinking; (2) on the fact that many of his concepts are more familiar than they at first appear, but are radicalised by his use of the operator 'not yet'; and (3) on the activist political motivation present throughout.

The term 'process philosophy' is generally used to describe philosophies which regard reality as a process or a series of processes.[1] It covers both traditional philosophies which emphasise the processual character of the world (for example, the philosophies of Heraclitus, Aristotle, Proclus, Plotinus, Scotus Erigena, Leibniz and Hegel), and also modern philosophies which use the idea of process to challenge radically traditional philosophical assumptions. In English the term 'process philosophy' is mainly used in connection with the modern process philosophies of Bergson and Whitehead, or in the context of process theology; but the term has wider application than this suggests. Modern process philosophers have included revisionary metaphysicians such as Peirce, Alexander, Bergson and Whitehead, speculative religious thinkers such as Solovyev, Berdyaev, Sri Aurobindo and Teilhard de Chardin, independents such as James Ward, William James, W. P. Montague and Charles Hartshorne, as well as *pensadores* such as Vasconcelos in Mexico and Iqbal in Pakistan, who exerted an influence on the intellectual and cultural history of their countries out of all proportion to the philosophical interest of their ideas. As revisionary metaphysics, modern process philosophy has concentrated on the need to break with philosophies which conceive of the world as complete or unchanging, and to develop new categories for a world of becoming. Apart from a commitment to internal relations in place of an ontology of simple particulars, modern process philosophers have been influenced by such doctrines as energeticism, emergence, real temporal becoming, contingency, novelty, holism and realism. Side by side with this involvement in revisionary metaphysics, however, modern process philosophy has also often been characterised by subjectivism and by explicit or concealed theology. Indeed, some modern process philosophers have used the claim that reality is a process to advance mystical, religious, or even pantheist doctrines as *avant-garde* process metaphysics. While claiming to be ultra-modern, even futuristic thinkers, they have reintroduced radically old ideas such as pan-organicism, pan-psychism, and teleology in a process philosophy form, and have postulated a process, more objective than 'facts' or 'things', which then guaranteed the subject's values and tended to higher levels of personality, or even to an emergent God term. By no means all modern process philosophers have confused process philosophy as revisionary metaphysics with a reassertion of the politics of the subject; but the danger of doing so may not be extrinsic. These remarks provide a background for the 'starting points' which Bloch used in developing Open System.

As a young man Bloch attempted to develop a speculative energeticism in response to Ostwald's *The Overcoming of Scientific Materialism* (1895) and Haeckel's *The Riddles of the Universe* (1899). He saw that an energeticism for which matter could be defined as force (*Kraft*) still needed to explain the cause of matter's movement, and, under the influence of Schopenhauer and Nietzsche, he attempted to identify the immanently developing 'thing in itself' as will.[2] In 1902 Bloch argued that 'the thing in itself' was the objective imagination (*Phantasie*) and that the contrast between ethics (*Sittlichkeit*) and sensuousness was a lie. He wrote:

> The philosophy of force does not merely dissolve all stuff and elements into energy, as in natural science, and denote the thing in itself as energetic universal will, which, as it were, has missed its vocation, and flows back without any purpose into itself and its cycles: rather the essence of the world is cheerful spirit and impetus to creative forms; the thing in itself is the objective imagination.[3]

This early monist problematic was to be transcended, but it signals the bias of Bloch's later philosophy towards a reconciliation of subject and object, as well as a possible basis for his use of anthropomorphic expressions, designed to prevent a separation of subject and object which cannot then be overcome.

Bloch was also in contact as a young man with currents of thought from which a process philosophy model of the world could be directly developed. Bloch was familiar with William James' process philosophy speculations, and he studied James'

A Pluralistic Universe in which James emphasised that the universe was an unfinished *multiversum*, not a *universum*.[4] Bloch was also influenced as a young man by the speculative process philosophies of Jakob Frohschammer and Eduard von Hartmann. Bloch's debt to the Catholic philosopher-priest and church historian Jakob Frohschammer is controversial, since Bloch does not mention Frohschammer in any of his works and the connection has also escaped modern German readers. Shortly before his death, however, Bloch admitted in conversation that he read Frohschammer in his youth, and that he may have used the term 'objective imagination' in his 1902 manuscript under Frohschammer's influence.[5] Frohschammer developed a teleological process philosophy, based on a variant of the vogue for a single principle (*Prinzip*) of the world process. For Frohschammer, the world was a teleological process developing towards entelechy, in which objective imagination (the teleological formative force in nature) and subjective imagination elicited new forms and so brought the world closer to completion. Moreover, Frohschammer analysed day dreams, art, religion and mythology in light of this model of the process.[6] Bloch was not in any sense a follower of Frohschammer, and the literary parallels between Frohschammer's model of the process and certain aspects of Bloch's thought should not obscure the fact that Bloch transformed what he borrowed and used it in a different sense.

Bloch's debt to von Hartmann was more direct. Eduard von Hartmann (1842–1906) is now remembered as the philosopher of the unconscious who influenced Freud, and as a pessimistic follower of Schopenhauer. In his lifetime, however, he was a highly respected philosopher, whose epistemological theory, known as Transcendental Realism, attracted international attention. Bloch corresponded with von Hartmann, but once again was not a follower. He was distant temperamentally from von Hartmann's pessimism, and while he knew and benefited from von Hartmann's model of the process, there is little evidence that he concerned himself with the details of von Hartmann's suffering God who needed to be liberated from the torments of the world process. Bloch learnt, however, from von Hartmann's sophisticated approach to the problem of the relationship between consciousness and being. He was decisively influenced by both von Hartmann's Transcendental Realism and by his philosophy of the unconscious with its manifold differentiations.

In addition, he accepted von Hartmann's insistence that the world could not be represented in solely logical terms. He also made use of several of von Hartmann's technical distinctions, including his dual theory of categories, which allowed for both intensive and logical dimensions in the categories, and his distinctions between the subjective-ideal, the objective-real, and the metaphysical spheres.[7] Above all, von Hartmann provided Bloch with a perspective on the late philosophy of Schelling. Von Hartmann criticised both Hegel's pan-logism and Schopenhauer's pan-thelism as one-sided, and argued that it was necessary to develop a system which treated Idea and Will as related attributes of the one substance. He believed that Schelling had outlined such a system in his late philosophy, especially in his *Philosophy of Mythology and Revelation*, and used Schelling's late philosophy to introduce his own concrete monism of the unconscious absolute.[8]

Whereas Bloch freely acknowledges his debt to von Hartmann, he is more circumspect about his debt to Schelling. Nonetheless, Bloch's debt to Schelling is immense and goes beyond the perspective offered by von Hartmann. In his late philosophy, Schelling attempted to rethink the central problems of metaphysics to take account of real temporal becoming, contingency, emergence and human freedom. He outlined a dynamic historical ontology for a world which developed and changed as a result of human action.[9] Bloch knew Schelling's late philosophy from his reading in the library of Mannheim castle and an underground of echoes and references runs through his work. His relationship to Schelling, however, was an active one, and he extrapolated model ideas and terminology with little regard for their meaning in Schelling's theological system, including: (1) the idea that philosophy should be historical, and can play a constitutive part in the making of history, since the future is not decided in advance by a quasi-objectivist structure of being, but depends on the projections and actions of men; (2) the idea that it is necessary to break with all perfectionist ontology and to develop a cosmogenesis model of reality, according to which the process develops from a state of imperfection to *omega* or *genesis*; (3) the idea that philosophy should not begin with an already solved, logical *prius*, but with an ungraspable, a-logical That, characterised by the needing-to-come-to-be of an objectively problematic and unsolved content (*Zwang der Sache*); (4) the idea that this unsolved content appears in the darkness of the unmediated moment; (5) the idea that the process is a process in search of the perfect mediation of its ground, in which the That drives towards its What; (6) the idea that the process is an unsolved identity process, in which identity is a *futurum* which anticipates itself in art and nature, even though it depends for its possible realisation on future contents and on adequate human action; (7) the idea that nature exhibits finality, and can be brought to a possible fulfilment through the emergence of a subject of nature; and (8) the idea that art can be the *organon* of philosophy.[10]

Bloch, however, did not confine his study of process philosophy models to Frohschammer, von Hartmann and Schelling. He also studied the process philosophies of Aristotle and Leibniz. In addition, he made an elaborate study of the modern revisionary process metaphysics being developed by Bergson. Bergson believed that traditional metaphysics had repressed the future, the possible and the new; he sought to develop a new process metaphysics based on a rejection of Eleatic metaphysics and Laplacean determinism, in which they would have a central place.[11] Bloch made an extensive study of Bergson's *Matter and Memory* (1896) and *Creative Evolution* (1907). He criticised Bergson's irrationalism, especially his doctrine of intuition and his quasi-mystical *élan vital*, and argued that for all his emphasis on indeterminism, irreversible duration and novelty, Bergson had no genuine concept of process, but only a non-finalistic concept of temporality and a process of endless rearrangement.[12] Nonetheless, although Bloch was critical of Bergson's doctrines, he took up the precedent of categorial innovations based on real temporality, and developed versions of novelty, possibility, contingency and temporality of his own, which he claimed did not suffer from Bergson's defects.

Bloch's widely misunderstood relation to Hegel needs to be seen in this process philosophy context. Although Bloch studied Hegel in his youth and claimed when he met Lukács that he knew 'only Hegel and Karl May',[13] there is little evidence that he was ever a strict Hegelian. Bloch sought to uncover the future in Hegel rather than to understand Hegel as a philosopher whose views were defensible *per se*. The basic pattern of his interpretation emerged in *Spirit of Utopia* (1918). Nonetheless, the details of Bloch's reformulation and wider working of Hegel were not clear until the publication of his study of Hegel, *Subject-Object*, in German in 1951. Even then, the structure and density of his argument impeded ready access, especially since he tended to mix Hegel interpretation with entries to his own system. Bloch's reading of Hegel is essentially different from the radical-ising interpretations of Lukács, Marcuse, Kojève and Hyppolite. Whereas Lukács and Marcuse tried to save Hegel for Marxism by representing him as less theological, mystical and meta-physical than Marx and Engels assumed he had been, Bloch argues that Hegel was not an atheistic *Aufklärer*, but an unorthodox Christian, influenced by Gnostic and Rosicrucian ideas.[14] So far from being Marx before Marx, Hegel was a metaphysical idealist and a 'mystical rationalist', who was sometimes most progressive when he was advancing metaphysical, mystical or theological doctrines. In a subtle gloss on Marx, Bloch implies that in Hegel the rational kernel appeared *in the mystical shell*. Consistent with this stress, he emphasises Hegel's mystical sources, his debt to Nicholas of Cusa and Boehme, and his place in the tradition of strong rationalism which runs from the neo-Platonists through Scotus Erigena. At the same time, he stresses the systematic character of Hegel's thought in every area, in opposition to attempts to make him simply a philosopher of history or an important political theorist.

Bloch interprets Hegel as *a process thinker* in the tradition of Aristotle, Plotinus, Nicholas of Cusa, Boehme and Leibniz,[15] and uses Hegel's emphasis on process to explain his superiority over thinkers who employ static concepts. According to Bloch, Hegel's central thought was that reality was a subject-object process.[16] With this idea, Hegel broke with the constellation of traditional problems generated by the dualism between an objective reality independent of men and a subjective reality denied objective status. He ' . . . introduced the true *objectivity* as that of a permanent dialectical subject-object relationship, by virtue of the *movement* already there before man, and human-historical *work* in and on the process'.[17] Like the Lukács of *History and Class Consciousness,* Bloch finds the basis for a practical as well as a theoretical advance beyond Kantian agnos-ticism and positivism in Hegel's subject-object process.[18] Un-like Lukács, however, Bloch sees that the advance is not waiting to be discovered in Hegel, that Hegel's own position is highly metaphysical, and that in Hegel this subject-object relationship is not confined to history but is present in the *Logik* and the *Realphilosophie*.[19] In effect, Bloch adopts an ultra-ontological interpretation of Hegel and then argues that it is this Hegel who needs to be 'rectified' in Marxism.

For Bloch, the *Phenomenology* provides the model of Hegel's process of world travel in both subject and object. Bloch, however, develops a parallel between the *Phenomenology* and Goethe's *Faust* which tends to conflate Hegel's dialectical development of the stages of consciousness with the satisfaction dialectic by which Faust journeys from moment to moment in search of an adequate object, or fulfilled moment.[20] Both the *Phenomenology* and *Faust*, Bloch claims, are based on the model of a journey of subject and object towards fulfilment, with a prevalence of the subject, a renewing birth of the goal ahead at each stage, and an exchange of countenance between subject and object at the end of the process.

Bloch also adopts ultra-ontological interpretations of Hegel's concepts of dialectic and totality. According to Bloch, Hegel's dialectic was an objective dialectic of the real (*Realdialektik*) in the tradition of Proclus, Nicholas of Cusa, Boehme and Leibniz. It was the law of movement of a process with immanent totality, and was based on the fundamental contradiction between reality at hand and the developing totality, not merely on local oppositions or resistances. So far from being merely 'negative', it functioned positively as a continual transcending of inadequate process forms, which extracted what was valuable from each phase, and always drove forward to new and richer content. Hegel's dialectic, Bloch argues, was the dialectic of an immanently developing *totum*.[21] Similarly, Hegel's concept of totality derived from Nicholas of Cusa and involved a form of emergent absolutism. For Hegel, totality was present *omnia ubique* throughout the process: *formally* in the all-pervading triadic structure of the process (the triad representing the Trinity), and *intensively* in the preappearance of 'essence' in each stage.[22] Here Bloch is close to modern critics of Hegel such as Colletti and Adorno. Whereas, however, Colletti and Adorno argue that Marxism must break with Hegel's wholly metaphysical and speculative system, Bloch takes a more hermeneutical view.[23]

Bloch attacks any attempt to import Hegel into Marx or to make Marxism pseudo-Hegelianism. He emphasises that all of Hegel's philosophy is idealist and panlogical, and can only be inherited by Marxism in an essentially different form.[24] On the other hand, large parts of Hegel's philosophy can be inherited by Marxism, Bloch argues, provided they are 'rectified' and relocated in an essentially different problematic. Indeed, on this basis, Bloch argues for a greater inheritance of Hegel than has been envisaged by any other Marxist. For Bloch, Hegel's psychology, ethics, aesthetics, philosophy of history, philosophy of law, philosophy of religion and even his philosophy of nature can all be critically reworked in Marxism in an active creative inheritance.[25]

Bloch, however, goes further. In an implied critique of the whole Marxist tradition Bloch argues that it is necessary to set Hegel's 'system' on its feet, and not just the dialectic.[26] Bloch's point is that although Marx and Engels both borrowed extensively from Hegel's system[27] (most obviously from his *Logik,* aesthetics, philosophy of right and philosophy of nature), a radical rethinking is necessary to make sense of the latent incoherence of the standard Marxist attempts to formulate a materialist 'dialectic' without having regard to the dependence of the model concept in Hegel on his system. If Marxism is an incomplete and often confused mediation of a materialist standpoint with Hegel's philosophy, it is partly because the exact relationship between Hegel's system and the new materialism was never adequately articulated by either Marx or Engels, both of whom also left the elaboration of the new materialist outlook radically incomplete. A further mediation of Marxism is therefore needed, Bloch argues, in which Hegel's system can play a decisive part, just as it has played a decisive part *in absentia* until now.[28] Bloch implies that ignorance of Hegel has been an important cause of the distortion of Marx's legacy and of the general lack of depth in the Marxist tradition. Ignorance of Hegel's system meant ignorance of Hegel, and granted ignorance of Hegel, Marx himself appeared in rags and it was possible to interpret Marxism as the overcoming of all 'philosophy'. As a result, Marxism in the West was often little more than a mixture of economic determinism and sociologism, while in the East a scholasticism emerged, which made Marxism *inter alia* an ideological interpretation of the results of the special sciences.

In contrast, Bloch argues that Marxists must know, understand and go beyond Hegel.[29] Without Hegel there would have been no Marx, but without Marx Hegel is not futuristic, and what is needed is a Marxist 'rectification' and wider working of the futuristic elements in Hegel. Bloch calls for a radically critical Marxist inheritance of Hegel's system (*Umfunktionierung*): for a new Marxist philosophy which inherits the power of Hegel's system, including its utopia of immanent totality, and the comprehensiveness and range of Hegel's world encyclopaedia, on new and in no way Hegelian foundations.[30] Marxism is still in the outline stage: there is no Marxist anthropology, ethics, philosophy of history, aesthetics, theory of categories, philosophy of law, philosophy of religion or philosophy of nature.[31] Of course, a Marxist occupation of these areas would not be 'philosophy' in the conventional sense, but the areas occupied up to now by philosophy are of crucial importance, and a Marxism which leaves them unoccupied is necessarily superficial and underdeveloped, or else acquiesces in patterns of thought in which its epistemological revolution has not been allowed to appear. According to Bloch, Hegel's system provides valuable elements for such a further mediation of Marxism, not only in the *Phenomenology* and in the *Logik*, but in the *Realphilosophie*.[32] Moreover, Bloch argues that Marxism can inherit the 'secret utopianism' of Hegel's system.[33]

Hegel postulated a process in which subject became substance and vice versa; he attempted to understand reality, not only as a dialectical process in which the subject came to self knowledge, but as a process in which there was an identity between the self (*Selbst*) and the truth as it could become through the revelation of the depth contents of the process.[34] According to Bloch, Marxism can inherit both Hegel's subject-object relationship and Hegel's subject-substance relationship in a new utopian system, which postulates that the subject can become substance through dialectical subject-object mediations in history.[35] Here Bloch breaks with the whole Marxist tradition. So far from 'Hegelianising' Marxism, however, Bloch utopianises Hegel. He interprets Hegel differently from Marx, and then makes the views which he finds in Hegel the views which are to be rectified and set on their feet in Marxism.

Bloch recognises that there are many objective difficulties in the way of such a development, and that Marx himself did not embark on anything so ambitious. According to Bloch, Marx set Hegel's process 'upright'. He identified the real subject of history as the working man (*homo faber*), and transformed Hegel's mystical subject-object process into the subject-object process of history, in which man, as the totality of social relationships, transforms both himself and the world through labour.[36] Nonetheless, Bloch recognises that Marx did not make the whole world a subject-object process. In so far as man stands within history, which encompasses nature, there is a single subject-object process in which everything of which men have knowledge is mediated by subject-object oscillations. But the problem of nature remains, despite the fact that nature itself is shaped and formed to some extent by human labour. Bloch argues that Marx made the process a material process, but he recognises that the relationship between the subject-object process of history and the process or processes of nature was not worked out in detail by Marx or Engels, and that Engels' attempt to explain how the dialectic worked in nature was less than successful.[37] This means that there is a problem, not only about how the utopian inheritance of Hegel which Bloch proposes could be effected, but about the relationship between such a proposal and Marxism understood as the totality of the *dicta* of Marx and Engels. Bloch often obscures this problem by citing Marx's *dicta* (as well as the *dicta* of Engels, Lenin and Stalin) as if his own views were a further concretisation of Marx's, and by speaking of 'Marxism', when he means Marxism which has already absorbed the development which he proposes.

Bloch emphasises that the Marxist supersession (*Aufhebung*) of Hegel which he proposes requires a critique of outmoded and inhibiting premises in Marxism, as well as new anthropological and historico-philosophical premises designed to take account of the development of the Marxist tradition since Marx's death.[38] He also recognises that such a development requires a more radical critique of Hegel than has prevailed so far. In the Marxist tradition, Hegel's 'idealism', panlogism and conceptual realism have been subjected to extensive criticism, but the fundamental point has been missed: the question of the availability of the world, and the consequent orientation of ontology and epistemology towards the past and the future.

Bloch takes up this point and argues that Hegel's whole philosophy is flawed by *anamnesis*.[39] *Anamnesis* was Plato's doctrine that knowledge took the form of recollection of Ideas seen in the transcendental world before birth. Bloch, however, uses the term to designate the tendency to: (1) restrict knowledge to

knowledge of what has become (backward looking epistemology); and (2) to backdate the structure and contents of the
world to a mythical beginning or 'first point', as if everything
was present *in potentia* and decided from the start (backward
looking ontology). According to Bloch, *anamnesis* pervades
both Hegel's epistemology and his ontology because Hegel lacks
any concept of the genuinely future or the genuinely new. He
conceives of knowledge as backward looking, ultimately as recollection; the owl of Minerva flies at dusk. Similarly, Hegel's
logic pre-exists in the mind of God, and his dialectic is a laying
out of what was present as unmediated possibility. Moreover,
Hegel's whole system is concluded *ab initio*: the process is
decided and well ordered from the start, and assumes an existing *Pan* or unified structure of being. The World Spirit has done
his work; the world spheres are fixed; and every detail of the
process is subordinated to an existing pattern of arrangement.
Moreover, Hegel's process is a tautology: a circle of circles,
which ends with the World Spirit returning to eternity to begin
the whole process all over again.[40]

It is possible to defend Hegel from these changes, in particular
to show that some of them presuppose a highly mythical interpretation. Such a defence, however, should not obscure Bloch's
contribution. Bloch's attack on Hegel's *anamnesis* implies that
any Marxist inheritance of Hegel's system must be based on a
break with all backward looking epistemology and ontology,
and not only on a break with Hegel's 'idealism' in the sense of
the primacy of thought or spirit. Most Marxists, he implies, have
not made this more radical break; they have substituted *backward looking* but allegedly 'materialist' epistemology and ontology for the *backward looking* idealist epistemology and ontology found in Hegel. Instead, Bloch argues, it is necessary to
break with all *anamnesis,* and to develop a Marxist philosophy
oriented to the future and the new.[41] Bloch calls this new philosophy: Open System.

OPEN SYSTEM

The idea that any future philosophical system needs to be an
open system because new contents will arise in the future, was
one of Rickert's basic teachings, and occurs in several modern

German philosophers, including Nicolai Hartmann.[42] Bloch's concept of 'Open System', however, is more radical. It is a new venture in both Marxism and in the history of metaphysics, which tries to break free from the thought patterns which it employs, and to which we are tempted to reduce it. Bloch's Open System is difficult to understand and strains the limits of the thought patterns which we have inherited at many points. Moreover, there is a danger that it will be domesticated by an interpretation which seeks to render coherent a pattern of thinking which is valuable precisely because it attempts to go beyond distinctions which seem inescapable, in order to open up patterns which are still at the stage of 'rough calculation'. Open System therefore needs to be approached with an eye for anticipation and with a consciousness of the difficulty of all horizon thinking, rather than seen through as an odd assemblage of philosophical bric-a-brac: a pathetic rehashing of age-old mistakes. It is not conventional philosophy, least of all the ungainly ménage which some interpreters have produced as a response to Bloch's texts.

Open System is Bloch's mature fusion of his utopian philosophy, process philosophy interests, and Marxism, and a direct continuation of the politics of philosophy which he outlined in *Spirit of Utopia*. It is an attempt to put the epistemological revolution which Bloch attributes to Marx into effect. Marx, Bloch argues, discovered the Archimedean point which makes it possible to exert a leverage on history by a theory-praxis oriented towards the contradictions in the world at hand.[43] Until Marx, knowledge was oriented to the already become. The new remained out of reach, and the present was an embarrassment, less knowable because the necessary distance and perspective were lacking, despite the fact that it was the region of decision making and purposive action.[44] Marx, in contrast, oriented knowledge to the present including the impeded future which it contained, and to what was to come. He broke with all purely contemplative, observational philosophy and with all theory pursued for its own sake, and developed *a revolutionary philosophy of changing the world,* based on the investigation of tendencies, knowledge of occurrences and a concrete relation to decision making.[45]

Open System aims to be Marxist philosophy in this sense: theory-praxis on the philosophical front, in contrast to all contemplative, observational philosophy which merely interprets the world which has become. Bloch recognises that Marxist philosophy cannot be more 'philosophy' in the old sense: that the revolutionary standpoint of the proletariat, partiality for the future, and an orientation to praxis combined with Marxist situation analysis, redefine what Marxist philosophy can be. Marxist philosophy, he argues, must stand at the front, knowledgeably active in the contemporary process of transformation, and provide a systematic interpretation of the tendencies developing in the world. It must provide the sense of the 'where to', without which there can be no authentic Marxist theory-praxis.[46] This is a conception of philosophy which is easier to state than to realise, and which raises many questions about the relationship between Marxist philosophy and philosophy as it has traditionally been understood.

Open System attempts to break with all backward looking epistemology and ontology. In contrast to Hegel's system, which according to Bloch only allowed philosophy to remember, Open System attempts to grasp the not yet known, not yet become, still arising elements in the world, and is oriented towards the future and the new.[47] It involves a radically non-classical interpretation of the nature and function of philosophy, and of the epistemological and ontological situation in which philosophy is attempted. Open System denies both the traditional assumption that the ontological structure of the world is settled, and the more deep seated assumption that man and the world are epistemologically available. According to Bloch, both man and the world are 'not yet': they are unfinished and in an unconcluded tendential state, and need to be changed in the direction of knowability.[48] Moreover, the world at hand is not 'true': it has not yet realised its truth (*Wahrheit*).[49] It is a *Vor-Welt*, the details of which are primarily important to the extent that they reveal the possibility of not-yet-actual true being (*ontōs on*). The world is in process and objectively problematic; its content (*Sache*) is 'not yet out', and our task is to push it forward by theory-praxis, not to enclose it within a system of ontological hypostasisations or settled meanings:

> Our task is to grasp the content (*Sache*) pending in the world process, to grasp it in its up to now not-yet-determination, and to *push it forward* to its still immanent real possible

success, instead of breaking it off with a principle (*Prinzip*) or an absolute which is already given as present, and so to fixate it in a false manner.

Bloch declares.[50] In this sense, philosophy must become 'the conscience of tomorrow, partiality for the future, knowledge of hope,'[51] without premising the closure of the world on which pre-Marxist philosophy depends. Open System attempts to be 'the conscience of tomorrow' in the sense of philosophy which provides direction and keeps men conscious of the new still to come and of the unreached goal; it is 'partiality for the future' in the sense of a pattern of thinking which aims to help the good 'not yet' into being; it is 'knowledge of hope' in the sense of a systematic attempt to grasp and bring into a dialectical system both what men intend, and what is becoming possible in the world.

Open System is not traditional metaphysics, but activist *viator* philosophy which aims at *metaphysical productivity* in subject and object alike. Its task is not that of an undertaker commissioned to take the measurements of a dead world, but that of a billeting officer; it aims to represent the world as 'open' and 'unfinished' in a way which helps the 'not yet' into being. For Bloch, there is a primacy of practical reason in the logic of philosophy, and Open System must be judged not only by its formal validity or by the epistemological justification for its categories, but by the extent to which it gives men an historically situated handlehold on an unfinished world, and helps them to shape it in a humanly successful direction.

As historical philosophy elaborated in the unfinished process which it seeks to influence, Open System is not an interpretation of reality *sub specie aeternitatis* which assumes that the world can be known apart from the class standpoints and particular social relationships of men. It is limited by the stage of development which the subject and the object have reached, and by the point in the process at which its pre-view of process possibilities is articulated. Open System, however, aims at transmission to a future phase of the process where, in another society and with a more developed material content in both subject and object, problems which are only pre-posed now in a necessarily mythological manner, may be posed more adequately and brought to a result.[52]

As transmission philosophy, Open System reworks thought experiments from the past, with a view not to formulating watertight finished doctrines, but to the transmission of models which will be later rectified or even replaced. Open System is *experimental philosophy,*[53] not only in the sense that it contains thought experiments which aim beyond the regnant paradigms, but also in the sense that it attempts to contribute to the experiment for content taking place in the process, rather than to the staticist utopia of correct philosophical doctrine. It contains 'outlines', 'postulates', 'model theses', 'creative calculations' and 'anticipatory designs'[54] which aim to begin the process of causation leading to the realisation of what they contain. It involves long term suppositions, which cannot be falsified by the facts at hand, and which aim at contents which will not come into manageable focus in the immediate future. Open System is *consciously utopian*, and aims at historically effective anticipation. It is speculative by design and with projective intent, and takes as its guiding principles: *exodus, expedition* and *utopian excess.*[55] This means that many, though not all, of the objections to Open System fall within the definition of its project. As *viator* philosophy which exploits the epistemological resources open to the traveller and systematises 'indications', 'signs', 'testimonies' and 'possibly significant details' which may give a clue to the path ahead, Open System is based on weak epistemological claims and derives its possibility as a system from *a decision* to systematise such claims. It therefore not only lacks some of the virtues of traditional philosophy, but involves the claim that some of those virtues are over-optimistic *vis-à-vis* our situation, and so misplaced.

As *viator* philosophy which aims at real world travel in both subject and object, Open System redefines the classical concept of truth. The 'truth' which 'Open System' seeks is a truth in travel; and the aim of Open System is to provide a plan of journey which will be revised once travel has taken place. Open System aims at material truth (*Wahrheit*), which remains to be produced and which depends for its verification on its production as a result.[56] At this point in time, this truth is not available in an unproblematic form: it is developing and in large part 'not yet'. The truth that is available now is the truth of correctedness and the truth of process trends. Man, however, also has access to normative truth, the postulatory truth of practical

reason which cannot be refuted by the 'facts' of a humanly inadequate world; and this truth must be summarised and acted
on now, if material truth is ever to be produced. Similarly, Open
System involves a revision of the classical conception of error.
In Open System concepts are not necessarily erroneous simply
because their outlines are mistaken. Error, in the historically
and philosophically serious sense, is not a mistaken projection
which leads Columbus to find India instead of the New World,
but a pattern of thinking which never sets sail.

In contrast to all previous Marxist philosophy, Open System
aims to grasp the world as a world which is open to a not yet
reached, still undecided *processual* future, which is not given or
pre-fixed in the past. It is an *open* system, not only in the sense
of a system which allows for new contents still to come, but in
the sense of a system which takes such new contents as intrinsic
to the character of the world, and attempts to rethink the fundamental categories of philosophy as a result. Open System represents the world as fundamentally unfinished and changeable: as
a system of developing open coherences, the laws and structure
of which change as it develops.[57] It represents the world as
an *experimental world* which can be shaped by human gearing
and goal setting, beyond the limits of any closed world conception and beyond the restrictions of any settled ontology. It is
a futuristic, eschatologically open system for a world which can
be brought to a good result through the actions of men.[58]

Open System, however, is an open *system*: a dialectical system of utopian material truth.[59] The new philosophy requires
system because it is the duty of philosophy to supply an interpretation of the world as a whole;[60] but this system cannot be
one which classifies the world as though it were finished and
settled, as though it had already reached its final ontological
form. On the contrary, in Open System there can be no *fixum*
or settled substratum, in which everything is contained *in
potentia*; no already finished 'substance', 'concluded entelechy',
or 'decided essence'; no imposed logical schemas; no fixed
world spheres; no concluded specification of nature; and no
subordination of details to a decided pattern of arrangement,
as though the world were an already existent *Pan*.[61] The world,
Bloch argues, is not a well ordered system with an already decided meaning, but 'unsolved', full of *allotrias* and disparities,
a *multiversum,* not a *universum* (William James), which contains
many chambers and different levels.[62]

Open System, therefore, can only be a *utopian* system for an unfinished world. Given that both epistemologically and onto-logically the completeness required for a traditional system is not available, Open System can only be a system constructed with a view to transmission, which seeks to bring all the elements in the world which can contribute to the good future into a process of realisation, by indicating at the level of theory (with praxis as its purpose content) what their relevance to a possible future cohesion might be. Nonetheless, Open System inherits the intention of 'system' in Hegel's sense, in that it represents the world contents as relating to a still utopian totality.[63] The immanent totality of Open System is 'not yet' and does not exist anywhere.[64] It is utopian in three senses: (1) it has 'no place' in the world at hand; (2) it premises the possibility of maximalist fulfilment; and (3) it has a critical function *vis-à-vis* the inadequate world at hand. The totality of Open System is to be produced in history by theory-praxis, but the world of Open System has the possibility of becoming a totality, the possibility of becoming a solved, unified world. It is not 'solved' now, and the very possibility of such a development cannot be stated apart from human action or as something given *ab initio*. An objective-real intention to such a development however pre-appears throughout the process:

> Actuality is *nominalism,* not conceptual realism, nonetheless nominalism, all the moments and details of which are kept together through the *unity of the objective real intention,* are founded through the *utopian unity of the goal.*[65]

This objective-real intention requires human activity and plan-ning over long historical periods if it is to cease to be utopian. It depends on dialectics, as a process of transmission beyond the contents at hand which can become a revolutionary realisation process when it is grasped and made the object of conscious planning by men.[66] Open System therefore requires a hermen-eutics which analyses the world contents for their possible rele-vance to dialectical transmission. It requires a new world ency-clopaedia: an encyclopaedia of possible 'instances' with a posi-tive or negative relationship to the outstanding totality, which, unlike Hegel's world encyclopaedia, is not panlogical or well or-dered from the start, and in which the contents are not subsumed under a preordained, purely schematic pattern of arrangement.[67]

In contrast to Hegel's world encyclopaedia, the encyclopaedia of Open System must give full representation to details, particulars and singularities with objective-real intention to a possible future cohesion, wherever they are to be found.[68]

This preliminary characterisation may be sufficient to indicate that those interpreters who attribute a neo-classical metaphysics to Bloch misrepresent his position, and that those Marxist critics who accuse Bloch of making Marxism 'philosophy' have not attended sufficiently to what 'philosophy' for Bloch means.[69] Open System is only 'metaphysics' in an unconventional sense. It is activist metaphysics which occupies the *topos* of traditional metaphysics for Marxist purposes.[70] As constitutive imagination (*Phantasie*) which interprets the world in terms of ideas which have no 'place' in it (*u-topia*), Open System aims to represent the possible 'truth' of the world: the *plus ultra* of unrealised possibility developing in the process.[71] It is philosophy as *theory of what needs to be (Philosophie, als Lehre was nottut)*, which mobilises optatives and suppositionals: *concrete philosophical architecture,* which represents the world as open to the possibility of concrete utopia.[72] But this conception of activist constitutive metaphysics transforms what metaphysics has hitherto been taken to be, especially since Bloch intends such 'metaphysics' to relate to what can be produced through Marxist theory-praxis.

Open System is *political metaphysics* aiming at the production of the good future, which accepts a duty of politically effective pre-figuration[73] and an obligation to 'over-take' the times. Consistent with this transformation of metaphysics into political metaphysics of the good 'meta' which the world contains, Open System has no ontology of a traditional sort. It is based on the principle of hope, in the sense that hope is not only its dominant knowledge interest, but its *archē* and the source of its final metaphysical grade.[74] It is a *metaphysics forwards,* for which the real is not located in a metaphysics *ante rem* or behind the world, but as a task for theory-praxis which lies on the horizon of the future.[75] This means that the sources or 'starting points' which Bloch uses in Open System operate with transformed functionality (*umfunktioniert*): as refunctioned covering concepts which no longer necessarily have the precise ontological reference they originally possessed. This is important because the radicalism of Open System is concealed for many readers by Bloch's use of older philosophical terminology. Thus, Open

System inherits Hegel's model of a process in which subject becomes substance as a plan of journey for the historical process. Bloch, however, modifies Hegel in light of Goethe's *Faust*. He finds 'genuine utopian metaphysics' in Faust's moment in which full existence is present without any mythological 'behind there': an immanentist-transcendentalist metaphysics which links man's subjective experience of fulfilment with a finalism of the object.[76] Hence, the historical journey becomes a subject-object process, in which the subject journeys in search of an adequate object, with the moment providing the conscience of the plan, stirring the subject to fresh dissatisfaction, and reminding him of the intensity which is the unreached goal. Similarly, Open System inherits Kant's postulates of practical reason, his stress on the primacy of hope, his postulate of an unreached Real and In General, and his relation of identity to 'the deep' or what men ultimately will, in a radically refunctioned form.[77] It also inherits Kierkegaard's stress on the need to understand oneself in existence[78] and Schelling's critique of Hegel's panlogism. Indeed, Bloch argues that it is necessary to set Schelling as well as Hegel on his feet in a Marxist context, and makes Schelling's doctrine that an unsolved, a-logical state is the source of all becoming basic to Open System.[79] Nonetheless, Open System is neither Kantian transcendental philosophy nor Kierkegaardian existentialism nor Schellingesque philosophy of history.

Open System can be regarded as Marxist metaphysics in two senses, each of which assumes that the meaning of 'metaphysics' undergoes a revision in a Marxist context. First, Open System can be regarded as Marxist metaphysics in the sense of an attempt to relate the present world to a beyond. Such an attempt has usually been regarded as alien to Marxism. Bloch, however, argues that Engels' polemic against 'metaphysics' has been misunderstood, as though Engels rejected all metaphysics, instead of only 'metaphysics' in his specific sense of static world conceptions.[80] Indeed, Bloch observes that those Marxists who have been quick to reject all 'metaphysics' have often lapsed into metaphysics in exactly the sense criticised by Engels, and have substituted fixed and backward looking materialist epistemology for the fixed and backward looking epistemology and ontology of idealism. Moreover, Bloch insists that Marxist dismissals of attempts to relate the world to a beyond are only valid against a mythological, vertical realm, not against an unconclu-

ded horizontal future which is already to some extent immanent.[81] In contrast to all static world conceptions, Open System
represents the world as an unfinished world with a dialectically
developing immanent beyond. Open System is 'new metaphysics' in this sense: it represents the world as a world with
immanent 'transcending' but no 'transcendence'.

Second, Open System can be regarded as Marxist metaphysics
in the sense of an attempt to outline a categorial scheme for an
unfinished world. Open System can thus be seen as a continuation of Engels' polemic against 'metaphysics' in the sense of
static thinking and static world conceptions.[82] The need for a
categorial scheme for an unfinished world was a theme of
Bloch's early utopian philosophy. As a Marxist, Bloch envisages
the need for a categorial scheme which will have a historical,
non-static character. Here Bloch's position is radical in a Marxist
context. Bloch raises the question of whether traditional categories are adequate for Marxist purposes, of whether Marxism
does not require a radical opening up of traditional categorial
analyses. In Open System Bloch provides Marxism with an activist, politically aimed categorial scheme which recognises the
need to relate now to future history, and not merely to be taken
by surprise when the world changes. Bloch emphasises that
Open System reflects the world of late capitalism, in which
socialism is becoming possible, and that no category can be regarded as fixed or final in pre-history.[83] Like other categories,
the categories of Open System have a transmission character;
but, unlike other categorial schemes, Open System envisages
this transmission. Its categories are allied to Marxist politics and
are designed to be 'burst open' in the future under socialism,
when they will cover new content not available now and reflect
new social conditions.[84]

In the remainder of this chapter an attempt will be made to
introduce some of the most important concepts which Bloch
employs in Open System: ontology of not-yet-being, the not-
yet-conscious, the moment, concrete utopia and hope.

ONTOLOGY OF NOT-YET-BEING

Open System is based on a new ontology of not-yet-being. Like
Heidegger, Bloch attempts to break with the Western metaphy-

sical tradition. The Western metaphysical tradition since Thales, Bloch argues, has been based on the assumption of a settled ontology, as though the world was in being as something given and settled from the start. It has tended to posit a *fixum*, or concluded substratum, in which the world contents were present *in potentia.*[85] Whether this substratum was called 'substance', 'idea','matter', or 'spirit', it was assumed that the ontological structure and possibility content of the world were in being. In all traditional philosophy, Bloch claims, there was a block against the future and the genuinely new. In contrast, Open System has no settled ontology 'up there' or 'behind there':

> The new philosophy, on the other hand, both despite and because of its real *meta,* is by no means just more old metaphysics. For its relationship to the not-yet-manifest does not allow of the slightest hint of an *ontōs on,* and consequently of an ontology which, being inwardly agreed and settled as the behind-there, has already got everything completely settled and behind it. To be sure, it is also an ontology of a sort (this field has not yet been cleared of positivism nor of other forms of agnostic eunuchry), but only the ontology of not-yet-being . . .[86]

Bloch's ontology of not-yet-being depends on three central assertions. First, Bloch argues that the world at hand is not yet solved. There is a real ontological world problem: a problem of being as well as cognition. The world is 'not yet',[87] and this 'not yet' keeps the world in an expectant, tendential state, because something is needed and awaiting its genesis in the tendency-latency of the process. In logical terms, S is not yet P: subject is not yet predicate; and in the language of the tradition of dynamicist process metaphysics deriving from Schelling and von Hartmann, the predicate of the 'That ground' (*Dassgrund*) of existing reality (*das Seiende*) has not yet been produced.[88] The world cannot therefore be adequately represented simply as a world in being, because the world at hand is only explicable in terms of the fact that something is 'not yet'. It is not yet what it needs to be and not yet what it can be. If this 'not yet' was settled or decided, there could be an ontology of a traditional sort. Bloch, however, holds that this 'not yet' is itself open and still developing, so that neither what the world needs to be nor what the world can be is concluded or decided in advance. In this sense, Open System involves a break with all static metaphysics.

Second, the world at hand (*das Seiende*) is full of realities which are 'not yet': existing reality is full of not-yet-existing reality (*Noch-Nicht-Seiendes*).[89] The world is full of objective real possibilities, which are not yet actual possibilities because they have not yet fulfilled all the conditions of their possibility, and may or may not ever become fully possible. According to Bloch, these possibilities have a grade of being: the new, and admittedly difficult grade of 'not-yet-being'. They are present as partially completed possibilities, which have achieved some of the conditions for their possibility. Moreover, such possibilities are tendential, even though they have not yet achieved their final form. In this sense, Open System implies a new open utopian ontology, beyond the limits of any classical world conception.

Third, Bloch argues that full or perfect being (*Sein*) is 'not yet', but developing in the course of the process.[90] Here Bloch's argument depends on the distinction in German between *Sein* and *das Seiende*. In English there is a difference between 'Being', a word with ultra-metaphysical connotations, and 'being'. In German, however, *Sein* is quite commonly used with a metaphysical or even mystical colouring, which is not present in the English word 'being' to the same degree. It is also common in German to distinguish between *Sein*, which has a metaphysical colouring and implies higher levels of being and value, and *das Seiende*, what has being, existing reality. Heidegger uses this distinction to contrast the being of beings (*das Seiende*) and Being (*Sein*). Western metaphysics, Heidegger claims, has 'forgotten' Being and confused it with 'the being of beings'.[91] Being, however, Heidegger argues, is not actual or ontic, but only 'Being-as-presence' (*Anwesenheit*), unconcealment, which shows itself momentarily in 'eks-static' experiences. Moreover, for Heidegger there is a radical ontological difference between 'Being' and 'the being of beings'.[92]

Bloch's position is a conscious rejoinder to Heidegger. Like Heidegger, Bloch distinguishes between *Sein* and *das Seiende*. For Bloch, however, there is no radical ontological difference between *Sein* and *das Seiende*, but there is a qualitative difference and a difference in fullness. *Sein* for Bloch, in the full meaning of its concept, is full or perfect being (*ontōs on*) as opposed to *das Seiende*, existing reality or not-yet-full being.[93]

Bloch, however, denies that *Sein* has been 'forgotten' or lost. On the contrary, rightly understood, as full or perfect being, it is what has never yet been, and is becoming possible in the course of the process:

> . . . being (*Sein*) — not in the formal, but in the full meaning of its concept — is not lost, but it has never yet been present at all; thus it is entirely dependent on existing reality (*das Seiende*) as its possible place of preparation.[94]

Being, in the sense of full being, is pre-illumined in the process, not as something actual, but as something 'in suspense', as an as-yet only dawning *Utopikum*.[95] It is foreshadowed as something attempted (*Versuch*) but not yet successful:

> Ontology of not-yet-being is an ontology of processual form-laden existing reality with constant reference to being as existing mediated arising being (*In-Aufgang-Sein*). This being . . . has its attempted mediation in the endeavours of both man and the world. But in itself, it has not even begun its *archē* as its full source, as its fully attained ground.[96]

Full being, however, is present more concretely as the object (*Gegenstand*) of all the statements of not-yet-being in existing reality,[97] and these statements provide an historical index of the extent to which full being is approaching possibility; they are also more comprehensive and determinate than the mere hovering suspension of pre-illumined full being.[98] Hence, ontology of not-yet-being is an ontology of a still developing, forward moving reality, grounded in the open forward moving meanings of being present in the developing process forms:

> As a theory, not of the most universal, but of the most essential determinations of being, ontology of being throughout existing reality (*das Seiende*) is merely one of existing reality as a moved series of open forms, *open forward meanings of being*.[99]

The difficulty is that Bloch seems to reject Heidegger's position in a way that preserves Heidegger's problem: the tension between a meta-ontic full being and ontic being at hand. Hence he produces a final metaphysical grade of full being which cannot be adequately glossed, as well as a permanently inchoate distinction between the 'ontological' and 'the ontic'. It is true that he attempts to ground his distinction in what is phenomenologically accessible, and argues that reference to a qualitatively higher 'ontological' level is present in the process forms. But even granted the need to preserve this 'conscience of totality' against positivism, it is difficult to see that a comprehensive thematisation of the world contents can be related to praxis, unless it involves a break with the traditional phenomenology on which Bloch relies.

Bloch's ontology of not-yet-being is little more than an outline needing further and more formal development. Bloch does not adequately delineate the problems which the notion of not-yet-being poses; it is also often difficult to be certain precisely what has not-yet-being. Bloch's analysis might be clearer if he distinguished more sharply between: (1) the not-yet-finished mode of being of the world at hand; (2) the not yet actual mode of being of objective real possibility; and (3) the 'not yet' as the mode of being of full or perfect being. His failure to do so partly arises from his central point: the world is not yet finished *because* it contains objective real possibility; objective real possibility is a mode of being *because* it is weakly actual in the world at hand; full or perfect being has a mode of being *because* it is developing in the world at hand and its objective real possibility. The radicalism of Bloch's ontology of not-yet-being is that he replaces any conception of a settled world with the thought experiment of a world kept open by the presence of futuristic properties within it. Because the world is full of the 'not yet' which is 'in suspense', it cannot be closed off in a settled ontological system. Rather its own ontological structure refers to what has only not-yet-being, and this open model of being, or partially conditioned ability to be, itself develops as the world goes forward.

THE NOT-YET-CONSCIOUS

Bloch emphasises that philosophical anthropology is not a key term for him,[100] and it is important not to reduce Open System to purely anthropological or psychological foundations. Nonetheless, Open System involves philosophical anthropology of a kind, in so far as Bloch makes the *humanum* or 'uncovered countenance' the norm by which the goal of a humanly successful world is to be judged. Bloch does not so much supply an image of man as a negative anthropology which emphasises the need to actively oppose ontological closure in the theory of human nature. For Bloch, man is 'not yet', an open experimental being, an x which is still to be fully determined: *homo absconditus*.[101] In anthropology as well, S is not yet P.

Like Sartre, Bloch sees man as characterised by lack and need, and as active in an attempt to overcome an inner void, a not-having. Man's true nature is still unmediated, latent, an *incognito* which remains to be illumined; and he is driven to search for satisfaction and fulfilment by hunger for what he lacks.[102] He has still to actualise many of his essential powers, and to win back those of his essential powers which have become alienated from him in class society. He is not in self-possession of his own full being: the *humanum* or not-yet-actual countenance. Man is what he can become in real possibility, and this is not a settled or decided now.[103] Nor can the problem of what man can become be understood in dualistic Cartesian terms, apart from the surrounding world which, as Marx saw, conditions men and so must be transformed and shaped by them. Hence, for Bloch the *humanum* is a proleptic *telos*; and he finds relevant material in subject and object alike for a future hominisation, which is as deeply anticipated in present human experience as it is presently fantastic.

For Bloch, adolescence provides the paradigm for the human condition, with its unidentified desires and unarticulated wants, pregnant with future content and half conscious of something to come.[104] Man lives in pre-history: he has hardly yet begun to be man. No man, Bloch argues, is truly there. 'I am, but I do not possess myself': the 'am' of 'I am' is still 'under', 'within', 'not yet out'.[105] Like Heidegger, Bloch emphasises the temporal character of all human being-in-the-world and the projective nature of human consciousness. Man lives primarily in the future, he declares, and is always on the way to something else.[106] Bloch, however, goes beyond Kierkegaard's emphasis on man as a being who lives forwards, and argues that man, in so far as he is most truly human, lives in utopia. Utopia is the fundamental characteristic of man as a projecting, intending, protending being.

There is a precedence not only of the future, but of the good future, in human psychology: an anticipatory awareness of, and a directedness towards, a fulfilment which has not yet been reached.[107] In this sense, utopian function operates generally in human psychology: in man's drives, wishes and affects as well as in human imagination.[108]

Bloch's awareness of this double motion of utopia, its anticipatory presence and its proleptic function, leads him to develop a philosophy and logic of objective imagination (*Phantasie*). Like Sartre, Bloch seeks to investigate the whole imaginative life of man, in the light of the intentionality of human consciousness and its tendency to populate the universe with irreal dimensions and imaginary realms.[109] Unlike Sartre, he relates the presence of an overwhelming counterfactual *plus ultra* in human consciousness to dialectical materialism. Bloch's theory of an anticipatory consciousness (the not-yet-conscious) needs to be seen in this context: as a theory for which human imagination is informed by the object, by what is still developing at the front of the process.[110]

Bloch presents the mature version of his theory of an anticipatory consciousness as a breakthrough grounded in the specificity of the history of capitalism, and as the basis for a positive Marxist critique of psychoanalysis.[111] Apart from rejecting Adler's power psychology and Jung's 'proto-fascist' theory of the collective unconscious, Bloch draws attention to the *anamnesis* and staticism of psychoanalysis, as well as the unreflexive incorporation of capitalist social relations in psychoanalytical theory.[112] He attacks the fundamentals of Freudian theory and opposes to it a philosophical anthropology in which openness to the future dominates over mechanisms which set non-abolishable limits to human fulfilment. Bloch rejects Freud's account of human drives as staticist, and argues that in so far as there is a fundamental drive, it is 'hunger' and not 'libido'.[113] He denies that there is any fixed or settled human nature apart from the mediation of particular socio-economic contexts; and argues that all human drives and drive structures are historically and socially conditioned.[114] Similarly, Bloch rejects Freud's pathological bias and over-emphasis on the neurotic character of human irrealism. He challenges the adequacy of Freud's treatment of day dreams as infantile substitutes for real experience, and, without underestimating the importance of subliminal and biological influences on psychic life, implies that Marxism requires a hermeneutical psychology which recognises the centrality of day dreams in human existence as well ordered fantasies concerned with ideal future states and with the improvement of the world.[115]

Bloch seeks to be the Freud of the day dreams of mankind: to explore the creative function of waking dreams of a better life in a way which overcomes any Marxist reception of the nihilism of the late bourgeoisie. Hence, he emphasises a praxis-oriented optimism rather than premature disillusionment as a basic orientation for Marxist research. In a bold refunctioning of Romantic psychological doctrine, with its stress on the productivity of the unconscious, the constitutive function of imagination (*Phantasie*), and the role of dreams as revelations of a meta-mundane order, Bloch argues that man possesses an anticipatory consciousness which provides him with not-yet-conscious knowledge of developing real possibilities. According to Bloch, the not-yet-conscious operates in human consciousness as an auroric 'pre-conscious', as a relatively 'under-conscious', which, unlike Freud's 'no longer conscious', has never yet become conscious.[116] Unlike Freud's recursive no-longer-conscious, it operates not in the cellar but at the height of human consciousness, and works in the darkness of the lived moment. It is the psychic representation of the not-yet-become: of the objective real possibilities developing in its time and in its world.[117]

Bloch does not only mean that human consciousness has an anticipatory dimension which enables men to envisage possibilities before they become actual. He means that the not-yet-become works in human consciousness before it becomes actual. The not-yet-conscious is a dawning forwards of a subject-object sort: the foreglow in the subject of what is objectively dawning in the world.[118] For Bloch, it is reality, and not merely consciousness, which has futuristic properties. The not-yet-conscious is the grade of consciousness in which the new announces itself, and works in human day dreams to produce determinate utopian imagination (*Phantasie*) with a correlate in the world.[119] Here Bloch's position overcomes the Cartesian dualism of subject and object, and the consequent reduction of subjectivity to a private enclave. It implies that Marxism requires a dialectical materialist depth psychology which, unlike psychoanalysis, recognises the object-related futurity of human consciousness.

It is possible to provide an analytical critique of Bloch's theory of the not-yet-conscious, to emphasise his dependence on Romantic phenomenology rather than scientific methods, and his reliance on an anachronistic conceptual framework taken from Husserl, Brentano's *Gegenstand* psychology, and the act psychology of Theodor Lipps. Despite his affirmative bias, however, Bloch does more than revive Romantic illusions. Bloch inherits the critique of utilitarian and intellectualistic psychologies implicit in Nietzsche's and Schopenhauer's recovery of the secret operation of will and desire in human consciousness. If Bloch's approach ultimately owes more to a futurist verson of von Hartmann's treatment of the unconscious than to Freud, it is praxis-related and hypothetical, and designed to illumine our immanence within an objectively unfinished world.

THE MOMENT

Bloch's phenomenology of the darkness of the lived moment was a major theme of his early utopian philosophy. In Open System this phenomenology reappears as support for Bloch's claim that the process contains concrete utopia. According to the traditional analysis found in Saint Augustine and Meister Eckhart, the moment contained the mystical foreglow of ultimate happiness, and also the threat of final destruction. In the moment, the soul experienced its likeness to God and its destiny to be what He is; the now of the moment was a foretaste of eternity: a *nunc stans.* In *Faust* Goethe interpreted this analysis to mean that man's search for fulfilment is a search for the complete fulfilment of what appears in the moment: for a completely fulfilled moment. In Open System, Bloch applies his operator 'not yet' to the content which appears as the highest intensity of the moment,[120] so that the reality experienced in the moment becomes a reality which is 'not yet'. As in his early utopian philosophy, Bloch follows Schelling in holding that the moment is the blind spot of our vision: the region of existence which is too near for the perspective necessary for something to be seen. We do not see the moment in which we live: there is an invisibility at the heart of our existence.[121] The moment is lived (*gelebt*), but not experienced (*erlebt*). It is 'empty', 'dark', 'unmediated', and only experienced before or after it has passed, especially in rare, short-lived experiences of an anticipatory 'still', in which a vertical lightning effect falls on the unmediated content of the moment, and makes it seem 'almost mediated'.[122] In such experiences, a symbolic intention to an unreached Real and In General is present in the darkness of the moment, and encourages us to seek its adequation in the world.[123] Hence, the moment gives the process its Faustian subject-object plan[124] by keeping man's utopian conscience alert and giving the subject an experience of the fulfilment which he lacks. What is sought for under the name of 'utopia' pre-appears in the moment: the 'far' is present in the near, and philosophy with a utopian conscience seeks to realise this content in the world.[125]

In Open System, however, Bloch attempts to relate this phenomenology to a model of the world process. Like Husserl, Bloch is concerned to give representation to man's internal consciousness of time: to his experience of the now or temporal instant, which is basic to the texture of human being-in-the-world, but ignored by positivist and externalist ontology. He is concerned to provide a categorial analysis of the moment which summarises the objectively vague nature of its content, while making a new attempt to interpret this content's meaning. Bloch follows Plato in treating time as a discontinuous continuum of discrete 'nows' and rejects the flow model of James and Bergson.[126] The now, he argues, constitutes itself anew in each moment and always takes the same form: the form of a sudden pulse, which drives forward to the next and then sinks.[127] Bloch interprets this process of the now as a section which reveals the structure and content of the world process. According to Bloch, the process is heliotropic and begins again in each moment: as a process to solve the question of its origin; and every moment contains both the *datum* of world completion and the *data* of its content.[128] In more formal terms, the process is an unsolved world process in which the intensive That drives towards its missing What or essence, and the structure of the moment reflects the structure of the process. Moreover, according to Bloch, both the foreglow of ultimate happiness (which Bloch identifies as the pre-appearance of concrete utopia) and the threat of final destruction (which Bloch identifies with his category *hazard*) pre-appear in the moment; and correlate with man's experience of positive and negative wonder (*Staunen*), and with the two possible results of the process: 'everything' (*Alles*) or 'nothing' (*Nichts*).[129]

This is possible because the moment is full of the not-yet-conscious, the not-yet-become. According to Bloch, the now of the moment is not the apparent present (*Gegenwart*) but a real now (cf. the medieval 'now') which is 'not yet'. It is a utopian reality which comes before the future and the past as well as the apparent present.[130] The now is the 'not there' in the moment, which presses forward to the next in search of an identified moment. In this sense, the moment reflects an anticipatory condition of the world itself.[131] The darkness of the moment copies the darkness of the world, or the fact that much which needs to be is still immanent. The knot of the riddle of existence, the 'subject' of existence, the still nowhere realised *agens* or kernel of process matter, is present in the moment: as the thrust (*Stoss*) of the now which has never come forth in time or space.[132]

Bloch returns again and again to the moment with chiliastic insistence as the fundamental paradox of our immanence: the *mysterium* or 'world secret' is present in the nearest near. For Bloch, it is the presence of concrete utopia in the moment which finally secures its 'concrete' character, and which provides the unity of the utopian *Evidenz* throughout the world. But the moment itself remains a dark chamber which cannot be illuminated and in which we are not-yet-conscious.

In a Marxist context Bloch's treatment of the moment is speculative. Bloch's analysis abounds with difficulties, and it is unclear how he can ground the move from phenomenology based on Husserlian *Wesensschau* to process metaphysics. If Bloch's meaning is restricted to the philosophy of history, there are relatively few problems. Bloch may be right to draw attention to the human experience of the moment, and to argue that Marxism should not ignore this aspect of our experience merely because traditionally it has been discussed in a mystical context. Again, his attempt to treat the 'foreglow' of the moment as an intensive indication of human finality may not be indefensible. It may be that the process of history is built out of actions which relate to decisions which can be construed as militant affirmations of the promise of possible success given in the moment. But in so far as Bloch extends his argument to a hypothetical process metaphysics, he elaborates a thought experiment which is based on hope. Even assuming that the traditional mystical claim that what man ultimately wills appears as the highest intensity of the moment is correct, it is far from easy to see what grounds a Marxist could have for claiming that this intensity was a preappearance of a possible final state of the world; or how such a claim could be admitted, without representing the world as a potential, but not-yet-actualised anthropodicy. It is not uncommon for process philosophers to treat certain subjective experiences as reflections of the structure of the process, but in a Marxist context this requires more elaboration than Bloch provides.

CONCRETE UTOPIA

In Open System, Bloch uses the term 'concrete utopia' to reintroduce metaphysics, in the sense of a doctrine relating the present world to a beyond, into Marxism. The concept of an inherent utopian tendency in the world and the need for a utopian metaphysics were themes of Bloch's early utopian philosophy.[133] In Open System these themes reappear in a stronger form.

Bloch's concept of 'concrete utopia' can be seen as a Marxist inheritance of the transcendentalist attempt to relate the present world to a beyond. Transcendentalism claims that present reality is full of ciphers or signals of a higher reality: of a reality with a higher level of value and being. Nihilism dismisses this claim, on the ground that there is no such higher reality. Bloch, however, implies that this dismissal, although justified *vis-à-vis* a mythical Transcendence 'up there' or 'behind there', is not justified in so far as the world itself is a process which is full of immanent transcending, immanent reference to a beyond which is 'not yet'.[134] Open System inherits the 'truth' of transcendentalism, in an immanentist-transcendentalist form, with its concept of concrete utopia. In this sense, concrete utopia and the new metaphysics are synonymous: transcending without Transcendence.[135] There is no mythological 'Transcendence' and no need for other-worldly assumptions, because the world itself contains immanent reference to a possible perfection towards which it is driving (*fieri*), and a forward driving *transcendere* pervades the process forms. For Bloch, it is the function of Marxism to grasp this *transcendere* and to bring it to a good result.[136]

According to Bloch, concrete utopia is 'concrete' because it is present in the now (*Jetzt*) of the moment as the still unmediated promise of fulfilment, as the content of metaphysical wonder (*Staunen*).[137] It is present in the process forms as the horizon of every process reality: as anticipation of 'essence', and as intention towards perfect being (*ontōs on*).[138] Concrete utopia, Bloch argues, is the *invariant direction* of the process: the goal of its tendency (*Tendenz*) and the content of its latency (*Latenz*). It anticipates itself in the *utopian surplus* present not only in human day dreams, great philosophy, religion and art, but in the ciphers of nature.[139] It is the process *motif,* the *incognito* in both man and the world, which, if it is realised, will be the solution to the world problem: to the problem objectively present in the world itself as an unfinished, unsolved world. In contrast to all 'abstract', 'static', 'undialectical' utopias, concrete utopia is a *processual* utopia, grounded in immanently developing tendencies working out of the present in the direction of something better.[140] In Marx's language, it is the 'something in the form of a dream' or, more strictly, the 'dream of a thing', which needs to be realised in reality; and, in more systematic language, it is the paradox of utopia with a basis in the object (*Objekthaft-Utopisches*) and corresponds to the mediated *novum*.[141] Concrete utopia is the immanent beyond which is 'not yet', the something hopeful in the distance, which is now only an undecided real possibility, but which comes before itself as *intention*, as the *novum* in the not-yet-conscious, and as *real* anticipation. Unlike an abstract utopia, it cannot be detailed now, except intensively, and in terms of the conditions which will not be present if it is realised.[142]

Bloch glosses concrete utopia in a large number of ciphers, including 'home', 'being-as-hope', 'perfect being', 'a humanly successful world'; and in more Marxist language, as the end of alienation, the naturalisation of man and the humanisation of nature, and as the realm of freedom.[143] Concrete utopia is neither absent from the world at hand nor something given without reference to human action. It denotes a dispositional possibility in the world which can only be realised through theory-praxis. It is the un-become which is present in the world as a utopian reality, but which depends on human work, intervention and planning for its possible realisation.

Concrete utopia is the paradox of *real* utopia with a basis in unfinished process matter.[144] As *real* utopia, in the sense of a frontal, not yet reached object determination of matter, concrete utopia is the last content of *dynamei on*: the final 'forwards', towards which process matter is driving. Hence, it has a grade of being: the grade of not-yet-being.[145] 'Utopia presses forward in the will of the subject and in the tendency-latency of the world, beyond any ontology of an already reached, settled there', Bloch declares.[146] Such a philosophical concept is impeded as long as men take the pre-Marxist heteronomy of a concluded world as beyond question. Bloch argues, however, that Marxism requires a new conception of reality which (1) represents the world as an unfinished process; (2) relates the realm of ideals to the world; and (3) recognises that the concrete imagination (*Phantasie*) and its mediated anticipations are developing in the process itself.[147]

These characterisations need to be understood in light of the function of ontological concepts in Open System. Concrete utopia is a projective ontological concept, not a metaphysical reality which is already actual. Here there is an antinomy between Bloch's desire to emphasise that concrete utopia is a reality *now,* which must not be excluded from a representation of the world as if it were merely subjective, and his desire to stress that, as a realised reality, concrete utopia is 'not yet'. For Bloch, there is no purely analytical resolution of this difficulty, and our ability to humanise the world requires a willingness to make use of such paradoxical, historically limited concepts. Concrete utopia is not a pre-Marxist metaphysical absolute, but a praxis-oriented work category. As Bloch puts it, ' . . . there is a great meaning and an intention to the still un-become throughout the whole world. Concrete utopia is the most important theory-praxis of this tendency'.[148] As a praxis-oriented work category, concrete utopia is the praxis of the mediated anticipations of the good which have emerged in both history and nature.

In post-Hegelian language, concrete utopia is the immanent utopian totality of Open System.[149] It is only totality, however, in a refunctioned (*umfunktioniert*) sense, which assumes Marx's stress on revolutionary activity as the means of deciding the form which the future will take. Open System has no totality in the idealist sense of a quasi-mythical holism. Bloch, however, argues that the concept of totality can be given a new meaning in Marxism as a theory-praxis concept which helps men to exert rational mastery over the process. Concrete utopia is not therefore identical with Karel Kosík's 'concrete totality', which implies that reality is already a structured, self forming dialectical whole in the process of coming into being.[150] For Bloch, reality has the dispositional possibility to become totality in this sense, but much remains to be done by men before the aporias and objective impediments in the world, not least in cosmic nature, can be overcome. Instead, concrete utopia is a critical, non-contemplative totality, an ontological concept which must first be brought into being: both (1) the possible final stage of the process, which is present *omnia ubique*; and (2) the *novum* of a goal which, if it were realised, would become something radically new.[151]

Here Bloch's position is open to objection, but it is important to emphasise the political meaning of Bloch's move. Bloch argues that Marxism enables men to grasp totality again, to reoccupy the possibility of a coherent, ordered and meaningful world, which has been occluded under capitalism:

> . . . Marxism reveals totality again, which is the method and subject matter of all authentic philosophy. But for the first time this totality appears not as something *static,* not as a *finished principle (Prinzip)* of the whole, but rather as a *utopian,* or more precisely, *concrete utopian* totality, as the *process latency of a still unfinished world.*[152]

Obviously Marxism does not allow men to grasp totality again in a naïve sense, as if they could be certain that what is intended can be realised. Bloch emphasises that concrete utopia is non-warrantable and founded on *militant optimism.*[153] Concrete utopia is open to *hazard,* and there is no security available on which to base the *militant optimism* which it embodies. Such a concept, however, can be effective in guiding praxis and in influencing the course of world travel which such praxis makes possible. According to Bloch, Marxism needs to break with the positivism which excludes from the world whatever cannot be represented in articulated meanings. It needs to take as its *telos* the utopian fullness of what preappears in the unmediated near, and relate this *telos* to a theory-praxis of the mediated anticipations of the good throughout history and nature. As a re-

definition of the goal which Marxism should take as its operative
telos, concrete utopia depends (1) on the claim that Marxism
should pursue maximalist ends, even though what can be realised
at any stage falls short of such ends; and (2) on the claim that
Marxism should postulate thai the possibility content of the
world is not necessarily alien to such ends, but contains something which, if it is realised, will be a justification of the original
excess.

Bloch's concept of concrete utopia is more metaphysical than
his identification of concrete utopia with Marx's 'realm of freedom' would suggest, or than a reassertion of transcendentalism
within Marxism would seem to require. Once, however, the
nature of Bloch's 'metaphysics' is understood, it can be seen that
Bloch uses the concept of concrete utopia to extend radically
the purview of Marxist praxis. Bloch argues that Marxism must
become the praxis of concrete utopia. This implies both that
Marxism should not prematurely restrict the range of what is
hoped for, and that Marxism should not be concerned solely
with social questions, divorced from their relevance to total
human liberation. Concrete utopia therefore involves a reassertion of a conscience of totality in Marxism: of a totality which
must be envisaged when it is still utopian if praxis oriented to
a good future is not to lapse into practicism or suffer a radical
foreshortening of the goal. It is true that concrete utopia is anything but 'concrete', in the sense of fully specifiable in analytical
terms. Clearly it would be helpful if Bloch distinguished more
clearly between (1) concrete utopia as a content given now in
human experience; (2) concrete utopia as the praxis of mediated anticipation of the good; and (3) concrete utopia as the
correlate of such praxis with real not-yet-being. It would then
be possible to avoid the division which has already emerged
among interpreters between one-sided ontological and equally
one-sided praxis interpretations.[154]

In the context of Bloch's project of an immanentist-transcendentalist metaphysics, however, concrete utopia has three
important implications. First, concrete utopia implies that
Marxism requires a utopian metaphysics for a forward moving
world which anticipates its own real possibilities in still open
process fragments:[155] a metaphysics for which the presence of
mediated anticipations of the good in the process is the only
transcendence, and utopia is the fundamental concept by which

being is defined in the order of essence.[156] In other words, Marxism requires a non-static metaphysics, for which 'the metaphysical' denotes a possible *futurum,* and not a metaphysical 'Transcendence' above or behind the world.[157] Second, concrete utopia implies that Marxism can inherit the intentionality of traditional metaphysics on new foundations. It implies that Marxism can inherit the traditional metaphysical problem of the meaning of the world and re-pose it as a problem for theory-praxis, the solution of which belongs to the more distant future, even though as a problem it is structural and gives other, more transient problems their colouring. For Bloch, Marxism needs to represent the world as changeable and in no way necessarily and permanently alien to human purposes. If Marxism is not to confine itself to social questions divorced from their relevance to total liberation and prematurely to restrict the range of what is hoped for, it must wager the utopian excess that the world can come to have a meaning, against thinking which takes defeat as its starting point and never moves beyond an implicit reconciliation to the world at hand. Third, concrete utopia implies that Marxism requires a meta-eschatological perspective. The intention to utopia found throughout the world and the pre-appearance of an end-relation in the moment, point to the need to posit a beyond in which more would be possible than can be envisaged now. Obviously utopia cannot be realised in the present world. It is no 'enduring circumstance', and the attempts to realise it throughout history give rise to 'a melancholy of fulfilment'. The dream was always better, and what comes to be always falls short of the utopian intention.[158] To this extent, the realism of utopia requires a meta-eschatological perspective which marshalls the 'present eschatology' of utopian *Evidenz* against the falling short of present possibility.[159]

HOPE

Open System is based on the principle of hope. Nonetheless, although Bloch is famous as 'the philosopher of hope', what Bloch means by hope is widely misunderstood. For Bloch, hope is not merely psychological, but a fundamental determination within objective reality in general:

Expectation, hope, intention to still unbecome possibility, is not only a fundamental characteristic of human consciousness. Concretely rectified and grasped, it is a fundamental determination within objective reality as a whole.[160]

Bloch distinguishes between subjective hope: the hope that hopes (*spes, qua speratur*), and objective hope, the correlate of subjective hope in developing real possibility: the hope that is hoped (*spes, quae speratur*).[161] If his discussion concentrates on subjective hope, it nonetheless assumes that subjective hope has an objective correlate (which remains to be identified and then produced) in so far as anticipatory consciousness works in it, to produce not-yet-conscious knowledge. Bloch differentiates between fulfilled affects such as envy, avarice and reverence which have their objects at hand, and expectation affects, such as anxiety, fear, hope and faith, whose objects are still in the future.[162] According to Bloch, hope is the most militant expectation affect: the functionaire of what has never been which summons men to stand at the front and to work for the realisation of what is home-like.[163] It is an act of a cognitive sort which indicates a 'where to': a direction in which something is intended and must be experimented for.[164]

Bloch emphasises that hope is not guaranteed. Hope can only be based on *militant optimism*, which recognises that the process contains not only the possibility of success, but also *hazard* or the possibility of destruction.[165] Moreover, the presence of objective hope in the world does not guarantee that such real possibilities will be realised. Bloch concedes that experience suggests that hope is bound to remain discontented and thwarted as long as the process lasts, and that what comes to be always falls short of the fullness of what was hoped for. Hope merely tops the horizon of the present in a way which grasps the trend, and shows what may become possible in the future. Nonetheless, hope is the best thing we have, and must be trusted if it is to succeed. The project of a humanised world requires 'faith in discontented hope', which makes theory-praxis in the long run the test of what is possible, and not judgements based on the reified and still encapsulated world at hand.[166] Moreover, hope can mediate with process trends and gradually correct and reformulate itself. It can become educated hope, *docta spes*: hope grasped and understood in a dialectical material-ist manner, with a firm basis in real possibility.[167]

Open System is based on the principle (*Prinzip*) of hope in the sense that hope, grasped and understood in a dialectical material-ist manner, provides the starting point from which to begin as well as the historico-philosophical utopian *a prioris*, or regula-tives, which Marxism seeks to realise in history.[168] According to Bloch, *utopian function* works in human consciousness to make men discontented with what is inadequate in the world at hand (negative utopian function), and to produce ideal antici-pations of what is needed (positive utopian function).[169] This productive anticipatory function has a basis in the object (*objekthaft*): in the existence of future properties in real-ity itself. It is not merely subjective, but the real in anticipation of itself.[170] Utopian function works in hope as an expectation affect to produce an objective presentiment of real possibilities with not-yet-being: to produce determinate utopian imagination with a correlate in dialectically developing real possibility.[171] This is a claim which must be tested by praxis.

Bloch argues that Marxism must become the theory-praxis of hope. The positive act content of hope must be raised to full consciousness and become consciously known (*bewusst-gewusst*). Hope needs to be understood in a dialectical materialist manner as productive utopian function which sets goals for theory-praxis.[172] According to Bloch, Marxism requires a hermeneutics of subjective and objective hope, resulting in an inventory of utopian function. Bloch developed a utopian hermeneutics in his early utopian philosophy, and in Open System this hermen-eutics reappears as a dialectical materialist hermeneutics of hope. Bloch concedes that the operations of utopian function are admixed with ideology, illusion and class interest and that a detectivistic Marxist *Ideologiekritik* is needed to de-code the genuine *utopian surplus*.[173] He attempts however to show that a positive hermeneutics (in contrast to Freud's negative her-meneutics of distrust and disenchantment) of superstructural contents is possible, which combines Marxist situational analysis with intentional research into the act content and real judge-ments (*Realurteile*) hope contains, in a way which yields intelli-gence about real possibilities and process trends.[174] Bloch offers a massive example of such an inventory of utopian func-tion in his encyclopaedia of hope.

In *The Principle of Hope* Bloch provides an unprecedented survey of human wish pictures and day dreams of a better life. The book begins with little day dreams (part I), followed by an exposition of Bloch's theory of anticipatory consciousness (part II). In part III Bloch applies his utopian hermeneutics to the wish pictures found in the mirror of ordinary life: to the utopian aura which surrounds a new dress, advertisements, beautiful masks, illustrated magazines, the costumes of the Klu Klux Klan, the festive excess of the annual market and the circus, fairy tales and kolportage, the mythology and literature of travel, antique furniture, ruins and museums, and the utopian imagination present in dance, pantomime, the cinema and the theatre. In part IV Bloch turns to the problem of the construction of a world adequate to hope and to various 'outlines of a better world'. He provides a 400 page analysis of medical, social, technical, architectural and geographical utopias, followed by an analysis of wish landscapes in painting, opera and poetry; utopian perspectives in the philosophies of Plato, Leibniz, Spinoza and Kant, and the utopianism implicit in movements agitating for peace and leisure. Finally, in part V Bloch turns to wish pictures of the fulfilled moment which reveal 'identity' to be the fundamental supposition of anticipatory consciousness. Once again, the sweep is breathtaking as Bloch ranges over happy and dangerous experiences in ordinary life; the problem of the antinomy between the individual and the community; the works of the young Goethe, *Don Giovanni, Faust, Don Quixote*, the plays of Shakespeare; morality and intensity in music; hope pictures against death, and man's increasing self-injection into the content of religious mystery.

Bloch's hermeneutics of hope is an outstanding achievement. Through the range and subtlety of his analyses, Bloch shows that a hermeneutics of hope can extend immeasurably the range of goals which Marxism seeks to achieve. He also shows that a processual analysis of the transmission of dream images and ideal postulates over many centuries can serve to bracket the premature dismissal which confronts such contents at the early stages of their careers. In this way, Bloch pioneers a concept of theory-praxis *in the long run* in Marxist theory, which counters absolutisations of current possibility, as well as the standard Marxist premature foreshortening of hope, which banishes large parts of human subjectivity to the no man's land of subjective illusion. At the same time, Bloch shows that there is no need for Marxists to abandon the field to the non-political hermeneutics of a Ricoeur or a Gadamer, let alone to a Jungian hermeneutics which relates allegories, ciphers and symbols to a collective unconscious. He demonstrates that a hermeneutics for which economic and social theory must be present in all its analyses, can also do justice to the phenomenological contents which the world contains.

Bloch succeeds brilliantly in showing that human consciousness is pervaded by a utopian dimension; he also provides evidence for the claim that man possesses intentionality towards utopia in the sense of a higher level of being. Moreover, the sheer weight of Bloch's evidence implies that this utopian intentionality is fundamental and transfigures conscious human purposes. The difficulty is that none of this evidence proves that such intentionality has a correlate in real possibility. Bloch rightly emphasises that many utopian dreams and fantasies later turn out to relate to more limited possibilities, and that the final test can only be praxis. Bloch, however, attempts to ground the excess of such dreams and fantasies in real possibility. To this extent, he is the historian of the pre-appearance of absolute or total hope in particular hopes. Partly for this reason, he places little emphasis on ordinary hopes or detailed technical possibilities, and concentrates much of his attention on irreal dimensions of ordinary hopes, on irreal hopes which go beyond present possibility, and on the pre-appearance of 'irreal hope' wherever it can be found. Indeed, it often seems as if it is not the act of hoping which is finally important for Bloch, but the pre-appearance of the intensity of *being as hope.*

Bloch draws much of his material from religion, mythology, mysticism, and cultural forms. By their very nature, these sources yield wish postulates and ideal goals rather than models for immediate praxis. Moreover, Bloch relates the intensity which appears in particular hopes to the intensity which appears in the moment.[175] This, however, deflects attention from the problem of the antinomies and contradictions between more limited specific hopes, and sets up the monistic goal of 'being as hope', or the actualisation of the intensive content which appears in the moment. Thus Bloch's hermeneutics of hope finally relates to an eschatological perspective. Bloch is not the only philosopher to concentrate on pre-appearances of absolute or total hope. The same tendency appears in the philosophies of hope of Berdyaev and Marcel. As explicitly religious thinkers, however, Berdyaev and Marcel admit that absolute or total hope contradicts external possibilities, and is ultimately a form of belief which transcends the present world.[176] Here Bloch's approach is consistent with his stress on a meta-eschatological perspective in Marxism, but it also means that he emphasises forms of utopian imagination which seem unlikely ever to correlate with real possibilities. Even if the postulates implicit in such imagination did turn out to correlate with possibilities, he fails to show that the real *surplus* in such postulates, that is, the intentionality to a perfect or utopian level of being, is anything more than surplus, albeit perhaps of a psychologically necessary kind.

This discussion of some of the most important concepts in Open System may raise doubts about the extent to which Bloch's 'Open System' can be reconciled with Marxism. It will also have emerged that Bloch's syncretism tends to make the precise inter-relations of Open System rather unclear. Moreover, there is an obvious tension between Bloch's objectivist terminology and the subject-object meaning which it turns out to bear. As activist *viator* philosophy Open System begins with the experience of the subject and never departs far from it. It is also true that Bloch, the Expressionist theurgist, is better at raising up unconstruable depths than at grasping the niceties of technical philosophical argument. Nonetheless, Bloch's fecundity is undeniable. If Bloch's utopian excess remains utopian at crucial points, it allows him to discover the utopian country of a Marxist philosophy of an unfinished world. No other Marxist uncovers so many model ideas which point beyond the modernist horizon in which they are articulated. The next chapter analyses Open System in more detail. An attempt is then made to assess Bloch's Open System as a whole.

4 Open System: Marxist Metaphysics II

The history of the world is itself an experiment, a real experiment in the world aiming at a possible right world. Such history therefore should be understood as a self operative test, as a *real test,* in countless *objective-real models*, for a still lacking example. For an omega example as was always intended in the philosophical concept of true being (*ontōs on,* substance, full identity of appearance and essence).

Tübingen Introduction to Philosophy

In developing his account of the process Bloch employs traditional categories in new or unexpected meanings; he also invents new 'categories' and neologisms. Some of the most important of these will now be discussed.

PROCESS

Open System is a form of process philosophy. Like many process philosophers, however, Bloch tends to underdefine what he means by 'process', and to move imperceptibly from one technical meaning to another. It may be useful therefore to consider these meanings separately, despite the fact that Bloch runs them together. First, Bloch argues that there are processes: dynamic relationships which are not yet finished, not 'facts' or 'static things'.[1] Second, Bloch argues that the real is process. This is a stronger claim, especially since Bloch identifies process with real temporal becoming. 'The real is process; this process is the widely intertwined mediation between the present, the unfinished past, and, above all, the possible future',[2] Bloch writes.

Third, Bloch claims that there is a world process.[3] The term 'world' here is ambiguous. Does it mean the historical world, 'the world' in the sense of the earth, or the whole universe, including the star system? According to Bloch, the whole of reality ('the world') is a process. Thus far, this process takes two forms: (1) the process of history, which possesses a subject and is a developed subject-object process; and (2) the process, or processes of nature, which is still repetitive and undeveloped, and in which subjectivity exists only dispositionally, as a drive to something not-yet-reached. At present, therefore, there is a disparity between the process of history, which can be given teleological direction through the activity of men, and the process of nature, which is not clearly related to human finality, and in some ways is opposed to it (the law of entropy).[4] Bloch, however, postulates that this disparity between the two 'world series' or forms of the process can be overcome in the future through theory-praxis.

Fourth, according to Bloch the process is a process to articulate or 'process out' (*herausprozessieren*) the possibility content of matter. There is a process because something is 'not yet'. Something is needed, and this need or lack, together with the fact that the process contains something which should not be, drives the process forward.[5] The process is a process to 'find' or 'illumine' the 'not yet' of process matter, where this 'not yet' is structural, and not merely the possibility of further content. In more difficult language, the process is a process to 'process out' the 'realising factor' or *agens* of material being.[6]

Fifth, the process is experimental in at least two senses. Firstly, the process is experimental in the sense that it is 'open', 'undecided', 'unconcluded', in 'a model state'.[7] The process is 'open', in the sense that (1) the present process forms are open to change; (2) new additional contents can arise in the future; and (3) the process result is as yet undecided. Secondly, the process is experimental in a much stronger sense. It is an experimental process to find the world's true form: to find the adequation of the That or intensive driving of the process forward: a process to solve the question of the origin which drives or incites in the moment, as the unillumined 'world knot' inherent in the That (*das Dass*) of existence:

. . . the world as a process is the experiment to solve the

always and everywhere driving question of the origin. Above, this unsolved problem, was described as the world knot (*Weltknoten*), which is inherent in the That (*das Dass*) of existence; thus the world in its unmediated being-there (*Da-sein*) constantly creates itself anew in each moment, and this continuous creation at the same time appears as the preservation of the world, of the world process.[8]

According to Bloch, the process begins again in each moment as a process to 'identify', 'find', 'illumine' and then 'realise' the ground or cause of its movement, as a process attempting to find an adequation to the intensive impetus (*Dass-Anstoss, Dass-Antrieb*) or That factor (*Dassfaktor*) driving it forward.[9] It is a process of 'tests' for a still outstanding example, a process seeking its 'saturation' or still outstanding true form.[10] In this sense, the world of the process is not only an experimental world, but a world experiment (*experimentum mundi*): an experiment for a right world; and the process forms are themselves *real* experiments for the not yet found 'essence' or 'true being'.[11] Thus far, the process is still unsuccessful, a process which has not yet succeeded. It is a process which can be 'given light' by men (*Heilungsprozess, Erhellungsprozess*), but also a process which must be 'given light' by men, if it is to be what it can be: a *laboratorium possibilis salutis.*[12]

Sixth, the process is a process of immanent transcending. For Bloch, process means 'transcending without Transcendence': the process goes beyond the given in search of its missing entelechtic form. It goes forward to more and to higher forms, although the danger of total destruction increases along with the possibility of realising utopia as the process goes forward.[13] The process is emergentist: a process of expansion with emergent content in the process forms. According to Bloch, utopia preappears in the process forms because the process itself is a utopian function which represents what is needed before it becomes a realised reality, and the process is full of *real* ciphers, *real* symbols, *real* models of utopia.[14]

Finally, the process is finite and comes to an end. It is not an endless flow, as in Bergson, but a process to process out 'something' (*Etwas*). According to Bloch, the process can end in one of two possible results; 'everything' (*Alles*) or 'nothing' (*Nichts*).[15] Bloch glosses 'everything' (*Alles*) in a number of dif-

ferent ciphers, emphasising alternatively the utopian, the eschatological and the identity aspects of the 'not yet'. 'Everything'
would be 'utopia', 'the whole', 'success', 'totum', 'totality', *ontōs on,* 'perfection', 'the best', 'home', 'highest good', *'eschaton'*,
'apocalypse', 'the end', 'the last', 'identity', 'fulfilment'. 'Nothing'
would be failure, destruction, the end of the process in the anni-
hilation of the world through entropy. Moreover, 'everything'
and 'nothing' are not merely possible results of the process, but
structural features which colour the process forms and pre-appear
in the darkness of the moment.[16]

In a Marxist context, Bloch's concept of reality as a process is
bold and highly speculative. Nonetheless, Bloch is not advancing
a pre-critical, dogmatic process metaphysics, but a projective
metaphysics which aims to represent the world in a way which
helps men to change it. Bloch is committed to process philosophy as an ontological schema as against positivism or empiricism.
As a Marxist, however, his concern is to set a process philosophy
model to work in the historical process: to develop a conception of reality which directs men to those points where the
world itself indicates that more is possible or that it can be
changed. The objectivism of Bloch's presentation therefore
needs to be interpreted, in a subject-object perspective, as
conscious utopian excess: as a suppositional framework for
Marxist theory-praxis which is dialectically aimed. Again and
again, Bloch refunctions the language he uses so that his characterisations of the process become modernist metaphors with
reference, but no exact, already made out sense. The point is
not to object to the conceptual slippage which this involves, but
to observe how Bloch challenges more standard Marxist approaches.

First, Bloch replaces the standard Marxist nihilism and agnosticism with an attempt to understand the world as a world in
which 'something' is in process: as a world in which 'true being'
or 'utopia' is present as an imperilled *fieri*, but not as a made out
reality. Second, Bloch challenges Marxists to model a unified
world conception, even though this unity has still to be achieved.
Third, Bloch invites Marxists to consider whether the thought
that the world is not 'there' in the classical sense, can be given
content in terms of a process philosophy model, and, in particular, in terms of a model of a process which has not yet succeeded,
has not yet 'clicked in'.[17] For Bloch, the world is an *emerging*

world process, still in an anticipatory stage, which needs to be illumined by men. But this is a speculation designed to promote theory-praxis to produce more than present possibility would lead men to expect. Fourth, Bloch challenges Marxists to reconsider the problem of the constitutive consequences of adopting a particular metaphysical schema, in the context of: (1) the need to leave the maximum space for more and better still to come; and (2) the need to give representation to human wish contents, instead of opposing them as world strange contents to a decided ontological order. This is the deeper meaning of Bloch's attempts to 'inherit' the wish content of the philosophies of Leibniz and Hegel in a utopian system, aiming at metaphysical productivity.[18]

TENDENCY-LATENCY

Bloch uses the category tendency to designate the energetic drive of process matter. Like Liebniz, Bloch does not mean by tendency a passive trend, but an active energetic straining, created by impeding possibilities. For Bloch, as for Leibniz, matter is active, not passive (everything possible strives to become actual), and the present is pregnant with the future, in the form of possibilities which become actual as soon as the impediments to their realisation are removed.[19] In this sense, the world is full of the 'not yet' which strains as tendency, and the process has a fundamental tendency to the manifestation of its cause.[20]

Bloch, however, applies his operator 'not yet' to the traditional category 'tendency', so that tendency becomes the open, dialectical, unconcluded tendency of the developing real possibility content of the process: the utopian tendency which manifests in times of change and in music, an historical-dialectical materialist 'truth' of Leibniz's *appetitio perfectionis*:[21]

> Tendency is the energetic of matter in action, driving forward in all its already reached forms via excerpt forms (*Auszugsgestalten*) to what is tendentially implied in the intended entelechtic goal, as it has not yet become, yet is nonetheless latent in a utopian manner.[22]

According to Bloch, tendency works in matter *per se*, but only weakly and in an under-developed anticipatory form in the extra-human world. The most important tendency is the tendency which works in human history, and this is a tendency of a historical-social sort, bound up with the tendencies of particular forms of society, which needs to be activated by men if it is to be realised. Clearly there are good as well as bad tendencies; but for Bloch there is a fundamental tendency in human history towards the manifestation of a content, and this tendency, as in Hegel, has a basis in the movement present before men in the dialectical process.[23]

Bloch uses the category 'latency' to designate the entelechy of matter in potentiality.[24] The 'latent' is what is 'still concealed', not directly visible, 'not yet out'. In Open System however, Bloch applies his operator 'not yet' to the traditional category 'latency', so that 'the latent' becomes latent real possibility with not-yet-being. As the latency of the dialectical tendency, the latency gives the tendency its direction, but it is not there as something mechanical, which needs to be unpacked. It is only 'there' in a non-classical sense appropriate to an ontology of not-yet-being: as the manner in which the not-yet-existing purpose content makes itself effective in the tendency.[25] It has a *novum* character as the reality of tomorrow which belongs to today, and is still 'utopian' in the sense of 'open' and 'undecided'.

As developing real possibility, the latency of the process requires further conditions for its possibility, including further dialectical leaps and the active intervention of human labour. What has 'not yet become' and is 'only latent in a utopian manner', above all, the absolute purpose content immanently developing in the process, has a difficult, not yet fully determined mode of being. It is the emergentist entelechy content immanently referred to, in a concrete utopian manner, by the excerpt forms which emerge in the process:

> Latency is the entelechy of matter in potentiality, utopian, but concrete utopian, via the excerpt forms in the process, substantiated by the In General of the entelechtic intended purpose, . . .[26]

FRONT

Bloch uses the neologism 'the front' in an attempt to overcome the bias of staticist thought against the new, and in favour of the already become. Bloch defines 'the front' as 'the farthest section of time, where we find ourselves living and active'.[27] Here Bloch has in mind the link between our relationship to the reified present, and our ability to intervene at those points where the future is being decided and can be shaped.

In Open System Bloch combines two previously separate notions of the front: the Aristotelian notion of the *nisus* which draws the process forward *a fronte*, and the military usage of 'the front', in the sense of the 'front line' with its implication of 'the place where the battle is being decided'. The front is where the become is driving forward towards the new. It is a non-classical ontological space to represent the furthermost region of reality (*Wirklichkeit*): the space of 'what is arising' and 'coming up', where existing reality is developing into the new.

Because, however, the process is heliotropic, the front is present in the darkness of the moment. It is present in the now of the not: 'Thus the front lies in every instance in the now, which in turn is the now of the not, which is thrusting out of itself and therefore always again rushing forward'.[28] Bloch speaks of the 'constantly breaking out' front, of the driving front which goes forward in every moment to what is next, of the front as the place where the next test for a successful solution to the process is taking place. He uses the term front multivocally to refer to: (1) the front in the sense of the front of the world process, where matter is 'in ferment' and driving forward to the new; (2) the front in the sense of the temporal front, which is always the now of the moment, in which we find ourselves living and active; (3) the front in the sense of the projected front: the space which lies ahead of what has become, into which frontal concepts with teleological mobilising power are projected; and (4) the human front, in the sense of space into which men project themselves forward in order to survey the present and plan ahead.

The result is a new categorial identification of the problems of praxis *vis-à-vis* a reified present, for which these different senses inter-relate. Against the tendency to understand the future as naturalistic, Bloch stresses the need for men to assume responsibility for guiding the world in a direction which will be good.[29] Successful praxis for Bloch, however, depends on placing oneself ahead of the things which have become. To stand 'at the front' of the process, it is necessary to grasp the trend, to anticipate what is coming up, to sense where the new in each area is coming into being, and where what is arising can be helped to birth.

At the same time, the ability to guide the world in a good direction depends on projecting mobilising goals into the frontal space which lies before us: on overreaching the mark in a way which maintains the right direction, in the face of temporary disappointments and counter evidence from the 'bad empiricism' of the world at hand. This, in turn, requires men who can overcome the conditioning which makes them passive and backward looking. Bloch concedes that thus far 'the human front' is 'weak', but he holds that this weakness can be explained in terms of man's weak relation to the now of the moment.[30] Because men do not relate strongly to the now in the present, they do not actively grasp what the present contains, project their own goals into the frontal space ahead, and lead what has become actual towards the good new.

NOVUM

Bloch uses the neologism the *novum* to designate the radical new which has never yet been. Many process philosophers have elaborated concepts of novelty in an attempt to give categorial status to the new, which they believed was repressed and under-represented in traditional Western metaphysics. Bloch's position is more radical, and he criticises Bergson for limiting novelty to new arrangements of content or developments of existing possibility.

Bloch's category *novum* derives from the Biblical concept of the eschatological new.[31] The Bible, at least on one view, contains a concept of the new not found in Greek metaphysics. This is the concept of the radical new brought about by the acts of God. God acts to fulfil his promises, in a way which goes beyond what was expected, and which introduces something which could not be extrapolated from what was already at hand. Moreover, this Biblical new is related to a system of finality. The new which arises from the acts of Yahweh can be related to a final new or *eschaton*, when Yahweh intervenes to end the present world and establish 'a new heaven and a new earth'; and this final eschatological future is 'now and not yet'.

In Open System Bloch refunctions this Biblical eschatological new in terms of his process metaphysics.

Bloch's category *novum* involves a complete break with any classical ontology of a closed or completed world. It is an intervention category, designed to effect a shift in ontology from a centring grounded on the past to a centring grounded on the 'not yet'. Moreover, Bloch's category *novum* contains subjective content meant to evoke the new as it is experienced phenomenologically in astonishment and wonder; it is not reducible to formal 'novelty'. Bloch uses the term *novum* to refer to both: (1) the radically new contents developing in the process; and (2) to the final good new with which the process can end, since on his account of the process these are immanently related. The process is emergentist and develops by dialectical leaps which produce genuinely new contents.[32] The new first comes to be as real possibility; it announces itself in the determinate utopian imagination (*Phantasie*) of the not-yet-conscious when it is still not-yet-become:

> . . . the *novum* should be defined: it takes place and grounds itself in the real possibility of the not-yet-conscious, not-yet-become, and indeed with a prevalence of something which promises to be good . . .[33]

The *novum* is the 'genuine future' or radically new content, which has emerged as a real possibility and is developing towards the fulfilment of its conditions. It passes through a period of incubation and then a period of preliminary identification before it emerges as something which can be clearly envisaged and contended for. As the dialectical *novum*, it has an inciting final causality as what has not-yet-being, and depends for its reality on the *real* self anticipation of process matter.[34] As the dialectical tendency of the impeded new, the tendency of the process has its *novum* before it (*vor sich*); the 'where to' of existing reality first appears in the *novum*:

> The world is rather full of disposition to something, tendency to something, latency of something, . . . But this tendency arises in flow as one which already has the *novum* before it. The 'where to' of actuality first shows its fundamental object determination in the *novum*, and summons humanity . . .[35]

In this sense, the *novum* is the 'perspective land' of the process which gives a view of what lies ahead.[36] The historical meaning of the *novum* is bound up with theory-praxis. If the *novum* is taken up and experimented for, if initial formulations about it are corrected in accordance with process trends, it becomes the mediated *novum*, which has acquired many but not all of its subjective and objective conditions; and then the ruling mediated *novum* which strains as tendency: the dialectical, explosive *novum* which is objectively pending and only requires the subjective factor to act for it to become actual.[37] Bloch concedes that the *novum* in this sense need not be good, and also that to become actual the new needs to mediate with the dominant social tendency. He also emphasises that the new is never quite new, that the new which becomes actual is the unexpected fulfilment of what has pre-appeared.[38] But he does not confine the *novum* to what has pre-appeared. Rather what has pre-appeared evidences the possibility of a qualitative leap, of a real exodus from the things at hand.

For Bloch, the *novum* in this intermediate sense is immanently related to the final good *novum*. The final *novum* is present in each good new which emerges in the process. Moreover, as *nova* are brought to realisation, the impediments to the realisation of the final good *novum* are removed. Hence, the theory-praxis of the *novum* is a meta-eschatological theory-praxis, which prepares the way for the ultimate radical new or final *novum*. In this sense, the *novum* is haunted by the border concept of an *ultimum*: the possibility of a final dialectical leap, which would overcome the disparity between *Logos* and *Cosmos,* and bring cosmic nature into a purposive relationship with man.[39] The ultimate in this sense would be the 'realisation' of the 'realising factor', the end of the process in *omega* or *genesis*, the creation at last of 'a new heaven and a new earth'.[40] The final *novum* can also be identified as the dialectical materialist 'truth' of the traditional concept of the apocalypse or the something wonderful still to come; and with the absolute purpose content which pre-appears in the utopian surplus of great art, philosophy and religion, and in the ciphers of nature.[41] Like the Biblical eschatological new, it would be both (1) the fulfilment of what is hoped for, the realisation of what is still possible despite its continuing failure to appear; and (2) a qualitative leap into the unexpected new, the most extreme infusion of new content.

Bloch's attempt to break with the heteronomy of Greek ontological thinking and to include a process metaphysics version of the Biblical eschatological new in Open System is politically motivated. Bloch deliberately fractures the possibility of ontological closure by representing the world as open to a final new. Because the world of Open System has the *novum* within it as well as before it, it strains everywhere to the 'more' and 'other' still to come.[42] Because the *novum* stirs and strains now, it undermines the inherited tendency to think of reality as settled and finished. Again, Bloch's category *novum* transforms the limits of the possible in a Marxist context, since many hopes which would otherwise have to be regarded as unrealistic, could become possible after the realisation of the final *novum*. It also gives Marxist theory-praxis an explosive, eschatological dimension: as work to remove impediments to a developing, emergentist total world transformation. Bloch emphasises that the *novum* is the genuinely historical concept,[43] which allows Marxism to understand history non-naturalistically: as an emergentist process of transmission with dialectical leaps to real new contents, and a continuing rebirth of the goal ahead. Here, his argument links up with the Christian claim that the Bible reveals the structure of history which was concealed from Greek metaphysics. Nonetheless, even if it were accepted that Biblical thinking provides models for historicity of a non-trivial kind (as Bultmann, C. H. Dodd, Richardson and many others have argued),[44] it is by no means clear that the eschatological new can be ontologised, or that the absolute *futurum* should be identified in this way.

GROUND

Bloch's treatment of the category 'ground' is demanding because he attempts to re-interpret the thought experiment of the most obscure tradition in German metaphysics in dialectical materialist terms. The 'ground' is that out of which things arise, that which 'grounds' them: the *ratio* in an ontological as well as in a logical sense. In Leibniz's identity logic the real ground is identified with the logical ground: the sufficient reason for a thing is present in its ground. Bloch however follows the Boehme-Schelling–von Hartmann problematic, which rejects the attempt to backdate later developments to a ground which contains the possibilities which arise out of it. Like Schelling, he adopts a model of a process which begins with a ground which is a non-ground (*Ungrund*), a state of imperfection, characterised by lack and will-like drive to what it lacks: ground or full ground. Bloch represents the process in categorial terms as a process in which the intensive That (*das Dass*) drives or incites towards its What or missing essence.

The claim that the process begins with a non-ground attempting to become ground, can be understood as a categorial representation of the nature of existing reality. Bloch follows Schelling and von Hartmann in reviving the scholastic distinction between *quodditas* and *quidditas* as a way of expressing the fact that the existence of something, *that* it is, cannot be deduced from reason or logical ideas about *what* it is.[45] That which exists is not 'ir-rational', but it is 'a-rational', in the technical sense that its 'thatness' cannot be wholly grasped by, or reduced to, logical ideas. It is heterogeneous and 'intensive' (cf. Duns Scotus). Existing reality (*das Seiende*) is 'will-like'. In scholastic terms, the 'intensive' is tensional or tendential to something. Existing reality is will-like, not in a psychologistic sense, but in the sense that it has an assertive, striving, directional character, like the will. It is defined by an intensive relation, present throughout, between existence and essence, between the That and the What.[46]

Existing reality is will-like (*dasshaft*) because it rests on a ground which is not a ground. This non-ground cannot be characterised as something with being. Rather, for Bloch, as for Schelling, the non-ground with which everything begins is before being; and the process does not begin with a ground in which everything is present *in potentia*, but with a That-ground (*Dassgrund*) with only That-being (*Dass-sein*), not there-being (*Da-sein*).[47] In this sense, the That, with which the process begins and from which everything goes forth, is the 'empty', 'dark', 'objectively vague' 'nullpoint' of all being, which grounds the process by not grounding it (*Ungrund*).[48] It is not a 'something', but an undetermined x, an alpha without determinations which, because it has not come to be, functions as active lack or directed negation.[49] As the lack or objective 'not' in the material cause, it is the objectively unsolved 'world knot': both the 'establishing factor' (*Setzungsfaktor*), which sets up the process, and the 'realising factor', which keeps it in motion and drives it forward in search of its unreached goal.[50] The That is the undetermined, unmediated still within itself of being, which does not yet possess itself (*sich nicht hat*), 'has not yet driven itself out of itself'; the restless That, on which everything rests and is not able to rest, which strives to externalise and manifest itself.[51] It is the a-logical tendency-impetus or driving force (*Dass-Antrieb, Dass-Anstoss*) of the process: the unidentified So That or insisting factor (*incitare, Insistieren-im-Werdensein*) which drives or incites in search of its missing content.[52] As the 'realising actor' or *agens* of material being, the That is the 'subjective factor' in the sense of the active causal factor (*Dass-Subjekt, das Subjekthafte*).[53] In Open System however the causal factor is impeded and unsolved, and agitates to bring itself into being when it is not yet there. It is the still unreached primordial utopian content (*Ur-sache*) which produces the Thatness (*Dassheit*) of existing reality as an assertive, will-like reality with unidentified purposive driving to what it lacks.[54]

Bloch's treatment of the That as a subject engaged in a world Odyssey towards a possible Ithaca[55] should not be misinterpreted. Bloch does not mean that there is a world subject of a traditional metaphysical sort. The subject of the world of Open System must be produced by theory-praxis:

> This open That is the productive driving force in all things, although it itself has not yet completely made itself out, driven out itself from itself. The That and its productivity is the productive, the intensive, the realising factor in the world.[56]

Bloch emphasises that no one knows what the That is. In history, it can be provisionally identified with the working man as the active subjective factor, but what it is in the world as a whole is an *incognito* which it is our task to illumine. The That is a categorial expression of the fact that something remains to be determined: a representation of the 'before itself' of the utopian cause which is still impeded, has not 'stepped forth'. It is the intensity in the nearest near, which drives to an identified moment or a completely solved That, when it itself is still future, not-yet-existing.[57] The That is present in the darkness of the moment and drives towards its missing What or 'essence'. It is present as a 'stirring', 'goading', 'inciting', 'throbbing', 'driving' 'not' (*Nicht*), as the 'not' of the That-ground which seeks its experimental determination in the process:[58]

> What occurs in itself and unmediated as the now, is therefore
> still empty. The That in the now is hollow, is only at first
> undetermined, as a fermenting *not*. As the not with which
> everything begins and establishes itself, around which every
> 'something' is still built.[59]

The That in the moment is a 'not having', a 'not there'; it is the
'not there' of a something, which 'cannot stand together with
itself', which drives forward to what it lacks as the lack of something and the flight from this lack.[60] As the 'not there' of a
'something', the That operates as *nisus* or exigency: as the x of
a still undetermined In General (*Uberhaupt*). So far from being
a materialist world soul:

> It is, rather, a simple x, an alpha present in all being. In-
> complete and unobjective in itself, it draws man on through
> the transient darkness of each moment . . . It is *the not-there*
> *of each present moment,* which, still veiled to itself and seek-
> ing itself, truly evolves into being in and through the world
> process and its experimental forms, for it is their primary
> stimulus and driving force.[61]

As the 'not there' with which the process begins, the That exerts
negative causality as a void or active lack, as *horror vacui*. It is
the intensive realising factor, which brings the world into
motion and sustains it in motion as the experiment to pour out
its That content, and the process begins again in every moment
with the hunger and not-having of the 'not' of the That.[62]

Bloch's attempt to rethink the category 'ground' without
panlogism or ontological closure is obscure. Nonetheless, stripped
of the mystifying Boehme–Schelling–von Hartmann terminology,
Bloch's rejection of a ground which already contains what arises
out of it, is not trivial. On the contrary, it is fundamental to an
open world, which is still unfinished and can be changed for the
better. Because the realising factor or impeded cause of the process contains something which has not yet realised itself, the
world is open to the possibility of an identified That or the realisation of the realising factor, when the utopian cause is no longer
impeded, and the unsuccessful process ends in success.

124   *The Marxist Philosophy of Ernst Bloch*

IDENTITY

According to Bloch, the whole process is tending to the realisation of identity. Here Bloch's position has been widely misunderstood. Contrary to the claims of the Frankfurt School, Bloch is not an identity philosopher and does not postulate a neo-classical identity process. Bloch uses the model or thought experiment of identity metaphysics, but he refunctions it (*umfunktioniert*) in order to make it serve a new purpose.

Like Heidegger, Bloch sees that a new understanding of the principle of identity is necessary if a break is to be made with the history of metaphysics. Bloch approaches the problem via a critique of Leibniz. In Open System, as in his early utopian philosophy, Bloch breaks with Leibniz's principle of identity according to which what emerges in the predicate is present in the logical subject (*praedicatum inest subjecto*).[63] S is not yet P, subject is not predicate, means more than that Bloch allows for emergence and rejects Leibniz's pan-logical tendencies. Bloch does not dispute with Leibniz within a classical identity problematic. He refunctions the concept of identity and attempts to employ it as a theory-praxis concept for a world being shaped and decided by human action. Hence, when Bloch declares that subject is not yet predicate, his language carries a new sense. S is not yet P means that the 'What', 'essence' or 'kernel' of existing reality has not yet been articulated.[64] Bloch does not merely mean that the process is not yet finished. He means that it is necessary to understand the world in a radical, non-classical way, as a world with its kernel or essence still before it.[65] For Bloch, identity is given as a category of our inherited logic and as the supposition implicit in the intentionality of the utopian *Evidenz* found throughout the process: especially in music, religion, and great philosophy, in the 'gold' of the moment and in the ciphers of nature.[66] But it is not given as something which has ever been. Rather, identity takes on future reference as something which is 'not yet'. Here Bloch's radicalism, like Heidegger's related attempt to understand identity as 'belonging together', strains at the thought model it inhabits and tries to win ground for an open-ended, future oriented thinking of an untraditional kind.

Refunctioned as a meta-eschatological *futurum*, identity retains its classical perfection, but as an imperative. Nonetheless, identity is not an abstraction or simply an ideal. It is a categorial relation which obtains in the process, a centring relation in accordance with which the still latent 'substantiality' of process matter is preformed;[67] and an unreached *perfectio* which pre-appears in the process and in the darkness of the moment.[68] First, identity (if it were achieved) would be the *novum* of the self identity of the ground with which the process begins, when the That finds its What and S is finally P. Identity would be an 'identified', a completely 'solved' That:[69]

> . . . identity . . . denotes the That (*Dass*) or intensive in material existence (*Dasein*), in so far as it some day must find its tendential goal content by theory-praxis, and the Thatground (*Dassgrund*) of all driving and realising factors finally drives itself out and realises itself in the goal.[70]

Identity in Open System, therefore, is not the tautological identity of formal logic, but the directionality of the unrealised 'realising factor' which makes the process an experimental process with growing identification in its forms.[71] Hence, identity for Bloch implies active processual identifying,[72] and, ultimately, the realisation of the realising factor itself, the production of the producer. In this latter sense, identity would mean a structural change in the intensive impetus keeping the process in motion, the 'clicking in' of the still unsuccessful process in 'an identified moment'.[73] Bloch emphasises that: 'It is particularly not an idea that is to be realised, but the kernel of matter, the source, the drive, the birth ground of its tendency-impetus'.[74] According to Bloch, the process can end with a last identifying of the What of the That: with the omega of a completely solved That, when the That no longer remains within itself and the material *agens* 'springs forth'.[75] The projection of such a radical outlet (*Mündung*) or meta-eschatological perspective arises because the possibility of an identified ground pre-appears in the darkness of the moment, because the process is full of preappearance (*Vor-Schein*) of a completely successful mediation of the That.[76]

Second, identity would mean the *novum* of the identity of subject and object: the successful completion of history as a dialectical subject-object process.[77] Bloch glosses identity in this sense as an unalienated subject in identity with an unalien-

ated object, as the end of alienation, 'the naturalisation of man
and the humanisation of nature', and as the beginning of Marx's
'realm' or 'kingdom' of freedom.[78] Identity in this sense would
not be confined to 'reconciliation' or 'alliance'; it would mean
an end to the disparity between man and cosmic nature, a
dialectical materialist fulfilment of the myth of the *Makanthropos*, the *unio* of subject and object in a convergence of *Logos*
and *Kosmos*, based on the mediation of man as the 'subject of
history' with the not-yet-actual 'subject of nature'.[79] Third,
identity would mean the *novum* of the self identity of the
humanum. Bloch glosses human self identity as 'self possession',
as 'the illumination of our *incognito*', as 'fulfilment' (*Erfüllung*),
and, in apocalyptical terms, as 'the eschaton of our immanence'.[80] For Bloch, all three senses of identity converge at the
end of the process if utopia or 'everything' is achieved. The process ends with the adequation of the 'That'; subject and object
achieve *unio*; the *humanum* achieves self identity in a humanly
adequate world (*Heimat*).

Bloch realises that 'identity', even reinterpreted as a meta-
eschatological *futurum,* is not credible now. He emphasises that
identity is a border ideal which lies 'beyond the border of saya-
bility', that it is the most extreme utopian postulate, the *utopis-
simum* of utopia, which cannot be specified now, except intensively, and in terms of the conditions which will not be present
if it is realised.[81] Similarly, to avoid settled dispositional identity, or the implication that the process is a closed identity process with identity only 'undecided' but still structural, Bloch
stresses that identity would be *Mündung* (literally, 'outlet'): a
radical convergence or flowing together of hitherto disparate
instances.[82] Identity would be the realisation of the intended In
General, the 'truth' of the Biblical postulate of a new world, the
novum of the creation of the world *in integrum* for the first
time.[83]

In Marxist terms, Bloch's concept of identity is bound to
seem over-metaphyiscal. Even if it were accepted that man intends identity and that this is what human finality means, it is
difficult to justify the claim that there is any disposition to the
realisation of such identity in the world. Moreover, despite
Bloch's attempts to minimise the claim of ontological identity
by emphasising that identity is still 'future' and 'open' in the
sense of 'undecided', it is difficult not to regard identity

as structurally presupposed as what is needed, even if what would constitute such identity is not fixed or ready, but develops in the process.

Perhaps Bloch's category identity could be interpreted to mean: (1) that the subject-object gap constitutive of modern experience is historical; (2) that the relation which centres human history is man's search for self identity or fulfilment; (3) that man experiences anticipatory identity, in this sense, in the darkness of the moment and in the process forms; (4) that human intentionality to identity gives direction to human labour and goal setting; and (5) that men experience the *telos* of an end to alienation in prehistory. Bloch himself goes further, however, and his position remains suspended between two parameters. To the extent that he seems to build identity into the present world, even if only as a real possibility, his process borders on theodicy; while to the extent that identity is really 'not yet' and still future, it is difficult to know what it would be, or how one could be confident that any given course of action would lead to it.

DIALECTIC

Like Sartre, Adorno and Kosík, Bloch attempts to develop a new concept of the dialectic in Marxism. He seeks to avoid both pre-critical objectivism and historicist subjectivism, without sacrificing either objective dialectics or the revolutionary function of the dialectically aimed interventions of the subject. According to Bloch, the materialist dialectic is a dialectic of the real: an ontological dialectic of the process contents (*Realdialektik*) in the tradition of Boehme, Nicholas of Cusa, Leibniz and Hegel. It is not simply the law of thought or 'a method', but the law of movement of material being:[84] a tendency dialectic which keeps the process in a state of dialectical unrest. For Bloch, the materialist dialectic is inherently teleological. In Hegel's language, it is a law-governed drive to manifest an unreached content, which arises because the content (*Sache*) in process is not yet.[85] It is a totality dialectic, based on a *unity of unity and contradiction*, with need as its driving force (*Anstoss*) and a relation to totality in each contradiction which is related to 'essence'.[86]

Despite these strong characterisations, Bloch recognises that the problem of how to conceive of the materialist dialectic is a difficult one; that the inherited model implies idealist and pan-logical features which are inconsistent with materialism; and that it is necessary to rethink radically the idea of a materialist dialectic in the context of an undecided, unfinished world. To distinguish the materialist dialectic from all panlogical dialectics, Bloch emphasises that the materialist dialectic does not begin with 'logical' contradiction, but with a material *prius* which is itself in an objectively unsolved, self contradictory state.[87] In categorial terms, the materialist dialectic begins with the 'not' present in the cause, which goes forth as a 'not yet' to the realisation of 'everything' or 'nothing'.[88] It is a dialectic of immanent exploding, of wider driving negation,[89] and takes the form of a subject-object relationship in which the subject attempts to manifest itself in an adequate object.[90] Similarly, the materialist dialectic is not based on conceptual realism; nor does it take a syllogistic thesis-antithesis-synthesis form.[91] Nor is it a dialectic which lays out content present from the start. On the contrary, the materialist dialectic is the dialectic of the developing *novum*: a dialectic of unrest based on the unsuitability of the at hand to the possible new, which mediates with the future as well as the past.[92] It is an anticipatory, synthetic dialectic, and works as the dialectical tendency to something of the impeded *novum*.[93] It is emergentist, expansive and discontinuous: a dialectical process of transmission, full of interruptions, disparities, breaks and sudden leaps to genuinely new contents (*nova*).[94] As an anticipatory dialectic, it strains before the cause of its straining has itself been realised; as a synthetic dialectic it produces what is not present *a priori* in the cause: both new contents and emergentist cohesions of previously disparate elements, which are in turn burst open to make way for fresh interruptions, leaps to new contents and unexpected cohesions.[95]

Bloch emphasises that the materialist dialectic develops as a lawlike, ordered process, but as a process full of changes, in which what occurs is in no way automatic:

> It is only that dialectic with the ground, not as *ratio* from the beginning, but as intensive Thatness (*Dassheit*), with what follows not as automatic consequence *per se*, but as a process which is able to be changed, which is full of changes,

albeit an ordered process, which transforms the causal principle from an *a priori* analytical one to a synthetic, expanding *a posteriori*.[96]

According to Bloch, the materialist dialectic involves a radical break with the causality appropriate to a finished world. It transforms the causal principle from an *a priori* analytical one (the effects are present in the cause and can be deduced from it in a logical manner) to one that is *a posteriori* and synthetic (the effects are not archaic, but emerge in the process in a converging synthesis which cannot be retraced in purely logical terms).[97] Bloch rejects the traditional principle that the cause must be adequate to its effects, and argues that the materialist dialectic allows for reciprocal causality of the effect back upon the cause, for interrupted causality and causality of contradictions, and for the structural causality in all instances of the final cause: the *agens-agendum* or still utopian primordial content (*Ur-Sache*).[98]

According to Bloch, the dialectic operates in history as a critical subject-object dialectic,[99] based on the working man, who finds himself and his labour inadequately objectified in the world around him.[100] It is driven forward by need and hope as the subject acts to overcome objectifications which are inadequate to his needs.[101] Like Sartre, Bloch attempts to free the dialectic in history from automaticism, and emphasises the crucial role of the intervention of the subject, who acts to activate contradictions and to raise developing contradictions to a higher stage. Unlike Sartre, however, Bloch does not reduce the dialectic in history to anthropology. The dialectic in history for Bloch is not subjective. It operates if and only if there is an objective contradiction on the side of the object, which has reached the point at which it can be 'exploded' by the active intervention of the subjective factor. The possibility of dialectical leaps in history rests on strict lawfulness, on impeded tendencies and the maturation of conditions, and has nothing to do with a voluntarism which does not confine itself to 'what has become due'.[102]

Equally, however, the subject's negating of the objective contradiction is the key to changing a changeable world. It opens the way for the realisation of the next 'ability to be', and sets new causes and conditions. For Bloch, the dialectic in history is the key to guiding the historical process, and to determining what can be brought within its developing finalism. Moreover, Bloch emphasises that such an activist, constitutive concept of the dialectic cannot be confined to the Hegelian model with which it begins. Instead, a more differentiated concept of the dialectic is needed, which allows for multi-spatial, multi-temporal lines of development, and for the presence of non-contemporaneous as well as contemporaneous contradictions.[103] In subject-object terms, the dialectic in history is not a mythical objectivist dynamic which operates regardless of the decisions of men, but a revolutionary method.

   This activist emphasis is also the key to Bloch's concept of the dialectic in nature, which plays a central and controversial role in Open System. Bloch recognises that there are dangers in any concept of a dialectic in nature which can be conceived in crude naturalistic or mechanical terms. He argues, however, that there is an objective-real dialectic in nature in the sense of a dialectic of unsatisfied need, based on the unsuitability of nature's already manifested forms to nature's latent possibility content.[104] For Bloch, there is dialectical processuality in nature which existed before man and continues to operate after him. Dialectical processuality, including dialectical leaps from quantity to quality, is the way of nature, Bloch argues.[105] Nonetheless, it is obviously not possible to extract much emancipatory potential from the dialectical processuality of nature in its present form; there is also a danger that such processuality will be arbitrarily transferred to history, despite the fact that in history, unlike nature, a subjective factor has emerged with conscious purposes. Bloch, however, attempts to find emancipatory potential in nature by relating his activist concept of the dialectic in history to unrealised possibilities in nature, which may be able to be released through human intervention and goal setting.

   Bloch finds such possibilities in the qualitative forms or figures (*Gestalten*) which nature contains. Bloch regards the qualitative forms in nature, which contain more than is present in their parts, as 'excerpt forms' (*Auszugsgestalten*) which anticipate the true form of nature which has nowhere been achieved. Moreover, he argues that such 'excerpt forms' are unfinished and developing dialectically to further qualitative forms.[106] In this sense, Bloch postulates that there is a dialectic of qualitatively qualified, self-manifesting form categories in nature:[107] a dialectic of still unconcluded entelechtic form categories which are experimental models of something which has not yet succeeded.[108] According to Bloch, the process is full of *real* ciphers, *real* allegories, *real* symbols of its not yet found 'true form', and such self-manifesting form categories are *real* fragments:

> The forms which are thrown up by the process, the ciphers, allegories and symbols in which it is so rich, are *still only fragments, real fragments, through which the process streams unconcluded, and proceeds dialectically to further fragmentary forms.*[109]

Such form categories anticipate and incite towards the not yet found solution of the process. They testify to the presence of a subject-object relation in nature which has not yet reached a developed form, and ultimately to the possibility that nature as well as history contains a still nowhere manifest 'subject':

> All forms are merely *tension* figures, *tendency* figures of a changeable, indeed explosive kind, and they are so on account of the still nowhere objectively laid out experimental constitution of the world as process.[110]

Bloch recognises that this concept of a dialectic of qualitatively qualified form categories in nature is speculative, and can only have a utopian foundation in terms of the nature currently at hand. In the context of Open System as projective metaphysics, however, such a concept serves to set up the horizon of a future transformation of nature as a result of human labour: to re-emphasise the final goal envisaged by the young Marx of the 'naturalisation of man and the humanisation of nature'. According to Bloch, the qualitative form categories in nature measure the utopian potentialities developing in the process.[111] As objective-real models of the missing What of the That, as *real* ciphers, symbols and allegories of a possible 'naturalisation of man and humanisation of nature',[112] they provide 'lineaments' of a possible end relation or end figure[113] and can be regarded as *real* experiments, *real* probes for the not yet manifest 'core' of the world: even as material self-anticipations of a still possible 'last matter'.[114] Such statements, however, have forward reference: they must be related to a still future form of theory-praxis. The dialectic of form categories in nature is only anticipatory and points to a possible future dialectical movement in nature, which is impeded as long as nature remains encapsulated and unmediated with man.[115] Hence the 'truth' of Bloch's speculation, grounded in utopian excess, remains to be produced in history, and Open System is not dogmatic philosophy of nature, but *viator* philosophy which reasserts the problem of nature as a future task for an illusion-free Marxist politics.

REAL POSSIBILITY

Bloch also provides a new analysis of the category possibility in Open System. The need for an analysis of possibility going beyond the classical concept of preformed possibility has been recognised by many modern philosophers. It was implicit in Kierkegaard's analysis of possibility in *Either-Or*, from which modern existentialism derives, and in the work of William James and Bergson, both of whom had a direct influence on Bloch. It also occurs in Heidegger and in modern analytical philosophy.[116] Bergson, James and other modern process philosophers argued that the concept of possibility was repressed and impeded in traditional metaphysics, and in modern philosophy influenced by Laplacean determinism. Granted a finished, completed world and strict determinism, possibility tended to become preformed possibility, which necessarily comes to be granted the presence of certain conditions, whereas it was necessary to admit a class of 'objective possibilities', which were not actual possibilities now, but which might or might not become so in the future.[117]

Bloch approaches the problem of possibility in this context of the need to overcome the bias of staticist thought against openness and the new. He recognises that possibility is the Benjamin of the great philosophical concepts, and reviews the history of the concept in the hands of the great philosophers from Aristotle to Hegel.[118] Bloch follows Aristotle in interpreting possibility, in the true sense, as a determination of objective reality. He rejects attempts to restrict possibility to epistemology or to anthropomorphic introjection, and sees the recovery of a concept of ontological possibility as fundamental to Marxist philosophy and its practical intention to change the world. Bloch denies both the traditional modal hierarchy (possibility, actuality, necessity) and the traditional assumption that what has become is higher than possibility. He argues that possibility is more fundamental than the become (cf. James), and that much more can become actual than has done so already.[119]

Bloch distinguishes four grades of possibility. First, *formal possibility (das formal Mögliche)*: formal thought possibilities which are not part of the object and which may be absurd: 'counter-sense' as opposed to 'non-sense'.[120] Second, *factual epistemological possibility (das sachlich-objektiv Mögliche)*: possibilities relating to factually evident conditions which are the object of hypothetical or problematic judgements. Possibility in this sense is a category of judgement, and the element of uncertainty arises in the judgement, because of incomplete knowledge of factually evident conditions, not in the object itself.[121] Third, *possibility according to the object (das sachhaft-objektgemäss Mögliche)*. Possibility according to the object is the open structural or dispositional possibility of the *Gegenstand* and its states of affairs, according to its genus and type, and taking account of its social and lawful variability. Bloch emphasises that the *Gegenstand* and its states of affairs differs from the object of knowledge as well as the real object and its states of affairs.[122] It is a realistic copy (*Abbild*) of the real object as it can become: a copy of what the object can hypothetically become through variability and inter-relation (including constitutive properties which can be produced by real definition) as a matter of present modal possibility.[123] Bloch, however, distinguishes a fourth class of possibility: *objective real possibility (das objektiv-real Mögliche)*. Objective real possibility is possibility whose conditions have not yet been completely assembled in the sphere of the object itself:

> Real possibility, on the other hand, is everything whose conditions have not yet been completely assembled in the sphere of the object itself; be it, that they are still in a process of ripening, or be it, above all, that new conditions — albeit mediated through those already present — spring up to herald the entry of a new reality.[124]

It is the paradox of 'open', 'undecided', 'unfinished' possibility which is 'in suspense' in the 'blue of the object'.[125]

According to Bloch, objective real possibility is the logical

expression for the categorial *vor sich* (before itself) of the
movement of process matter as a movement which is process-
like: an expression for process matter with *dynamei on.*[126] It is
what constitutes the specific regional character of existing
reality at the front of its happenings. By this Bloch means that
objective real possibilities are future-laden determinations, *real*
material self anticipations of process matter.[127]

Bloch's initiative is more radical than this presentation suggests. Bloch's objective real possibility is not simply an additional fourth class of possibility. Indeed, it is difficult to speak
of possibility, actuality or necessity in Open System in a traditional sense, since (1) there is no (non-formal) concluded possibility; (2) there is no 'actuality' in a sense which implies a
clear separation from future possibility, since existing reality is
full of the 'not yet', and (3) necessity, in the strict sense of concluded 'essential' necessity, is 'not yet', something which would
arise if the process ended in success.[128] Bloch's objective real
possibility changes the character of all non-formal possibility. In
effect, Bloch combines Bergson's concept of objective possibility
with Meinong's theory of incompletely determined objects in
order to arrive at partial conditionality which is both 'starting
to be' and 'already under way'.[129] If, however, the world is indeed unfinished, if S is indeed not yet P, then the final determination of ontology is shifted to the future. Possibility remains determinate in the sense that there are always limits to
what is 'in suspense'. The fact, however, that these limits change,
that real possibility goes forward, means that what things are
cannot be defined once and for all from what they are now. It
means that the world is metaphysically open and that things are
what they can become, where this cannot be wholly known in
advance, or determined apart from the contingency of possible
future human action. In this sense, the real possibility of x is
not something fixed. It is 'open', 'in suspense', 'still developing'.
Thus man, for example, is the real possibility of all that he can
become, including what he cannot become now (present modal
possibility), even as a result of lawful variation and human activity.[130]

In a Marxist context, Bloch's concept of real possibility is
very important. First, Bloch provides a categorial grade for what
is coming into possibility designed to overcome the tendency to
prejudge possibility in terms of existing reality. A categorial

representation of 'weakly actual' and 'starting to be' has obvious relevance to Marxism, with its postulates of 'the classless society' and 'the realm of freedom', and is also admitted by some analytical philosophers. Second, Bloch's concept of real possibility points to the need for Marxist theory-praxis to be based on what may be coming into possibility, on what exists in partial conditionality, and not merely on what is fully possible now. For Bloch, Marxism becomes the praxis of objective real possibility at the front of the world. His approach raises the reflexive character of real possibility to full consciousness, since what men project as possible may have a causal influence on what becomes a real possibility, especially as a result of dialectics. There is a primacy of theory-praxis in determining what things may become, and real possibility is possibility which extends its *potentia-possibilitatis* through dialectical leaps.[131] Third, Bloch's concept of real possibility undermines the foundation of nihilism in Marxism by removing the crucial premise that the possible is pre-set, something given as fate, to which human hopes must be adjusted. Bloch sees that both the Marxist concept of praxis and the doctrine of dialectical leaps imply a break with a classical world conception. He emphasises the *changeability* of the changeable world, the extent to which human intervention and gearing mean that the ability of things to be other than they are is open and developing. Bloch distinguishes between the possibility of actively changing the world and the capacity of the world to change in potentiality, and stresses that the process allows for contingency in the sense of dialectically mediated, lawful variability.[132] The possibility of human intervention in and mediation with existing conditions to change them, combined with the potentiality in the world for dialectical leaps, undermines the traditional closure of the possibility and opens the way for possibilities which still require further dialectical leaps to achieve full conditionality.

The problem remains: how can we know that something is a real possibility and not merely a formal one? The problem is acute because Bloch (1) tends to describe ideal projections as 'real possibilities', which most other Marxists would doubt could ever become possible; and (2) uses the term 'real possibility' to refer to both real essential possibilities and to open possibilities in general. This means that the criteria for identifying something as a real possibility must be stricter than Bloch provides, and cannot simply be the continued appearance of an ideal in utopian imagination. Nonetheless, Bloch's attempt to supplement Marxism with a wider possibility concept may have an importance apart from his own formulation of it, as an anticipation which more formally minded philosophers may translate into more acceptable terms.

MATTER

All the categories of Open System finally relate to Bloch's concept of matter. Like other categories in Open System, 'matter' takes on an unfamiliar function and meaning. Bloch interprets Marxist materialism as 'materialism forwards', in contrast to all previous recursive materialisms. He argues that for Marxism the totality of matter is not given from the start, but arises on the horizon of the future as something 'not yet', which can be decisively influenced by the goal setting and activity of men.[133] Bloch conceives of matter as open, dialectical, utopian process matter, with *real* anticipation, unconcluded entelechy and a forward trend.

First, matter is 'open' in the sense that it is not a substratum of preformed possibilities, but something which develops to new and further contents. It is not mechanical solidity, but, according to the implied meaning of the Aristotelian definition of matter, both 'being-according-to-possibility' (*kata to dynaton*) and 'being-in-possibility' (*dynamei on*); both what has come to be (which determines potential phenomena according to existing possibility), and what is not yet fully possible: futuristic real possibility which constitutes the open and developing active substratum of the process.[134] Hence, matter is both the precondition for phenomena, and something dynamically active in the direction of the future which has not yet entered into full phenomenal existence. It follows that matter is historical and extends its limits over time. It is always limited, but it is not always limited in the same way. Hence its definition is futurological, like the definition of man himself: 'Matter is the real possibility to all the forms which are latent in its womb and can be brought out through the process'.[135]

Second, matter is dialectical in the sense that it develops through contradictions and dialectical leaps from quantity to quality and to the genuinely new contents.[136] Third, matter is inherently processual: process matter, both in the sense of something still in process, and in the sense of matter which must be defined by the processuality of its moments, not by what it has become at any given point in time. It is utopian process matter in so far as it has a utopian *totum* or possible perfection (*Vollkommenheit*) as its latency and final goal, as what is implicit in *dynamei on*.[137] Bloch does not mean that matter contains utopia as an already realised possibility now. He means that matter contains immanent reference to the horizon of a 'last matter' in the ciphers of nature[138] or self manifesting form categories which would be utopia if it were realised:[139] that matter itself is not yet what it can be, and has not yet produced its 'core', which is hypothetically the same in man and nature.[140] Bloch recognises that utopia cannot be realised within the restrictions of the present world, but he argues that matter already witnesses to utopia as its latency, even though the realisation of utopia would first require a last dialectical leap releasing the final *novum* and bringing nature as a whole into a purposive relationship with man.[141]

Fourth, matter is uncompleted entelechy, and this is reflected in the energetic drive of the tendency and the entelechtic latency of the process. Here Bloch refunctions Aristotle's explanation of movement as a drive to realise entelechy. Whereas for Aristotle, however, entelechy was settled and only remained to be actualised, Bloch argues that the entelechy of matter itself is dialectically developing in the process, and that 'not only the movement of matter, but *matter as a whole . . . is still uncompleted entelechy*'.[142] Here Bloch's position depends on the notion of a positive lack. The entelechy of matter is 'not yet', in the sense that what the final state of matter can be is undetermined. But the entelechy of matter is now, in the sense that matter at hand is uncompleted entelechy with immanent reference to entelechtic completion as a structural characteristic. Bloch's matter is matter with *real* anticipation, in the sense of matter with an immanent *horizon* which anticipates its own future real possibility;[143] it is matter with a forward trend in the sense of matter which is dynamically active in the direction of the future and which drives towards the possible completion of its uncompleted entelechy.[144]

Bloch's concept of matter is one of the most difficult features of Open System and is further discussed in chapter 5. Nonetheless, it is important to note that matter for Bloch is a suppositional foundation for whatever can be brought forth in nature and history, not a mysterious ontological substance. Hence, Bloch's decision to adopt a maximalist, affirmativist matter concept is a projective move against premature disillusionment designed to ground further theory-praxis, and not an overoptimistic interpretation of a settled matter at hand.

ANTICIPATION

According to Bloch, the process contains the *plus ultra* of *real* anticipation. There is anticipation in the process because matter itself has an immanent horizon, and anticipation is an objective attribute of process matter.[145] By this Bloch means that there is objective imagination in the world itself:

> Mediated anticipation and objective imagination give us and the world process the *plus ultra* of the homecoming implicit in its expressive forms, excerpt forms; objective imagination is the organ of real possibility.[146]

Objective imagination is the 'dream of a thing' developing in the world. It is the thing in itself which is anticipated in great art and in the process forms:

> . . . the concrete imagination and the imagery of its mediated anticipations are fermenting in the process of reality itself, and represent themselves in the concrete dream directed towards the future: anticipatory elements are components of reality itself.[147]

Anticipation for Bloch has a subject-object character. Bloch deliberately stresses the objective side of anticipation as part of his move against the subjectivism of post-Cartesian thought; but he does not mean that there is anticipation, as men experience it, inside matter. He means: (1) that the process forms themselves refer to a *Gegenstand* which is still concealed or encapsulated in the object; and (2) that such reference indicates a dispositionality which can correlate with and ground human labour designed to realise it.

The process is full of objective-real pre-appearance (*Vor-Schein*) of the Real and In General developing in the world.[148] It is full of *real* ciphers, allegories and symbols which anticipate what is 'not yet'.[149] Such *real* ciphers, symbols and allegories are not merely subjective, but refer in an anticipatory manner to an intentional object (*Gegenstand*) which is still concealed in the object itself. Bloch does not imagine that what is denoted by such reference can come about without the intervention of human labour, or that such reference provides a concrete glimpse of a future development. He emphasises that such anticipation is unmediated, non-specific and has a difficult horizon character, which derives its potential importance from theory-praxis.[150] For Bloch, such pre-appearance is found not only in the aesthetic, ethical and religious materials, but in the ciphers of nature.[151] Such pre-appearance arises in human consciousness as something subjective; it is also conditioned by ideology. Nonetheless, *Vor-Schein* is grounded productive imagination with an objective-real intention to something which can be realised in the future.[152]

Bloch's concept of anticipation is essentially hypothetical and praxis-related. It is based on the original conception of the relation between subject and object which is central to Open System. Bloch attempts to overcome the modern dualism between subject and object . For Bloch, subject and object are not dualistically separated, but dialectically related as different aspects of the same moving 'something':[153]

That which is within is, and remains the key to that which is without; yet the key is not the substance, and the substance of the key lies as well in the object house (as yet hardly on its way to completion) that is the world.[154]

The identity of subject and object, in other words, must be produced. It is a *futurum*, but a *futurum* which anticipates itself in a way which provokes human action and goal setting to bring it into being.

FINALITY

Bloch attempts to rehabilitate the concept of finality in Marxism against both the staticist objectivism of traditional teleology and the positivist denial of purpose. He concedes that there is no 'finality' in the traditional sense of pre-ordained goals and purposes. For Bloch, however, the thought experiment of finality does not fail with the unsuccessful attempts to identify it. Moreover, the danger of 'excess' involved in finalistic thinking is preferable to the 'bad infinite' which follows from the abandonment of the attempt to think of the world as tending towards an end.

First, for Bloch there is human finality in two important and related senses. Apart from the teleology implicit in Marx's concept of 'the human essence' and the 'social powers' of the rich social individual, there is human finality in the sense of fundamental intentionality to the unconditioned: to an absolute purpose content which can be glossed as 'utopia', 'fulfilment', 'self encounter', 'being as hope'.[155] Moreover, this finalism colours all human experience, and man lives in a constant recursion to the still unidentified goal or purpose content present in the darkness of the moment.[156] It is true that man's intentionality to utopia, to radical self fulfilment which would include an adequate object, is substantially unrealistic, that the world at this point remains in many respects alien to human purposes. Nonetheless, this intentionality is anticipatory and causal in so far as it leads men to transform the world, which is open and changeable through theory-praxis. Thus, there is human finality in the second sense of goal-oriented human labour. Here Bloch has in mind not only the teleological starting point of labour (which Marx recognised in *Capital* when he emphasised that the presence of a plan in human imagination distinguished human labour from the activity of animals).[157] but the way in which human goal setting and gearing constitute an active teleology and set the possible.

Like Lukács in *The Ontology of Social Being*, Bloch emphasises the teleological character of the labour process, and the decisive role of human goal-setting and conscious planning in determining what the world can become.[158] Bloch, however, rejects Lukács' reliance on Nicolai Hartmann's staticist concept of teleology, and attempts to posit emergentist finality of a subject-object sort. Granted that there are no pre-ordained purposes, as in the old teleology, Bloch argues that there is emergentist finality in the sense of the emergence of goals and ends, towards which process forms tend.[159] Such goals are not subjective, but objective attributes of process tendencies, which set the conditions for their realisation. Bloch concedes that such goals are heterogeneous, in the sense that they are transformed in the process of realisation;[160] but he emphasises against Lukács the degree to which there are predispositions in matter towards the realisation of the goals which are set by men.[161]

Bloch, however, also argues for finality in a much stronger sense. He tries to refunction the idea that there is finality at work in the world as a whole, by applying his operator 'not yet' to the traditional category finality. Although there is no *telos* in the sense of a settled or decided purpose given from the start, Bloch argues that reality is tendential to a purpose which has not yet been found. For Bloch, the process has the real possibility of realising a final purpose.[162] According to Bloch, the world is objectively incomplete.[163] Reality is tendential to an unidentified 'what for', and this 'what for' functions in the process as the unidentified intended cause (*Zweckursache*): as the possibility of an absolute purpose content which exists in latency and transmits itself along the causal chains of the process as a purpose content which is still not reached.[164] Something (*Etwas*) is attempting to realise itself, to achieve 'substantiality' in the process, and this still utopian but developing 'substantiality' keeps the process in a state of dialectical unrest.[165] In this sense, there is an inciting 'self-seeking substantiality of events', an *agens agendum* which exerts a structural causality in all instances.[166]

At this point in time, it is not possible to indicate finality in any stronger form. For Bloch, the world is objectively unsolved and contains the real problem of its own meaning: the problem of the tendential, but nowhere yet identified purpose content of the That.[167] But it does not have this purpose content as something given from the start. Rather the possible final purpose (including the possibility of utter finality if the realising factor is realised) develops in the experimental identifying of the process forms, and emerges in a staggered development of the teleological impulse from end to purpose to meaning (*Zweck, Ziel, Sinn*).[168] Thus, although the world is an experiment for the 'substance' of matter, this 'substance' is 'not yet' and only arises if the process ends in an adequation of the That. At this point, this 'substance' has a basis in the substantiality developing in the process forms[169] and in *dynamei on*,[170] but it is nowhere present. The unidentified purpose content of the process anticipates itself in excerpt froms (*Auszugsgestalten*) with finalistic entelechtic reference,[171] and in the intention of the That to strike into the purpose content of its That-ground.[172] But even if the world contains the ability to be utopia in its objective imagination, in its objective real possibility,[173] this purpose is still 'not yet'. The world has its 'core' still before it;[174] and the pre-appearance of its final purpose content in the utopian *Evidenz* of the process,[175] especially in the constant return to the still unbecome purpose content in the moment,[176] does not mean that this purpose content is more than a utopian reality with not-yet-being. The pre-appearance of an end relation in the process is an impetus to theory-praxis,[177] and not something which can be represented except in terms of an ontology of not-yet-being.

Bloch's revival of finality in a utopian form has parallels with the rehabilitation of finality in realist philosophy of science with its stress on latent potency and the natural agency of causal powers. Indeed, Bloch's doctrine of real dispositions and tendencies could be restated in a less speculative form as a realist interpretation of Marx. Bloch may be right to argue for a renewed finalist dimension in Marxism in the sense of a conscious setting of teleological goal content, but once again he seems to go too far in a speculative direction.

SUBJECT OF NATURE

The most controversial aspect of Open System is Bloch's concept of a 'subject' of nature. The concept of a 'subject' of nature has a long history in theosophical speculation and in Renaissance *Naturphilosophie,* and played a leading part in the philosophies of Franz von Baader and Schelling. In Open System Bloch applies his operator 'not yet' to the traditional concept, and postulates a possible 'subject' of nature, which is 'not yet.'

Bloch does not mean that there is a 'subject' of nature inside matter; he is not postulating some kind of materialist world soul. He realises that in the face of modern scientific theories any postulate of a 'subject' of nature is bound to seem fantastic. Indeed, he describes it himself as a hypothetical, half mythological postulate.[178] Moreover, he does not attempt to detail the 'subject' of nature, as though there was some way of knowing in advance what the final state of nature would be. Bloch does not postulate a 'subject' of nature because he is simple minded or credulous, but because he believes that much of the Marxist tradition is unrealistic. If, as Marx held, nature is reflected in history and history takes place on the basis of natural conditions, then it is an illusion, Bloch argues, to envisage a utopian transformation of man and society without a transformation of man's relationship to nature.[179] Bloch seeks to overcome the separation of nature and history in Marxism, with the fatalism and pessimism which it involves, and to raise Marx's insight that there is no absolute separation of history and nature to the level of a programme for theory-praxis.[180] Bloch argues that it is necessary to put nature back on the agenda for change under socialism. He stresses that all conceptions of nature are historically and socially conditioned, and that Marxists should not take the concept of a meaningless mechanical nature which prevails under capitalism as beyond question.[181] There is no iron law in Marxism, Bloch argues, which establishes that nature is incapable of change. On the contrary, the dream of such a development has appeared throughout history,[182] and a socialist concept of nature must take account of such optatives, as well as the less encouraging conditions immediately at hand. For Bloch, the future history of nature needs to be understood as a task for human labour: as something to be brought within the ambit of human planning and goal setting. Bloch concedes that nature at hand is caught up in meaningless repetition and contains the horizon of total destruction as a result of the law of entropy,[183] but he argues that Marxism should not capitulate in the face of this evident disparity between nature and human finality.

In Marxist terms, Bloch argues that nature could change under socialism as a result of dialectics. If, as Engels claimed, the dialectic applies to nature, then nature may be capable of further dialectical leaps. Moreover, if nature has produced man by a dialectical leap and, as Bloch claims, there is a unity of material being, then it is theoretically possible that nature could produce further forms of 'subjectivity' in the future.[184] Bloch is not the only Marxist to envisage a possibility of this kind. A related speculation occurs in the thought of Mao Tse-tung.[185] The difficulty is that granted even the most improbable changes in nature, there can be no guarantee that these changes would be favourable, let alone that they would produce a 'subject'.

Bloch's concept of a possible 'subject' of nature goes beyond the postulate of a possible change in nature, although it requires it. It depends on a Marxist inheritance of a pre-modern philosophical theory. Bloch rejects mechanistic accounts of movement as non-explanatory, and follows the traditional analysis according to which movement resulted from the active causality of a teleological 'subject'. Hence, for Bloch the 'subject' of nature is the active causal factor or source of activity and movement in nature.[186] Bloch concedes that this 'subject' has not yet been identified, but he argues that such a postulate expresses the 'truth' of what was meant by the Renaissance distinction between *natura naturata* and *natura naturans*. In modern terms, Bloch implies that there is a causal substratum in nature more basic than phenomena. Bloch argues that a concrete pattern of mediation with this causal substratum could become possible under socialism.[187] Here Bloch implies that Marxism requires a praxis-oriented philosophy of technology. He envisages a future non-Euclidian nuclear technology, based on radiation industries, which would be capable of mediating with the 'subject' or causal substratum of nature, and not only its immediate phenomenal field.[188] Under socialism, Bloch argues, a new technology could arise which would replace the capitalist domination of nature, and lack of mediation with nature's substratum, with a concrete 'alliance technology' and an organicist transformation or 'dis-organization' (*Entorganisierung*) of machinery.[189] Once again this is a development with a pre-history in dream and legend.[190] Bloch envisages that a radical productivity could result from such a concrete mediation of man with the causal substratum of nature (*Mitproduktivität*), leading both to a radical intensification of the human subject (which would fulfil the intention of the ancient oriental will technologies), and to a heightened nature capable of producing new and higher forms, even a *natura supernaturans*.[191]

Here Bloch's position is important because it implies that socialism cannot be achieved by means of a capitalist technological utopia: that Marxism must change the technology it inherits in the light of the social relations implicit in capitalist technology, and actively involve itself in the prospects for the scientific-industrial transformation of nature. Bloch, however, goes even further and explicitly revives Marx's youthful postulate of a 'humanisation of nature'. Bloch argues that the *humanum* as the utopian goal of the process ultimately requires a new Marxist cosmology.[192]

According to Bloch, the project of a new Marxist cosmology depends on the problem of a possible mediation of man and his labour with the possible 'subject' of nature.[193] In categorial terms, the hypothetical 'subject' of nature is a synonym for the not yet manifested That drive in the world as a whole.[194] In history, the 'realising factor' has achieved subjectivity in man, but there is also a disposition to subjectivity in nature, and if men were to escape from the alienation in which they have been encapsulated until now, then this still nowhere manifest 'subject' of nature might become accessible:

The hinge in human history is its producer — the working man, finally no longer alienated, estranged, reified, . . . But the hinge in the history of nature . . . is that still hypothetical *agens* of extra-human happenings, which is as yet hardly mediated with us, what is abstractly called the force of nature, and which has been untenably and pantheistically called *natura naturans,* which however can be made concretely accessible in that moment in which the working man, that strongest, most highly conscious (in no way separated from the rest of nature) part of the universal material *agens,* begins to emerge from the half *incognito* of his alienation up till now.[195]

A mediation of this finally identified 'subject' of nature with man as the 'subject' of history could then follow, leading ultimately to identity: to a *regnum humanum.*[196]

Bloch's meaning is more straightforward than his baroque language suggests. Bloch's 'subject' of nature is an anticipatory, still encapsulated identification of the kernel or 'core' of matter, which is 'not yet'. At this point of time, there is no actual 'subject' of nature. What there is, is a nature at hand which is widely interpreted as permanently heteronomous *vis-à-vis* man. Against this interpretation, Bloch attempts to set the utopian postulate of a 'subject' of nature which is still awaiting its genesis; but he claims no more than that there is a real possibility of a 'subject' of nature, to which the ciphers of nature bear witness.[197] According to Bloch, there is a utopian *totum* attempting to manifest itself in nature,[198] and this *totum* anticipates itself in the qualitative form categories of the process or the ciphers of nature. In this sense, the 'subject' of nature is what is sought for in the still undeveloped subject-object relationships present in nature,[199] and a forward oriented Marxism can include a Marxist philosphy of nature, designed to take account of the *signatura rerum* or utopian figures nature contains.

Nonetheless, Bloch does not claim that the 'subject' of nature can be produced without human intervention and goal setting. For Bloch, nature is the end problem of human history, a still arising apocalyptical *omega*, and it is only by bringing nature within the sphere of history in a conscious way that history itself can end in success.[200] But the subject-object relation of history must delegate for the still secret, concealed subject-object relationship in nature if that relationship is ever to emerge from its anticipatory phase.[201] Likewise, Bloch does not claim that the 'core' of man and nature are the same now. What he claims is that men experience such an identity now, as a result of the operation of anticipatory consciousness, and that the pre-appearance of this identity in utopian *Evidenz* can ground the supposition that they are the same as an hypothesis for theory-praxis.[202]

NEO-RIEMANNIAN TIME

Bloch's vision of a process leading to possible identity must seem fantastic, granted the normal conception of time. How could the short time of human history make way for an event capable of altering the infinitely slow time of nature, let alone the milliards of geological history? Bloch attempts to overcome this difficulty by outlining a theory of neo-Riemannian time.

Like other modern process philosophers, Bloch relies on a form of realism in order to attribute some of the phenomenal properties of the human experience of time to time itself. Bloch rejects the transcendental idealist denial of the real character of time, as well as attempts to treat experienced time as purely psychological. Real time, Bloch argues, is not an abstract schema, but something concrete and elastic which changes with the material movement taking place in it.[203] It is not illusory or a hypostasised thing in itself, not abstract uniform, homogeneous clock time, but objectively qualitative and heterogeneous: the mode of

existence of the That driving the process forward.[204] Following
Leibniz, Bloch implies that time is the mode of being of a tendential event. There is only time, Bloch claims, where something
happens.[205]

Bloch uses the idea that time varies with the material movement present in it, to develop a theory of neo-Riemannian time
for history. Riemann's contribution was to elaborate a theory
of qualitatively heterogeneous, multi-dimensional space, which,
unlike uniform Euclidean space, varied with the distribution of
matter. By analogy, Bloch envisages a theory of time which
would allow for qualitatively different, multi-dimensional times,
of different shapes, proportions and intensities, varying according to their different distributions of 'historical matter'.[206] Bloch
admits that the parallel is not exact, but he uses the concept of
qualitatively different times, which reflect different distributions
of matter, to undermine the apparent disproportion between (1)
the slow empty time of nature and the short full time of history;
and (2) between long uneventful periods in history and short
periods of great significance.[207]

Bloch's theory of neo-Riemannian time enables him to postulate a flexible non-Euclidean time manifold and to allow for a
topology of differing, non-rigid, polyrhythmical historical times,
varying elastically with their distributions of matter. Moreover,
he attempts to use the same principles to re-open the question
of natural time, in a way which implies that a future cohesion
of historical and natural time is a real possibility developing in
the process. He concedes that there is a qualitative difference
between natural and historical time, and also that there is no
representation of time as the mode of being of a tendential event
in abstract mathematical physics.[208] Nonetheless, Bloch argues
that natural time is also heterogeneous, and that two very different times are present in natural time: (1) a predominant,
empty, repetitive natural time; and (2) a qualitative, natural
time, replete with possible future, which is polyrhythmically in-
terwoven with it.[209] The anticipatory 'tomorrow of nature' is
present in its symbolic, qualitative Goethean dimensions as the
time of 'the humanisation of nature' which has not yet begun.[210]
The possibility of realising this qualitative time in nature, however, depends on human goal setting and action to bring this
possible future of nature within the tendential time of history.

But even this utopian imagination does not open the way for

an end of time: for a meta-eschatological exodus from natural time and the historical 'times' limited by it. Bloch, the student of Biblical eschatology and Christian moment mysticism, is anxious not to leave this radical intention without a postulate: to give some representation to the possible 'last moment' or 'identified moment', in which the qualitative times of history and nature could flow together (*Mündung*). Like his friends Benjamin, Kracauer and Tillich, Bloch draws on the Biblical eschatological concept of full times (*kairoi*) in which the end of history pre-appears, and uses this notion to imply that the past, in so far as it is still unfinished, can come to completion in the future. Like Benjamin, he uses the term *Jetztzeit* for a moment of radical convergence at the end of history, when the 'nows' which were not fully actualised in the past are realised in a final moment, in which the 'now' is at last fully present.[211]

In a Marxist context, Bloch's theory of neo-Riemannian time is important as an anticipation of a more differentiated Marxist theory of time. Bloch's achievement is to relate the development of a theory of time to its socio-economic context, and to see that Marxism needs to take an active stand on the reflexive effect of time theory on what men seek to realise and think possible. Marxism, Bloch implies, needs not only to expose 'undialectical', 'abstract' or 'idealist' aspects of existing theories of time, but to accept full responsibility for the constitutive function of time postulates in the making of human history.

EXTRA-TERRITORIALITY

Bloch's revolt against every closure of the world leads him to rebel against the concept of fixed limits to the ontological order. Instead, he attempts to win a frontal space ahead of what has become, which does not constitute a barrier or boundary, but a weakly actual reference point that can be given content by human goal oriented action in history. Bloch uses the term 'extra-territoriality' for this radical opening up of traditional ontology.

Extra-territoriality means that some realities are outside or extra-territorial to the world of manifest process forms, because they have not yet become actual, and only have not-yet-being.[212] What has never come to be, Bloch argues, cannot pass away. Bloch uses this argument to claim that both the 'core of man' and the 'core of the earth' are extra-territorial. They are not manifest process forms, but real possibilities which are still 'not yet'; they are therefore not directly involved in the destruction of those process forms which have become manifest:

> The kernel of existence has not yet entered the process; therefore it is not affected by the transient features of the process. When faced with death, it is within a protective circle of that which is not-yet-living.[213]

In this sense, there is a dialectical materialist 'truth' of the wish pictures against death which postulate some form of survival. What men call 'soul' is ultimately the content of the That, the most immanent immanence of matter which is 'not there', but latent in a utopian manner:

> *De te, homo nondum naturans, supernaturans, fabula narratur.* The *"fabula"* in question tells what man is really about, and tells it for the first time. The intensive core of his intentionally-directed being . . . has only ever appeared in small hints, in attempts at home and in resurrection utopias. For at the inmost kernel of our being we are *homo absconditus,* and that alone: we are the one authentic mystery of our own most immediate immediacy, and that mystery has never objectified itself. So, never having really come to be, it can never really pass away. The *homo intensivus sed absconditus*, the still not brought out closest closeness of our deepest depths, is, *by virtue of being not yet become being,* utterly and completely *extra-territorial to the great destroyer of being called death.*[214]

It is not uncommon for process philosophers to attempt to show that traditional religious and moral problems take on a new dimension, granted their account of the process. As a Marxist alternative to immortality, however, Bloch's concept of extra-territoriality is problematic. Bloch cannot offer a formula for personal survival. He can argue that the intensity of life which men value is only an anticipation of what exists in possibility and has not yet come to be, and therefore can still emerge in full strength, even though its anticipatory forms are destroyed. Immortality, however, means the survival of what has appeared, not of what has never come to be. Moreover, the complete

destruction of all manifest process forms presumably would effect what has not come to be, by removing the conditions necessary for it to enter actuality. Nor does extra-territoriality help
Bloch with the traditional problems of good and evil. Bloch can
imply a form of recompense for suffering, in the sense that present defeat is alleged not to effect the extra-territorial human
core. He can also imply a form of reward for goodness, in the
sense that good actions may contribute to the final success. But
he cannot show either that the traditional antinomies and moral
dilemmas are elucidated by his system, or that the profoundest
moral intuitions of mankind can be grounded on his premises.
This may not be as important, however, as the Pascalian claim
that the intentionality of certain traditional moral and religious
doctrines is normative, despite the difficulties or even impossibility of grounding them in systems of discursive reasoning.
Bloch's aim is Promethean, not doctrinal. It is to establish a postulated space for causally effective hope contents against the
heteronomy of the apparent ontological order, in the name of a
projective ontological order which is 'not yet'. Such a historico-
philosophical counter-move cannot hope for favourable reception from exact philosophy; but it relates to a genuine problem
for the philosophy of history: that of the finalistic causality exerted by 'transcendental loci' (Lukács) or value orientations
which persist for millennia, even though they cannot be ration-
ally grounded. For Bloch, it is the maintenance of direction
which justifies the ontological adventurism necessary to keep
open a relevant frontal space.

A related difficulty arises with regard to the structure of
Bloch's account of the process as a whole. Unlike many process
philosophers, Bloch avoids explicit theodicy, including the claim
that evil is necessary for the good of the whole. Nonetheless,
his movement from the intentional structure of peak experiences
produces a process which has the aura and numinous quality of
a possible anthropodicy, despite his denials. At a superficial
level, the point can be argued on the basis of the invariant direction and two possible ends of the process; by reference to Bloch's
flirtations with the doctrine that nothing good is ever lost; or
by observing Bloch's attempt to preserve the centrality of Jesus
in process philosophy form as the man in whom the *humanum*
pre-appears: the sign that *docta spes* is grounded in the real
possibility content of the process.[215] The substantive point,

however, is the supposition that constitutive philosophy will need to repeat the structuration of theology and mysticism at those points where this structuration has causal power in the making of history, as long as the basis of this power in objective pre-historical conditions lasts.

OPEN SYSTEM AS MARXIST METAPHYSICS

Bloch's Open System is a wide ranging and complex achievement. Given that there are endemic and far reaching problems about the degree to which Open System can be reconciled with Marx's ideas, Open System can be considered a bold attempt to supplement Marxism with a utopian system of a new type. It is true that Bloch conflates Marx's positions with his own, and does little to clarify the problems which Marx's ideas involve. Nonetheless, Bloch's attempt to provide Marxism with a new conception of reality may be capable of reconstruction.

If Open System is not read down to Bloch's starting points, then the obvious critique which arises in answer to a Schellingesque metaphysics can be bracketed as over-ontological and pre-critical. The underdeveloped potential of Bloch's idea of an activist political metaphysics can then be explored. Even on a modernist interpretation, however, Open System is open to charges of incoherence, confusion and evasion. Moreover, like Benjamin and Adorno, Bloch is imprisoned within the antinomic structure of his recursive modernism and consistently promises more than he can perform, partly because the materials which he refunctions have an unclear sense once their original reference is removed. Bloch can reply that as long as truth is understood traditionally as a system which authenticates itself by flowing back into itself, it is difficult to relate to an open system of dialectical truth, in which the limit meanings of concepts are not decided, and which aims at content which is not yet at hand. To this extent, it would be wrong to reject a thought experiment which points to a future oriented thematisation of the world contents, and uncovers a recurrent structure of interiority in the most diverse cultural materials simply because it is unorthodox. The problem is that Bloch's recursive modernism forces him to retreat into cipher talk at so many analytically crucial points that Open System runs the risk of being poetry philosophy, a theurgic aestheticist *Weltanschauung*: a system of faith in hope with splendid meta-mystical meditations, but little explanatory power. Even Bloch's refunctioning of thought experiments from Plato, Aristotle, Leibniz, Kant, Hegel and Schelling lends philosophical weight which turns out to be more rhetorical than real. This is especially true of Bloch's borrowings from Hegel, which seem to dilute what was powerful in Hegel's system and to leave a symbolic remainder with no clear conceptual advance over Hegel. Moreover, Bloch's attempt to refunction Hegel, assuming his own and not Marx's interpretation, leads to confusion, and suggests that Lukács was right to argue, in correction of his own earlier views, that Marxism cannot be a rectification of Hegel's subject-object process. Similarly, in so far as Bloch refunctions thought experiments from Schelling, the objection arises that Engels (who attended Schelling's lectures in Berlin on the philosophy of revelation) rejected these ideas in 1841–2. Indeed, in many cases Engels rejected precisely the positions which Bloch takes up: (1) the project of a positive philosophy which begins with the sheer fact of existing and develops as an empiricism of *a prioris*; (2) the idea of a *prius* which is 'before itself' (*vor sich*) and impossible to preconceive in advance of its articulation; (3) the speculative dialectic according to which the latent will appear: (4) the revival of the scholastic distinction between the That and the What; (5) the decision to develop merely 'hypothetical doctrines'; (6) the stress on the need for strong will if reality is to be rightly apprehended; (7) the decision to base a philosophy on possibility; and (8) the idea of matter which develops the maximum.[216] Again, Engels' attacks on Schelling's methodological irrationalism, use of the language of the emotions in philosophy, lack of conceptual rigour, and 'gnostic-oriental dream thinking' could all be applied to Bloch.[217] Bloch could reply that Engels was attacking the reactionary use of Schelling to discredit Hegelianism rather than offering a technical study of Schelling's philosophy, and that Engels' local judgements as a young man are hardly normative. But even if Engels' strictures on Schelling are often glib, the hermetic style of Bloch's philosophy is open to criticism in so far as he claims to be a Marxist.

As metaphysics in the sense of a doctrine relating the present world to a beyond. Open System is open to objection. There is a certain grandeur in Bloch's attempt to reformulate immanentist-transcendentalism on materialist foundations, and it may even be psychologically correct to claim that man has an intentionality to the unconditioned. But any attempt to claim that this intentionality has a foundation in the ontological structure of the world requires more justification than Bloch provides. Certainly Bloch may be right to stress that Marxism should not accept a disillusioned view of the world without question, but it is another thing to opt for an enchanted view of the world which remains purely speculative.

Here Open System resembles certain forms of religious thought. The idea that human consciousness possesses a primary intuition of being, which colours all other knowledge, is central to the whole neo-Augustinian tradition in philosophy and runs through much French and Italian spiritism; while the claim that human consciousness intends an absolute is basic to Transcendental Thomism, and to the work of Coreth, Maréchal and Rahner in particular.[218] Rahner, for example, argues that man has the absolute as his immanent horizon, even though he has no knowledge of the absolute except *per excessum*.[219] Likewise, there is no singularity in the claim that human life is a satisfaction dialectic governed by a structuring absence. The metaphysical possibilities of such a move were brilliantly explored by Maurice Blondel in his philosophy of action. Moreover, like Bloch, Blondel saw that the influence of the will on human life, combined with the constitutive effect of action, meant that the character and directionality of human existence could not be adequately grasped by an abstract rationalism.[220] There are also extensive parallels between Bloch's work and that of Gabriel Marcel, whose phenomenology of existence was designed to evoke metaphysical intimations rather than to solve analytical problems, and included 'A Phenomenology and A Metaphysics of Hope'.[221] Moreover, a related strategic structure can also be traced in 'right-wing existentialists' such as Louis Lavelle or Le Senne, and in the work of the influential contemporary Jewish philosopher Emmanuel Levinas.[222]

These parallels can be over-stressed. Bloch's positions are distinguishable from those of religious thinkers. Nonetheless, in the context of Marxism even formal resemblances between Open System and the speculations of professed idealists or religious mystics are disturbing. Bloch can reply that such parallels are trivial, since Open System differs from such speculations in its materialist premises and in its orientation to Marxist theory-praxis. This is true, but it does not meet the objection that fundamental human experiences can be labelled in many different ways, so that it is necessary to show that Bloch's labelling is preferable to others which might be suggested. In practice, Bloch's labels often seem as arbitrary and confessional as those of religious thinkers, who cite fundamental experiences as evidence for their claims when precise epistemological justification is required to establish that one label and not another is appropriate. Bloch often appears to think that a system which contains no explicit religious or idealist concepts, and is based on materialism, avoids the objections which can be made to religious and idealist ideas. But on the contrary, the objection remains that what is asserted is simply speculation. Bloch can reply that Marxist metaphysics in the sense of a doctrine relating the present world to a beyond, must be speculative, since the future is substantially undetermined, and will in fact be partly determined by men's speculation about what it could contain. Here there is an antinomy at the heart of Bloch's position. On the one hand, Bloch wants to stress that the world is open and experimental, and that it is important to develop 'outlines', 'suppositions' and 'handleholds' which can guide praxis in its attempt to shape the world in a humanly successful direction. On the other hand, he wants to guarantee the possibility of success.

This is the familiar modernist dilemma of a thinker who wants to affirm the security and meta-mundane orientations of pre-modern metaphysics, while retreating from attempts to ground such orientations, except psychologically and in language obscure enough to amount to equivocation. Here, Open System can be compared with the different thought experiments of his friends, the theologian Paul Tillich and the Austrian novelist Hermann Broch. Both Tillich and Broch were interested in the problem of an eschatological utopianism, and both attempted to preserve maximalist metaphysical reference in post-theologies in which metaphysical language was affirmed, but not in its original sense. Like Bloch, Tillich developed an evocative existentialist theology based on the claim that man's *Existenz* disclosed an intentionality towards a non-objective Being or absolute.[223] Like Bloch, he combined oratorical powers with a flair for enchanted language, full of foreboding and ontological significance, which finally remains cipher talk, metaphorical drama which cannot be precisely glossed. Similarly, like Bloch, the Austrian novelist Hermann Broch developed a form of religious atheism, based on an 'earthly absolute', and emphasised both human intentionality to the infinite, and the need for a meta-political, meta-religious outlook which replaced modern nihilism with absolute values. Moreover, like Bloch, Broch summoned up a world pervaded by ontological mystery, and used Expressionist devices to evoke the mystical experiences of the deep subject.[224] Apart from the question of Bloch's influence on both men, it is legitimate to ask how far it matters which cipher language is used, since Bloch's 'concrete utopia', Tillich's 'being' and Broch's 'earthly absolute' are all equally *recherché*.

There are also links between Open System and the work of Bloch's contemporaries, Jaspers and Heidegger. All three were influenced by Rickert and the late Schelling, and attempted to develop post-intellectualistic philosophies in the age of technology. Bloch knew Jaspers in Heidelberg before 1914 and wrote a withering attack on his philosophy in *Heritage of this Time*.[225] Nonetheless, there are clear parallels between Jaspers' philosophical elucidation of *Existenz* and Open System. If Jaspers rejected the possibility of a satisfactory ontological system, he relied as heavily as Bloch on an immanentist-transcendentalist phenomenology, and developed a philosophy of *Existenz,* in which the interpretation of religious symbols and the reading of the 'ciphers of nature' played a central role.[226] Bloch did not meet Heidegger until 1961, although a polemic against Heidegger runs through his works. Heidegger's avant-gardism, like that of Bloch, involved fusions of the phenomenology of Husserl and Scheler with the late Schelling and Kierkegaard. Moreover, like Bloch, Heidegger turned from positivism to medieval logic, in particular to Duns Scotus. Again, like Bloch, Heidegger adopted a projectivist approach to the future and attempted to rework the relation between the That and the What on which Western metaphysics is based.[227] It is true that the late Heidegger, unlike Bloch, attempts to step behind this distinction, and develops a problematic based on the rejection of Being-as-presence, which carries the argument into a different arena. Nonetheless, if Heidegger is more radical than Bloch, just as Jaspers has a finer Kantian sense of antinomies and a greater analytical sharpness, there are problems of modernist philosophical method common to all three which are not overcome simply because Bloch breaks with 'Transcendence' and develops a praxis-oriented projective metaphysics.

Finally, there are also significant resemblances between Open System and the cosmogenesis process philosophies of Solovyev, Berdyaev and Teilhard de Chardin. All three were religious mystics, influenced by the metaphysical radicalism of Boehme and Schelling, and developed systems which involved: (1) an imperfect first term or non-ground; (2) a process developing towards increasing hominisation; (3) a central role for Jesus; (4) a transformation of nature in the direction of pan-organicism; (5) an emergent God term; and (6) a new creation or genesis at the end. Unlike Bloch, Solovyev provided an account of the process which rested explicitly on Russian orthodox eschatology and mysticism. Solovyev had no reservations about making the world an anthropodicy or about allowing Sophia to appear in the process to entice men towards the final goal.[228]

The parallel with Berdyaev touches Bloch more directly since Berdyaev, like Bloch, studied with Oswald Külpe and was influenced by Franz von Baader and Bergson. Moreover, like Bloch, Berdyaev developed a philosophy of hope as well as an eschatological process metaphysics, although, unlike Bloch, he broke with Marxism on the grounds that it was incompatible with transcendentalism and settled in Christianity.[229] The parallel with Teilhard is more complex because Teilhard advanced his cosmogenesis process philosophy as a reconciliation of Christianity with science. Nonetheless, like Bloch, Teilhard mixed the Boehme–Schelling model with borrowings from Bergson, and combined an emphasis on activism based on optimism and hope in the future, with a model of the process which allowed for the emergence of a 'Spirit of the Earth'.[230] These parallels suggest that the Open System owes more structurally to speculative process philosophy than Bloch admits. They also raise doubts about the degree to which Bloch can show an indisputable basis in the world for the structure of Open System, and not simply a basis in historically given starting points.

As metaphysics in the sense of a categorial scheme, Open System suggests that Bloch can be considered a revisionary process metaphysician in the tradition of Bergson and Whitehead. It is true that Bloch's reworking of categories from Plato, Aristotle, Boehme, Leibniz, Hegel, Schelling and von Hartmann suggests a

capacity for variation rather than origination, and that anticipations of many of his categorial innovations can be found in
the work of other modern process philosophers such as Bergson,
Whitehead, Vasconcelos, Berdyaev or Samuel Alexander.[231]
However, with his attempt to refunction categories from
Plato, Aristotle, Boehme, Leibniz, Kant, Schelling, Hegel and
von Hartmann, Bloch provides models for a new Marxist philosophy which understands the world as an open system. In particular, his attack on *anamnesis* in epistemology and ontology,
his attempt to develop an ontology of not-yet-being, and his
attempt to elaborate a doctrine of real possibility, raise important political as well as philosophical issues. The difficulty is that
Bloch's utopian mentality leads him again and again to give a
useful categorial initiative an unclear or speculative dimension.
As a result, there are insoluble conceptual difficulties involved
in Bloch's category formation and attempts at entity characterisation. Bloch's categories tendency, latency, front, *novum*, identity and anticipation all have original features and could be usefully reformulated in a more analytical, less speculative form.
Moreover, Bloch's concept of reality as a process raises legitimate questions involved in any consistent dialectical materialism. The problem is that Bloch's use of the process philosophy
model is high handed. In fairness to Bloch, it must be said that
his advocacy of ontological realism is provocative, and has parallels with scholastic interpretations of the implications of
Marx's ideas. Again, Bloch draws attention to philosophical
problems about the status of the future and the productivity of
human goal setting and treats these problems in ways which
may have anticipatory value in the context of Marxism.

On the other hand, Bloch's treatment of ground is unneces-
sarily mystifying. Bloch may be right to argue that Marxism requires a non-panlogical concept of ground, but his model of a
process in which the That drives towards its What or missing
essence is hermetic. Similarly, Bloch's concept of matter, on
which his whole analysis finally rests, repeats many of the difficulties of the traditional monist problematic. Moreover, by
making matter a friend rather than a permanent limit to human
hopes, Bloch dissolves one of the main merits of philosophical
materialism. Bloch's concept of matter functions almost like a
God term in other process philosophies, in that it secures the
possibility of the fulfilment of maximalist human hopes,

grounds ethical and meta-religious values, and ceases to delimit the possible since possibilities which are not possible now may become so after the *eschaton*. Again, Bloch subverts the original radicalism of his project to the extent that he concedes that there is in fact *anamnesis* throughout the process, in the sense of return to what has never yet been:

> . . . the *genuine* reference-and-return is towards what is still in the future and therefore *what has not come to be in the past;* ultimately it is a return to the *still underived derivation* of all that happens. To the impelling That — or the intensive origin from and by reason of which life occurs . . . The substance of the What is actually the same as the intensity of the That: the intensity which will be disclosed at the 'end of history', and which drives as the realising factor in the world.[232]

It is also difficult to accept that Bloch's process involves a consistent break with stasis ontology. Bloch claims that the process is open, but the possible structure, possible results, and the hierarchy of values in Bloch's process all appear to be closed. Moreover, Bloch seems to make his own values structural features of the process, under the cover of advancing *avant-garde* process metaphysics. At the very least, he fails to indicate how his account of the process can be defended against such a charge. Hence, the suspicion arises that Open System shares some of the weaknesses of the modern process philosophy tradition on which it draws, including the tendency to an excessive categorial innovation which proclaims the discovery of a new category too often to be convincing, and the tendency to confuse revisionary metaphysics with a reassertion of the politics of the subject.

5 Bloch's Developments of Marxism

Only the horizon of the future as Marxism brings it into knowledge, with the past as the ante-room to the future, gives reality its real dimension.

The Principle of Hope

Bloch also attempts to counter the *lacunae* of the Marxist tradition with a series of developments of Marxism, designed to take account of the failures of the Marxist tradition since Marx's death. These developments of Marxism are based on a new approach to the problem of the future. In contrast to the French tradition (running from Blondel, Bergson, Le Senne and de Jouvenel to Gaston Berger), which emphasises the causality of prospection and the possibility of prediction, especially in the context of social planning, Bloch is not concerned to detail the immediate future. He is critical of futurology, at least in its American form, and shows little interest in contemporary rational utopians, such as Buckminster Fuller, who attempt to invent the possible future. He is equally distant from analytical philosophical approaches to the logical and ontological status of the future, although inevitably he covers some of the same ground.[1] Instead, Bloch draws on: (1) *the projectivist approach to the future* (cf. Heidegger in *Being and Time*), which emphasises that men project themselves into the future and base their lives on imaginations about what it can contain; (2) *the presentist approach to the future*, according to which the good future is present now (in a utopian manner) and must be brought to bear on praxis and on the selection of long- and short-term goals; (3) *the recursive approach to the future*, according to which the future is latent in the unrealised past; and (4) *the eschatological approach to the future*, according to which the future is *not* yet: a *futurum vis-à-vis* present delineations of the possible. Bloch fuses these approaches in an approach to the future based on a praxis of anticipation.

Bloch transforms the approach to the future in Marxism by supplementing Marxism with a positive critique of ideology. In the Marxist tradition the critique of ideology has mainly been understood negatively, as if ideology was a foreign body which could be eliminated and replaced by a scientific world outlook. Bloch rebels against the abstract utopianism and the underlying staticism of this view, which assumes that the truth is true in a timeless present. Instead, Bloch attempts to assert an immanentist perspective for which the truth itself is in process, and must be judged by the level of development which it has reached. Bloch argues that a Marxist critique of ideology cannot confine itself to the unmasking of class interest and the illusions to which it gives rise. It cannot simply provide a residue of timeless truth which can be immediately integrated into an illusion free, quasi-scientific theory. Instead, a Marxist critique of ideology must recognise that the ideological formations of the super-structure often remain encapsulated, even after the most obvious distortions of class interest and illusion have been eliminated.[2] A Marxist critique of ideology, Bloch argues, needs to uncover the *utopian surplus* in the ideological formations of the super-structure which outlast the society and specific class interests in which they arise. It needs actively to inherit (*Erbe*) this utopian surplus as potentially constitutive of future developments.[3]

But this means that the relationship between truth, time and ideology must be rethought in Marxism, not only because such utopian surplus first appears in an ideological form and even, Bloch emphasises, in ideology itself; but because (1) without ideology, such surplus might not appear at all; and (2) because such surplus in some cases remains 'encapsulated', even after it has been demystified and released from its original ideological constellation.[4] This means, however, that Marxism requires not only a critique of the utopian surplus which has appeared so far, but also a conceptual framework in which utopian surplus which cannot yet be adequately glossed can be kept in view as anticipation and allowed to function as goal-related material with a potential transmission character. For Bloch, 'philosophy' can provide this projective conceptual apparatus in which the utopian function present in ideological formations can be raised to full consciousness.[5] As philosophy of the future in an untraditional sense, Marxist philosophy must recognise that there is ideology in a good sense; and that Marxism must accept its immanence within a form of ideology as long as pre-history lasts. It can then reset the concept of truth in the context of socialist ideology (Lenin) which seeks to refunction forwards the utopian surplus in the present and the past.[6]

Bloch argues that Marxism needs to conceive of the future in subject-object terms. He holds that the future is partly real now: as partially conditioned objective real possibility. Future contingents, as Aristotle taught, are undetermined events which have not happened yet; but for Bloch there is already dispositionality to what is unreached: developing partially conditioned ability-to-be, which requires further conditions before it can be realised. Moreover, even though the form the future will take is undetermined, the future is not merely mystical haze, but something which can be brought within the ambit of planning and goal setting through a Marxist analysis of (1) tendencies; and (2) the pre-appearance (*Vor-Schein*) or utopian anticipation which the world already contains.[7] Because, however, both man and the world are open and unfinished, it is crucial not to conceive of the future as automatic or naturalistic. The future has an objective reality of a difficult kind even now (not-yet-being), but what it will be, depends on the productive actions of men and on their projections of what it may contain. In Marxist terms, the determination of the teleological content of socialism must be a praxis of anticipation. It follows that Marxism has need of *educated hope*, in the form of goals for theory-praxis which have a basis in what is developing in the world, and in the subject-object mediations by which what comes to be possible is constantly extended.

Bloch's emphasis on a constitutive, subject-object approach to the future leads him to attempt to supplement Marxism with new initiatives in (1) Marxist ethics and natural law; (2) Marxist aesthetics; (3) Marxist meta-religion; and (4) Marxist materialism. In each case, he is concerned to break with the standard Marxist closure of the world, and to win new goals for theory-praxis from materials with constitutive potential. In each case, his approach assumes that Marxism needs to inherit 'the truth' of idealism in a rectified form. It implies that Marxism requires a utopian rationalism, oriented towards what is becoming possible, which grasps the rational in the irrational, and brings the utopian anticipations of the process within the *ratio* of hope: a committed integral rationalism biased in favour of the objective partisanship of what is developing in the world.[8] It also implies a new concept of realism in Marxism, which combines both reflection and production in an active co-knowledge (*Mitwissenheit*) of the unfolding course of the world: a realism which copies what things can become as a result of human labour (*Fortbildung*).[9] Marxist realism, Bloch argues, must be constitutive process realism: forward imagination which grasps the tendency-latency of the process, and not simply the reified 'facts' at hand. It can do so because consciousness can be 'causally affected' by the thing in itself which is 'not yet' (cf. transcendental realism) in the sense that imagination forwards can be informed by the object in a way which leads to the production of what it contains.[10] Bloch refunctions the ancient Stoic doctrine of *phantasia kataleptike*, according to which subject and object 'embrace' in the act of knowledge. He argues that the act of judgement can be 'causally affected' in such a way that there is a productive bridge between the subjective-ideal judgement and its objective-real correlate.[11] Bloch calls the knowledge which results from such productive interaction of subject and object constitutive knowledge, because such knowledge can be the basis for effective action which produces what it intends, albeit in a different form.

MARXIST ETHICS AND NATURAL LAW

Bloch attempts to supplement Marxism with a more developed ethics. As a Marxist, Bloch holds that ethical problems cannot be separated from determinate levels of social relations and of the forces of production. There is no timeless 'good', even if there are virtues which are recognised in most societies. As Hegel saw, ethical development cannot be separated from social development and particular instantiations of ethical norms in social and legal arrangements (*Sittlichkeit*).[12] Nonetheless, Bloch emphasises the need for Marxists to actively inherit and refunction the ethical doctrines of the great philosophers, especially Aristotle, Kant and Hegel. Thus, it is possible to use Aristotle's distinction between ethical and dianoetic virtues to illumine the functionality of evil in producing new good; to extend Kant's emphasis on man's will to an unrealised Real and In

General to cover the still developing *telos* of what men ultimately intend; to implement Hegel's socially instantiated ethics
as a programme for the supersession (*Aufhebung*) of existing
class societies.[13]

For Bloch, the two crucial movements beyond the Marxist
tradition are: (1) the overcoming of the reductionist, socio-
logistic approach to ethics; and (2) the development of a Marxist axiology or value theory with a dialectical materialist perspective. Bloch claims that Marxism can actively inherit the
utopian surplus of the ethical values and ideals which have
emerged in the past: that such surplus has a transmission character beyond the societies and situations in which it arose.[14] He
also argues that a Marxist axiology or value theory needs to recognise that values have a dispositional basis in matter (*Wert-
materie*): in what can be objectively realised in the world, even
though the greater part of such value must first be produced by
human labour.[15] Such a dialectical materialist approach situates
the problem of values within the labour process. It allows for
both historicity (including the mutability and social determination of values), and for an objectivist dimension which leads
the argument beyond abstract rationalism or irrationalist attempts to derive values from the will.

Bloch allows for the rational constitution of values, while
denying the possibility of deducing values from a single rational-
istic principle. He emphasises that values have a thelic dimension
which cannot be reduced to a purely intellectualistic system.[16]
His basic position, however, is a developing ethical finalism,
which allows for ontological emergence as present values are
transformed in the process of realisation and new and other values
come into being. Here Bloch is influenced by Franz von Baader
and by Max Scheler's emergentist processual ethics, which combined historicity with a material axiology of heterogeneous
values based on Husserl's eidetic knowledge of essences (*Wesensschau*).[17] In a dialectical materialist perspective, however, the
discovery of not-yet-conscious knowledge in the emergence of
human ethical attitudes must be combined with an ontological
analysis for which there is emergence in what can be realised as
value in the world itself.

Bloch's fusion of historical transmission and axiology leads
him to make a highly original attempt to overcome the failure
in the Marxist tradition to develop adequate moral and legal

norms for socialist society. This attempt is based on the claim
that Marxism can inherit what was intended by natural law. In
view of Marx's attack on the bourgeois 'Rights of Man' in *On
the Jewish Question* (1843), many Marxists have assumed that
Marxism is incompatible with any concept of natural law. In
contrast, Bloch emphasises that in *On the Jewish Question*,
Marx drew a sharp distinction between the bourgeois 'Rights of
Man' and the ideal of the *citoyen*.[18] Marx, Bloch argues, ex-
posed the egoistic content of the bourgeois 'Rights of Man', but
he also recognised the need for man to reappropriate for himself
the contents which first appeared in the ideal of the *citoyen* in
an abstract form.[19] Marx, Bloch claims did not deny that there
were human rights (although he made the socialised individual
the bearer of such rights, not the egoistic bourgeois), and criticised capitalism by the standard of the human right to freedom.[20] Bloch has no difficulty in showing that a strong ethical
position is central to the young Marx, and that a conception of
how human beings should live is fundamental to both Marx's
critique of alienation and to his conception of communism. He
cites Marx's attack on the *a posteriori* methods and relativism of
the historical school of German jurists as indicating that Marx
assumed that some things were wrong *per se*, and cites Marx's
Critique of Hegel's Philosophy of Right as evidence that Marx
provided no specific definition of right because he was opposed
not only to specific injustices, but to injustice in general.[21] Above
all, he quotes Marx's famous categorical imperative (to rebel
against all conditions in which man is a wretched, enslaved and
degraded creature) to show that a form of natural law lived on in
Marx in a creative, active form.[22]

Even assuming, however, that there is a form of natural law
implicit in Marx, natural law has hardly figured as a central
theme in the Marxist tradition. Bloch takes up this point, and
uses it to imply that the neglect of natural law has led to an im-
balance in Marxist thought, with serious political and moral
consequences. An immanentist perspective requires an awareness of the way in which particular traditions bring forward
contents not elaborated as fully elsewhere, even as they repress
and distort others; it excludes any perfectionism of a single
tradition or tendency. Marxism, however, Bloch implies, suffers
from a failure to apprehend the specificity of one of its own
basic sources and its relationship to other traditions. It has in-

herited the intention, including the value orientations, of the social utopias; but it has not consciously inherited the intention of natural law, despite the fact that natural law revived during a hiatus in the history of the social utopias and provides counter-balancing perspectives.[23] Bloch does not undervalue the social utopias. He is the most distinguished Marxist historian of utopian thought.[24] Nonetheless, Bloch emphasises that the social utopias alone provide a one-sided and in some ways distorted basis for the determination of the purpose content of socialism. He stresses the inherent weakness of social utopian thought about polit-ical and social problems; the reformist tendencies implicit in abstract social projections which ignore the qualitative changes and dialectical leaps which Marxism implies; the distortions con-sequent upon the tendency for the utopias of freedom to be separate from the utopias of order; and the manifest danger implicit in the centralist social utopias of Cabet and Saint-Simon.[25] Whereas the social utopias developed the postulates of human happiness, Bloch argues that the postulates of human dignity were developed, in most cases, by natural law.[26] More-over, in some respects, natural law was more radical than the social utopias, in that it provided general postulates rather than abstract detailing.[27]

Bloch does not claim that an active Marxist inheritance of natural law is possible without a radical and revolutionary trans-formation of the contents of traditional natural law. He rejects any notion of a timeless static natural law derived from God, nature, reason or a static finished human nature.[28] Similarly, Bloch recognises that a Marxist philosophy of right cannot be based on existing positive law (which in class society expresses the interests of the ruling class), on the nature of the existing com-munity, or on the nature of the case (*Natur der Sache*) statically conceived.[29] For Marxism, right is 'not yet'. Nonetheless, a Marxist philosophy of right which inherits the intention of natural law can be based on a praxis of anticipation. It can be based on the pre-appearance of ideals of what is right through-out history which express the concrete tendency of history to a possible realm of freedom.[30] For Marxism, there is no natural law of a traditional kind, but there is a developing historical apriorism of 'rights'; and these rights emerge and exert an effect prior to any situation in which they can be fully realised. Bloch follows Marx's *dictum* that right can never be higher than the

economic form of society and the level of cultural development
determined by it; but he argues that there is a transmission of a
utopian surplus of concrete ideals and postulates which outlasts
the social systems in which they arise.[31] Marxism, Bloch insists,
only rejects abstract ideals. It does not reject concrete ideals,
such as socialism, with a basis in the tendency of history. On
the contrary, Marxism itself requires concrete ideals without
idealism, which it criticises for their illusion and class interest
and refunctions forwards.[32] In this sense, Marxism completes
the best thoughts of the past (Letter to Ruge, September,
1843). It takes the maxim *verum est index sui et falsi* as an imperative, in so far as the truth which has pre-appeared can
come to concretion through Marxist theory-praxis to shape a
good future.[33]

Bloch's attempt to outline a Marxist inheritance of natural
law is found in *Natural Law and Human Dignity* (*Naturrecht
und menschliche Würde*), which was published in West Germany
in 1961, although much of the preparatory work was done in
the DDR.[34] In *Natural Law and Human Dignity* Bloch provides
a history of concepts of natural law from the Greeks to modern
times, which combines Marxist *Ideologiekritik* and situation
analysis with an attempt to indicate a utopian surplus. He offers
immanent critiques of the great legal philosophers (including
Plato, Aristotle, Cicero, Aquinas, Althusius, Hobbes, Grotius,
Wolff, Pufendorf, Rousseau, Fichte, Kant, Hegel, Schelling,
Anselm Feuerbach, Kohlhaas, Savigny, Bachofen, Stammler,
Ihering and Kelsen); and uncovers a wealth of postulates and
ideals of 'right' which, in a 'rectified' form, could provide
starting points for a Marxist theory of right, including a framework of norms which a socialist society could seek to realise.[35]

Consistent with his emphasis on finding the future in the past,
Bloch argues that Marxist right, as 'right forwards' which operates through open-ended matrices, can inherit the intention of
such postulates as the human rights to freedom, happiness, dignity, justice, community, peace and leisure, and the free expression of racial, religious and national differences; as well as such
ideals as a harmonious relationship between man and nature,
internationalism and the unity of mankind.[36] Moreover, Marxist
right can also inherit the intention of such postulates as Kant's
postulate of the autonomy of the self determining individual,
and Lessing's maxim that no man should be compelled; the class-

less meaning of the bourgeois rights to freedom of speech, assembly, information and the press, and equality before the law; as well as emergent optatives such as the ideal of world law and women's liberation.[37] For Bloch, there are no limits to the postulates and ideals which Marxism can extract from mankind's anticipatory conscience of what is right and reset as the purpose content of socialism. But he emphasises that in each case Marxism refunctions what it inherits as futuristic right, which extends to new contents not envisaged in their original class-bound historical articulations.

Because Marxist right must always be integrated with the potentiality opened up by concrete social and economic developments, Bloch places special emphasis on the need for Marxism to inherit the ideals of the Enlightenment and the revolutionary bourgeoisie. According to Bloch, Marxism needs to inherit the revolutionary ideals of the French Revolution, and to refunction them in a rectified form as futuristic postulates with developing content, which will only be fully realised in a classless society. Freed of their 'bourgeois' class content, liberty, equality and fraternity acquire a new functionality as horizon concepts in socialist ideology. Liberty comes to mean the substantial freedom to determine one's own life as an autonomous moral being, and to realise one's capacities in conditions exempt from external necessity; equality comes to mean the equality of each with the not yet realised human essence, and an end to the inequalities of class society; fraternity comes to mean the solidarity of all in the attempt to end all forms of oppression and realise the classless society.[38]

For Bloch, the Marxist inheritance from the revolutionary bourgeoisie is not confined to the ideals of the French Revolution. As Bloch emphasises in his monograph on Christian Thomasius, the revolutionary bourgeoisie added a new emphasis on human dignity to natural law: an emphasis on the need for non-heteronomous law and on the rights of the individual.[39] According to Bloch, Marxism needs to inherit the classless intention implicit in the bourgeois doctrine of 'subjective right', or the delineation in 'bourgeois' jurisprudence of the legal entitlements of the subject against what the state is entitled to require or forbid.[40] A socialist society, Bloch claims, must inherit both the freedoms won by the bourgeoisie which serve to limit the lawmaker's power (such as freedom of religion, freedom of the press, freedom of association, freedom of assembly, freedom from arbitrary arrest and freedom of information) and also the general principle that the legal subject possesses rights in every instance *vis-à-vis* the law making power.[41] Indeed, Bloch makes such an inheritance of subjective right fundamental to a socialist legal system. Objective right without subjective right is not law, he insists, and no society based on a heteronomy of objective right can be socialist.[42] Moreover, according to Bloch, Marxism also inherits subjective public right in the wider sense of the right of men to realise their capacities and to satisfy their needs. Indeed, subjective right in this sense is the password of the revolutionary struggle, and under socialism the bourgeois antagonism between subjective and objective right is gradually overcome until the *facultas agendi* of the unalienated individual becomes the *norma agendi* of socialist society.[43]

Bloch's emphasis on concrete ideals in socialism, on natural law in the sense of an increasing determination of what men and women have a right to claim as the precondition for the realisation of their humanity, assumes that the human countenance is 'not yet' and that the form of the classless society (*Gemeinschaft*) (in which individual and collective interpenetrate beyond bourgeois individualism and abstract collectivism) is not yet fully specifiable. It is an attempt to keep the radicalism of the socialist dream open against all premature reductions of socialist right to the heteronomy of the socialist state. Bloch tries to renew the practical power of the socialist dream in the face of its postponement and replacement by bureaucratic machinery and administrative apparatuses. He attempts to go back to the 'good socialism' of Rosa Luxemburg: to base socialism firmly on a commitment to freedom and democracy. He renews Rosa Luxemburg's insistence that there can be no socialism without democracy, just as there can be no true democracy without true socialism.[44] For Bloch, socialism is the ideal of a non-antagonistic society in which the antinomies of pre-history being to be overcome and the anticipatory aura of what men have always sought for under the name of 'morality' begins to be realised.[45] Under socialism, in place of the bourgeois separation of law from morality, law ceases to be formalistic, abstract and divorced from men's real needs, and morality ceases to be purely private, heteronomous and passive. Instead, socialist legality seeks to make situations right, and increasingly takes on a moral pathos as it reflects the developing shared ethical life (*Sittlichkeit*) of socialist society.[46] Similarly, under socialism the traditional antinomies between freedom and order, the individual and the collective begin to be overcome in a 'concrete' (i.e. mediated) moral external order, which guarantees the concrete freedom of all.[47] In place of the antagonism and anarchy of bourgeois society, in which the other man is a competitor, under socialism the other man is the guarantee of one's own freedom in a solidarity which realises the ideal of brotherhood in practical life.[48]

Clearly, such ideal characterisations of socialism run the risk of moralism: of a totalist attitude which replaces the need to confront the frustrations and conflicts of social life with the dream of perfect social unity, in which civil and political society would coincide. If, however, the ideal of a *polis* without *politea* has its dangers, Bloch's point is that socialism requires postulates which strengthen the visibility of the goal and the will to it, including new postulates of human dignity and upright carriage, both as a basis for action which seeks to concretely anticipate future good instead of postponing it to the *deus ex machina* of the classless society, and because such ideals exert a goal-forming causality with more chance of success than a one-sided reliance on an automaticism of the forces of production. Moreover, Bloch intends such ideal characterisations of socialism as a critique of state socialist legal philosophy and practice as it has developed in the Soviet Union and in Eastern Europe. Bloch provides immanent critiques of the classical Soviet texts on Marxism and law by Pashukanis, Vyshinsky, Reisner, Stuchka and Kerimov.[49] He rejects the fundamental assumptions of the state socialist approach to socialist legality, including (1) the denial of human rights 'in general'; (2) the attempt to make human rights derive from and depend on 'the socialist state'; (3) the reduction of particular pre-socialist legislation and forms of law to 'class interests'; and (4) the denial of any supra-political dimension, in either social or personal life. Bloch attempts to renew the utopian rejection of the state as an *arcana dominationis* in Marxism. In direct contradiction to state socialist philosophy of law he rejects any concept of a socialist *Rechtsstaat* and argues that a 'true' state is a contradiction in terms. Where there is a state, there is no freedom, he claims, and where there is freedom, there is no state.[50] Bloch grounds this radical rejection of the state, once its transitional functions are fulfilled, in the Marxist classics. He cites Engels' *dictum* that the first act of the socialist state would be its last, after which the state would wither away; he also refers to Engels' expectation that all reification of power would end under socialism, and his claim, in his letter to Bebel in 1875, that the state would cease to exist as soon as it was possible to speak of freedom.[51] Similarly, he cites Lenin's claims in *The State and the Revolution* that under socialism the state would be merely a central planning organisation, administering things, not persons; that this 'state' would function so smoothly that 'a cook' could run it; and that under socialism all power over persons would cease. Bloch admits that Lenin held that it would be necessary to make use of the bourgeois state during the period of transition, but he emphasises that Lenin assumed that this transitional state would be unlike any previous state, and that the period of transition would be relatively short.[52]

Bloch's attempt to outline a Marxist inheritance of natural law goes to the fundamental neglect of moral values and human rights in the Marxist tradition. Bloch may be right to claim that there is a form of natural law implicit in some of Marx's writings. Marx was deeply concerned with affronts to human dignity and his Promethean assertion of man as the highest being for man could be read as having axiological implications.[53] In another sense, however, natural law is precisely what is lacking in Marx. In so far as traditional natural law was concerned to regulate the means to be pursued in realising noble ends, it included an ethical concern which is hardly prominent in Marx. Marx condemned situations in which man was a wretched or oppressed being, and he also set maximalist goals which communists were to try to realise. Marx, however, was neither moralistic nor sentimental about the means to be employed in realising these goals, and regarded capitalism, with its ethically lamentable features, as an important phase on the way to communism. In contrast, Bloch tends to make his active inheritance of natural law cover both the final goals to be achieved and the means, at least after the initial revolution, to be adopted in realising them. Bloch's stress on the futuristic rights has had an influence on German jurisprudence;[54] there are also Soviet parallels to Bloch's axiological approach to Marxist ethics.[55] Again, Bloch's emphasis on open anthropology has important implications both for particular legal doctrines and for general concepts of reasonableness and humanity. The openness of Bloch's stance emerges from a comparison with Cunow or della Volpe, whose efforts in the direction of a Marxist philosophy of law and the state assumed a high degree of closure.[56] Nonetheless, Bloch's work also has a conservative aspect and his treatment of specifics often reveals a teleological emphasis which could become a single political truth.

Bloch's distance from the fallibilist tradition in political and social thought leads him to treat freedom, equality and fraternity as positive values requiring moral agreement, rather than as arrangements for dealing with pluralism and moral conflict. His relative neglect of the problem of conflict between values and ends suggests that he has not entirely broken with the tradition of 'totalitarian democracy'.[57] Again, although Bloch makes an initiative towards a new Marxist penology, in general he gives little consideration to technical law, either in the form of statutes or cases. Instead, he concentrates on the philosophical aspects of German jurisprudence, and ignores contemporary developments in English, French and Swedish jurisprudence, in which technical considerations have received more consideration. Similarly, Bloch fails to descend to the technical legal and administrative procedures which could perhaps allow the norms which he prescribes for a socialist society to take effect. Indeed, he provides almost no practical indications about how this socialist society is to be organised; and no procedural suggestions as to how a socialist society, committed to high moral goals, is to be prevented from resorting to amoral means to achieve them. Bloch could perhaps argue that a pattern of concrete ethical life (*Sittlichkeit*) exercises its own restraint, once it has developed, but he offers no guarantees that a temporary socialist state would in practice create such a pattern of ethical life. As a result, the danger which Bloch himself recognises, remains a danger still. Anti-Rome will not be built in a day, Bloch rightly declares;[58] but the problem remains that there is no guarantee that it is anti-Rome which will be built.

MARXIST AESTHETICS

Bloch also pioneers a new 'warm stream' Marxist aesthetics against the vulgar sociologism, historicism and reductionism of the Marxist tradition. Bloch is not primarily a philosopher of aesthetics, despite his life-long pre-occupation with cultural materials, and his hermeneutical analyses are designed to uncover the 'metaphysical' significance of cultural materials rather than to rank them in a critical system. Nonetheless, Bloch's conception of the world as an open system allows him to make original initiatives in Marxist aesthetics which challenge the closure of the world implicit in the Marxist tradition.

Where orthodox Marxist writing on aesthetics has assimilated the disillusionment of post-Romantic bourgeois aesthetics, and turned the pre-Marxist attempt to analyse the social origins of a work of art into a dogma, Bloch reclaims for Marxism the idea that art has a 'transcendent' quality and also the objectively hierarchical approach to aesthetics (genius, laws of beauty) implicit in Marx himself.[59] He outlines a Marxist aesthetics which finds the future in art: as the truth of the beautiful, which is still to be built. Marxism, Bloch argues, overcomes the bourgeois antinomies between beauty and truth, sensuousness and morality.[60] It locates aesthetic materials within the labour process, without losing sight of the reference such materials contain to dispositionalities and possibilities which can be elicited from the world. In the context of theory-praxis, it understands beauty as a form of truth: as true anticipation with a basis in the not-yet-become in the object.[61]

Bloch attempts to assert a subject-object perspective in Marxist aesthetics by drawing on thought experiments in Schelling, Hegel, Husserl and Freud. Bloch refunctions Schelling's emphasis on the truth function of art against the subjectivism of 'bourgeois' aesthetics; he also follows Schelling's extension of aesthetics to cover the aesthetic dimension of reality in general, and not simply art objects.[62] Similarly, he refunctions Hegel's 'material' (i.e. non-formal) aesthetics, with its finalistic stress on the appearance of the infinite within borders, against the formalism of both 'bourgeois' and Marxist aesthetic theories.[63] In an attempt to assert a dialectical materialist perspective in Marxist aesthetics, Bloch relates art to the possibility content of the world by refunctioning Husserl in a way which allows him to uncover models for theory-praxis in aesthetic materials. He also reworks Freud's emphasis on the wish fulfilment present in cultural productions, as part of a hermeneutics of aesthetic materials which seeks to raise the utopian function they contain to full consciousness.[64]

For Bloch art is a product of man's utopian consciousness and contains not-yet-conscious knowledge. It is allegorical pre-appearance (*Vor-Schein*): anticipatory appearance which provides a pre-view, a pre-semblance of possible success.[65] Because art has a subject-object character, it is not merely subjective. On the contrary, aesthetic imagination, Bloch emphasises, has the capacity (*Potenz*) to produce objective-real fragments which anticipate what they intend, and have a correlate in real possibilities which can be elicited from the world by theory-praxis. Art outlines or pre-images (*vorgestaltet*) not yet realised possibilities in its time, and its pre-appearance has a finalistic character. It represents objects in a way which is more 'immanently successful' or 'essential' than the objects in the existing world.[66] Bloch concedes that such *Vor-Schein* never loses its experimental character as 'an attempt', and that what becomes actual will be very different from what pre-appears in an ideological, encapsulated form; but he also insists on the need for an objective ontological dimension. Art, Bloch argues, is formed from the material of the world. It is a laboratory and festival of real possibilities: Luciferic completion of the object, based on insight into what it can become, which relates to real dispositionality in the object.[67] The *Vor-Schein* of art has a work character and points to the perfectibility of the object.

Bloch's emphasis on art as anticipation involves a new concept of realism in Marxist aesthetics, based on the claim that Marxist realism must be process realism, which 'reflects' the tendency-latency of the process in which something is 'not yet'.[68] All great art has a utopian window, Bloch claims, and realism must reflect the fact that every process reality has a utopian horizon.[69] Because reality is in process, Bloch rejects any representation of the world as finished and settled. Reality is objectively fragmentary, he claims, and no interpretation of the world without interruptions and openness can be realistic.[70] Equally, the process reality of the world means that the world cannot be represented as already manifest. Realism requires a recognition of the not-yet-manifest within the world, and the not-yet-manifest before the world in the form of perspective. For Bloch, to be 'realist' art must have not only social perspective (Lukács), but concrete reference to the *plus ultra* or utopian surplus which the process contains.[71] Bloch's point is not to set up an approved stylism, but to argue that great art does have this character, whatever style it employs. Bloch applies this concept of realism over a vast area to uncover realism in apparently irreal art forms as well as in the irreal dimensions of realist art forms; and here his views have already had a major impact on Marxist aesthetics.[72]

Bloch also attempts to break with the historicism of Marxist aesthetics and to reassert the repressed difference of the past as a task for theory-praxis. Marxism, Bloch argues, must actively inherit the great culture of the past and 'make true' (*wahrmachen*) what was unfinished or only implicit in it, in a transformative motion which critically appropriates what it inherits for socialist purposes.[73] For Bloch, such an active inheritance includes a Marxist inheritance of Romanticism. Nonetheless, it is misleading to suggest that Bloch is simply a Marxist Romantic. For all his enthusiasm for Jean Paul, Hoffmann and Novalis, Bloch is a critic of Romantic powerlessness, illusion and excess,[74] and emphasises that Romanticism is not the model for such a socialist reprieve, but only one cultural movement which can be transformed and set to work in a concrete utopian perspective. There is no normative dimension to Romanticism as such:

> Romanticism does not understand utopia, not even its own utopia, but utopia which has become concrete understands Romanticism, and penetrates into it, as far and as wide as the archaic and historical content of its archetypes and works contains something which has not yet become articulate, and is not yet finished.[75]

Similarly, Bloch emphasises that Marxism must actively inherit the total cultural heritage, including primitive art forms and the non-European cultures of Africa, South America and South East Asia.[76] He breaks with the Eurocentrism and high bourgeois bias of the Marxist tradition in aesthetics and stresses that both teleological contents for socialism and materials for the qualitative critique of capitalism can be found in all periods and cultures.

Bloch also attempts to break down the sociologism of Marxist aesthetics. He does not deny that all cultural production is situational and himself analyses cultural productions as reflections of struggles between social classes. But he denies (1) that the 'truth' of art can be confined to social truth; and (2) that a recursive analysis of the social origins of art is sufficient in a Marxist context. For Bloch, the truth of art has an ontological, and not only a social dimension, in the context of Marxist theory-praxis to change the world, and not only society; and he illustrates this claim with studies of literary, musical and visual art forms.[77] Moreover, in contrast to most Western Marxists, he attempts to ground Marxist aesthetics in dialectical materialism: in a specific philosophical conception of form-laden matter.[78]

Bloch's subject-object approach, as well as his immanentist-transcendentalist bias, can be seen in his philosophy of music.[79] Bloch modified his early work on the philosophy of music to take account of perspectives from Adorno's sociology of music; but despite his wide sympathies, extending to Bruckner, Berg and Kurt Weill, his emphasis centres on the ontological significance of music as anticipation.[80] For Bloch, music is the most utopian of the arts. It is speech which men can understand: a subject-like correlate outside of us which embodies our own intensity, and in which we experience an anticipatory transcendence of the existing interval or distance (*Abstand*) between subject and object. 'Identity', the 'last moment', 'a world for us', 'utopia' is present in music: as the anticipatory presence and pre-experience (*Vorgefühl*) of the possibility of self encounter in an adequate object.[81] Bloch does not deny that musical forms reflect the dominant social tendency and economic trends in an ideological way. For Bloch, however, it is not the reflection of an antagonistic social reality or the revelation of 'social truth' which is of fundamental importance, but the metaphysical meaning of music: as anticipation which reveals the still hidden 'uncovered countenance'. Hence, Bloch's utopian philosophy of music is an anthropology and an eschatology of music at once. Bloch insists that the expressionist character of music is not confined to human self expression.[82] Music expresses something 'not yet'. It copies what is objectively undetermined in the world.[83] There is a human world in music which has not yet become actual: a pre-appearance of a possible *regnum humanum*. For Bloch, music is the most public organon of the *incognito* or subjective factor in the world as a whole, and it provides an anticipatory experience of the subject-like (*subjekthaft*) *agens* as if it had become objectified in the external world.[84]

In this sense, there is a pre-appearance (*Vor-Schein*) of the realisation of the realising factor in music: a proleptic promise of a new heaven and a new earth.[85]

Bloch's approach combines a phenomenological analysis of musical forms, and of the specific objects (*Gegenstände*) intended by particular works and composers, with a projective ontological orientation which preserves the specificity of musical experience against positivism. He attempts to overtake the philosophies of music of Wagner, Nietzsche and, above all, Schopenhauer, with a philosophy of music for which music provides privileged access to 'the thing in itself' which is 'not yet'.[86] Bloch attempts to relate this philosophy of music to dialectical materialism. Granted that any attempt to ground the nature of music in the nature of matter must have a utopian character, and that the ontological nature of music is not yet known, Bloch claims that the dialectic of the not yet is the organon at work in musical forms, and relates the utopian-eschatological character of music to the 'realising factor' at work in process matter.[87] For Bloch, the constitutive potential of music needs to be related to a dialectical materialist theory-praxis, and music itself must be interpreted forwards: as an art capable of a radical utopian further development which has not yet occurred.

Bloch's warm stream aesthetics implies the need for a new Marxist cultural politics, friendly to imagination and hostile to the abstract 'cold' of capitalism. From the 1930s onwards Bloch rejected the cultural Popery and narrow 'Roman Communism' of orthodox Marxist cultural politics, and called for an alliance between the political *avant-garde* and the cultural *avant-garde*, in so far as it promoted a rebellion against bourgeois philistinism and the reification of life under capitalism. For Bloch, a Marxist cultural politics had to support revolutionary cultural initiatives: to combine (1) a productive inheritance of the great culture of mankind; with (2) initiatives to revolutionise traditional culture in the light of the latest technological developments.[88] Bloch's famous defence of Expressionism needs to be seen in this context. Instead of concentrating on Bloch's contribution to the debate in *Das Wort*, it is important to emphasise that Bloch first championed Expressionism in *Spirit of Utopia* (1918) and that the debate between Lukács and Bloch on aesthetics was originally a private one, which manifested in criticisms of the *Theory of the Novel* and of Lukács' essay on 'The

Metaphysics of Tragedy'.[89] This debate was continued in later essays and in *Heritage of this Time* (1935). This was why Bloch replied to Lukács in *Das Wort*, and not to Kurella; it was also why Lukács replied to *Heritage of this Time,* and not simply to Bloch's essay in *Das Wort.* In retrospect, their internal debate about first principles seems more significant than the disagreement over Expressionism.[90]

On the immediate question there can be little doubt that Bloch was the better critic and the more informed judge. Lukács, he pointed out, supported his dismissal from the Expressionist manifestos and ignored the actual achievements of the Expressionist poets, painters and composers.[91] This was not only unfair: it reflected a falsely monistic approach which confused the detection of social tendency with the actual diffusion of progressive and reactionary elements in a particular work. Despite its weaknesses and excesses, Expressionism could not be dismissed as a form of bourgeois decadence with proto-fascist dimensions, Bloch argued. On the contrary, it was a Promethean rebellion against the abstract 'cold' of capitalism and its emotional outbursts contained critical revolutionary fantasies and images of a no longer alienated world.[92] Where Lukács saw a decline from classical standards, Bloch saw the immaturity and confusion appropriate to the birth of the new. Bloch did not deny that Lukács was right about the subjectivist, pseudo-activist nature of the Expressionist revolt; but he wanted a more differentiated analysis, which took account of the revolutionary strand in Expressionism and the constitutive potential which it contained.

The wider issue, however, was the need for a dialectical materialist theory of reflection. Lukács rejected modernism in general, and not only Expressionism, as a manifestation of the decadence of the Imperialist bourgeoisie. He emphasised its irrationalist and pessimistic tendencies, and that it set up an unmediated subjectivism which ignored the social world and the laws of development governing its movement. For Lukács, Bloch did as a theorist what the modernists did as artists: he confused the contents of consciousness with objective reality, and failed to go beyond unmediated appearance to the social forces which produced it.[93] Bloch, however, did not deny that there was a dominant social tendency governing capitalism (and every other mode of production), or doubt that capitalism had holistic, structural features which over-determined particulars in a systematic way. Like Adorno, Bloch denied that life under capitalism could be understood as panlogical, homogeneous, 'seamless' totality.[94] Instead, he argued that existing reality was only 'roughly mediated' and full of dissonance, discrepancies and breaks, that the structuration of existing reality was not a structuration of logically arranged contradictions, but a processual structuration, full of disparities, discontinuities and dialectical leaps through which the impeded new was attempting to burst forth. Bloch did not deny that modernism was subjective and full of reactionary elements, but he denied that objective reality could be identified with the existing social world or interpreted as something fully actual.[95] He argued, against Lukács, that Marxism involved a non-classical conception of reality as essentially unfinished and open to dialectical leaps, which allowed for anticipation and for superstructural representation of developing real possibilities.[96] For Bloch, Lukács' sociologism and schematicism led to a premature theoreticism, which missed the anticipatory moments in the superstructure which were capable of further development and needed to be set to work.[97] Bloch's critical sympathy for modernism, including Russian Formalism, Surrealism, Constructivism and Dada as well as Expressionism, implied both (1) a different analysis of the development of capitalism, for which mediated montage and disfunctioning of classical harmonies were appropriate critical techniques drawing attention to the new which appeared in the cracks and fissures of bourgeois society;[98] and (2) a different account of the nature of the reality which art 'reflected'. In a dialectical materialist context, Bloch held that great art 'reflected' the tendency-latency of an open, unfinished world through the medium of a more immediate 'reflection' of the society at hand.[99]

Bloch's quarrel with Lukács needs to be related to his continuing attempt to relate Marxism to the development of capitalism and to the revolutionary implications of the growth of technology. Bloch follows Marx in insisting that capitalism is inimical to certain forms of aesthetic production.[100] He argues against Benjamin that Marxists should not passively assimilate the abstraction of cultural production under capitalism, including the development of aleatory forms and the loss of the 'aura' of traditional art; but actively oppose to it artistic production which anticipates the new world and the possible socialist fulfilment towards which the development of the forces of production are leading. Indeed, to the extent that capitalism succeeds in externalising its own 'hollow space' as the 'reality' with which adults must come to terms, it is important for artists to maintain the perspective of life beyond capitalism: to anticipate a world without alienation in a critique of capitalism which agitates against current alienations in the name of what is still possible and 'not yet'. Hence, in the context of increasing 'alienation' and 'reification', Bloch developed from the outstanding Marxist champion of the artistic *avant-garde* in the first third of the century into a critic of the *avant-garde*'s assimilation of the alienation and unmediated technology which resulted from the stabilisation of capitalism from the 1930s onwards.[101] Unlike Benjamin, Bloch rejects any uncritical assimilation of the cultural logic of capitalist technology. Even if there is negative emergence involving the end of traditional aesthetics, he emphasises that Marxism looks beyond capitalist *Technik* to a socialist technology which would allow the emergence of new utopian art forms. Clearly such a perspective has implications for art in socialist societies, and this stress on art as critical anticipation formed the basis for Bloch's contribution to East German aesthetics during his years in the DDR.[102]

Bloch's work on aesthetic materials is unparalleled in its range and tolerance in the Marxist tradition. In contrast to Lukács, Bloch breaks with the high culture bias in Marxist aesthetics. He analyses the significance of kitsch in both popular and high culture, and deals not only with literature, but with music, painting, design, interior decoration, gardening, sculpture, architecture, dance, photography and film.[103] Bloch wrote a series of very early articles on music in the cinema, and later he continued to explore the utopian meaning of the cinema in the art film.[104] He also analyses the history of opera and the history of architecture from Egypt to the Bauhaus, including studies of the modern utopias of housing and town planning.[105] Again, in contrast to the Frankfurt School, Bloch provides a positive hermeneutics of popular culture, including advertisements, illustrated magazines, dance crazes, the products of the Hollywood dream factories, pantomimes, circuses, detective stories and popular music.[106] He emphasises the ambiguous political functionality of the mass culture industry and the need for Marxist media studies. Unlike Adorno, however, Bloch concentrates on the revolutionary potential of popular culture, and not simply on its soporific function, or on cultural pessimism. He draws attention to the way human intentionality continues to assert itself, even in the reified forms provided by a profit-oriented culture industry. A hermeneutics of popular cultural manifestations, he implies, can correct over-intellectualistic conceptions in Marxist circles of people's real needs.

Bloch's work implies that Marxism requires a new cultural hermeneutics which looks beyond evaluationist criteria and the cult of recursion to social origins. Such a hermeneutics would concentrate on (1) the political functionality of cultural manifestations; (2) the repressed needs, desires and intention to fulfilment which such manifestations embody; and (3) the objective possibility contents which such manifestations intend. It would decode the aesthetics of everyday life in a way which revealed the alienations and political distortions of cultural production and reception (cf. Bloch's decoding of Nazi culture and its perversion of the German cultural heritage); it would also detect the revolutionary potentiality of non-contemporaneous elements such as ornament and folk art, as well as the transfer of utopian perspectives under capitalism to technological fantasies and kolportage.[107]

Granted that Bloch's attempt to widen Marxist aesthetics is 'philosophical' in form, Bloch does not simply restate 'idealist' aesthetics in a materialist form. On the contrary, Bloch pioneers a praxis-oriented, activist approach to aesthetics, which seeks to refunction the cultural materials which emerge in the process, and to activate their constitutive potential for the determination of the teleological content of socialism. For Bloch, aesthetic materials reveal remote contents which need to be included on the agenda of goals which socialism seeks to realise. Bloch accepts the need for a radical critique of the contemplative character of bourgeois aesthetics in so far as it confines cultural production to entertainment, flight from the world at hand, or an elevated spiritual realm. He also concedes the need to break with the 'bourgeois' cult of art religion, with 'art for art's sake', and with the museumist approach to 'cultural treasures'.[108] For Bloch, the *utopian surplus* of cultural production has a present political functionality as well as a possible future functionality in a Marxist cultural politics; and he argues that it is necessary to give such surplus an explicitly socialist functionality *now*, related to the needs and repressed desires of particular classes and social strata.[109] Like Benjamin, he also stresses the need for an activist approach to the fragments and ruins of the culture of the past. Productive criticism must take the form of mortification of the work which releases what is capable of future development and allows a late ripening of its utopian surplus.[110]

For Bloch, Brecht's work illustrates this combination of a re-working of the utopian surplus of the past with an innovating radicalism which gives aesthetic productions a socialist function-ality. Bloch's enthusiasim for Brecht's work in all its phases is well known, In contrast to Adorno's critical attitude to Brecht's 'archaism', Bloch uncovers the hermeneutical movement in Brecht's break with Aristotelian dramaturgy and the illusionist theatre of the bourgeoisie. He interprets Brecht's use of non-contemporaneous materials as consistent with his own views. For Bloch, Brecht provides the outstanding example of the fusion of utopia and critique which is needed.[111] Bloch, however, goes beyond Brecht and develops his own theory of drama as an experimental laboratory of possibilities: a paradigmatic institution (cf. Schiller) in which real models are developed beyond any bourgeois confinement of art to contemplation or escapist illusion.[112] He also attempts to widen Brecht's concept of *Verfremdung* to cover distancing experiences with a not-yet-conscious utopian meaning.[113] Brecht used the term *Verfrem-dung* to refer to the distancing effects in his epic theatre. For Bloch, however, *Verfremdung* can have a wider and more positive meaning. *Verfremdung* in German usually means something strange or disconcerting, something distanced from its expected or familiar context, in contrast to *Entfremdung* or self alienation. Bloch, however, uses *Verfremdung* more in the sense of *Befrem-dung*, to refer to experiences of the 'beautiful strange': discon-certing experiences of something 'far off' mediated by the at hand, which produce astonishment and wonder (*Staunen*). In contrast to the alienation of *Entfremdung*, *Verfremdung* in Bloch's sense implies the possibility of external as well as internal fulfilment.[114] Bloch finds evidence of *Verfremdung*, in this sense, not only in cultural forms, but in nature, and he devotes the second volume of his *Verfremdungen* (1964) to 'geograph-ica'.[115] With characteristic initiative, Bloch pioneers a Marxist aesthetic of art in nature (*Naturkunst*), designed to overcome the separation of history and nature in Marxist aesthetics

(Lukács). He shows that model ideas in Baader, Schelling and Goethe can be refunctioned in the context of a Marxist theory-praxis which interprets nature as unfinished and changeable. Here Bloch goes beyond Adorno's emphasis on natural teleology in Marxist aesthetics in the direction of a dialectical materialist praxis of the utopian potentialities concealed in nature, to which the aesthetic ciphers, symbols and allegories of nature bear witness.[116]

Bloch's stress on the utopian character of art has parallels in the work of Adorno and Benjamin, and also in Marx himself in so far as Marx took artistic activity as a model of unalienated human labour. Like Adorno and Benjamin, however, Bloch is limited by the non-discursive character of the utopian moments to which he refers and finds it difficult to provide concrete models for the praxis whose pathos he invokes. Moreover, Bloch's approach to aesthetics is over nostalgic. Like Lukács, he shuns empirical research and sets up a discourse remote from positive knowledge. A critic could also charge that his work on aesthetics remains within the problematic of the aesthetics of subjective experience; that it ignores the radicalism of hermeneutical philosophy as an ontology of interpretation (Gadamer); the problem of reception or the actual communication received (Jauss); the background and horizons of specific readers (Escarpit); and the possibility of a systematic informational analysis (Bense). It is also true that Bloch carries over the aesthetics of his early utopian philosophy (including the material on the philosophy of music, art history, architecture, drama and humour) into Marxism without giving this material a genuinely Marxist form; that he neglects the problem of specifically proletarian art forms and the history of working class traditions (although he knew Asja Lacis and had links with German experimentalist theatre through Piscator); and that he fails to deal adequately with explicitly political literature. Because Bloch remains within the self definition of a philosopher, he fails to consider the possibility of a Marxism which breaks *in toto* with philosophical aesthetics or to take full account of technical considerations, especially in music, to which the categories of nineteenth century philosophical aesthetics are inadequate. He also fails to come to terms with many of the most untraditional features of the technological civilisation of the twentieth century, or to appreciate the need for a detailed analysis of particular culture industries.

Nonetheless, Bloch vastly extends the range of Marxist aesthetics and challenges its latent positivism in a way which implies that new initiatives are needed to take account of the constitutive potential of cultural materials, wherever they are to be found. He also re-poses the problem of ontological materialism in Marxist aesthetics in a way which challenges the differently conceived 'materialist criticism' of della Volpe and Macherey, and reopens the question of whether Lenin's emphasis on a realism of the future in the present[117] may not be capable of a praxis-oriented dialectical materialist reinterpretation.

MARXIST META-RELIGION

Bloch also breaks with the tradition of vulgar anti-religion in Marxism, and attempts to develop a more positive Marxist critique of religion, based on the 'warm stream' which he claims was implicit in Marx's own views. Under the influence of Engels and even more Lenin, Marxists have often assumed that religion is illusion and superstition, which Marxism first exposes and then actively struggles to abolish. Bloch regards this view as undialectical and naïve, and emphasises that Marx's view of religion in his *Critique of Hegel's Philosophy of Right* was more complex. Marx, Bloch argues, held that religion was the fantastic realisation of the human essence, which, in an alienated society, had not become actual in the world. It was therefore important, not only as the starting point for Marx's general critique, but as an indication of the goal of political activity. Marx held that religion was the heart of a heartless world, and would not disappear until man's relations to man and nature were rational and intelligible. For Marx, Bloch argues, religion was not merely illusion, but an illusory representation of what was needed. If religion was an opiate, which often operated to keep men in their chains, the prime need was not to abolish religion, but to abolish the social conditions which gave rise to religion, in a way which would realise the 'truth' of what was represented in religion in an illusory way.[118] Bloch, however, develops an interpretation of religion which goes beyond anything in Marx. He concedes that religion is illusory, that it postulates mythical entities, that it has often reconciled men to unjust social conditions and been a form of oppression. Nonetheless, the problem remains that relig-

ion has prevailed in almost all cultures over an enormous period
of time, despite the fact that the world to which it refers mani-
festly does not exist as an actual visible reality now. For Bloch,
this 'irrealism' of religion is the key to its importance and its
meaning.

In a Marxist context, Bloch's view of religion is unprecedented
and important. Bloch implies that religion is not only illusory,
but healthy, normal and to a degree non-abolishable as long as
what hope intends is unfulfilled. For Bloch, religion embodies
not-yet-conscious knowledge which needs to be made the object
of a praxis of anticipation. Bloch's originality is to interpret the
counter-factual excess of religion as secretly wise, and as potentially constitutive for theory-praxis. Religion, Bloch argues, is
full of utopianism and where there is hope, there is religion.[119]
What was intended by the great religions was absolute or total
hope.[120] Consistent with this view, Bloch argues that Marxism
needs a new praxis-oriented approach to religion which actively
inherits the symbolic pre-appearance (*Vor-Schein*), found in the
religious history of mankind.[121] Such an inheritance requires a
Marxist critique of the ideology and illusion present in religious
projections, which relates such projections to the development
of classes and to particular modes of production. But it also
requires a hermeneutic of the 'act content' such projections
contain, which cannot be appropriated in any simplistic ideology
free form. Instead, for Bloch, there is a translation of the genuine
intentionality which the religious imagination of mankind has
uncovered into a revolutionary socialist ideology which aims at
theory-praxis in the long run.

To fulfil this programme, Bloch provides a detailed analysis
of the major world religions, and interprets the history of religions as the history of man's increasing self injection into the
content of religious mystery. Bloch does not hesitate to find
not-yet-conscious knowledge in religions as diverse as Zoro-
astrianism, Buddhism, Taoism, Confucianism, the astral religions
of Babylonia and Chaldaea, the ancient religions of Egypt and
classical Greece, and Islam.[122] He combines a Marxist sociology
of religion with a hermeneutical interrogation of the particular
utopias which different forms of religious imagination produce,
in the context of the need to relate religious imagination to an
open anthropology and to the open ontology of an unfinished
world. According to Bloch, Marxism requires a new anthropology

of religion in order to take account of the depth and intensity of religious desire, and a new eschatology of religion to take account of the intention to perfect being which the religious sphere posits.[123]

Bloch's project of an active Marxist inheritance of religion involves a new concept of Marxist atheism. According to Bloch, Marxist atheism is not philistine 'half enlightenment' or the shallow anti-religion of rationalism.[124] It does not imply a defeat for human values or a limitation on hope. It is not a form of ontological reductionism, and the assertion that 'there is no God' does not delimit the qualitative content of being. Marxist atheism, Bloch argues, is substantial atheism, which actively inherits what was intended by religion with the philosophical concept of concrete utopia.[125] It is not the negation of religion, in so far as religion is a manifestation of hope, but an active humanism which seeks to realise the 'hope treasures' of religion in reality.[126] Bloch attempts to give Marxist atheism an active, positive meaning. He refunctions the anthropological critique of religion developed by Hegel and Feuerbach, in a way which avoids reductionism and opens the way for theory-praxis. Bloch rejects Feuerbach's abstract 'species man', along with all other attempts to reduce the God postulate to existing men (including their un-realised existing possibilities) or to existing social conditions. The God postulate, Bloch argues, is a hypostasised utopian ideal of the *humanum*, to which the 'otherness' and numinous quality attributed to God rightly belongs.[127] Because the *humanum* is still a *futurum*, Marxist atheism does not cancel the maximalism or the ontological radicalism of the God postulate. Instead it inherits the speculative anthropology of the German mystics, so that the *deus absconditus* is preserved as a *homo absconditus* which is 'not yet'.[128] The ideal of 'man' takes on the form of an ensemble of utopian relationships adequate to what has been projected as the God postulate, with the result that the making of future man acquires a centrality and a utopian meaning in Marxism which it has not hitherto possessed.[129]

Similarly, according to Bloch Marxist atheism needs to inherit the *topos* into which the God postulate was projected. The idea of a space beyond the present world in which human hope contents have a place, is not necessarily illusory because men have only imagined illusory entities to fill it. Instead, the history of men's ideas of God is the history of the highest frontal content which they could imagine. Granted that these entities were illusory, Bloch argues that Marxism needs to retain the *topos* into which they were projected: as a *topos* for a possible future reality still to come.[130] Marxism replaces the God postulate with the *humanum* and with the utopia of a kingdom of freedom into which it could fit. Such a kingdom of freedom, however, requires that the space into which God was projected be real, and not illusory.[131] Marxist atheism, however, can only inherit this *topos* as the still open frontal space for the utopia of the kingdom, if it breaks with the backward reference implicit in theism, and not only with its God postulate. In so far as religion binds its adherents to a mythical God of the beginning and encourages men to think of the world as already in being, Marxism needs to break with the ontological closure implicit in the *anamnesis* of religion. It needs to replace this ontological closure with meta-religion which inherits the revolutionary utopian meaning of religion, and refunctions it forwards: as teleological content for theory-praxis.[132]

Bloch emphasises that an active Marxist inheritance of religion involves the end of religion. Nonetheless, it does not involve an abstract rupture with those functional aspects of religion which continue to have relevance as long as pre-history lasts. Here, it is necessary to distinguish between (1) the functionality of religion as alienated self consciousness; and (2) the functionality of religion as a projectivism which affirms the goal against the anti-utopian world at hand. In the latter sense, Bloch argues that Marxist meta-religion can inherit some of the functionality of religion, including its explosive, counter-factual hope content. Marxist meta-religion inherits the problem of the meaning of life, which religion poses in a mystified form, as a task for theory-praxis. It recognises that religious imagination cannot be entirely dismissed, even after a successful disenchantment of the world, in so far as it embodies not-yet-conscious knowledge and intentionality to a better world than the world at hand.[133] In a radical refunctioning, Marxist meta-religion inherits the depth dimension of religion, including its unconscious goal,[134] and activates it towards the future. The forward look replaces the upward look; and the true reference of religious faith is identified as hopeful faith in something unmistakably wonderful still to come.[135] For Bloch, Marxist meta-religion, including a

Marxist 'dogmatics' or 'faith without lies', even perhaps a 'socialist church',[136] is necessary to bear witness to the genuine mystery in the world, the mystery of ourselves, in the face of the continuing defeats and discouragements of the world at hand. It is realistic, even though the orientation to utopia function which it inherits, including the intention to perfect being, cannot be maintained without a dialectically moderated element of intoxication. In this sense, a Marxist meta-religion which inherits the symbolic pre-appearance (*Vor-Schein*) of religion as teleological purpose content for socialism involves a change of psychological style in Marxism:

> *Religion inherited* (meta-religion) comes to be the conscience of the last utopian function *in toto*: that function is the self-transcending of man, the transcending in league with the dialectically transcending tendency of man-made history, the *transcending without any heavenly transcendence, but with full understanding of that transcendence: as a hypostasised anticipation of being-for-itself.*[137]

Bloch finds the elements for such an active inheritance of religion not in the standard Marxist anti-religious criticism of religion, but in the religious critique of religion which emerged within religion itself, above all in the Bible.[138] The Bible, Bloch claims, is a great manual of utopianism and contains a unique 'total explosion of hope'.[139] It has a stronger utopian conscience than the social utopias and teaches men to think of transcendence as future and to long for total 'newness of life'. Moreover, the Bible introduced an eschatological conscience into the world with no precedent in Greek philosophy.[140] In order to bring out the utopian meaning of the Bible, Bloch develops a new kind of detectivistic Marxist Biblical criticism, based on (1) situation analysis of the economic and political background to the Biblical texts; and (2) on an attempt to find radical ontological implications in familiar materials. In contrast to Bultmann, Bloch argues that it is the myths of the Bible which are true, and that what is needed is to break with the conventional priestly interpretations of them in order to reveal their astonishingly heretical meaning.[141]

According to Bloch, the Bible records an extraordinary exodus from Yahweh. This exodus began when Moses transformed Yahweh from a Sinai volcano god into an entirely new kind of God: an exodus God, who promised to lead his people out of bondage and to reveal himself to them in the future.[142] Moreover, Moses' self injection into Yahweh produced a fundamental qualitative shift in the history of religion:

> The injection of Moses changed the substance of the salvation that had made up the external, wholly completed goal of the pagan religions, the astral-mythical ones in particular. *Now, instead of the finished goal, a promised one appears, one yet to be acquired; and instead of the visible nature God, there appears an invisible one of justice, of a kingdom of justice.*[143]

Inevitably, this self injection was adulterated in the subsequent history of Israel, especially in Canaan, where a class society arose, and Yahweh degenerated into a pagan creator God. Nonetheless, underground opposition to this false, priestly Yahweh continued throughout the Old Testament. The Nazirites preserved the social egalitarianism of Bedouin communism and this strand was continued by the prophets, with their radical stress on social justice, their reinterpretation of Yahweh as a *futurum* who brings a moral-social apocalypse, and their teaching that men could determine the outcome of history by their actions.[144] From Daniel onwards, Bloch claims, the creation of a finally just world was increasingly looked for in the future. Bloch finds further evidence of this exodus in Job, the Hebrew Prometheus who was more righteous than his Creator, and in the transformation of the Messiah in Jewish apocalyptical literature into the Son of Man: a *Makanthropos* who would inaugurate a new aeon and create a new heaven and a new earth.[145] The most important exodus occurred, Bloch argues, in Jesus who claimed equality with Yahweh, usurped his place, and then outbid him by promising immortality and showing that he was morally superior to the Creator God who allowed him to be crucified.[146] In Jesus, Bloch claims following Hegel, God became man. Moreover, the exodus from Yahweh continued after Jesus' death, when the man Jesus was identified with the cosmic Son of Man, and his *parousia* replaced the 'day of the Lord' as the *futurum*.[147] Thus, according to Bloch, there is meta-religion implicit in the Bible itself and, in particular, in Christianity which revealed for the first time what religion really is: an explosion of absolute hope.[148]

Bloch's Biblical criticism implies that Marxism can discover purpose content not only in the Biblical narratives with their *topoi* and utopian postulates, but also in the theological wish pictures through which they were interpreted in subsequent centuries. Bloch provides a Marxist critique of the theologies of Barth and Bultmann, and attempts to oppose a Marxist Christology to the heteronomous theology of the Christian churches.[149] Like Lamennais and Weitling, Bloch sees Jesus as a revolutionary who preached a communism of the poor against the rich and promised to bring 'not peace, but a sword'. Nonetheless, he recognises that Jesus' gospel was not primarily social or moral, but eschatological;[150] and he follows Schweitzer's interpretation of Jesus as an eschatological figure, influenced by John the Baptist, who expected the imminent end of the world. Jesus was dangerous, Bloch implies, not because he claimed to be Messiah, but because he preached the end of the present world and the beginning of a new aeon.[151] Nonetheless, despite this eschatological emphasis, Bloch resists any dissolution of the Christian *muthos* itself. Thus, for Bloch, Jesus' miracles are authentic signs of the end, of the fact that the world contains the possibility of dialectical leaps; and the Resurrection, Ascension and Parousia are wish mysteries which point respectively to (1) the fact that the soul is extra-territorial to death; (2) an insertion of man into heaven; and (3) the possibility of a final hominisation of the world.[152] The objection remains that such a hermeneutics merely translates the Christian myth structure into other terms, without exploding what is really mythical in it. Bloch's interpretation mixes clichés of the *Aufklärung* with a gnostic bias derived from Hegel, and even more obviously, Schelling. In Bloch's political version of an esoteric interpretation, Jesus' eschatological communism was replaced by Paul's sacrifice theology, the heteronomous Lord of the church replaced the Son of Man, and Christianity ceased to be revolutionary political theology for centuries.[153] Nonetheless, 'true' Christianity burst through again in the doctrines of the heretical sects such as the Anabaptists and the Hussites, and, above all, in Thomas Münzer, who combined the *eritis sicut deus* theme with the *telos* of a coming earthly kingdom.[154]

Bloch argues that Marxism needs to inherit this 'subject-laden' revolutionary Christianity of the Christian heretics, with its postulates of the Son of Man and the exodus, and its explosive

Messianism of a meta-cosmic kingdom, not the vaguely ethical, safely contained Christianity of the churches.[155] Rightly understood, adherence to the exodus-figure called 'I will be what I will be', and to the Christianity of the Son of Man and of the eschaton, is no longer religion.[156] Bloch claims that an alliance between an illusion-free Christianity and a Marxism which has recovered its depth dimension,[157] will become possible when Christians and Marxists recognise that Christianity and Marxism require each other for the fulfilment of what they intend: the substantial atheism of an end to heteronomy and the realistic goal of a future kingdom of freedom. In this sense, Bloch writes: 'Only an atheist can be a good Christian, only a Christian can be a good atheist'.[158]

Bloch's attempt to outline a Marxist inheritance of religion is open to serious criticism. Bloch provides no genuine critique of the psychology or methodology of religion. Instead, he tends to reinterpret religious postulates in utopian, and allegedly materialist terms. He introduces Marxist analyses to explain social and ideological aspects of religion, but he provides no Marxist explanation of why it was Moses who invented the idea of an exodus God, or why it should have been Jesus who 'made God man'. Moreover, he gives Judaism, Christianity and, above all, Jesus, a centrality in his treatment for which there is biographical rather than methodological justification. Bloch tries to distinguish Marxist meta-religion from the religiosity of Russian 'Godbuilders' such as Lunacharsky or Bazarov (the parallels with 'God-seekers' such as Berdyaev or Gippius are also revealing),[159] but the suspicion remains that Bloch confuses Marxism with a projective meta-religious outlook of an essentially religious kind. It may be true that Marxism can inherit something of the hopefulness of religion, but it cannot do so unless it qualifies that hope, without turning itself into a form of religion, albeit of a materialist variety. Bloch insists that his Marxist meta-religion is not 'religion'. Nonetheless, it often seems like a substitute for religion rather than something genuinely meta-religious or Marxist. Bloch's postulate of the not-yet-actual *humanum* has highly religious overtones, and implies a heteronomous primacy of moralistic and maximalist values, while his concept of extraterritoriality seems a substitute for immortality. Bloch also has an essentially religious conception of good and evil. He praises Jesus' stress on love for poor and insignificant things, and implies that such love could ultimately have some effect in the context of moment mysticism. He also accepts the validity of the religious option to project a maximalist negative and, like Adorno, argues that Auschwitz shows the need for a postulate of radical evil or 'Satan', if metaphysics is not to lose its depth.[160]

Bloch can reply that the experience of the 'socialist' countries suggests that attempts to repress the religious needs of mankind have proved harmful; that our immanence precludes any complete sublation of religion in pre-history; and that religion can have a transitional functionality even under socialism. Bloch is surely right to insist that it is a mistake to attempt to suppress manifestations of the imagination when the conditions to which they relate still obtain, and also to emphasise the potential function of religious ideas in the struggles of repressed social strata. Clearly, it is inadequate to reduce the role and function of religion to 'alienated self consciousness' or to merely a socially determined epiphenomenon concealing class interests. But the objection remains that Bloch's own modernist treatment of religion does justice neither to the religious intention nor to the possibility of a rational advance beyond it. In so far as the force of religion lies in its meta-empirical dimension, it could be argued that what is needed is a recognition of the continuing relevance of such a dimension, and not a historicisation of it in a futurist form.

These deficiences can be set against Bloch's contribution to the contemporary reinterpretation of Christianity. Bloch has provided theologians with models for a post-theistic, post-individualist redefinition of Christianity, in which futurism becomes the model for faith, hope becomes the supreme theological virtue, and God becomes a *futurum* ahead of man with the future as his mode of being. The central text of the so-called 'theology of hope' movement, Jürgen Moltmann's *Theology of Hope* (1964), was written under Bloch's influence, and Moltmann went on to assimilate Bloch's ideas in a Christian context in such volumes as *Man, A Christian Anthropology* and *The Experiment Hope*.[161] Wolfgang Pannenberg has also stressed the relevance of Bloch's thought to a future development of Christianity:

Perhaps Christian theology will one day have to thank Ernst Bloch's philosophy of hope for giving it the courage to recover in the full sense its central category of eschatology . . . Bloch has taught us about the overwhelming power of the still-open future and of the hope that reaches out to it in anticipation . . . [162]

Nor is Bloch's influence confined to Protestant theologians.[163] Bloch has also made a major contribution to the development of contemporary political theology. Johannes Metz wrote one of the classic texts of political theology, *Theology of the World* (1968), under Bloch's influence,[164] and later Bloch's ideas were taken up by leading Latin American political theologians such as Bonino, Gutiérrez, Alves and Segundo,[165] through whom they had an impact not only in South America, but in Africa and Asia. Here, Bloch's work coincided with a general politicisation of Christianity in the direction of a theology of corporate redemption and social justice; but it also contributed directly to a more reflexive Christianity which attempted to take account of Marxist insights,[166] and to an increasing Christian-Marxist convergence in several countries. Obviously, it is possible to question this politicisation of Christianity and to wonder how lasting its orientations will prove to be. Nonetheless, a situation in which many Christian thinkers have to differentiate their views from those of Marxists was unthinkable when Bloch wrote *Thomas Münzer.*

MARXIST MATERIALISM

Bloch also attempts to supplement Marxism with a more sophisticated Marxist materialism, which reasserts the 'warm stream' implicit in the views of Marx and Engels against the reductionism and mechanical materialism of the Marxist tradition. He resets the problem of materialism in the context of an unfinished world in which man can influence what matter can become through a praxis of anticipation.

Bloch rethinks the nature of historical materialism as a critical, subject-object materialism, based on the revolutionary spontaneity of the subjective factor. He takes his starting point from the young Marx who, he claims, developed an entirely new concept of materialism, which he equated with real humanism. According to Bloch, Marx's new concept of materialism went beyond Feuerbach's anthropological materialism and developed a theory of the determination of history by man and his activity.[167] In *Theses on Feuerbach,* Bloch argues, Marx returned from Feuerbach to Hegel and made Hegel's subject-object relationship fundamental to his new materialism, for which 'the material base' was man and his activity or the subject-object relationship of human labour.[168] Marx's new materialism, Bloch insists, was not a dualistic externalist materialism, for which human life and consciousness were passively determined by factors external to man. On the contrary, in *Theses on Feuerbach* Marx emphasised the activity of the subjective factor, which had been developed abstractly by idealism.[169] For Marx, Bloch insists, there was no dualism of subject and object, mind and matter. Instead, Marx emphasised the subject-object oscillations in operation at every point. He held that the subject and its activity were part of the external world, which everywhere represented a reciprocal mediation of subject and object; and stressed that men determined circumstances (subject) just as they were determined by them (object).[170] Similarly, in opposition to previous materialisms, Marx stressed the role of subjective activity in perception.[171] Again, where previous materialism tended to devalue thought and to oppose it dualistically to 'objective being', Marx, like Hegel, held that sensuous appearance was 'abstract', whereas thought was 'concrete'. So far from devaluing thought in favour of things, Marx recognised in his Letter to Ruge of September, 1843 that thought had an anticipatory function and gave thought a more important role than it possessed in any previous materialism: the power to apprehend relations between things which were not given in appearance, and the power to change the world.[172] Moreover, Bloch notes that Marx held that ideas could become 'a material force' when they were grasped by the masses.[173]

Bloch recognises that Marx went beyond his early formulations in *Theses on Feuerbach* and developed a complex 'economic materialism'; but he insists that Marx never retreated from the critical standpoint of the *Theses*, least of all in *Capital* or in *A Contribution to the Critique of Political Economy*. Bloch does not prove that Marx's later formulations are compatible with the *Theses,* but he insists on the moral impetus in all Marx's work, and implies that the young Marx's revolutionary break with all previous materialism should prevail over the later Marx's occasionally more positivist statements. The 'economic material-ism' of the mature Marx had its origins in the young Marx and was, he emphasises, in no way purely 'economic'. Apart from Engels' famous clarification that he and Marx only held econ-omic factors to be decisive 'in the last instance', Marx's political economy was not political economy in the bourgeois sense, but an account of the whole of human existence, under a specific mode of production, which extended to art, religion, politics and law, as well as to technical economic relationships.[174] So far from being value free or a form of scientism, Marx's political economy was essentially critical and centred on evaluative con-cepts such as fetishism, alienation and self production. Bloch sees that precisely because the critical superiority of Marxism rests on Marx's analysis of capitalism, it is crucial not to allow 'Marxist economics' to be divorced from the critical character of Marx's materialism in general, based on the emancipatory potential of a return to the producer, who is forgotten in his product as long as history is dominated by quasi-automaticist processes. Hence, he stresses that for Marx economic categories were expressions of determinate relationships between man and man and man and nature, and that Marx's economic materialism had a critical meaning in terms of the antagonistic social relation-ships between social classes. For Marx, Bloch claims, there was no isolation of the economy from society as a whole, understood as a totality of subject-object relationships reflecting a particular mode of organisation of human labour.[175]

Just as Bloch resists the attempt to interpret Marx's historical materialism as narrowly economic, so he attempts to combat the claim that Marx's historical materialism sets up objectivistic 'laws of history', to which men are subject. Bloch denies that there are any naturalistic laws of history, and argues that all historical laws must be understood as ruling tendencies.[176] Similarly, he denies that historical materialism implies an ob-jectivistic determination which is incompatible with human freedom. Rightly understood, Bloch argues, Marxism is the phil-osophy of powerful, active freedom, which shows men how to overcome the determinism of external, quasi-automatic proces-ses; and when Engels equated freedom with 'insight into neces-sity', he meant that Marxism made it possible to have insight into how unmediated, external necessity could be overcome.[177] Marxism, Bloch claims, understands freedom as a moment of dialectical materialist lawfulness.[178] It recognises both objective ruling law-like necessity and contingency, where objective necessity is changeable as a result of the intervening action of the subjective factor, and where the subjective factor's ability to change objective necessity is based on the partial conditionality of conditions.[179] It follows for Bloch that contingency, understood as the crossing of otherwise separate causal chains, and the activity of the subjective factor acting in accordance with dialectical lawfulness, are central to historical materialism.[180] Likewise, Bloch rejects naturalistic causality in history and argues for dialectical causality, based on the causality of conditions and a clear distinction between conditions and causes. Causes, Bloch claims, are material presuppositions of law-like necessary realisations, and determine the realisation of the possible according to the degree of its conditionality. Conditions, on the other hand, are material presuppositions, which will not come to pass without the activity of an intervening subject. Conditions maintain themselves in suspense and mature over time, whereas there is no partial causality. They merely set the possible, and require the activity of the subjective factor to intervene as an active cause in a way which mobilises existing causes and creates new ones.[181] Because, however, the subjective factor can intervene and change the level and state of contradictions in accordance with conditions, historical materialism is a philosophy of freedom, for which revolutionary spontaneity is the key to changing the prevailing lawfulness in the direction of more freedom from external necessity.

Bloch also attempts to reformulate the standard base-superstructure distinction in historical materialism. He rejects any absolute contrast between the superstructure and the base, and argues that Marx envisaged a subject-object relationship, for which the superstructure acted on the base as well as reflected it.[182] Like Althusser, he stresses that the notion of the superstructure 'reflecting' the base must not be crudely stated; that the superstructure is a relatively autonomous region with its own structures and regional laws; and that different areas such as religion, art, philosophy and law, have specific regional problems which require localised approaches.[183] What is reflected in the superstructure, he emphasises, is *the base and the superstructure*, and the base itself is unintelligible without reference to ordering superstructural elements present in it.[184] Moreover, this 'reflection' is active and internal. Granted that some of Engels' *dicta* suggest a narrower view, Bloch argues that in his remarks on Greek art Marx recognised that some superstructural elements possessed a validity which transcended the society in which they arose.[185] For Bloch, the superstructure is creative in a way which leads to the emergence of elements not present in the base, and contains genuine utopian surplus which is futuristic and ahead of the world at hand.[186] Moreover, such utopian surplus needs to be refunctioned and appropriated for socialist purposes, if it is not to be mobilised by the forces of reaction.[187] Bloch does not deny that all such superstructural contents reflect existing relations between social classes, but he attempts to underline the need for historical materialism to take account of the constitutive potential of such contents, and not to rest content with detecting the reflection of class interests present in them.

Bloch also recognises that historical materialism needs to be rethought as a philosophy of history. For Bloch, historical materialism is not a philosophy of history of a traditional type, but a constitutive leading of an open, undecided world. Because the meaning of history has first to be built, Bloch argues that Marxism needs to inherit the various philosophies of history which have emerged as anticipations: as tasks for theory-praxis (the unity of mankind in the Stoics, universal history in Hegel). Nonetheless, it cannot close history off with a settled interpretation.[188] Bloch stresses that the categories of industrial capitalism cannot be projected on the past, and that close attention to regional variations and to the knotted patterns of the relationships which pertain is necessary. He also recognises that it is necessary to challenge the Euro-centric bias of the Marxist tradition (reflected not least in its category formation), and to give full weight to the immense mass of non-European material, even though this necessarily destroys any simple pattern, introduces complex curves of development, including delays and new starts, and undermines the basic conceptual schema (oriented to England, France, Germany, Russia and classical antiquity) with which Marxism began.[189]

Bloch attempts to overcome the influence of historicism on Marxism, in the sense of a relativism which absolutises the standpoint of its own 'higher' moment in history. He seeks to recover the whole of the past for Marxist research, and to show that it is possible to shape the future by uncovering the unrealised future in the past. In the context of a praxis of anticipation, Bloch argues that it is necessary to construct a horizon of possibilities which points beyond the given, and that the past provides a wealth of models for such constructions: a plethora of possible 'tasks'. Such an approach, based on 'utopian tolerance' and a redemptive intention not confined to the immediate needs of the present, recognises the integrity of the past, in a perspective for which the unrealised past as well as the future is 'not yet'. In this context, Bloch calls for a more differentiated concept of 'progress' in Marxism, which recognises the relative invalidity of any simple concept of progress in regard to superstructural contents; that what is next is not necessarily better; that there are 'losses on the march forward'; that advanced superstructural achievements may occur in societies in which the base is relatively backward; and that there are vastly different rates and patterns of development in different intellectual and cultural areas.[190] He breaks with the fetish of linear progress and with developmentalist interpretations of the historical process, and argues that a spatial dimension is necessary to allow for the multiverse of polyphonous phenomena history contains, especially the disproportionate development of the multi-layers of time found in particular societies.[191] Such a differentiated concept of progress would allow Marxism to take account of the specificity of particular societies, including the different time structures of different superstructures, and to interpret them as experiments for the *humanum* with constitutive potential. In so far as Bloch claims that history has an invariant utopian direction and can end in 'fulfilment', his position remains 'historicist' in Popper's sense;[192] but it is a utopian historicism for which the meaning of history is not pre-set, but a task for praxis.

Bloch also attempts to renew the ontological dimension in Marxist materialism against the Western Marxist reduction of Marxist materialism to social materialism. Once again, he finds starting points in the classical Marxist texts. Bloch emphasises that Marx, and not only Engels, was an ontological materialist. He cites Marx's doctoral thesis on the difference between Democritus' and Epicurus' concepts of matter, in which Marx rejected Democritus' determinist mechanical materialism in favour of Epicurus' theory of free swerving atoms, allowing for an element of voluntarism and for an energising 'subjective' factor in matter.[193] He also points out that Marx favoured a qualitative ontological materialism in *The Holy Family*, that he was critical of the 'one-sided' materialism of Hobbes and the French Enlightenment, and that he quoted with approval both Boehme's characterisation of matter as 'drive' (*Trieb*), 'life spirit' (*Lebensgeist*), 'tension' (*Spannkraft*), and 'torment' (*Qual*), and Bacon's claim that matter turned a smiling, poetic sensuous face to man.[194] Again, Bloch implies that there can be no absolute distinction between historical and dialectical materialism in Marx, and that there is sufficient evidence for at least the project of a dialectical materialism in Marx's writings.[195] Indeed, for Bloch, Marx's *dicta* on his relationship to Hegel are only intelligible if Marx envisaged a materialism with dialectical features.

In practice, however, Bloch finds the elements of a Marxist dialectical materialism in Engels and Lenin. Bloch follows Engels in holding that ontological materialism implies: (1) the genetic thesis that matter comes before spirit (*Geist*); (2) the epistemological thesis that consciousness 'reflects' the external world, which exists independently of it; and (3) the cosmological claim that what there is, is matter in motion characterised by a universal law of dialectical movement and a unity of material being.[196] Bloch follows Engels' claim that there is no 'matter in general', but only qualitatively different forms of matter, concretely qualified material 'starting points'.[197] He concedes that Lenin spoke of 'matter in general' and 'a philosophical concept of matter'; but he argues that this was only in the context of epistemological materialism, in which 'matter' referred to the external world existing independently of consciousness.[198] Again, Bloch accepts Lenin's claim that the external world exists independently of human consciousness, although he fails to notice that this is a thesis compatible with some forms of idealism, and is not necessarily a 'materialist' claim. Moreover, he attempts to save Lenin's theory of reflection, by emphasising that Lenin held that the reflection of the external world was a complex process in which thought figures and human imagination played a creative role. For Lenin, Bloch claims, the senses and reason were in dialectical oscillation and the categories were subjective 'copies' of the real world, with both sensory and logical features.[199] Nonetheless, even if there is an external world which exists independently of consciousness and which consciousness reflects, consciousness is needed to describe that world. It is also difficult to explain what the specific 'matter' of consciousness is.

Bloch attempts to locate this problem within Engels' emergentist materialism. For Bloch, all matter moves dialectically and there is a qualitative hierarchy of the different levels which this material movement has reached.[200] The matter of the world is dialectical process matter, which leaps from quantity to quality, to higher forms of movement. Bloch finds evidence of such dialectical leaps in the transitions from quanta to the cell and then to consciousness or 'psychic matter'.[201] He accepts Engels' view that consciousness is the highest manifestation of matter, and also his claim that inorganic matter contains a predisposition to produce consciousness; and interprets this to mean that consciousness is a highly qualified form of matter.[202] Moreover, in contrast to Lukács and most Western Marxists, Bloch deals sympathetically with Engels' *The Dialectics of Nature*. He concedes that Engels confused Marx's dialectic with Goethe's concept of polarity, and that his application of dialectics to nature was largely external. He also criticises Engels for postulating the eternal circulation of matter, and for accepting the fatalistic conclusion that the world is bound to end as a dustball.[203] On the other hand, he praises Engels for his critique of staticist thinking ('metaphysics') in the natural sciences, for his preference (like Marx) for Goethe's quality realism against Newton, and for his emphasis on process against mechanism. Bloch's originality is to emphasise the extent to which Engels laid the foundations for a Marxist philosophy of nature, drawing on Renaissance and Romantic sources, which was more than a rewrite of the results of the natural sciences. He stresses that Engels tried to uncover a 'rational kernel' in Oken's theosophical nature philosophy; he also underlines the subversive meaning of Engels' *dictum* (in the preface to *Anti-Dühring*) that romantic nature philosophy stands in the same relation to dialectical materialism as the social utopias do to modern Communism.[204]

Bloch recognises that there are many difficulties associated with Engels' views, and that the problems which ontological materialism raises cannot be solved by a return to the classical Marxist texts. Bloch attempts, however, to set these problems in a new context by rethinking the Marxist concept of matter. He rejects the counter-strategy, which dismisses dialectical materialism as a form of 'materialist idealism'. Bloch concedes that there are objective aporias in the way of any concept of dialectical matter, and also problems about the relationship between dialectical materialism and the natural sciences. However, he argues that the emancipatory critical character of Marxism demands a projective attempt to make sense of the world, even if this attempt needs to be constantly revised in light of subsequent developments.

Granted that Marxism must integrate the results of the natural sciences and affirm the progressive character of the natural sciences for social development,[205] Bloch holds that Marxism cannot leave the interpretation of the world to the natural sciences. On the contrary, Marxism relates the history of the natural sciences to the development of the forces of production, and to the determinate relations between man and man and man and nature under a given mode of production. It reveals the social, class-related character of natural scientific theoretical production, and poses the critical question of the social relations implicit in both the natural sciences and the technology of a given society.[206] Marxism cannot ignore either the abstract relation to the material substratum implicit in capitalist science and technology, or the commodity, abstract mathematical form which the natural sciences have taken under the capitalist mode of production since Galileo.[207] He follows Engels in insisting that Marxism must provide a critique of the 'metaphysical staticism' and 'abstraction' of the natural sciences, not *qua* sciences, but as ontological accounts of the world. He offers himself a detailed critique of the relativism of modern physics and, in particular, 'idealist' interpretations of it.[208] Like other dialectical materialists, he is not adverse to interpreting quantum physics, with its electrical fields, micro-physical indeterminism and space-time continuum, as a confirmation of dialectical materialism. But he also insists on a Marxist critique of contemporary philosophies of science, which shows that the problem of a qualitative nature remains after Galileo and even Einstein, together with other traditional problems in philosophical physics which contemporary science avoids but does not solve.[209] Here Bloch's position is consistent with trends in contemporary realism.[210]

In an attempt to reopen the problem of how to conceive of matter in a Marxist context, Bloch provides a Marxist history of philosophical concepts of matter which combines immanent critique with the uncovering of anticipation.[211] He uses Lenin's famous *dictum* that clever idealism is closer to clever material-ism than unintelligent materialism, to justify a history of material-ism which contrasts with the usual run-through materialist thinkers from Democritus to Plekhanov. The history of philo-sophical concepts of matter, Bloch argues, illustrates the para-dox that it is often the idealists who are the best teachers from whom to learn what matter is, just as it is the materialists who are the best teachers from whom to learn about thought.[212] On the basis of this insight, Bloch provides the most original history of materialism in the Marxist tradition, in which the concepts of matter developed by idealist philosophers are treated as more philosophically significant than the matter concepts of the phil-osophers who were materialists. Almost all the great philosophers after Democritus were not materialists or not-yet-materialists, Bloch emphasises, and it is from these philosophers (rather than from the *epigoni* who were materialists) that Marxists need to learn.[213] Thus, according to Bloch, Marxists need to learn from the voluntaristic materialism of Epicurus; from the Stoic concept of a *logos spermatikos* or a direction giving principle in matter; from Plotinus' paradox of 'intelligible matter'; from Leibniz's concept of matter with impeded tendency and objective pre-dispositions; from Schelling's doctrine of potencies and view of nature as capable of a qualitative transformation or 'resurrection'; from Hegel's qualitative 'gothic' matter with dialectical leaps from quantity to quality; even from the theosophical matter concepts of Oken and Baader, with their implication that matter can undergo an eschatological transformation or 'nature sab-bath'. By drawing attention to the pre-appearance (*Vor-Schein*) of materials with constitutive potential in the history of material-ism, Bloch extends the limits of the normal understanding of matter and places the more familiar materialisms of Democritus, Hobbes, Lamettrie and Holbach in a wider historical context. He also relates the problem of how to conceive of matter to the need to provide continuing determinations of goals for theory-praxis. In this subject-object praxis-related perspective, Bloch makes a series of original moves in Marxist materialism which serve to draw attention to fundamental problems evaded or glossed over in the Marxist tradition.

First, Bloch takes up the problem of how to conceive of the relationship between matter and consciousness, which has not been solved in any philosophical system. In an extension of the Marxist tradition, Bloch argues that *logikon* or the logical is an objective attribute of matter.[214] According to Bloch, the logical is not something added or introjected by human consciousness on a reason-strange world, but the world itself has logical-like features and contains relations approximate to the relations of human reason.[215] For Bloch, a form of this position is required by the success of thinking in knowing and changing the world, not least through the natural sciences. In a refunctioning of Abelard's doctrine of *conformitas*, Bloch implies that the logical in human consciousness can find what conforms or corresponds to it in the world.[216] This conformity is not mechanical or always already given; it must be tested and produced by praxis. But for Bloch, the fact that rectified or corrected thinking can find such a conformity in the world, implies that world has a logical-like character, a predisposition to categorial formation and to the realisation of goals set by men.[217] Bloch, however, goes further. He claims that a dialectical materialism is necessarily a logical materialism and that matter is qualified with direction and finality.[218] For Bloch, there is a direction giving principle in matter: a dialectical materialist 'truth' of the Stoic *logos spermatikos* in the form of the materialist dialectic (*Realdialektik*) as the only ground and universal law of the world.[219] He interprets the leaps from quantity to quality postulated by dialectical materialism as evidence of a drive to self realisation or self qualification, and the leap from inorganic matter to consciousness as evidence of a drive in matter to self reflection. Similarly, he argues that matter is form-laden and contains an energetic drive (*Formtrieb*) to higher forms.[220] There is a logical dimension in matter as a dialectical process which develops towards something still not reached, especially in the teleological operation of the driving tendency and the entelechtic latency:

> The logical, in contrast to the circulation of what is alien to purpose, hostile to purpose, takes place in the grasped process of dialectical matter — above all teleologically, certainly with a *prius* of the causal, but nonetheless with an immanent primacy of the teleological, that is, of the driving tendency, the entelechtic latency.[221]

Here Bloch the recursive modernist attempts to set Aristotle's doctrine of entelechy 'on its feet' in dialectical materialism. He refunctions Aristotle's backward looking conception of entelechy and argues that the entelechy developing in the world is open and 'not yet'. Not only the movement of matter, but matter as a whole, Bloch argues, is uncompleted entelechy; and none of the purpose realising forms present in matter has yet reached adequation. As a result, the whole of matter is open to developing finality, and has an invariant utopian direction towards entelechy, which is not yet.[222] Bloch's position here assumes a subject-object perspective, and is designed to relate to future possibilities for praxis. His aim is not to set up a naturalistic ontological materialism, but to eliminate dualism from dialectical materialism. Because Marxist materialism is a subject-object materialism for which the subject belongs to the world, Bloch argues that dialectical materialism overcomes the traditional dualisms between spirit and matter, thinking and being, reason and sensuousness,[223] even though the correlate of the logical in the extra-human world cannot be reduced to the human categories which pre-grasp it, and even though the world-informed character of human consciousness must always be tested by praxis.

Second, in an attempt to break with the concealed panlogism of Marxist materialism, Bloch argues for a new primacy of particulars in a Marxism which recognizes that materialism is not yet matter. He provides a detailed Marxist analysis of the treatment of the problem of particulars and universals in the history of philosophy,[224] and argues that Marxism makes possible an advance on the traditional problem by interpreting the antinomies between particulars and universals as objective features of matter which can only be resolved by theory-praxis to develop matter to a stage at which they do not occur.[225] Because the world is still unfinished and contains such objective antinomies, there can be no wholly satisfactory, already made out ontological materialism, Bloch implies. Marxist materialism must be open-ended and problem directed, not a finished monism or a historiosophy of social universals. Hence, Marxism needs to take account of both (1) the discrepancies and gaps which the world contains, including the many alterities which seem alien to any projection of purpose; and (2) the intensive particulars in which a tendency to a possible *universum* appears.[226]

Third, Bloch takes up the vexed problem of a materialist

theory of categories in the context of historical-dialectical materialism. As a Marxist Bloch stresses the socio-economic background to the history of theories of categories, and that each mode of production produces its own categorial cohesion. He denies, however, the standard Marxist claim that categories simply reflect the relations of production and exchange in a given society, and argues that categories reflect the world at hand in a creative way, which (1) designates possible tasks for praxis; and (2) anticipates future collections and cohesions of the process.[227] All categories are open and changeable, Bloch argues, and take part in a process of transmission in which they can be burst open in the future and made to cover new contents.[228] They are active and constitutive, and build themselves as they 'lead' and 'organize' the process.[229] At the same time a materialist theory of categories recognises that categories, as the most general terms of relation, are statements which reflect the most general forms of existence (*Daseinsweisen*).[230] It follows that Marxism requires a materialist theory of categories which takes account of both these perspectives.

Bloch attempts to provide such a theory of categories in his great late work, *Experimentum Mundi* (1975). Bloch argues that Marxism cannot inherit Hegel's panlogical theory of categories even in a materialist form, and requires an entirely new initiative, which breaks with all panlogism as well as with the contemplative staticism of traditional categorial analysis.[231] In *Experimentum Mundi* Bloch relates the problem of a materialist theory of categories to the need to give a praxis of anticipation the primacy in determining the future of an experimental world. He distinguishes between frame categories such as causality, finality and latent substantiality; self-manifesting form categories; and intercentring communication categories such as region (history, man, nature) and principle.[232] In each case, he insists on a finalistic dimension, but he also outlines an unprecedented categorial openness, which represents the world as changeable and not as a finished ontological system. Moreover, in contrast to all panlogical materialism, Bloch stresses the need for Marxism to recognise that the world contains intensive features ('the thelic') which cannot be represented in purely logical terms, and calls for an inheritance of von Hartmann's dual theory of categories in Marxism. All the categories of the process, Bloch claims, are not yet successful attempts to identify the What of the That, and every category is a tensional relation between a-logical intensity and logical law.[233] Every category involves a 'lifting up and turning out' of the unmediated through logically preformed predication and there is thelic material in the categories just as the thelic itself has logical features.[234] Granted that the speculative features of Bloch's von Hartmannesque theory of categories may need to be bracketed, Bloch's attempt to provide a constitutive theory of categories for a changeable, unfinished world is immensely rich in theoretical innovations which are capable of further development.

Finally, Bloch attempts to overcome the inheritance of the bourgeois devaluation of matter in Marxism, with the pessimism and resignation it implies, and to supplement Marxist materialism with a new *speculative* materialism. Because Marxist materialism is a 'materialism forwards', for which the totality of dialectical process matter exists on the horizon of the future, Bloch emphasises that what can be brought out of matter depends on the purpose content which men project as a basis for theory-praxis. It follows that what matter can become is a question for theory-praxis, and not a theoretical question for contemplative philosophy. Materialism, for Bloch, means the explanation of the world from itself,[235] but the world is still open and unfinished, and a Marxism oriented to praxis does not foreclose the nature of the world with premature ontological characterisations. On the contrary, Bloch argues that Marxist materialism must become a utopian materialism: a materialism for which utopia and matter belong together.[236] Utopia, Bloch claims, is a function of matter with *real* anticipation, and Marxist materialism needs to be expanded to take account of utopian function, which provides immanent anticipations of what is becoming possible in the process.[237]

In a radical reorientation of Marxist materialism towards an open future which can be determined by human action, Bloch argues that Marxism requires a materialism based on the theory-praxis of utopian function, for which matter contains a utopian *totum* as its immanent horizon (*speculari*).[238] It requires a materialism which derives perspective and goals for theory-praxis from the *real* anticipation which the world contains, including a Marxist inheritance of the mythical nature pictures which have emerged in the process.[239] Men cannot think too highly of matter, Bloch claims, and must rebel against every matter concept which falls short of what may still be possible, especially since matter with *real* anticipation contains the utopian horizon of a possible 'last matter'.[240]

Bloch grounds the utopian excess of a *materia ultima* on the pre-appearance (*Vor-Schein*) found in the process, and on a Marxist inheritance of the speculative matter concept of the Aristotelian Left.[241] According to Bloch, Aristotle distinguished between being-according-to-possibility (*kata to dynaton*) and being-in-possibility (*dynamei on*), but made both forms of possibility passive and confined activity to the immaterial forms. Under the influence of Avicebron's doctrine of universal matter however, the Aristotelian Left, especially Avicenna and Averroes, interpreted the forms as material. Hence, for the Aristotelian Left, matter became self creative, active form-laden matter, a fermenting womb which produced new contents as it developed.[242] Bloch admits that this concept of the immanent creativity of matter, which passed into European thought through Amalric of Bena, David of Dinant and Bruno, was bound up with mystical and even pantheist speculations; but he argues that Marxism needs to inherit the rational kernel in this mystical shell if Marxist materialism is to escape from static ontology and a backward looking conception of the world as settled and finished.

Refunctioned in the context of a new speculative materialism, *dynamei on* means: (1) that the womb of matter is not exhausted by what has already come to be; (2) that more and better can become actual than has done so already; and (3) that the possibility content of matter can be further extended by human labour. For Bloch, matter is a forward moving, active substratum of dialectically developing possibilities with possible finalistic structuration, and grounds the horizon concept of a possible realm of freedom in which the thing in itself could become the thing for us. *Dynamei on* is the substratum not only of developing matter, but of the developing final *novum*, which, if it were realised, could create the conditions for the realisation of the realising factor.[243] Thus, Bloch's speculative materialism ends with the subject-object perspective of a future in which the experiment for a utopian world stuff (beyond the limitations of any present 'matter') could end in success.

Bloch's attempts to supplement Marxist materialism are intricate, and inevitably controversial. Bloch makes the unusual

move of affirming both the humanist materialism of the young
Marx and dialectical materialism. As a result, he complicates the
standard discussion by introducing an ontological materialist
perspective into the discussion of historical materialism, and a
historical materialist perspective into the discussion of dialectical
materialism. Many of Bloch's attempts to rethink historical
materialism are perceptive, although his work is betrayed by a
lack of analytical sharpness and an inability to come to terms
with detailed economic questions. His grasp of concrete
historical detail is exceptional, and he provides one of the most
subtle treatments of superstructural phenomena to be found
anywhere. On the other hand, his approach is syncretist, and he
fails to come to terms with the possibility that Marxism does
involve an externalist determinism which defeats man's more
radical hopes. Bloch's work on ontological materialism is characteristically bold rather than satisfactory. Nonetheless, it provides
models capable of further development, and strikes at the ontological closure at the heart of the Marxist tradition. It also re-
emphasises human responsibility for the future, and the truth
that no one knows what possibilities may finally be brought
forth from history and nature. The difficulty is that Bloch
sophisticates ontological materialism to a point which threatens
to deprive it of coherence. Materialism is usually taken to imply
a prevalence of what is actual now. Moreover, Bloch's emphasis
on utopia and finality in a 'materialism forwards' means that
the world is explained, in important respects, by what is 'not
yet', and only a distant possibility. It involves a radical shift of
emphasis from the 'materiality' of the actual to the 'materiality'
of the 'not yet'. Again, materialism is usually thought to imply
some objective limitation on human hope. Bloch's equation of
matter with dialectically developing real possibility, however,
removes the force of such limitations, both because nothing
can be ruled out *a priori* as a possibility after the *eschaton*, and
because whatever men hope for and project over long periods is
deemed to have a correlate in real possibility. Moreover, Bloch's
approach suggests that it *is* possible to think too highly of
matter, because if matter is transformed from an objective limiting factor into a not-yet-fully actual substratum of utopian real
possibilities, then it becomes as speculative as utopia itself, and
functions to guarantee the possibility of developments which
Marxists would normally regard as hopelessly unrealistic. Apart

from his immense philosophical learning, which again and again widens the ambit of the standard discussion, Bloch's strength is that he grasps both the impossibility of transcending the subject-object relation and the continuing force of the perspectives historically associated with 'idealism'. He is also painfully aware that materialism is and remains a problem in a Marxist context, which no adoption of an allegedly scientific materialist method can wholly resolve. Bloch himself, however, fails to elucidate precisely what 'materialism' involves. Indeed, his attempt to combine and reconcile the views of Marx, Engels and Lenin, as if they formed a consistent materialism, and were not, at certain points, in tension or even contradiction, leads him to use the term 'matter' in ways which deprive it of clear meaning. Bloch speaks of 'human matter', 'conscious matter', 'historical matter', 'thought matter', even of 'the last matter of the kingdom of freedom', in a way which blurs the distinction between consciousness and the external world, and between materialism as a theory of external determination and materialism as a theory of what there is. He is convinced that 'what there is' is matter, but he does not show that 'matter' is what there is, or that 'what there is' is usefully described as 'material'. On the contrary, to the extent that he tends to label whatever is real as 'matter', some term other than materialism could usefully be used to characterise his position.

Granted these deficiences, Bloch's attempt to develop Marxist materialism in a subject-object direction is one of the most original initiatives in the Marxist tradition. It challenges the one-sided externalist materialism at the heart of the Marxist tradition in a way which implies that the project of a Marxist materialism is full of problems which require more rigorous consideration.

6 Exodus

The true genesis comes not at
the beginning but at the end.
The Principle of Hope

Ernst Bloch — Marxist philosopher or modernist seer? Bloch is
both. He is a thinker of the deep will in an age which thinks too
quickly. Like Heidegger, Bloch invites criticism, much of it just;
but he survives his critics because of the meditative power of his
thinking, which strikes into areas which others barely touch. His
final significance depends on the fecundity of his utopian
imagination.

   A study which seeks to introduce Bloch cannot hope to provide an exhaustive exegesis of his position in each area. Nor can
it usefully attempt a detailed internal critique of his positions,
which assumes that these positions are fully evident. The tendency to advance such a critique dominates the existing German
literature at a time when the understanding of Bloch's views is
too minimal to make such a critique cogent. Moreover, the need
for such critique scarcely arises if Bloch is indeed advancing the
naïve, dogmatically ontological positions usually ascribed to
him. Obviously, Bloch is neither a philosopher nor a Marxist if
he advances an intellectually irresponsible gnostic futurism, or a
wholly out-of-date identity metaphysics.[1] Indeed, granted this
interpretation, the problem is not to show that Bloch is not a Marxist, but to explain how he could ever have imagined that he was
a Marxist at all. Clearly there is no basis in Marx for any speculation
about an ontological world problem, or for the idea that utopia
pre-appears in the darkness of the moment. Marx had no notion
of totality developing in the world as a whole or of a dialectic
of the real with eschatological implications, and it is difficult to
believe that he would have valued a thinker with such views
more highly than he valued Weitling or Moses Hess. But this
study suggests that Bloch's views are more complex than such a
reading implies, and that Bloch raises very important issues,
which do not fall with the mechanics of his treatment of them
in terms of his own system.

Bloch is a utopian in the philosophical mode who should be read for the challenges he provides to regnant assumptions and for the perspectives he opens up. Read in this way, Bloch may prove to be one of the most seminal minds in the Marxist tradition. Bloch is a heretic *par excellence*, and it is beyond argument that he strains the bonds which link him to the Marxist tradition at crucial points. His importance is that he does so in a way which reveals deficiences of the *doxa*, and calls into question familiar conceptions of its content. Bloch's Marxism is problematic because he attempts to combine Marxism with his own utopian philosophy, and a case can be made for characterising it as a form of 'philosophical revisionism'.[2] This case has an exegetical foundation, in so far as Bloch tends to advance ideas in tension or conflict with Marx's assumptions; it also has a biographical truth, to the extent that Bloch combined his early utopian philosophy with Marxism without the extensive reformulations which such a project would seem to require. Nonetheless, this case should not be used to locate Bloch in a museum of 'revisionisms'.

Bloch is open to the charge that he develops one more 'philosophical Marxism', based on the categories of idealism, which regresses behind Marx in the direction of affirmativist illusions. It is also possible to allege: (1) that he collapses the critical edge of Marx's analyses and replaces it with an over-rhetorical, aestheticist discourse, which perpetuates the history it seeks to overcome, and sets up a methodological irrationalism, based on a failure to define rigorously fundamental concepts or to argue for assertions in full; (2) that he makes no significant contribution to the analysis of the development of capitalism during its greatest period of innovation and expansion, and makes the formation of scientific concepts almost impossible by a conflation of phenomenological appearance with underlying law; (3) that he confuses Marxism with speculative humanism, and with an *avant-garde* philosophical modernism, based on a psychologistic recursion to a teleology of hopes and needs, which has little foundation in a systematic investigation of social and economic developments. Such objections can be rebutted in detail, and also in terms of the schematisms which they assume; but the underlying insight that Bloch always remained a 'bourgeois' intellectual with left adventurist sympathies is not without foundation. Bloch's syncretism and his immanence within

a form of utopian consciousness create insurmountable difficulties throughout his work, which remains remarkably infor-
mal, despite its quasi-philosophical form. It is also fair to charge
that Bloch remained isolated throughout his life from working
class organisations, and failed to contribute to the solution of
central problems of Marxist theory, such as the nature of the
revolutionary party, the Marxist theory of the state, the exact
temporality of the causal interaction between the relations of
production and the forces of production, and the scientific
status of notions such as 'alienation', 'fetishism' and 'surplus
value'.

Such tendency critique can be extended in a liberal 'sociology of knowledge' perspective by an attempt to locate Bloch
within the social history of pre-war German intellectuals: as a
mandarin with little knowledge of practical life, who accepted
Marxism as the master key to complex political and economic
questions; and as an assimilated Jewish intellectual, who recovered
his heritage by fusing Messianism with classical German philosophy. Or it can be continued along more Althusserian lines by
arguing that Bloch's work reveals many of the symptomatic
characteristics of 'Western Marxism'.[3] Bloch does illustrate the
tendency for 'bourgeois' intellectuals from literary and philosophical backgrounds to identify Marxism with humanism, to over-
emphasise the *dicta* of the young Marx, and to concentrate on
philosophical and cultural materials to the exclusion of technical
work on social and economic questions. He is close to Czech
philosophers of the Prague Spring, such as Karel Kosík and
Milan Machovec, who attempt to rework traditional religious
and philosophical questions in a Marxist context, and to those
Yugoslav philosophers who interpret Marxism as a utopian
philosophy of praxis rather than a scientistic determinism. His
stress on 'the occlusion of the subject' under capitalism has parallels in the work of phenomenological Marxists such as Banfi
and Paci, and in the existentialist Marxism of Merleau-Ponty
and Sartre. There are also parallels between Bloch's positions
and those of French Marxists such as Rubel, who emphasise
the ethical humanist philosophy of history of the young Marx;
and with the *Arguments* group, with their stress on 'meta-philo-
sophy' (Lefebvre), an 'open system' (Axelos), the critique of
everyday life, and a critical approach to technology. Again, Bloch
is close to those neo-Marxists who emphasise that the obstacles

to a good society are much greater than Marx imagined, whether because 'alienation' is not purely social, or because questions of sexuality require new and more radical solutions, or because the creation of a free society requires more radical initiatives than simply the abolition of private ownership of the means of production. Such tendency critique, however, is misleadingly self confirming, and does not bring out Bloch's originality or the significance of his achievement in the context of Marxism. That Bloch shares Lukács' imprisonment within the terminology of German idealism, that he participates in the controversial emphasis on superstructural factors common to Gramsci and Adorno, that he adulterates Marxism with speculative humanism in the manner of Sartre or Goldmann, that he resurrects the open sympathy for ethical socialism and religion common to Max Adler, Garaudy and Kolakowski, that like Benjamin and Marcuse he fuses Marxism and utopianism without sufficiently clarifying the precise cognitive content of either, may not be as important as the radicalism on which his contribution depends.

Bloch is the Marxist philosopher of the 'not yet'. Granted that the syncretic nature of Bloch's operator 'not yet' deprives his work of the conceptual sharpness it requires, Bloch's 'not yet' involves a conjunction of perspectives of great importance for the Marxist tradition. Bloch's 'not yet' combines *a radical conservative perspective*, which implies that what has already preappeared can have a radical future, with *a revolutionary futurist perspective*, which implies that what has come to be is still changeable. In isolation, these perspectives are familiar, if not always in Marxism. Bloch's contribution is to conjoin them in a way which implies that the Marxist tradition is *not conservative enough*, in that it underestimates the potential relevance of existing and past experience for the making of a good future; and that it is *too conservative,* in that it uncritically burdens the good future with negative features of present and past experience which can potentially be changed. Bloch attempts to introduce an orientation towards the future into almost every area of Marxist thought. At the same time, he attempts to reorient Marxism towards first the hermeneutical analysis, and then the activation of the anticipations of the good future which occur. Bloch does not underestimate the possibility that the 'not yet' may not be utopia. The originality of his Marxism is to relate the openness of the future to maximalist anticipation, in a way which places what the future will contain in the hands of men.

This is also the key to the possible productivity of Bloch's work in the context of a reconstruction of Marxism. The need for a reconstruction of Marxism is widely recognised, both by Marxists, who recognise that it is impossible to remain content with Marx's own nascently incoherent formulations, and by non-Marxists, who recognise the continuing function of Marxism as an ideology of revolution and that Marx's historical materialism is crucial for contemporary political and social theory. No satisfactory reconstruction of Marxism could be based on Bloch, but a reconstruction of Marxism is unlikely to succeed unless it resolves some of the many problems to which Bloch draws attention. Because, in a sense, Bloch comes to Marxism as someone who is on the other side, he is able to highlight failures and weaknesses in the Marxist tradition, which other Marxists overlook, in a way which relates the need to overcome those failures and weaknesses to the historical development of Marxism itself. Because Bloch approaches every question via his operator 'not yet', he is able to challenge Marxists to inherit the total past without historicism, and to assimilate the 'truth' of conservative thought, in so far as it emphasises intra-historical immanence, the continuing effectivity of past experience, and the need to work out of the particularity of historically determined situations. Similarly, Bloch's sympathies with the 'irrational', in the sense of those aspects of epistemological experience which are repressed or de-represented by regnant epistemology, allow him to confront the epistemological passivity of the Marxist tradition and its underlying positivism in a way which challenges the abstract rationalism of the post-Enlightenment left, and indicates the need for a wider Marxist rationalism, which seeks the rational in the irrational, and takes account of the whole of human experience. If there is an element of self intoxication in Bloch inseparable from the rhetoric of his style, the charge of irrationalism is premature. More than any other Marxist, Bloch pioneers a philosophy of the irrational, including the not yet rational, which takes account of what cannot yet be reduced to entirely sober terms. He also challenges the naïvety of both Marxist and non-Marxist over-idealised approaches to the philosophy of language, which ignore what cannot be said and also what is said when it is still strictly unconstruable.

Again, Bloch's reassertion of a utopian dimension in Marxism is valuable, both as a critique of the assimilation of the negative features of capitalism into Marxism, and as an attack on the reduction of Marx's broad horizons to a narrow Communism, characterised by sectarianism, philistinism and resentment. More than any other Marxist, Bloch points to the need for a pathology of Marxism as it has developed, which relates its mixture of bad utopianism and sterile objectivism to an historical and social conditioning which does not cease to operate because Marxists believe they have broken with 'bourgeois ideology' and capitalism. In this sense, Bloch's work suggests that a post-capitalist Marxism is both needed, and more difficult to achieve than Marxists have hitherto imagined. It is true that Bloch's own critique of utopia is limited, that he fails to elucidate the real dangers of utopian thought, and sometimes repeats them in a cognitive form. Bloch refunctions the utopianism of the past without radically extending the range of things hoped for, and without providing convincing anticipations of additional developments. His utopianism has a conservative character, and contains no systematic critique of either affirmativist maximalism or expressionist appearance. Moreover, because Bloch relates his critique of utopia almost exclusively to Marxism, his critique is omissive of the universal rehabilitation of utopia which is possible, and which could provide a powerful critique of contemporary philosophy as well as Marxism. On the other hand, Bloch's rehabilitation of utopia in Marxism draws attention to the need for a new psychological and cultural style in Marxism, and sets limits to what a one-sidedly rationalist Marxism can hope to achieve. More than any other Marxist, Bloch reasserts the extent to which fantasy, dreams and illusions belong to the future social history of mankind, both as a functional ingredient in social change and as a non-defeasible feature of human existence.

Bloch's work also serves to challenge the tendency in the Marxist tradition for regional doctrines to become displaced beyond the area of their proper application. Here Bloch's work goes to the underlying failure of Althusser's attempted reconstruction of Marxism. Bloch and Althusser converge in their willingness to go beyond Marx's *dicta*, in their insistence on the need to reformulate historical materialism to allow for more complex accounts of causality and contradiction, and in their rejection of the classless site of knowledge on which pre-

Marxist philosophy depends. Bloch, however, offers a correction of Althusserian theoreticism by drawing attention to the inheritance of traditional, especially Aristotelian, ontological and anthropological frameworks in Marx, so that the reconstructionist question becomes how Marxism confronts the aporias present in each regional area, and not how it whisks them away with a theoreticist rupture, intimidating terminology, or an ungroundable methodologism. On the crucial question of the scientific status of Marxism, it is Bloch rather than Althusser who grasps the social immanence of the sciences, and the need for a break with self-guaranteed foundings of Marxism's emancipatory intention. Bloch also challenges the Marxist tradition, as Althusser does not, to rethink the need for a new qualitative relationship to nature, including the need for a Marxist concept of nature which goes beyond passivity and the ontologisation of the natural sciences. Again, if Bloch as well as Althusser fails to provide the rigorous critique of the materialism-idealism distinction necessary for a reconstruction of Marxism, he draws attention to some of the fundamental problems which such a critique would reveal, including the objective difficulty of any distinction between idealism and realism, the complexity of any attempt to rethink the identity of thought and being, and the impossibility of 'liquidating idealism', in all senses, without making Marxism an intellectual adventurism of the most dangerous kind.

Then, Bloch's Marxist process philosophy is full of model ideas, which are capable of further development. Bloch strikes at the ontological closure at the heart of the Marxist tradition, in the name of an eschatology of the 'uncovered countenance' or a humanly adequate world, and in the name of a negative anthropology, for which man is 'not yet' and needs to be changed as much as society. He pioneers an activist political metaphysics. Despite the intra-systematic weakness of this metaphysics, Bloch's Open System raises the possibility that Marxism requires a new conception of reality based on the postulate of an open world, in which what things can become can, in part, be determined by theory-praxis. It is possible to argue that, on the contrary, Marxism needs to be strictly confined to a proto-science of social development, that the errors and evasions of classical Marxism are intrinsic — and that political and social progress beyond Marx requires different orientations and stricter canons of philosophical rigour and scientificity than Marxism provides.

In so far, however, as Marxism is established both as a critical discourse and as an ideology of revolution, Open System serves to open up the problems of a Marxist ontology and theory of categories, in a way which implies that these problems require a more thorough consideration than they have yet received. No other Marxist has done so much to draw attention to the possible presence of a process philosophy dimension in Marxism, or posed the problem of Marxism's quiescent attitude to the history of Western metaphysics in so sharp a form.

Similarly, Bloch's hermeneutical analyses represent an achievement in contemporary hermeneutics. Bloch attempts to thematise the unconstruable elements in the world, which otherwise can be given a reactionary functionality. He gives the hermeneutical task a political significance which is original in terms of the Marxist tradition. Here, in a post-modernist perspective, Bloch's analyses could be extended in the light of the work of French theorists such as Marin, Lyotard, Deleuze, Boutang and Kristeva.[4] Bloch provides critical materials for a history and geography of desire and for an analysis of utopian figures and texts which indicate a referent not present in their discourse. He also develops a concept of traces which could be usefully challenged in light of a Derridarian semantics with its emphasis on difference and erasure. Bloch's work as a whole is subject to a Derridarian critique; it also contains elements for a positive deconstruction of Western metaphysics against Derrida, based on the insight that the meaning which is never completely present has positive rather than negative connotations. Bloch's work could also be brought into conjunction with Kristeva's *sémanalyse*. Kristeva seeks to explore the prelinguistic 'semiotic chora' below the symbolic order, and to elucidate its content as an arrangement of drives. Her work opens up (1) the question of the interpretation of those signifying practices (especially magic, art and religion) which cannot be reduced to the symbolic order; and (2) the question of how the 'semiotic chora' relates to the symbolic ordering of social formations, questions which Bloch's own work raises from a different standpoint.

Finally, Bloch lays the foundation for a new approach to the problem of the future in Marxism, based on anticipation. Here, Bloch goes beyond the philosophies of the future of Cieszkowski, Feuerbach and Moses Hess. If Bloch fails to prove that Marxism is in fact a tendency science which indicates the next step, and

provides no clear methodology for distinguishing genuine anticipations from recurrent illusions, he does suggest that a more
complex temporal analysis can liberate Marxism from a will to a
disjunction between the future and the past. He also pioneers a
new approach to historical materials in Marxism with his concept of praxis, which releases anticipations in the past as anticipations in the present. If Bloch shares the standard Marxist tendency to historicise the problem of transcendence and to set up
the alienation of a future horizon in which the reality of human
finitude is mythologically resolved, he also witnesses to the
productivity of a deeply willed revolutionary optimism. Here,
Bloch's naïvety is not necessarily naïve. It can be understood as
a Kantian claim that the structure of human finitude is such
that only an optimistic stance brings into activity the most
creative recesses of practical reason. Or it can be understood as
post-Nietzschean historical shrewdness, which recognises that the
constitutive power of human hope makes possible more than a
thoroughly disenchanted consciousness can permit. Such a perspective is dangerous unless it is more closely allied with analytical rigour and a procedurally oriented rationalism than it is in
Bloch. It is also powerless as long as it is confined to purely rhetorical satisfactions. On the other hand, a reconstruction of
Marxism which came to terms with Hume, Quine and Kripke,
which admitted the moral seriousness of intellectual caution
and committed itself to new and discouraging standards of clar-
ity and exactitude, could find in Bloch indications for a reworking of Kant's practical reason as well as post-Heideggerian questions of the most demanding kind. In so far as Bloch's optimism
takes a methodological form, it is fair to conclude that such optimism produces a maelstrom of ill-digested material in which
what is seminal is hard to disentangle from the rhetorical excess:
that Bloch's utopian tolerance towards his own thoughts means
that he fails to develop systematically what is really new. But
even here Bloch's failure is corrective of contemporary illusions
about a pristine way to truth, and reminds more careful thinkers
of other bold men from whom they have much to learn.

A Marxism which understood the phenomenon of Ernst
Bloch and allowed such an understanding to modify its strate-
gies would have made a considerable advance. Armed with a
non-naturalistic understanding of history and equipped with a
hard-won awareness of the misdirection of even the best inten-

tioned human efforts, such a Marxism could mobilise the insight that the future is open to more and not less severe confrontations with the parameters of human servitude. To this extent, Bloch's optimism could become emancipatory if it were interpreted to mean that hope is not defeated when it confronts its failures, but finds in them the 'educated hope' which must finally be defined as success. A more specialised study would show that Bloch's optimism allows him to go beyond Benjamin: to envisage a Marxist inheritance of theology and esoterism free from the pessimistic nostalgia and the concessions to disenchantment to which Benjamin is subject. It would also show that the same optimism allows him to go beyond Adorno's sociology of illusion and abstractionist break with the concept of identity which culminates in an acceptance of a permanent heteronomy of the object. Such optimism is tragic, but it also leads to a heightening of the circumstances in which it fails. It is difficult to believe that Bloch is right when he endorses Augustine's *dictum* that 'we ourselves shall become the seventh day'; but it is possible to think that the excess of such an affirmation illumines the grandeur of our finitude in a way which a serious reconstruction of Marxism should not ignore.

Notes

CHAPTER 1

1. See J. H. Horn (ed.), *Ernst Blochs Revision des Marxismus* (East Berlin: VEB Deutscher Verlag der Wissenschaften, 1957) especially pp. 25–33, 52; for a Soviet view, see M. Iovchuk, *Philosophical Traditions Today* (Moscow: Progress Publishers, 1973) pp. 235, 269, 293, and for more recent works on Bloch see D. Horster, *Bloch zur Einführung* (Hannover: SOAK-Verlag, 1977); H. H. Holz, *Logos spermatikos Ernst Blochs Philosophie der unfertigen Welt* (Darmstadt und Neuwied: Luchterhand, 1975); H. L. Reinicke, *Materie und Revolution. Eine materialistisch-erkenntnistheoretische Untersuchung zur Philosophie von Ernst Bloch* (Kronberg: Scriptor-Verlag, 1974); P. Widmer, *Die Anthropologie Ernst Blochs* (Frankfurt a. M.: Akademische Verlagsgesellschaft, 1974).
2. See, for example, Jürgen Moltmann's perceptive introduction to *Man On His Own*, trans. E. B. Ashton (New York: Herder and Herder, 1970) pp. 19–29, an English translation of an anthology of selections from Bloch; *Religion im Erbe. Eine Auswahl aus seinen religionsphilosophischen Schriften* (Frankfurt a. M.: Suhrkamp, 1959); I. Frenzel, 'Philosophie zwischen Traum und Apokalypse', in *Über Ernst Bloch*, 3rd ed. (Frankfurt a. M.: Suhrkamp, 1971) pp. 17–41, especially pp. 36–7; J. Rühle, 'The Philosopher of Hope: Ernst Bloch' in L. Labedz (ed.), *Revisionism. Essays on the History of Marxist Ideas* (London: George Allen and Unwin, 1962) pp. 166–78, especially p. 172; M. Solomon, 'Marx and Bloch: Reflections on Utopia and Art', *Telos*, no. 13, Fall (1972) pp. 68–85; W. A. Johnson, *The Search for Transcendence* (New York: Harper and Row, 1974) ch. 4: 'Transcendence as "Future" — Ernst Bloch', especially p. 106 ff; J. Moltmann, 'Messianismus and Marxismus', in *Über Ernst Bloch*, op. cit., pp. 42–60; H. Kimmerle, *Die Zukunftsbedeutung der Hoffnung* (Bonn: Bouvier, 1966); A. Jäger, *Reich ohne Gott. Zur Eschatologie Ernst Blochs* (Zurich: EVZ-Verlag, 1969); E. Roeder von Diersburg, *Zur Ontologie und Logik offener Systeme* (Hamburg: Felix Meiner, 1967); R. Damus, *Ernst Bloch: Hoffnung als Prinzip-Prinzip ohne Hoffnung* (Meisenheim am Glan: Anton Hain, 1971); Karl Kränzle, *Utopie und Ideologie. Gesellschaftskritik und politisches Engagement im Werk Ernst Blochs* (Bern: Verlag H. Lang und CIE, 1970); F. Jameson, *Marxism and Form Dialectical Theories of Literature* (Princeton University Press, 1971) p. 117; H. G. Bütow, *Philosophie und Gesellschaft im Denken Ernst Blochs* (Berlin: Ost-Europa Institut, 1963); C. H. Ratschow, *Atheismus im Christentum? Eine Auseinandersetzung mit Ernst Bloch*, 2nd ed. (Gütersloh: Gütersloher Ver-

lagshaus Gerd Mohn, 1971); J. Habermas, 'Ein marxistischer Schelling', in *Über Ernst Bloch*, op. cit., pp. 61-8, originally published in *Merkur*, no. 11 (1960).

3. For Bloch's style, see T. W. Adorno, 'Grosse Blochmusik', in *Neue deutsche Hefte*, no. 69, April (1960) pp. 14 ff; G. Steiner, 'The Pythagorean Genre', in S. Unseld (ed.), *Ernst Bloch zu ehren (sic)* (Frankfurt a. M.: Suhrkamp, 1965) pp. 327-43, and H. H. Holz, 'Das Wesen metaphorischen Sprechens', in *Festschrift, Ernst Bloch zum 70. Geburtstag* (East Berlin: VEB Deutscher Verlag der Wissenschaften, 1955) pp. 101-20.

4. Ehrhard Bahr, *Ernst Bloch* (Berlin: Colloquium, 1974) p. 17, in the *Köpfe des XX. Jahrhunderts* series. This volume contains useful, though highly selective, biographical material, much of it supplied by Karola Bloch. For Bloch's life generally, see Silvia Markun, *Ernst Bloch* (Hamburg: Rowohlt, 1977), and A. Münster (ed.), *Tagträume vom aufrechten Gang. Sechs Interviews mit Ernst Bloch* (Frankfurt a. M.: Suhrkamp, 1977) pp. 20-118.

5. *Spuren* (Berlin: Paul Cassirer, 1930) p. 91; cf. Ernst Bloch, *Gesamtausgabe* (Frankfurt a. M.: Suhrkamp, 1959-77) in sixteen volumes (hereafter *GA*) vol. I, p. 67.

6. *Spuren* (1930), p. 96. cf. *GA*, vol. 1, p. 70.

7. A. Münster (ed.) *Tagträume vom aufrechten Gang*, op. cit., p. 32.

8. *Spuren*, op. cit., p. 97, cf. *GA*, vol. I, p. 71.

9. A. Münster (ed.), *Tagträume vom aufrechten Gang*, op. cit., pp. 27-8.

10. ibid., pp. 26-7.

11. R. Traub and H. Wieser (ed.), *Gespräche mit Ernst Bloch* (Frankfurt a. M.: Suhrkamp, 1975) p. 300.

12. Ehrhard Bahr, op. cit., p. 19. See also 'Nachruf auf Theodor Lipps' (1914), in *Philosophische Aufsätze, GA*, vol. 10, pp. 53-5.

13. A. Münster (ed.), op. cit., p. 110.

14. R. Traub and H. Wieser (ed.), op. cit., p. 300.

15. *Kritische Erörterungen über Rickert und das Problem der modernen Erkenntnistheorie* (Ludwigshafen, 1909) pp. 68 ff.

16. See 'Weisen des "Vielleicht" bei Simmel' (1958), in *Philosophische Aufsätze, GA*, vol 10. pp. 57-60, and G. Simmel, *Fragmente und Aufsätze*, Gertrud Kantorowicz (ed.), (Munich: Drei Masken Verlag, 1923), and *Brücke und Tür* (Stuttgart: Koehler, 1957) pp. 1-16, 29-58, 141-52.

17. *The New Hungarian Quarterly*, Vol. XIII, no. 47, Autumn (1972) p. 90.

18. A. Münster (ed.), op. cit., pp. 104-6.

19. Ehrhard Bahr, op. cit., p. 22.

20. Author's interview with Karola Bloch, 8 December 1977.

21. Margarete Susman's far sighted review in the *Frankfurter Zeitung*, 12 January 1919, is reprinted in S. Unseld (ed.), *Ernst Bloch zu ehren*, op. cit., pp. 383-94.

22. *Geist der Utopie* (1918), *GA*, vol. 16, pp. 298-9, 304 ff, 408-11.

23. *Thomas Münzer als Theologe der Revolution*, *GA*, vol. 2, p. 230.

24. See 'Aktualität und Utopie. Zu Lukács' "Geschichte und Klassenbewusstsein" ' (1923), in *Philosophische Aufsätze, GA*, vol. 10, pp.

598-621. This review originally appeared under the title 'Aktualität und Utopie. Zu Lukács' Philosophie des Marxismus' in *Der neue Merkur*, VII, no. 7 (1924) pp. 457-77.

25. G. Scholem, *Walter Benjamin — die Geschichte einer Freundschaft* (Frankfurt a. M.: Suhrkamp, 1975) pp. 102-3, 109, 113, 139. For a useful preliminary discussion of the Benjamin-Bloch relationship, see Philippe Ivernel, 'Soupçons - D'Ernst Bloch à Walter Benjamin', in *Utopie - Marxisme selon Ernst Bloch*, G. Raulet (ed.), (Paris: Payot, 1967) pp. 265-77.

26. A. Münster (ed.), op. cit., pp.48-50, and S. Markun, *Ernst Bloch*, op. cit., pp. 32-3.

27. For Benjamin's and Bloch's hashish experiments, see W. Benjamin, *Über Haschisch: Novellistisches, Berichte, Materialen*, ed. T. Rexroth (Frankfurt a. M.: Suhrkamp, 1972) pp. 69 ff.

28. *Erbschaft dieser Zeit, GA* vol. 4, pp. 368-71.

29. W. Benjamin, *Briefe*, ed. G. Scholem and T. W. Adorno (Frankfurt a. M.: Suhrkamp, 1966) vol. II, p. 603, cf. p. 424.

30. A. Münster (ed.), op. cit., p. 47.

31. ibid., p. 48.

32. *Erbschaft dieser Zeit, GA*, vol. 4, pp. 33-5.

33. Bloch to Kracauer, 29 June 1926, Bloch-Kracauer correspondence in the Schiller National Museum, Marbach am Neckar.

34. Bloch to Kracauer, 29 April 1931,

35. S. Unseld (ed.), *Ernst Bloch zu ehren*, op. cit., pp. 145-50.

36. A. Münster (ed.), op. cit., pp. 50-1.

37. See, for example, the conversation between Bloch and Adorno 'Etwas fehlt . . . Über die Widersprüche der utopischen Sehnsucht' (1964), in R. Traub and H. Wieser (ed.), op. cit., pp. 58-77.

38. A. Münster (ed.), op. cit., pp. 53-6.

39. ibid., p. 52.

40. *Ernst Blochs Wirkung. Ein Arbeitsbuch zum 90. Geburtstag* (Frankfurt a. M.: Suhrkamp, 1975) p. 48.

41. See Hans Günther's review in *Internationale Literatur*, no. 3 Moscow (1936), and Bloch's reply 'Bemerkungen zur "Erbschaft dieser Zeit" ', *Philosophische Aufsätze, GA*, vol. 10, pp. 31-53.

42. For Bloch's famous debate with Lukács over Expressionism, see 'Diskussionen über Expressionismus' in *Das Wort*, Moscow (1938) 3, no. 6, pp. 103-112, reprinted in the expanded 1962 edition of *Erbschaft dieser Zeit, GA*, vol. 4, pp. 264-75; and Chapter 5 below.

43. For the National Bolsheviks, see K. von Klemperer, *Germany's New Conservatism* (Princeton University Press, 1968), ch. 4, and more generally A. Möhler, *Die Konservative Revolution in Deutschland 1918-32 (sic)* (Stuttgart: Friedrich Vorwerk Verlag, 1950), F. R. Stern, *The Politics of Cultural Despair. A Study in the Rise of German Ideology* (Berkeley: University of California Press, 1961), and G. L. Mosse, *Germans and Jews* (New York: Howard Fertig, 1970) chs 4 and 7.

44. See 'Thomas Manns Manifest' (1937) in *Politische Messungen, GA*, vol. 11, pp. 148-59, especially p. 158.

45. 'Zur Methodenlehre der Nazis' (1936) pp. 176-84, and 'Wiederkehr

der Ideale' (1937) pp. 192-7, both in *Politische Messungen, GA*, vol. 11.

46. 'Poesie in Hohlraum' (1931) in *Literarische Aufsätze, GA*, vol. 9 pp. 117-35, especially pp. 128-9.

47. See Bloch's address to the Congress for the Defence of Culture in Paris in 1935, 'Marxismus und Dichtung' in *Literarische Aufsätze, GA*, vol. 9, pp. 135-43, and 'Rettung der Moral' (1937) in *Politische Messungen, GA*, vol. 11, pp. 236-55.

48. For Bloch's attacks on the Nazis 1932-8, see the section 'Durchbruch und Hölle der Nazis' in *Politische Messungen, GA*, vol. 11, pp. 87-259; and 'Deutschfrommes Verbot der Kunstkritik' (1937) in *Literarische Aufsätze, GA*, vol. 9, pp. 43-56.

49. On the problem of Bloch's attitude to Stalin and his political position generally in the 1930s, see the collection of unrevised essays, *Vom Hasard zur Katastrophe. Politische Aufsätze aus den Jahren 1934-1939*, (issued in response to criticism of the revised texts in *Politische Messungen*), especially 'Kritik einer Prozesskritik' (1937) pp. 175-84, 'Feuchtwangers "Moskau 1937" ' (1937) pp. 230-5 and 'Der Intellektuelle und die Politik' (1938) pp. 336-43; and in English, Bloch's essay 'A Jubilee for Renegades' (1937) trans. D. Bathrick and N. V. Schults, and Oskar Negt's 'Ernst Bloch — The German Philosopher of the October Revolution' trans. J. Zipes, *New German Critique*, no. 4, Winter (1975) pp. 17-25 and 3-16.

50. See 'Über die deutsche Ostorientierung' (1923) in *Politische Messungen, GA*, vol. 11, pp. 70-4.

51. 'Deutsche Armee des Friedens', *Aufbau*, no. 11 (1952), and 'Wahre Rettung abendländischer Kultur' (1954) in *Politische Messungen, GA*, vol. 11, pp. 337-42.

52. See, for example, W. Schubardt, 'Kritische Bemerkungen zu dem Buch "Subjekt-Objekt" von Ernst Bloch', *Einheit*, 7, (1952) 6, p. 600ff; G. Mende, 'Klassisches Erbe der Philosophie', *Aufbau*, no. 10 (1954) p. 277 ff; R. O. Gropp, 'Die marxistische dialektische Methode und ihr Gegensatz zur idealistischen Dialektik Hegels', *Deutsche Zeitschrift für Philosophie*, 2 (1954) 1, pp. 69-112.

53. The title *Das Prinzip Hoffnung* is difficult to translate. *The Principle of Hope* is the standard translation and also the translation preferred by Bloch. Nonetheless, it may be a little misleading since Bloch uses *Prinzip* in the technical sense of *principium* or *archē*. Hope, the *Principle* and *The Hope Principle* are also current. *The Principle — Hope* is more accurate, but perhaps a little too ontological. *Das Prinzip Hoffnung* hints at the technical meaning without committing Bloch to it. Hence, I prefer to retain the standard translation and to correct any misunderstanding with a technical gloss.

54. For the extensive East German literature criticising Bloch, see H. G. Bütow, *Philosophie und Gesellschaft im Denken Ernst Blochs*, op. cit., ch. 3, and Literaturverzeichnis, pp. 154-7.

55. See 'Über Kulturbünde und Verwandtes' (1951) in *Politische Messungen, GA*, vol. 11, pp. 350-7; and 'Parteilichkeit in Wissenschaft und Welt' (1951) in *Philosophische Aufsätze, GA*, vol. 10, pp. 330-44, especially p. 340.

56. ibid., p. 354 and 'Universität, Marxismus, Philosophie' (1949) in *Philosophische Aufsätze, GA*. vol. 10, pp. 270-91, especially p. 278.
57. See 'Über den Begriff Weisheit' (1953), pp. 355-95, and 'Was ist Philosophie, als suchend und versucherisch?' (1955), pp. 395-401, especially p. 400, both in *Philosophische Aufsätze, GA*, vol. 10.
58. See 'Über die Bedeutung der XX Parteitags' (1956), pp. 357-65, especially pp. 359 ff, and 'Brot und Tanz' (1956), pp. 373-4, both in *Politische Messungen, GA*, vol. 11.
59. See 'Hegel und die Gewalt des Systems' (1956), pp. 481-500, and 'Problem der Engelsschen Trennung von "Methode" und "System" bei Hegel' (1956), pp. 461-81, both in *Philosophische Aufsätze, GA*, vol. 10.
60. Ehrhard Bahr, op. cit., p. 72.
61. See the volume of essays against Bloch, J. H. Horn (ed.), *Ernst Blochs Revision des Marxismus*, op. cit., and J. Rühle, 'The Philosophy of Hope: Ernst Bloch', in L. Labedz (ed.), op. cit., pp. 176-8.
62. See the section *Widerstand und Friede* (1961-70) in *Politische Messungen, GA*, vol. 11, pp. 375-483, especially pp. 390-4, 418-24, 471-5, 478-83.
63. 'Marx, aufrechter Gang, konkrete Utopie' (1968) in *Politische Messungen, GA*, vol. 11, pp. 445-58, especially p. 454.
64. Obituary, *The Times*, 6 August 1977. For the German obituaries and funeral speeches, see *Ernst Bloch lebt weiter* (ASTA, Tübingen, 1977) especially pp. 91, 99. A further volume, *Tendenz - Latenz - Utopie* (1978) was published posthumously, containing a diary dating from 1921, parts of Bloch's doctoral dissertation on Rickert and other miscellaneous pieces.

CHAPTER 2

1. For Bloch's emphasis on Nietzsche as the thinker who pointed to a new moral metaphysical philosophy illumined from a world that did not exist, see 'Der Impuls Nietzsches' (1913) in *Durch die Wüste. Frühe kritische Aufsätze* (Frankfurt a. M.: Suhrkamp, 1964 revised edition) pp. 105-9.
2. *Kritische Erörterungen über Rickert und das Problem der modernen Erkenntnistheorie*, op. cit., p. 71. Republished, for the most part, in *Tendez - Latenz - Utopie* (Frankfurt a. M.: Suhrkamp, 1978).
3. *Geist der Utopie* (1918) *GA*, vol. 16, pp. 733, 294, 442, 420ff.
4. *Kritische Erörterungen*, op. cit., pp. 72-9, and *Geist der Utopie* (1923) *GA*, vol. 3, pp. 237-247.
5. For Bloch's early articles on psycho-analysis, see A. Grinstein, *The Index of Psychoanalytical Writings*, vol. I, (New York: International Universities Press, 1956) pp. 186-7. These included: 'Ein Beitrag zur Freudschen Sexualtheorie der Neurosen', *Wiener klinische Wochenschrift*, no. 52 (1907); 'Beitrag zu den Träumen nach Coitus interruptus', *Zentralblatt für Psychoanalyse und Psychotherapie*, no. 2 (1912) pp. 276-7; 'Über Intelligenzprüfungen (nach der Methode von Binet und Simon) an normalen Volksschulkindern und Hilfsschulkindern', *Zeitschrift für die gesamte Neurologie und Psychiatrie*, 17,

224 The Marxist Philosophy of Ernst Bloch

(1) (1913); 'Freie Assoziationen bei Kindern', *Zentralblatt für Psychoanalyse und Psychotherapie*, 3 (1913) pp. 208–9; 'Über das noch nicht bewusste Wissen', *Die weissen Blätter*, 2 (1919) p. 355.

6. *Kritische Erörterungen*, op. cit., pp. 71–9, and *Geist der Utopie* (1918) *GA* vol. 16, pp. 332–42.
7. *Kritische Erörterungen*, op. cit., p. 79.
8. ibid., p. 74.
9. ibid., cf. p. 69.
10. ibid., pp. 70, 75.
11. *Geist der Utopie* (1918) *GA* vol. 16, pp. 332–42, 339, 227.
12. ibid., pp. 275–6.
13. A. Münster (ed.), *Tagträume vom aufrechten Gang*, op. cit., p. 36.
14. *Geist der Utopie* (1918) *GA*, vol. 16, pp. 226, 293–4 and cf. *Philosophische Aufsätze*, *GA* vol. 10, pp. 211–15.
15. *Kritische Erörterungen*, op. cit., pp. 66, 76–7.
16. ibid., pp. 70, 75–80.
17. *Geist der Utopie* (1918) *GA* vol. 16, pp. 332–342.
18. *Kritische Erörterungen*, op. cit., pp. 67–8.
19. ibid., pp. 66–8.
20. ibid., pp. 62–3.
21. *Geist der Utopie* (1918), *GA* vol. 16, p. 388.
22. *Kritische Erörterungen*, op. cit., pp. 8–65.
23. ibid., p. 57.
24. ibid., p. 72 ff.
25. *Geist der Utopie* (1918), *GA* vol. 16, p. 369.
26. ibid., p. 275.
27. *Geist der Utopie* (1923), *GA*, vol. 3, p. 235.
28. *Geist der Utopie* (1918), *GA*, vol. 16, pp. 271–6.
29. ibid.
30. *Geist der Utopie* (1923), *GA*, vol. 3, p. 225.
31. *Geist der Utopie* (1918), *GA*, vol. 16, p. 281.
32. ibid., pp. 276–9.
33. ibid., pp. 280–94, and *Geist der Utopie* (1923), *GA*, vol. 3, p. 229.
34. *Geist der Utopie* (1918), *GA*, vol. 16, pp. 280–94, and *Geist der Utopie* (1923), *GA*, vol. 3, pp. 235–6.
35. *Philosophische Aufsätze*, *GA*, vol. 10, pp. 210–9, especially p. 219; cf. *Geist der Utopie* (1918), *GA*, vol. 16, pp. 370–3, 383–9; and *Geist der Utopie* (1923), *GA*, vol. 3, pp. 251–6, 283–7.
36. *Kritische Erörterungen*, op. cit., p. 74.
37. *Geist der Utopie* (1918), *GA*, vol. 16, pp. 363–73, 388; cf. *Geist der Utopie* (1923), *GA*, vol. 3, pp. 256–62.
38. *Geist der Utopie* (1923), *GA*, vol. 3, p. 260.
39. *Geist der Utopie* (1918), *GA*, vol. 16, pp. 363–73; *Geist der Utopie* (1923), *GA*, vol. 3, pp. 237–67.
40. *Geist der Utopie* (1918), *GA*, vol. 16, pp. 255–61.
41. ibid., p. 338, and R. Traub and H. Wieser (ed.) *Gespräche mit Ernst Bloch*, op. cit., p. 300.
42. *Geist der Utopie* (1923), *GA*, vol. 3, p.345
43. For a discussion of Bloch's philosophy of music, see T. Kneif, 'Ernst

Bloch und der musikalische Expressionismus', in S. Unseld (ed.) *Ernst Bloch zu ehren,* op cit., pp. 277–326.
44. *Geist der Utopie* (1918), *GA,* vol. 16, pp. 227–34.
45. ibid., pp. 227, 228–34.
46. ibid., pp. 19–77.
47. ibid., pp. 268, 274, 121–2, 411.
48. ibid., p. 294.
49. ibid., pp. 339, 341.
50. ibid., p. 274. A form of subject utopianism can also be found in the works of some of the leading theoreticians of Expressionism, including Kurt Pinthus and Ernst Toller. Pinthus wrote of his generation as 'those condemned to their aspirations', with nothing left but their hope in Man and their belief in Utopia'. See the famous Expressionist anthologies *Menschheitsdämmerung* (Rowohlt, 1919) and *Die Erhebung* (Fischer, 1919–20); and J. Willett, *Expressionism* (London: World University Library, 1970) pp. 145–7, 115–17, 124–9.
51. *Geist der Utopie* (1918), *GA,* vol. 16, pp. 341, 339.
52. ibid., p. 9.
53. For the tendency to combine utopianism with eschatology in twentieth century German thought, see L. Bossle, *Utopie und Wirklichkeit im politischen Denken von Reinhold Schneider* (Mainz: Hase & Koehler Verlag, 1965), and Tillich's important essay 'Critique and Justification of Utopia' in F. E. Manuel (ed.), *Utopias and Utopian Thought* (London: Souvenir Press, 1973) pp. 296–309. For a useful comparison of Bloch's and Tillich's fusions of utopianism and eschatology, see H-J. Gerhards, *Utopie als innergeschichtlicher Aspekt der Eschatologie* (Gütersloh: Gütersloher Verlagshaus Gerd Mohn, 1973).
54. *Geist der Utopie* (1918), *GA,* vol. 16, pp. 430–42.
55. *Geist der Utopie* (1923), *GA,* vol. 3, p. 346.
56. K. A. Kutzbach (ed.), *Paul Ernst und Georg Lukács. Dokumente einer Freundschaft* (Düsseldorf: Paul Ernst Gesellschaft, 1973–4) p. 95, and *Geist der Utopie* (1918), *GA,* vol. 16, p. 337.
57. *Geist der Utopie* (1918), *GA,* vol. 16, p. 52.
58. ibid., p. 429.
59. ibid., pp. 238–43. For other discussions by Bloch of Steiner's ideas, see *Literarische Aufsätze, GA,* vol. 9, pp. 27–30; *Erbschaft dieser Zeit, GA,* vol. 4, pp. 128–39; and *Das Prinzip Hoffnung, GA,* vol. 5, pp. 393–8.
60. *Geist der Utopie,* (1918), *GA,* vol. 16, pp. 267–70.
61. ibid., pp. 373–82.
62. ibid., p. 445.
63. *Kritische Erörterungen,* op. cit., pp. 78–9.
64. *Geist der Utopie* (1918), pp. 386–7, 436, and *Philosophische Aufsätze, GA,* vol. 10, pp. 218, 211–17, 209–10, 370–3.
65. A. Münster (ed.) op. cit., p. 27.
66. ibid.
67. For Bloch's early radicalism, see 'Ein Panthersprung' (1911) in *Politische Messungen, GA,* vol. 11, pp. 16–18.

68. *Geist der Utopie* (1918), *GA*, vol. 16, pp. 304-19.
69. A. Münster (ed.) op. cit., p. 44.
70. *Politische Messungen, GA*, vol. 11, pp. 57-9.
71. *Durch die Wüste* (Frankfurt a. M.: Suhrkamp, 1964) p. 35.
72. *Thomas Münzer als Theologe der Revolution, GA*, vol. 2, p. 210.
73. ibid., p. 227.
74. In the 1923 edition Bloch omitted the section entitled *Über die Gedankenatmosphäre dieser Zeit*, and added an introduction to his theory of the not-yet-conscious, and a section on the countenance of the will.
75. *Geist der Utopie* (1923), *GA*, vol. 3, pp. 303-7.
76. ibid., p. 307.
77. ibid., pp. 309, 318.
78. *Durch die Wüste*, op. cit., p. 54.
79. ibid., pp. 301, 303, and *Geist der Utopie* (1918), *GA*, vol. 16, pp. 393-411.
80. ibid., pp. 304-5.
81. ibid., pp. 300, 304.
82. ibid., p. 301.
83. ibid., p. 304.
84. ibid., pp. 304-5, cf. *Geist der Utopie* (1918), *GA*, vol. 16, p. 407.
85. *Geist der Utopie* (1923), *GA*, vol. 3, p. 305.
86. ibid., pp. 304-5.
87. ibid., p. 346.
88. A. Münster (ed.), op. cit., p. 102.
89. Lukács to Bloch, 30 April 1965, Bloch-Lukács correspondence, Lukács Archive Budapest.
90. 1969 Preface to *Magyar irodalom, magyar kultúra* (Budapest, 1970), quoted in *The New Hungarian Quarterly*, vol. XIII, no. 47, Autumn (1972), 'In Memoriam György Lukács (1885-1971), p. 114.
91. A. Münster (ed.), op. cit., p. 106.
92. ibid., p. 103.
93. K. A. Kutzbach (ed.), *Paul Ernst und Georg Lukács*, op. cit., p. 73, Lukács to Ernst, 4 May 1915.
94. ibid., p. 66, Lukács to Ernst, 14 April 1915.
95. See, for example, Bloch to Lukács, 29 February 1911, 19 July 1911, 18 October 1911, 8 February 1912, 20 February 1913, 18 December 1914, 24 August 1916, 22 October 1916, 11 November 1916, 22 January 1917, 23 June 1917, Lukács Archive Budapest.
96. G. Lukács, *The Theory of the Novel*, trans. A. Bostock (London: Merlin Press, 1971) pp. 45, 92, 63.
97. ibid., pp. 144-5.
98. ibid., p. 115.
99. ibid.
100. Bloch to Lukács, 15 March 1915, 5 June 1915, 26 September 1916, 1 December 1916, Lukács Archive Budapest.
101. *Geist der Utopie* (1918), *GA*, vol. 16, p. 347.
102. ibid., pp. 291, 338, 410.
103. ibid., pp. 66-77.

104. cf. Ferenc Fehér, 'The Last Phase of Romantic Anti-Capitalism: Lukács' Response to the War', trans. J. Wikoff, in *New German Critique*, no. 10, Winter (1977) pp. 139–54.
105. A. Münster (ed.), op. cit., p. 107 and M. Lowy, 'Interview with Ernst Bloch' in *New German Critique*, no. 9, Fall (1976) p. 37.
106. R. Traub and H. Wieser (ed.), *Gespräche mit Ernst Bloch*, op. cit., p. 36.
107. M. Lowy, 'Interview with Ernst Bloch', op. cit., pp. 37–8.
108. ibid., p. 38.
109. G. Lukács, *History and Class Consciousness*, trans. R. Livingstone (London: Merlin Press, 1971) pp. 121–49.
110. ibid., pp. 203–4, 222, fn. 68, 157–8.
111. ibid., pp. 160, 177, 192, 205.
112. ibid., p. 194. Lukács might also have applied his strictures on Moses Hess to Bloch see G. Lukács, 'Moses Hess and the Problems of Idealist Dialectics', *Political Writings 1919–29* ed. R. Livingstone, trans. M. McColgan (London: N.L.B., 1972) pp. 181–223.
113. G. Lukács, *History and Class Consciousness*, op. cit., p. 192.
114. ibid., p. 193.
115. 'Aktualität und Utopie zu Lukács' "Geschichte und Klassenbewusstsein" ' (1923), in *Philosophische Aufsätze, GA*, vol. 10, p. 620.
116. ibid., p. 618.
117. ibid.
118. ibid., p. 619.
119. ibid.
120. ibid., p. 621. In the absence of the Paris Manuscripts, Bloch already cited Marx's letter to Ruge in support of his position against Lukács, ibid., p. 621.
121. ibid., pp. 620–1, cf. *Durch die Wüste*, op. cit., pp. 119, 122.
122. G. Lukács, *History and Class Consciousness*, op. cit., p. xviii.
123. G. Lukács, *The Theory of the Novel*, op. cit., pp. 20–1.
124. R. Traub and H. Wieser (ed.), op. cit., p. 34.
125. *Geist der Utopie* (1916), *GA*, vol. 16, p. 406.
126. *Durch die Wüste*, op. cit., p. 18.
127. ibid., pp. 43–56, and 'Hitlers Gewalt' in *Das Tage-Buch*, no. 15, April (1924), reprinted in *Erbschaft dieser Zeit, GA*, vol 4, pp. 160–4.
128. *Durch die Wüste*, op. cit., pp. 54–5.
129. See Bloch's essays 'Sokrates und die Propaganda', 'Die Frau im Dritten Reich', 'Rettung der Moral', 'Vom Hasard zur Katastrophe', 'Kritik der Propaganda', 'Wiederkehr der Ideale', 'Der Expressionismus', 'Avantgarde-Kunst und Volksfront' and 'Der Intellektuelle und die Politik' in *Vom Hasard zur Katastrophe. Politische Aufsätze aus den Jahren 1934–1939* (Frankfurt a. M.: Suhrkamp, 1972), and *Erbschaft dieser Zeit, GA*, vol. 4, pp. 148–9, 173–81, 367–71.
130. *Erbschaft dieser Zeit, GA*, vol. 4, pp. 152–86, and *Literarische Aufsätze, GA*, vol. 9, pp. 117–35.
131. *Erbschaft dieser Zeit, GA*, vol. 4, pp. 104–126, especially p. 113. See Ernst Bloch, 'Nonsynchronism and the Obligation to Its Dialectics', trans. M. Ritter, in *New German Critique*, no. 11, Spring (1977) pp.

22-8. Bloch distinguishes between false and genuine, subjective and objective non-contemporaneity, and between contemporaneous, non-contemporaneous and over-contemporaneous contradictions, see *Erbschaft dieser Zeit*, pp. 116-20. I prefer to translate *Ungleichzeitigkeit* as non-contemporaneity, and not non-synchronism, because Bloch emphasises the non-contemporaneity of social strata with the now (*Jetzt*), even though such strata occupy the same synchronous formal time.

132. *Erbschaft dieser Zeit*, *GA*, vol. 4, pp. 33-5, 105-11.
133. ibid., pp. 75-103, 126-52, 160-4, 202-4. See also A. Rabinbach, 'Ernst Bloch's "Heritage of Our Times" and Fascism' in *New German Critique*, no. 11, Spring (1977) pp. 5-21.
134. See especially the essay 'Zur Originalgeschichte des Dritten Reiches' in *Erbschaft dieser Zeit*, *GA*, vol. 4, pp. 126-45.
135. ibid., p. 111.
136. ibid., p. 154.
137. ibid., pp. 66, 149, 153-5, 197, 217-18, 389, 392, 402.
138. ibid., p. 148.
139. ibid., pp. 146-52, 155-7.
140. ibid., pp. 70-5, 126, 149.
141. See 'Sokrates und die Propaganda' in *Vom Hasard zur Katastrophe*, op. cit., especially p. 103.
142. See 'Wiederkehr der Ideale' in *Vom Hasard zur Katastrophe*, op. cit., pp. 261-70, the interview 'Über Ungleichzeitigkeit, Provinz und Propaganda', in R. Traub and H. Wieser, op. cit., pp. 196-207; and Oskar Negt, 'The Non-Synchronous Heritage and the Problem of Propaganda' in *New German Critique*, no. 9, Fall (1976) pp. 46-70.
143. See Bloch's important reply to Hans Günther's review in *Internationale Literatur*, no. 3, Moscow (1936), 'Bemerkungen zur "Erbschaft dieser Zeit" ' in *Philosophische Aufsätze*, *GA*, vol. 10, pp. 31-53.
144. *Erbschaft dieser Zeit*, *GA*, vol. 4, pp. 405-9.
145. ibid., pp. 387-96.
146. ibid., pp. 387-96 and 146-52, especially pp. 395-6, and 151-2.
147. *Politische Messungen*, *GA*, vol. 11, pp. 225-35, the translations Ernst Bloch, 'A Jubilee for Renegades', trans. D. Bathrick and N. V. Shults, and Oskar Negt, 'Ernst Bloch — The German Philosopher of the October Revolution,' trans. J. Zipes, *New German Critique*, no. 4, Winter (1975) pp. 17-25 and 3-16.
148. F. Engels, *Anti-Dühring* (1878) English trans. (London: Lawrence and Wishart, 1969) pp. 34, 169, 393-4, 436.
149. *Subjekt-Objekt*, *GA*, vol. 8, pp. 55, 162, 383, and *Das Prinzip Hoffnung*, *GA*, vol. 5, pp. 781, 239.
150. Author's interview with Karola Bloch, 8 December 1977.
151. *Politische Messungen*, *GA*, vol. 11, pp. 357-65.
152. ibid., pp. 449, 453.
153. Interview with author, 27 May 1971.
154. *Philosophische Aufsätze*, *GA*, vol. 10, pp. 132-3, and *Das Materialismusproblem*, *GA*, vol. 7, pp. 470-8.

155. *Das Prinzip Hoffnung, GA,* vol. 5, p. 726.
156. The impact of *Spirit of Utopia* on thinkers such as Adorno, Marcuse, Benjamin and Kracauer is beginning to be documented. Bloch himself claimed that it changed the understanding of utopia in Germany. See Bloch to Kracauer 30 April 1929, *Kracauer Nachlass* Schiller National Museum, Marbach am Neckar.
157. K. Mannheim, *Ideology and Utopia,* trans. L. Wirth and E. Shils (London: Routledge & Kegan Paul, 1976) pp. 177–9.
158. ibid., pp. 173–9.
159. See for example K. Popper, *The Open Society and its Enemies* 4th ed., vol. I (London: Routledge and Kegan Paul, 1962) ch. 9. For general studies of utopia see F. E. Manuel, *Utopias and Utopian Thought,* op. cit.; H. J. Krysmanski, *Die utopische Methode* (Cologne and Opladen: Westdeutscher Verlag, 1963); A. Neusüss (ed.), *Utopie: Begriff und Phänomen des Utopischen* (Neuwied: Luchterhand, 1968); R. Ruyer, *L'Utopie et les utopies* (Paris: Presses universitaires de France, 1950).
160. A. Münster (ed.), op. cit., p. 123.
161. *Das Prinzip Hoffnung, GA,* vol. 5, p. 247.
162. ibid., p. 367.
163. *Tübinger Einleitung in die Philosophie, GA,* vol. 13, p. 94.
164. *Das Prinzip Hoffnung, GA,* vol. 5, p. 728.
165. ibid., p. 727.
166. ibid., pp. 334–68, cf. *Tendenz - Latenz - Utopie,* op. cit., pp. 414–17.
167. K. Mannheim, *Ideology and Utopia,* op. cit., p. 195. Mannheim's important discussion of chiliasm as a form of utopianism was influenced by Bloch's *Thomas Münzer als Theologe der Revolution* and he observed an inner affinity between Münzer and Bloch, see pp. 190-1 fn 2, 194 fn 2, and generally 190–7 ff.
168. ibid., p. 193.
169. *Tübinger Einleitung in die Philosophie, GA,* vol. 13, pp. 96–7.
170. *Das Prinzip Hoffnung, GA,* vol. 5, ch. 15.
171. *Politische Messungen, GA,* vol. 11, p. 456.
172. For Bloch's critique of Mannheim's position, see *Erbschaft dieser Zeit, GA,* vol. 4, pp. 285–9.
173. *Literarische Aufsätze, GA,* vol. 9, p. 131.
174. A. Münster (ed.), op. cit., p. 111.
175. *Das Prinzip Hoffnung, GA,* vol. 5, p. 160.
176. ibid., pp. 677-80, 723–9.
177. ibid., p. 727.
178. *Atheismus im Christentum, GA,* vol. 14, p. 346.
179. *Das Prinzip Hoffnung, GA,* vol. 5, p. 726.
180. ibid., pp. 724–5.
181. ibid.
182. A. Schmidt, *The Concept of Nature in Marx,* trans. B. Fowkes (London: New Left Books, 1971) ch. 4, especially p. 133.
183. Marx-Engels, *Selected Works* (Moscow: Progress Publishers, 1969) vol. 1, p. 135.
184. Marx-Engels, *Selected Correspondence,* trans I. Lasker, (Moscow: Progress Publishers, 1975) p. 172.

230   *The Marxist Philosophy of Ernst Bloch*

185. F. Engels, *Socialism: Utopian and Scientific*, first English edition 1892 in Marx - Engels, *Selected Works* (Moscow: Progress Publishers, 1970) vol. 3, pp. 117, 119–20.
186. ibid., pp. 121, 126.
187. ibid., p. 133.
188. L. D. Easton and K. H. Guddat (ed. and trans.), *Writings of the Young Marx on Philosophy and Society* (New York: Anchor Books, 1967) p. 304.
189. A. Schmidt, *The Concept of Nature in Marx*, op. cit., ch. 4, cf. B. Ollman, 'Marx's Vision of Communism: A Reconstruction' in *Critique*, no. 8, Summer (1976) pp. 4–41.
190. A. Schmidt, *The Concept of Nature in Marx*, op. cit., p. 138.
191. *Das Prinzip Hoffnung, GA*, vol. 5, pp. 240–2.
192. ibid., p. 1619.
193. K. Marx, *Critique of the Gotha Program* (1875), in Marx-Engels, *Selected Works* (Moscow: Progress Publishers, 1970) vol 3, p. 19 and *Das Prinzip Hoffnung, GA*, vol. 5, p. 1621.
194. See *Philosophische Aufsätze, GA*, vol. 10, pp. 406–11, and cf. J. Habermas, *Theory and Praxis*, trans. J. Viertel (London: Heinemann, 1974) pp. 239, 248.
195. *Das Prinzip Hoffnung, GA*, vol. 5, p. 598 and *MEGA I*, 2, p. 225 f.
196. *Philosophische Aufsätze, GA*, vol. 10, p. 406. (Bloch's abridgement).
197. *Philosophische Aufsätze, GA*, vol. 10, p. 407. (Bloch's abridgement).
198. *Philosophische Aufsätze, GA*, vol. 10, p. 411. (Bloch's abridgement).
199. *Das Prinzip Hoffnung, GA*, vol. 5, pp. 723–7.
200. *Philosophische Aufsätze, GA*, vol. 10, pp. 287–8.
201. *Das Prinzip Hoffnung, GA*, vol. 5, pp. 725–7.
202. ibid., p. 331–2.
203. *Das Prinzip Hoffnung, GA*, vol. 5, p. 1613. (Bloch's abridgement).
204. *Das Prinzip Hoffnung, GA*, vol. 5, pp. 1609–15, especially p. 1621.
205. ibid., p. 1621.
206. *Das Prinzip Hoffnung, GA*, vol 5, pp. 1605, 1612–13.
207. *Philosophische Aufsätze, GA*, vol. 10, p. 406.
208. ibid., p. 411. For an important study of the sympathies of the young Marx, see A. T. van Leeuwen, *Critique of Heaven* (London: Lutterworth, 1972). In a subsequent volume, van Leeuwen, like Bloch, finds an anti-mundane, qualitative stress in the older Marx, including borrowings from Boehme, see A. T. van Leeuwen, *Critique of Earth* (London: Lutterworth, 1974) ch. 1.
209. See, for example, *Das Prinzip Hoffnung, GA*, vol. 5, pp. 730–83.
210. *Zwischenwelten in der Philosophiegeschichte, GA*, vol. 12, p. 316. For a fuller discussion, see D. Horster, *Die Subjekt-Objekt-Beziehung im Deutschen Idealismus und in der Marxschen Philosophie* (Frankfurt: Campus Verlag, 1979).
211. *Das Prinzip Hoffnung, GA*, vol. 5, pp. 1607–8, cf. H. F. Lefebvre, *Karl Marx: sa vie, son oeuvre* (Paris: Presses universitaires de France, 1964).
212. *Das Prinzip Hoffnung, GA*, vol. 5, pp. 1607–8.
213. *Philosophische Aufsätze, GA*, vol. 10, p. 355.

214. *Subjekt-Objekt, GA,* vol. 8, p. 409.
215. ibid., pp. 409-10.
216. ibid., p. 409.
217. ibid., p. 414.
218. ibid., p. 409.
219. cf. *Philosophy in the USSR. Problems of Dialectical Materialism,* trans. R. Daglish (Moscow: Progress Publishers, 1977) 15ff, 22ff, 43ff.
220. *Philosophische Aufsätze, GA,* vol. 10, p. 353.
221. *Subjekt-Objekt, GA,* vol. 8, p. 412.
222. *Das Prinzip Hoffnung, GA,* vol. 5, p. 291. For a discussion of Bloch's original interpretation of *Theses on Feuerbach,* see ch. 5 *infra.*

CHAPTER 3

1. For useful discussions of process philosophy, see *Process and Divinity: The Hartshorne Festschrift,* W. L. Reese and E. Freeman ed., (La Salle: Open Court, 1964); A. P. Stiernotte, 'Process Philosophies and Mysticism', *International Philosophical Quarterly,* vol. IX, no. 4, Dec. (1969) pp. 560-71; and J. Macquarrie, *Twentieth Century Religious Thought* (London: S.C.M., 1963) ch. XVII.
2. A. Münster (ed.), *Tagträume vom aufrechten Gang* (Frankfurt a. M.: Suhrkamp, 1977), pp. 23-4.
3. *Philosophische Aufsätze, GA,* vol. 10, frontpiece, cf. *Spuren, GA,* vol. 1, p. 97.
4. For James' relationship to process philosophy, see M.Čapek, 'Simple Location and Fragmentation of Reality', *The Monist,* vol. 48, no. 2, April (1964) pp. 195-218. For Bloch's critique of James, see *Philosophische Aufsätze, GA,* vol. 10, pp. 60-5.
5. Interview with the author on 14 January 1977.
6. For Frohschammer's process philosophy, see J. Frohschammer, *Die Phantasie als Grundprincip des Weltprocesses (sic)* (Munich: Theodor Achermann, 1877), B. Münz, *Jakob Frohschammer, der Philosoph der Weltphantasie* (Breslau, 1894), and A. Attensperger (ed.), *Jakob Frohschammers philosophisches System im Grundriss* (Zweibrücken, 1899).
7. See E. von Hartmann, *Philosophy of the Unconscious* (1896), trans. W. C. Coupland, new ed. (London: Kegan Paul, Trench, Trubner. 1931); and for Bloch's debt to von Hartmann, see *Geist der Utopie* (1918), *GA,* vol. 16, pp. 261-7; *Philosophische Aufsätze, GA,* vol. 10, pp. 197-203: 'Eduard von Hartmanns Weltprozess' (1923); *Das Materialismusproblem, GA,* vol. 7, pp. 92-9, 282-8.
8. See E. von Hartmann, *Schellings positive Philosophie als Einheit von Hegel und Schopenhauer* (Berlin: Otto Loewenstein, 1869), and D. N. K. Darnoi, *The Unconscious and Eduard von Hartmann. A Historico-Critical Monograph* (The Hague: Martinus Nijhoff, 1967) pp. 14-19.
9. There is still no satisfactory account of Schelling's late philosophy in English. See, however, P. C. Hayner, *Reason and Existence, Schel-*

ling's *Philosophy of History* (Leiden: E. J. Brill, 1967) pp. 34-61, 92-124; F. W. Bolman Jr., Introduction to his translation of Schelling's *The Ages of the World* (New York: Columbia University Press, 1942), and Robert F. Brown, *The Later Philosophy of Schelling. The Influence of Boehme on the Works of 1809-1815* (London: Associated Universities Presses, 1977). In German, see K. F. A. Schelling (ed.), *Sämmtliche Werke*, 14 volumes in two divisions, (Stuttgart & Augsburg: J. G. Cotta, 1856-61) especially vol. 13, pp. 57, 127, 203; and A. M. Koktanek, *Schellings Seinslehre und Kierkegaard* (Munich: R. Oldenbourg 1962); C. Wild, *Reflexion und Erfahrung. Eine Interpretation der Früh- und Spätphilosophie Schellings* (Symposion, 25) (Freiburg/Munich: Verlag Karl Alber, 1968); B. Loer, *Das Absolute und die Wirklichkeit in Schellings Philosophie* (Berlin: Walter de Gruyter, 1974); Dieter Jähnig, *Schelling. Die Kunst in der Philosophie*, 2 vols (Pfullingen: Neske, 1969), H. Fuhrmans, *Schellings letzte Philosophie. Die negative und positive Philosophie im Einsatz des Spätidealismus* (Berlin: Junker and Dünnhaupt Verlag, 1940), and W. Schulz, *Die Vollendung des deutschen Idealismus in der Spätphilosophie Schellings* (Pfullingen: Neske, 1975) 2nd ed., especially pp. 21-30, 307-20.

10. The interpretation of Schelling's philosophy is the subject of dispute. For recent radicalising interpretations, see F. W. Schmidt, *Zum Begriff der Negativität bei Schelling und Hegel* (Stuttgart: J. B. Metzler, 1971); M. Frank, *Der unendliche Mangel an Sein, Schellings Hegelkritik und die Anfänge der Marxschen Dialektik* (Frankfurt a. M.: Suhrkamp, 1975) and M. Frank and G. Kurz (ed.) *Materialen zu Schellings philosophischen Anfängen* (Frankfurt a. M.: Suhrkamp, 1975). For Bloch's assessments of Schelling, see *Subjekt-Objekt, GA,* vol. 8, pp. 395-400, *Das Materialismusproblem, GA,* vol. 7, pp. 73-7, 216-29, and *Zwischenwelten in der Philosophiegeschichte, GA,* vol. 12, pp. 306-19.

11. For a discussion of Bergson's process philosophy, see M. Čapek, *The Philosophical Impact of Contemporary Physics* (Princeton, N.J.: D. Van Nostrand, 1961) ch. 17, especially pp. 336-9.

12. For Bloch's critique of Bergson, see *Geist der Utopie* (1918), *GA,* vol. 16, pp. 249-55; *Das Materialismusproblem, GA,* vol. 7, pp. 278-82.

13. R. Traub and H. Wieser (ed.), *Gespräche mit Ernst Bloch* (Frankfurt a. M.: Suhrkamp, 1975) p. 32.

14. See G. Lukács, *The Young Hegel* (1948) trans. R. Livingstone (London: Merlin Press, 1975) and H. Marcuse, *Reason and Revolution,* 2nd ed. (London: Routledge and Kegan Paul, 1969), and *Subjekt-Objekt, GA,* vol. 8, pp. 51-2, ch. 16.

15. *Subjekt-Objekt, GA,* vol. 8, p. 472, chs 9 and 11.

16. ibid., pp. 32-43.

17. *Tübinger Einleitung in die Philosophie, GA,* vol. 13, p. 43.

18. *Subjekt-Objekt, GA,* vol. 8, pp. 39ff, 109-20.

19. ibid., pp. 32-43, 121 ff, 198-200.

20. *Tübinger Einleitung in die Philosophie, GA,* vol. 13, ch. 9.

21. *Subjekt-Objekt, GA*, vol. 8, p. 138 ff, and *Tübinger Einleitung in die Philosophie, GA*, vol. 13, ch. 20.
22. *Subjekt-Objekt, GA*, vol. 8, pp. 140-5.
23. cf. L. Colletti, *Marxism and Hegel*, trans. L. Garner (London: New Left Books, 1973) chs 3 and 4, and T. Adorno, *Negative Dialectics*, trans. E. B. Ashton (London: Routledge and Kegan Paul, 1973).
24. *Philosophische Aufsätze, GA*, vol. 10, pp. 472 ff, 480.
25. *Subjekt-Objekt, GA*, vol. 8, chs 7-16, and *Philosophische Aufsätze, GA*, vol. 10, pp. 475-81.
26. *Philosophische Aufsätze, GA*, vol. 10, pp. 480-500.
27. ibid., pp. 271-2.
28. ibid., pp. 493-500.
29. *Subjekt-Objekt, GA*, vol. 8, *Die Aufhebung*.
30. ibid., pp. 453-73, 505-9.
31. *Philosophische Aufsätze, GA*, vol. 10, pp. 475-81.
32. ibid., pp. 481-500.
33. *Subjekt-Objekt, GA*, vol. 8, pp. 453-73.
34. cf. N. Rotenstreich, *From Substance to Subject* (The Hague: Martinus Nijhoff, 1974) especially chs 1 and 4.
35. *Über Methode und System bei Hegel* (Frankfurt a. M.: Suhrkamp, 1970) pp. 33-4, 55-69, 82-90, 93-4, 98-9, 117-19; cf. *Subjekt-Objekt, GA*, vol. 8, pp. 412-72.
36. *Subjekt-Objekt, GA*, vol. 8, ch. 19.
37. ibid., p. 414 and *Das Materialismusproblem, GA*, vol. 7, pp. 359-71.
38. *Philosophische Aufsätze, GA*, vol. 10, pp. 474-81, 493-500.
39. *Subjekt-Objekt, GA*, vol. 8, ch. 23.
40. ibid., pp. 453-4, 473-82, 504-5.
41. ibid., chs 22 and 23.
42. F. J. von Rintelen, *Contemporary German Philosophy and its Background* (Bonn: Bouvier, 1970) pp. 25, 153 ff.
43. *Das Prinzip Hoffnung, GA*, vol. 5, pp. 328-34.
44. ibid., pp. 330-1.
45. ibid., p. 331.
46. ibid., p. 1627.
47. *Subjekt-Objekt, GA*, vol. 8, pp. 467-73.
48. *Tübinger Einleitung in die Philosophie, GA*, vol. 13, p. 161.
49. ibid., ch. 19.
50. *Subjekt-Objekt, GA*, vol. 8, pp. 363-4.
51. *Das Prinzip Hoffnung, GA*, vol. 5, p. 5.
52 *Experimentum Mundi, GA*, vol. 15, pp. 114 ff, 144 ff.
53. R. Traub and H. Wieser (ed.), *Gespräche mit Ernst Bloch*, op. cit., p. 301.
54. *Tübinger Einleitung in die Philosophie, GA*, vol. 13, pp. 85-9, 105-18.
55. *Subjekt-Objekt, GA*, vol. 8, p. 473.
56. *Tübinger Einleitung in die Philosophie, GA*, vol. 13, 170 ff.
57. ibid., ch. 29, and *Experimentum Mundi, GA*, vol. 15, ch. 34.
58. R. Traub and H. Wieser (ed.), *Gespräche mit Ernst Bloch*, op. cit., p. 301.

59. *Subjekt-Objekt*, *GA*, vol. 8, pp. 469–73, and *Das Prinzip Hoffnung*, *GA*, vol. 5, p. 1200.
60. *Subjekt-Objekt*, *GA*, vol. 8, p. 460.
61. ibid., pp. 462–72.
62. ibid., p. 508, and *Das Materialismusproblem*, *GA*, vol. 7, ch. 17.
63. *Subjekt-Objekt*, *GA*, vol. 8, p. 470.
64. ibid., pp. 462, 499.
65. ibid., p. 508.
66. ibid., p. 506.
67. ibid., pp. 499–510.
68. ibid., pp. 505–6.
69. ibid., p. 519.
70. *Tübinger Einleitung in die Philosophie*, *GA*, vol. 13, ch. 31.
71. ibid., pp. 112–18.
72. *Politische Messungen*, *GA*, vol. 11, pp. 458–61, and *Subjekt-Objekt*, *GA*, vol. 8, ch. 22.
73 *Tübinger Einleitung in die Philosophie*, *GA*, vol. 13, pp. 90–2, and *Das Prinzip Hoffnung*, *GA*, vol. 5, p. 1627.
74. *Experimentum Mundi*, *GA*, vol. 15, pp. 178–81.
75. *Das Prinzip Hoffnung*, *GA*, vol. 5, pp. 1011–16.
76. ibid., pp. 1194–1201.
77. *Subjekt-Objekt*, *GA*, vol. 8, ch. 24.
78. ibid., pp. 393–5.
79. ibid., pp. 395–8, and *Zwischenwelten in der Philosophiegeschichte*, *GA*, vol. 12, pp. 306–19.
80. *Atheismus im Christentum*, *GA*, vol. 14, p. 97.
81. ibid., p. 98.
82. F. Engels, *Anti-Dühring* (1878), English trans. (Moscow: Progress Publishers, 1969) pp. 31–3.
83. *Subjekt-Objekt*, *GA*, vol. 8, p. 508.
84. *Experimentum Mundi*, *GA*, vol. 15, p. 52.
85. *Subjekt-Objekt*, *GA*, vol. 8, p. 363.
86. *Atheismus im Christentum*, *GA*, vol. 14, p. 96.
87. *Tübinger Einleitung in die Philosophie*, *GA*, vol. 13, pp. 222–7.
88. ibid., pp. 219–22.
89. ibid., p. 216.
90. ibid., pp. 288–302.
91. J. L. Mehta, *The Philosophy of Martin Heidegger* (revised ed.) (New York: Harper and Row, 1971) ch. 3.
92. ibid.
93. *Tübinger Einleitung in die Philosophie*, *GA*, vol. 13, p. 216–17, 285–96.
94. ibid., p. 216.
95. ibid., p. 217.
96. ibid., p. 217.
97. ibid., p. 216.
98. ibid.
99. ibid.

100. M. Landmann, 'Talking with Ernst Bloch: Korčula, 1968', trans. D. Parent, in *Telos*, no. 25, Fall (1975) pp. 165–85, especially p. 182.
101. cf. P. Widmer, *Die Anthropologie Ernst Blochs*, op. cit., pp. 22–72.
102. *Das Prinzip Hoffnung, GA*, vol. 5, pp. 74–9.
103. ibid., p. 271.
104. cf. ibid., p. 132.
105. *Tübinger Einleitung in die Philosophie, GA*, vol. 13, p. 13.
106. *Das Prinzip Hoffnung, GA*, vol. 5, p. 2.
107. ibid., pp. 161–223.
108. ibid.
109. cf. J-P. Sartre, *The Psychology of the Imagination* (London: Methuen, 1972), especially ch. 4.
110. See 'Antizipierendes Bewusstsein, Objektive Phantasie' in *Philosophische Aufsätze, GA*, vol. 10, pp. 74–189.
111. ibid., pp. 86–115.
112. *Das Prinzip Hoffnung, GA*, vol. 5, pp. 54–96, 182–9.
113. ibid., pp. 72–86.
114. ibid., ch. 11, and *Naturrecht und menschliche Würde, GA*, vol. 6, p. 219.
115. For Bloch's detailed differentiation of day dreams from night dreams, see *Das Prinzip Hoffnung, GA*, vol. 5, ch. 14.
116. ibid., ch. 15.
117. ibid., p. 143.
118. *Philosophische Aufsätze, GA*, vol. 10, pp. 122–31.
119. ibid., pp. 161–71 and ch. 17.
120. ibid., pp. 339–49.
121. ibid., ch. 20.
122. ibid., p. 336 ff.
123. ibid., pp. 336–43.
124. ibid., p. 1200.
125. ibid., pp. 364–8.
126. ibid., pp. 338–43.
127. ibid., p. 350.
128. ibid., p. 359.
129. ibid., pp. 356–64.
130. *Tübinger Einleitung in die Philosophie, GA*, vol. 13, p. 227, and *Experimentum Mundi, GA*, vol. 15, ch. 22.
131. *Das Prinzip Hoffnung, GA*, vol. 5, p. 343.
132. ibid., pp. 347, 341.
133. *Geist der Utopie* (1923), *GA*, vol. 3, p. 305.
134. *Atheismus im Christentum, GA*, vol. 14, p. 97.
135. *Tübinger Einleitung in die Philosophie, GA*, vol. 13, p. 356.
136. *Das Prinzip Hoffnung, GA*, vol. 5, p. 241.
137. *Das Prinzip Hoffnung, GA*, vol. 5, 336ff, 350–6, 364–8.
138. ibid., p. 258.
139. *Das Prinzip Hoffnung, GA*, vol. 5, p. 727, *Subjekt-Objekt, GA*, vol. 8, p. 470.
140. ibid., p. 727.

141. ibid., p. 226.
142. *Subjekt-Objekt, GA*, vol. 8, pp. 499–500, 513.
143. *Das Prinzip Hoffnung, GA*, vol. 5, pp. 364, 1086, 1628.
144. *Tübinger Einleitung in die Philosophie, GA*, vol. 13, p. 208.
145. *Das Prinzip Hoffnung, GA*, vol. 5, p. 235.
146. ibid., p. 363.
147. ibid., pp. 226–7.
148. ibid., p. 727.
149. *Subjekt-Objekt, GA*, vol. 8, pp. 462, 498–510.
150. K. Kosík, *Dialectics of the Concrete*, trans. K. Kovanda and J. Schmidt (Dordrecht: D. Reidel, 1976) p. 19.
151. *Erbschaft dieser Zeit, GA*, vol. 4, pp. 125, 151.
152. *Philosophische Aufsätze, GA*, vol. 10. p. 288.
153. *Das Prinzip Hoffnung, GA*, vol. 5, p. 229.
154. cf. H. D. Bahr, 'Ontologie und Utopie' (1968), in B. Schmidt (ed.), *Materialen zu Ernst Blochs 'Prinzip Hoffnung'* (Frankfurt a. M.: Suhrkamp, 1978) pp. 291–305.
155. *Das Prinzip Hoffnung, GA*, vol. 5, p. 255.
156. ibid., p. 166, and *Atheismus im Christentum, GA*, vol. 14, p. 96.
157. *Atheismus im Christentum, GA*, vol. 14, p. 96.
158. *Das Prinzip Hoffnung, GA*, vol. 5, pp. 364–8.
159. *Tübinger Einleitung in die Philosophie, GA*, vol. 13, p. 185.
160. *Das Prinzip Hoffnung, GA*, vol. 5, p. 5.
161. ibid., p. 1624.
162. ibid., pp. 77–186, 121–8.
163. ibid., pp. 126–8.
164. ibid., p. 10.
165. ibid., pp. 227–30, cf. *Literarische Aufsätze, GA*, vol. 9, pp. 385–92.
166. cf. *Tübinger Einleitung in die Philosophie, GA*, vol. 13, ch. 32.
167. *Das Prinzip Hoffnung, GA*, vol. 5, p. 8.
168. R. Traub and H. Wieser (ed.), *Gespräche mit Ernst Bloch*, op. cit., p. 235, and *Experimentum Mundi, GA*, vol. 15, pp. 178–81.
169. *Das Prinzip Hoffnung, GA*, vol. 5, pp. 161–71.
170. ibid., pp. 164–6.
171. ibid., p. 164.
172. ibid., pp. 161–6.
173. ibid., pp. 171–203.
174. ibid., p. 166.
175. cf. ibid., pp. 1296–7, 1540–50.
176. See G. Marcel, 'Sketch of a Phenomenology and a Metaphysic of Hope' in *Homo Viator*, trans E. Craufurd (New York: Harper and Row, 1962) pp. 29–67, and C. S. Calian, *Berdyaev's Philosophy of Hope* (Leiden: E. J. Brill, 1968).

CHAPTER 4

1. *Das Prinzip Hoffnung, GA*, vol. 5, p. 225.
2. ibid.

3. *Tübinger Einleitung in die Philosophie, GA*, vol. 13, p. 221.
4. ibid., pp. 138–43.
5. ibid., pp. 356–64.
6. *Tübinger Einleitung in die Philosophie, GA*, vol. 13, pp. 221–3.
7. ibid., pp. 89, 21, 343, and *Experimentum Mundi, GA*, vol. 15, ch. 47.
8. *Das Prinzip Hoffnung, GA*, vol. 5, p. 358.
9. *Experimentum Mundi, GA*, vol. 15, p. 241.
10. *Tübinger Einleitung in die Philosophie, GA*, vol. 13, pp. 219, 226.
11. ibid., pp. 334–44.
12. ibid., p. 221.
13. *Das Prinzip Hoffnung, GA*, vol. 5, p. 341, and *Tübinger Einleitung in die Philosophie, GA*, vol. 13, ch. 29.
14. *Das Prinzip Hoffnung, GA*, vol. 5, p. 203.
15. *Tübinger Einleitung in die Philosophie, GA*, vol. 13, p. 219, and *Das Prinzip Hoffnung, GA*, vol. 5, pp. 356–64.
16. *Subjekt-Objekt, GA*, vol. 8, pp. 108, 446, 501–10; *Das Prinzip Hoffnung, GA*, vol. 5, pp. 336, 346–8, 1551 ff, 1628.
17. *Experimentum Mundi, GA*, vol. 15, pp. 254, 257.
18. cf. *Das Prinzip Hoffnung, GA*, vol. 5, ch. 41.
19. On Leibniz's process metaphysics, see L. E. Loemker, 'On Substance and Process in Leibniz' in *Process and Divinity: The Hartshorne Festschrift* (ed. W. L. Reese and E. Freeman), op. cit., pp. 403–25.
20. *Das Prinzip Hoffnung, GA*, vol. 5, pp. 357–8.
21. *Experimentum Mundi, GA*, vol. 15, ch. 31.
22. *Das Materialismusproblem, GA*, vol. 7, p. 469.
23. *Das Prinzip Hoffnung, GA*, vol. 5, p. 357, and *Experimentum Mundi, GA*, vol. 15, p. 263.
24. *Das Materialismusproblem, GA*, vol. 7, p. 469.
25. ibid., p. 148.
26. ibid., p. 469.
27. *Tübinger Einleitung in die Philosophie, GA*, vol. 13, p. 227 ff.
28. ibid., p. 227.
29. *Experimentum Mundi, GA*, vol. 15, p. 242.
30. Interview with author, 14 January 1977.
31. *Atheismus in Christentum, GA*, vol. 14, p. 86.
32. *Tübinger Einleitung in die Philosophie, GA*, vol. 13, p. 193.
33. ibid., p. 228
34. *Das Materialismusproblem, GA*, vol. 7, pp. 466–9.
35. *Das Prinzip Hoffnung, GA*, vol. 5, p. 17.
36. *Tübinger Einleitung in die Philosophie, GA*, vol. 13, p. 229.
37. *Das Prinzip Hoffnung, GA*, vol. 5, p. 7.
38. ibid., p. 228.
39. *Tübinger Einleitung in die Philosophie, GA*, vol. 13, p. 229, and *Das Materialismusproblem, GA*, vol. 7, pp. 477–8.
40. *Das Materialismusproblem, GA*, vol. 7, pp. 477–8.
41. *Tübinger Einleitung in die Philosophie, GA*, vol. 13, pp. 299, 366, and *Experimentum Mundi, GA*, vol. 15, p. 225.
42. *Experimentum Mundi, GA*, vol. 15, p. 143.
43. *Das Prinzip Hoffnung, GA*, vol. 5, p. 1626.

44. See, for example, R. Bultmann, *History and Eschatology*. The Gifford Lectures, 1955 (Edinburgh: The University Press, 1957), C. H. Dodd, *History and the Gospel* (London: Nisbet, 1938), and A. Richardson, *History Sacred and Profane* (London: S.C.M. Press, 1964).
45. *Das Prinzip Hoffnung, GA*, vol. 5, pp. 1009–10, 221–3, 336–49; *Experimentum Mundi, GA*, vol. 15, pp. 31, 70–6, 239–48, 253–61; *Subjekt-Objekt, GA*, vol. 8, pp. 363–5, 395–8.
46. *Experimentum Mundi, GA*, vol. 15, pp. 76–9.
47. ibid., pp. 74–5, and *Das Prinzip Hoffnung, GA*, vol. 5, p. 1387.
48. *Das Prinzip Hoffnung, GA*, vol. 5, p. 358.
49. *Atheismus im Christentum, GA*, vol. 14, p. 293, and *Subjekt-Objekt, GA*, vol. 8, p. 483.
50. *Experimentum Mundi, GA*, vol. 15, p. 254.
51. ibid., pp. 218, 73, 108.
52. ibid., pp. 70–9.
53. ibid., pp. 254, 98.
54. ibid., pp. 67, 132, and *Das Prinzip Hoffnung, GA*, vol. 5, p. 357.
55. *Erbschaft dieser Zeit, GA*, vol. 4, p. 396.
56. *Subjekt-Objekt, GA*, vol. 8, pp. 363–4.
57. *Das Prinzip Hoffnung, GA*, vol. 5, pp. 349, 354; *Experimentum Mundi, GA*, vol. 15, pp. 74–5, 255.
58. *Das Prinzip Hoffnung, GA*, vol. 5, pp. 356–64; *Tübinger Einleitung in die Philosophie, GA*, vol. 13, pp. 273–5.
59. *Das Prinzip Hoffnung, GA*, vol. 5, p. 356; cf. *Tübinger Einleitung in die Philosophie, GA*, vol. 13, p. 218.
60. ibid.
61. *Atheism in Christianity*, trans. J. T. Swann (New York: Herder and Herder, 1972) p. 221; cf. *Atheismus im Christentum, GA*, vol. 14, p. 293.
62. *Das Prinzip Hoffnung, GA*, vol. 5, p. 358.
63. *Tübinger Einleitung in die Philosophie, GA*, vol. 13, pp. 195, 219–20, 245–6.
64. *Subjekt-Objekt, GA*, vol. 8. p. 517.
65. *Tübinger Einleitung in die Philosophie, GA*, vol. 13, p. 222.
66. *Das Prinzip Hoffnung, GA*, vol. 5, pt. V.
67. *Experimentum Mundi, GA*, vol. 15, p. 246.
68. *Das Prinzip Hoffnung, GA*, vol. 5, p. 355.
69. ibid.
70. *Subjekt-Objekt, GA*, vol. 8, p. 364.
71. *Experimentum Mundi, GA*, vol. 15, pp. 240–6.
72. ibid., p. 363.
73. ibid., p. 365.
74. *Subjekt-Objekt, GA*, vol. 8, p. 364.
75. *Experimentum Mundi, GA*, vol. 15, p. 243, and *Das Prinzip Hoffnung, GA*, vol. 5, p. 235.
76. *Experimentum Mundi, GA*, vol. 15, pp. 221, 75, 98, 259.
77. *Subjekt-Objekt, GA*, vol. 8, p. 365.
78. ibid., pp. 364–5, 510 and *Das Prinzip Hoffnung, GA*, vol. 5, pp. 235 and 364.

79. *Experimentum Mundi, GA,* vol. 15, pp. 177–8, 223–38; *Das Prinzip Hoffnung, GA,* vol. 5, ch. 37; *Atheismus im Christentum, GA,* vol. 14, pp. 294–307.
80. *Experimentum Mundi, GA,* vol. 15, p. 262; *Das Prinzip Hoffnung, GA,* vol. 5, p. 364; *Atheismus im Christentum, GA,* vol. 14, pp. 338–44.
81. *Das Prinzip Hoffnung, GA,* vol. 5, p. 368, and *Tübinger Einleitung in die Philosophie, GA,* vol. 13, p. 277.
82. *Subjekt-Objekt, GA,* vol. 8, p. 487.
83. *Experimentum Mundi, GA,* vol. 15, p. 230, and *Tübinger Einleitung in die Philosophie, GA,* vol. 13, pp. 185, 196, 375–6; *Atheismus im Christentum, GA,* vol. 14, pp. 393–7.
84. *Tübinger Einleitung in die Philosophie, GA,* vol. 13, pp. 186–96, and *Experimentum Mundi, GA,* vol. 15, p. 79.
85. *Tübinger Einleitung in die Philosophie, GA,* vol. 13, pp. 194–5, 257–66.
86. ibid., pp. 195–6, and *Subjekt-Objekt, GA,* vol. 8, pp. 138–41, 512.
87. *Subjekt-Objekt, GA,* vol. 8, p. 506, and *Tübinger Einleitung in die Philosophie, GA,* vol. 13, pp. 217–19, 224–7.
88. *Tübinger Einleitung in die Philosophie, GA,* vol. 13, pp. 356–64.
89. *Das Prinzip Hoffnung, GA,* vol. 5, pp. 360–3.
90. *Tübinger Einleitung in die Philosophie, GA,* vol. 13, ch. 24, especially pp. 265–6.
91. ibid., p. 193.
92. cf. *Subjekt-Objekt, GA,* vol. 8, pp. 131–5.
93. *Tübinger Einleitung in die Philosophie, GA,* vol. 13, pp. 330–3.
94. ibid., p. 193.
95. ibid.
96. *Experimentum Mundi, GA,* vol. 15, p. 132.
97. ibid.
98. ibid.
99. *Subjekt-Objekt, GA,* vol. 8, ch. 25. See also the translation, Ernst Bloch, 'Dialectics and Hope', trans. M. Ritter, in *New German Critique,* no. 9, Fall, (1976) pp. 3–10.
100. *Subjekt-Objekt, GA,* vol. 8, p. 512.
101. ibid.
102. ibid., p. 516.
103. *Erbschaft dieser Zeit, GA,* vol. 4, pp. 122–6, 395–6.
104. *Experimentum Mundi, GA,* vol. 15, p. 218.
105. ibid. cf. *Das Materialismusproblem, GA,* vol. 7, ch. 39.
106. *Tübinger Einleitung in die Philosophie, GA,* vol. 13, p. 333.
107. *Experimentum Mundi, GA,* vol. 15, pp. 218–19.
108. *Experimentum Mundi, GA,* vol. 15, p. 155.
109. *Das Prinzip Hoffnung, GA,* vol. 5, p. 255.
110. *Tübinger Einleitung in die Philosophie, GA,* vol. 13, p. 331.
111. *Experimentum Mundi, GA,* vol. 15, ch. 33 and 34.
112. ibid., pp. 165, 225–6.
113. ibid., pp. 219–20, and *Tübinger Einleitung in die Philosophie, GA,* vol. 13, ch. 29.

114. *Experimentum Mundi, GA*, vol. 15, pp. 219-30, and *Tübinger Einleitung in die Philosophie, GA*, vol. 13, pp. 327-44.
115. *Experimentum Mundi, GA*, vol. 15, pp. 154-5.
116. For treatments of possibility by analytical philosophers, see N. Rescher, *Conceptual Idealism* (Oxford: Basil Blackwell, 1973) chs II and III; J. Hintikka, *Time and Necessity. Studies in Aristotle's Theory of Modality* (Oxford: Clarendon Press, 1973). Like Bloch, Hintikka recognises the problem of a categorial representation of 'becoming possible'.
117. M. Čapek, *The Philosophical Impact of Contemporary Physics*, op. cit., pp. 336-9.
118. *Das Prinzip Hoffnung, GA*, vol. 5, pp. 280-4.
119. M. Landmann, 'Talking with Ernst Bloch: Korčula, 1968', trans. D. Parent, op. cit., p. 176, and *Experimentum Mundi, GA*, vol. 15, p. 129.
120. *Das Prinzip Hoffnung, GA*, vol. 5, pp. 258-9.
121. ibid., pp. 259-64.
122. ibid., pp. 264-71.
123. ibid., p. 268.
124. ibid., pp. 225-6.
125. ibid., pp. 271-8.
126. ibid., pp. 271, 274.
127. ibid., p. 271.
128. ibid., p. 277.
129. For Meinong's theory of incompletely determined objects, see J. W. Findlay, *Meinong's Theory of Objects* (London: Oxford University Press, 1933).
130. *Das Prinzip Hoffnung, GA*, vol. 5, p. 271.
131. *Experimentum Mundi, GA*, vol. 15, pp. 141-3.
132. *Das Prinzip Hoffnung, GA*, vol. 5, pp. 267-70.
133. ibid., p. 310, and *Subjekt-Objekt, GA*, vol. 8, p. 410.
134. *Tübinger Einleitung in die Philosophie, GA*, vol. 13, pp. 230-3.
135. *Das Prinzip Hoffnung, GA*, vol. 5, p. 271.
136. *Tübinger Einleitung in die Philosophie, GA*, vol. 13, pp. 186-96.
137. ibid., p. 208.
138. *Experimentum Mundi, GA*, vol. 15, pp. 228-30.
139. ibid., p. 139.
140. ibid., p. 230.
141. *Das Materialismusproblem, GA*, vol. 7, pp. 477-8, and *Tübinger Einleitung in die Philosophie, GA*, vol. 13, pp. 234-6.
142. *Das Materialismusproblem, GA*, vol. 7, p. 476.
143. *Das Prinzip Hoffnung, GA*, vol. 5, pp. 273-4.
144. *Das Materialismusproblem, GA*, vol. 7, p. 476.
145. *Das Prinzip Hoffnung, GA*, vol. 5, pp. 273-4.
146. *Philosophische Aufsätze, GA*, vol. 10, p. 131.
147. *Das Prinzip Hoffnung, GA*, vol. 5, p. 227.
148. *Vor-Schein* is a fundamental category of Bloch's philosophy. *Vorschein* ordinarily means pre-appearance or preview. Bloch however uses the term in a sense which emphasises the objectively

anticipatory aspect. *Vor-Schein* is anticipatory *Schein* (cf. Hegel's 'show'): anticipatory appearance, pre-semblance, pre-view of objective real possibilities with a relation to essence.

149. *Tübinger Einleitung in die Philosophie, GA*, vol. 13, ch. 29, and *Das Prinzip Hoffnung, GA*, vol. 5, pp. 250–5.
150. *Tübinger Einleitung in die Philosophie, GA*, vol. 13, pp. 320–1 and ch. 30.
151. *Experimentum Mundi, GA*, vol. 15, chs. 41–4.
152. *Das Prinzip Hoffnung, GA*, vol. 5, pp. 252–5.
153. ibid., p. 366.
154. *Tübinger Einleitung in die Philosophie, GA*, vol. 13, p. 44.
155. *Das Prinzip Hoffnung, GA*, vol. 5, pp. 336–56.
156. ibid., p. 347.
157. K. Marx, *Capital*, vol I (1867) trans. S. Moore and E. Aveling (London: Lawrence and Wishart, 1970) p. 178, and *Das Prinzip Hoffnung, GA*, vol. 5, pp. 84–5.
158. See G. Lukács, *Marx's Basic Ontological Principles*, trans. D. Fernbach (London: Merlin Press, 1978).
159. *Das Prinzip Hoffnung, GA*, vol. 5, p. 1626.
160. *Experimentum Mundi, GA*, vol. 15, ch. 28; cf. 'Über Heterogonie der Zwecke' (Leipzig, 1955) in *Philosophische Aufsätze, GA*, vol. 10, pp. 431–42.
161. B. Schmidt, 'Vom teleologischen Prinzip in der Materie', in *Ernst Blochs Wirkung* (Frankfurt a. M.: Suhrkamp, 1975) pp. 362–80.
162. *Das Materialismusproblem, GA*, vol. 7, p. 478.
163. ibid., ch. 47, and *Experimentum Mundi, GA*, vol. 15, p. 263.
164. *Experimentum Mundi, GA*, vol. 15, p. 125.
165. ibid., pp. 125–32.
166. ibid., p. 132.
167. *Tübinger Einleitung in die Philosophie, GA*, vol. 13, p. 314, and *Subjekt-Objekt, GA*, vol. 8, p. 364.
168. *Experimentum Mundi, GA*, vol. 15, p. 125 ff.
169. ibid., pp. 242–8.
170. *Das Materialismusproblem, GA*, vol. 7, p. 473.
171. *Experimentum Mundi, GA*, vol. 15, pp. 155–71.
172. *Das Materialismusproblem, GA*, vol. 7, p. 474.
173. *Das Materialismusproblem, GA*, vol. 7, p. 478.
174. *Tübinger Einleitung in die Philosophie, GA*, vol. 13, p. 272.
175. *Das Prinzip Hoffnung, GA*, vol. 5, ch. 20, especially p. 347.
176. *Tübinger Einleitung in die Philosophie, GA*, vol. 13, pp. 364–8, 347.
177. *Experimentum Mundi, GA*, vol. 15, p. 182.
178. *Das Prinzip Hoffnung, GA*, vol. 5, p. 777.
179. *Tübinger Einleitung in die Philosophie, GA*, vol. 13, pp. 143–5.
180. K. Marx and F. Engels, *The German Ideology* (1845–61) 2nd ed., English trans. (Moscow: Progress Publishers, 1968) pp. 28 and 42.
181. ibid., pp. 778 ff, 784 ff, and *Das Materialismusproblem, GA*, vol. 7, pp. 435 ff.
182. *Das Prinzip Hoffnung, GA*, vol. 5, ch. 37.
183. ibid., p. 781.

184. *Das Materialismusproblem, GA,* vol. 7, p. 464.
185. S. Schram (ed. and intro.) *Mao Tse-tung Unrehearsed,* trans. J. Chinnery and Tieyun (Harmondsworth: Penguin, 1974) pp. 220-1, 228.
186. *Experimentum Mundi, GA,* vol. 15, p. 228.
187. *Das Prinzip Hoffnung, GA,* vol. 5, pp. 786-7.
188. ibid., pp. 775-8.
189. ibid., pp. 771-88, 802-13.
190. ibid., ch. 37.
191. ibid., pp. 788-817, and *Atheismus im Christentum, GA,* vol. 14, p. 341.
192. *Tübinger Einleitung in die Philosophie, GA,* vol. 13, p. 145.
193. *Das Prinzip Hoffnung, GA,* vol. 5, p. 1383.
194. *Das Prinzip Hoffnung, GA,* vol. 5, p. 786.
195. ibid., pp. 287-8.
196. ibid., pp. 778, 807, 817, 1618-19.
197. *Experimentum Mundi, GA,* vol. 15, p. 225.
198. ibid., p. 221.
199. ibid., pp. 229-30.
200. *Das Prinzip Hoffnung, GA,* vol. 5, p. 810.
201. *Experimentum Mundi, GA,* vol. 15, pp. 223-30.
202. ibid., pp. 218-23.
203. *Experimentum Mundi, GA,* vol. 15, pp. 106-7.
204. ibid., p. 106.
205. *Tübinger Einleitung in die Philosophie, GA,* vol. 13, pp. 129, 136.
206. ibid., pp. 129-38.
207. ibid., pp. 133-8.
208. ibid., pp. 138, 132.
209. ibid., p. 142.
210. ibid.
211. *Literarische Aufsätze, GA,* vol. 9, pp. 152-6. Bloch specifically refers to Benjamin's use of *Jetztzeit* in his *Theses on the Philosophy of History,* see pp. 154-5.
212. *Atheismus im Christentum, GA,* vol. 14, pp. 238-44.
213. *Das Prinzip Hoffnung, GA,* vol. 5, p. 1390.
214. *Atheismus im Christentum, GA,* vol. 14, p. 341; cf. Eng. trans. 1972.
215. *Geist der Utopie, GA,* vol. 3 (1923), pp. 267-73.
216. See F. Engels, *Schelling on Hegel* (1841), *Schelling and Revelation* (1842), and *Schelling, Philosopher in Christ* (1842) trans. B. Ruhemann, in Marx-Engels, *Collected Works* (London: Lawrence and Wishart, 1975) var. trans., vol. II, pp. 181-7, 191-240, 243-64, especially pp. 186, 206-7, 220-1.
217. ibid., especially pp. 206-7, 222. Nor did Engels change his mind when he ceased to be a Young Hegelian, see *Anti-Dühring,* op. cit., p. 67.
218. For a detailed treatment of this aspect of Transcendental Thomism, see O. Muck S. J., *The Transcendental Method,* trans. W. D. Seidensticker (New York: Herder and Herder, 1968) especially pts I and III.
219. For Rahner's theological anthropology, see L. Roberts, *The Achie-*

vement of Karl Rahner (New York: Herder and Herder, 1967) especially chs 1 and 5.

220. See M. Blondel, *L'Action* (Paris: Félix Alcan, 1893); H. Duméry, *Raison et Religion dans la Philosophie de l'action* (Paris: Éditions du Seuil, 1963) pt III; J. J. McNeill, *The Blondelian Synthesis* (Leiden: E. J. Brill, 1966) chs IV, V, VII, XII, XIII.

221. See G. Marcel, *Homo Viator*, op. cit., especially pp. 29–67.

222. See E. Wyschogrod, *Emmanuel Levinas. The Problem of Ethical Metaphysics* (The Hague, Nijhoff, 1974), and Levinas' contribution to G. Raulet (ed.), *Utopie – Marxisme Selon Ernst Bloch* (Paris: Payot, 1976) 'Sur la mort dans la pensée de Ernst Bloch', pp. 318–26.

223. For a comparison between Tillich and Bloch, see H-J. Gerhards, *Utopie als innergeschichtlicher Aspekt der Eschatologie*, op. cit.

224. Bloch was friendly with Broch in the United States, and may have influenced his philosophical views. See E. Schlant, *Die Philosophie Hermann Brochs* (Bern/Munich: Francke Verlag, 1971).

225. *Erbschaft dieser Zeit*, GA, vol. 4, pp. 311–16.

226. See, for example, K. Jaspers, *Philosophical Faith and Revelation*, trans. E. B. Ashton (London: Collins, 1967) pp. 169–86.

227. W. J. Richardson, S.J., *Heidegger Through Phenomenology to Thought*, 3rd ed. (The Hague: Nijhoff, 1974) and O. Pöggeler, *Der Denkweg Martin Heideggers* (Pfullingen: Neske, 1963) chs VII and VIII.

228. See E. Klum, *Natur, Kunst und Liebe in der Philosophie Vladimir Solov'evs* (Munich: Otto Sagner, 1965); L. Müller, *Das religionsphilosophische System Vladimir Solovjevs* (Berlin: Evangelische Verlagsanstalt, 1956); and S. L. Frank (arr.) *A Solovyov Anthology*, trans. N. Duddington (London: S.C.M. Press, 1950).

229. See D. B. Richardson, *Berdyaev's Philosophy of History* (The Hague: Martinus Nijhoff, 1968) especially pp. 66–86, and C. S. Calian, *Berdyaev's Philosophy of Hope*, op. cit., especially pp. 9–41, 57–121.

230. For the process philosophy aspect of Teilhard's views, see D. P. Gray, *The One and the Many, Teilhard de Chardin's Vision of Unity* (London: Burns and Oates, 1969); and, more generally, Émile Rideau, *La pensée du Père Teilhard de Chardin* (Paris: Éditions du Seuil, 1965).

231. Cf. for Bergson, M. Čapek, *The Philosophical Impact of Contemporary Physics*, op. cit.; for a useful analysis of the process philosophy of José Vasconcelos, see P. Romanell, *The Making of the Mexican Mind* (Notre Dame: University of Notre Dame Press, 1967) ch. 4; S. Alexander, *Space, Time and Deity* 2 vols (London: Macmillan, 1920).

232. *Tübinger Einleitung in die Philosophie*, GA, vol. 13, p. 366.

CHAPTER 5

1. For the treatment of the future in analytical philosophy, see for example R. M. Gale (ed.), *The Philosophy of Time. A Collection of Essays* (op. cit.).

2. *Das Materialismusproblem*, GA, vol. 7, ch. 43.

3. ibid., pp. 409–17.

4. ibid., pp. 401–17.

5. ibid., pp. 409, 415.

6. *Philosophische Aufsätze, GA*, vol. 10, p. 350, and *Experimentum Mundi, GA*, vol. 15, pp. 52–3.

7. *Experimentum Mundi, GA*, vol. 15, pp. 188–230.

8. *Das Prinzip Hoffnung, GA*, vol. 5, p. 342, and *Philosophische Aufsätze, GA*, vol. 10, pp. 330–44.

9. *Experimentum Mundi, GA*, vol. 15, ch. 13; cf. *Tübinger Einleitung in die Philosophie, GA*, vol. 13, ch. 17.

10. *Experimentum Mundi, GA*, vol. 15, pp. 54–6.

11. *Experimentum Mundi, GA*, vol. 15, pp. 63–5.

12. *Subjekt-Objekt, GA*, vol. 8, chs 14 and 21.

13. *Philosophische Aufsätze, GA*, vol. 10, pp. 219–23, *Subjekt-Objekt, GA*, vol. 8, pp. 441–53 and ch. 14, and *Naturrecht und menschliche Würde, GA*, vol. 6, chs 12, 17, 22.

14. *Experimentum Mundi, GA*, vol. 15, ch. 41, and *Das Prinzip Hoffnung, GA*, vol. 5, ch. 47.

15. *Das Prinzip Hoffnung, GA*, vol. 5, ch. 54, especially p. 1568.

16. ibid., pp. 1555–62, 1575–7.

17. ibid., pp. 1562–67, and *Subjekt-Objekt, GA*, vol. 8, ch. 24 and for Scheler's ethics, see Alfons Deeken, *Process and Permanence in Ethics: Max Scheler's Moral Philosophy* (New York: Paulist Press, 1974).

18. *Naturrecht und menschliche Würde, GA*, vol. 6, pp. 200–6, especially p. 201.

19. ibid., pp. 202–3.

20. ibid., pp. 203–4.

21. ibid., pp. 213, 237.

22. ibid., p. 214.

23. ibid., pp. 233–8, cf. *Das Prinzip Hoffnung, GA*, vol. 5, pp. 621–37.

24. *Das Prinzip Hoffnung, GA*, vol. 5, pt IV.

25. ibid., pp. 674–80.

26 *Naturrecht und menschliche Würde, GA*, vol. 6, pp. 212, 233–8.

27. ibid., p. 237, and *Das Prinzip Hoffnung, GA*, vol. 5, pp. 629–37.

28. *Naturrecht und menschliche Würde, GA*, vol. 6, pp. 16–20, 23–29, 38–49, 50–75.

29. ibid., ch. 18.

30. *Experimentum Mundi, GA*, vol. 15, ch. 41, and *Philosophische Aufsätze, GA*, vol. 10, pp. 26–30.

31. *Das Prinzip Hoffnung, GA*, vol. 5, p. 1621, and *Naturrecht und menschliche Würde, GA*, vol. 6, pp. 211–15.

32. *Philosophische Aufsätze, GA*, vol. 10, pp. 26–30.

33. *Naturrecht und menschliche Würde, GA*, vol. 6, p. 215, and *Experimentum Mundi, GA*, vol. 15, p. 262.

34. For an example of Bloch's work on the Marxist inheritance of bourgeois human rights in his DDR period, including a citation from Stalin, see 'Marx und die bürgerlichen Menschenrechte', (1953) in *Politische Messungen, GA*, vol. 11, pp. 342–50, especially p. 344.

35. *Naturrecht und menschliche Würde, GA,* vol. 6, pp. 211–15.
36. See for example, ibid., pp. 27–8, 32, 79–80, chs 16, 21 and 25, and *Das Prinzip Hoffnung, GA,* vol. 5, ch. 42.
37. *Naturrecht und menschliche Würde, GA,* vol. 6, pp. 12–13, 81–7, ch. 21, and *Das Prinzip Hoffnung, GA,* vol. 5, pp. 569–75, 687–98.
38. *Naturrecht und menschliche Würde, GA,* vol. 6, pp. 175–200.
39. See *Christian Thomasius, ein deutscher Gelehrter ohne Misere* (East Berlin, 1953), reprinted in *Naturrecht und menschliche Würde, GA,* vol. 6, pp. 315–56. Bloch praises Thomasius' three rules for happiness and peace (*iustum, decorum, honestum*), his equation of natural religion with morality, and his attempt to widen natural law to include the idea of a community in which there would be neither rich nor poor, pp. 333–7.
40. *Naturrecht und menschliche Würde, GA,* vol. 6, pp. 241–2.
41. ibid., pp. 234–45, 252.
42. ibid., p. 242.
43. ibid., pp. 247, 258.
44. ibid., p. 227.
45. ibid., pp. 270–6.
46. ibid., p. 274.
47. ibid., pp. 258–9, cf. *Das Prinzip Hoffnung, GA,* vol. 5, pp. 598–637, 134–43.
48. *Naturrecht und menschliche Würde, GA,* vol. 6, pp. 252, 275–6, and ch. 25.
49. ibid., pp. 253–9, 271–3.
50. ibid., p. 259.
51. ibid., pp. 301–10, 257.
52. ibid., pp. 254–9.
53. Cf. E. Kamenka, *Marxism and Ethics* (London: Macmillan, 1969) chs I and II.
54. For Bloch's influence on contemporary Germany jurisprudence, see W. Maihofer, 'Demokratie und Sozialismus', in *Ernst Bloch zu ehren,* op. cit., pp. 31–67; W. Maihofer (ed.), *Ideologie und Recht* (Frankfurt a. M.: Vittorio Klostermann, 1969) pp. 1–35, 121 ff.
55. For a recent Soviet discussion of the problem of natural law, see V. A. Tumanov, *Contemporary Bourgeois Legal Thought,* trans. J. Gibbons (Moscow: Progress Publishers, 1974). Tumanov cites German work on natural law influenced by Bloch (pp. 291–4) and accepts the need for a Marxist axiology which inherits the concept of natural law and the rights of man (pp. 286–91).
56. See H. Cunow, *Die Marxsche Geschichts- Gesellschafts- und Staatstheorie,* 2 vols (Berlin: Buchhandlung Vorwärts, Paul Singer, 1920–1), and J. Fraser, *An Introduction to the thought of Galvano della Volpe* (London: Lawrence and Wishart, 1976) ch. 5.
57. Cf. J. L. Talmon, *Political Messianism: The Romantic Phase* (London: Secker and Warburg, 1960), Introduction and Conclusions.
58. *Naturrecht und menschliche Würde, GA,* vol. 6, p. 253.
59. For Marx's views on aesthetics, see M. Lifschitz (ed.), Marx (Karl) und Engels (Friedrich), *Über Kunst und Literatur* (Berlin: Verlag

Bruno Henschel und Sohn, 1950); L. Baxandall and S. Morawski (ed.), *Karl Marx and Frederick Engels, on literature and art* (New York: International General, 1974) and S. S. Prawer, *Karl Marx and World Literature* (Oxford: Clarendon Press, 1976).

60. *Literarische Aufsätze, GA*, vol. 9, pp. 111–4.
61. ibid., p. 113.
62. *Tübinger Einleitung in die Philosophie, GA*, vol. 13, pp. 175–8.
63. *Subjekt-Objekt, GA*, vol. 8, ch. 15.
64. For a selection of Bloch's work on aesthetics and useful introductions, see G. Ueding (ed.), Ernst Bloch. *Ästhetik des Vor-Scheins* (2 vols) (Frankfurt a. M.: Suhrkamp, 1974).
65. *Das Prinzip Hoffnung, GA*, vol. 5, pp. 242–58, and *Experimentum Mundi, GA*, vol. 15, ch. 42.
66. *Das Prinzip Hoffnung, GA*, vol. 5, p. 255.
67. ibid., p. 249.
68. *Das Prinzip Hoffnung, GA*, vol. 5, pp. 256–8, and *Literarische Aufsätze, GA*, vol. 9, pp. 137–41.
69. *Das Prinzip Hoffnung, GA*, vol, 5, p. 258.
70. *Literarische Aufsätze, GA*, vol. 9, p. 141.
71. ibid., pp. 135–60.
72. For Bloch's influence on Western Marxist aesthetics, see H. Arvon, *Marxist Esthetics*, trans. H. R. Lane (Ithaca: Cornell University Press, 1973) p. 116, where Arvon suggests that the aesthetics of Marx and Engels may need to be quickened with Bloch's 'utopian spirit'; and E. Fischer, *Art Against Ideology*, trans. A. Bostock (London: Allen Lane, The Penguin Press, 1969) pp. 48–50, 172, 196.
73. *Das Materialismusproblem, GA*, vol. 7, pp. 409–17.
74. See Bloch's discriminations in 'Hebel, Gotthelf und bäurisches Tao' (1926) in *Literarische Aufsätze, GA*, vol. 9, pp. 365–84.
75. *Das Prinzip Hoffnung, GA*, vol. 5, p. 160.
76. Cf. *Literarische Aufsätze, GA*, vol. 9. pp. 190–6.
77. See, for example, 'Marxismus und Dichtung' (1935); Bloch's brilliant analysis of detective novels in *Literarische Aufsätze, GA*, vol. 9, pp. 135–43 and 242–63, and *Das Prinzip Hoffnung, GA*, vol. 5, ch. 40.
78. See Bloch's important discussion 'Kunst, die Stoff-Form entbindend' in *Das Materialismusproblem, GA*, vol. 7, pp. 521–4.
79. For Bloch's work on music see *Geist der Utopie* (1918), *GA*, vol. 16, pp. 81–234 and the collection of essays, *Zur Philosophie der Musik*, selected and edited by K. Bloch (Frankfurt a. M.: Suhrkamp, 1976).
80. For a comparison between Bloch and Adorno on music, see W. Gramar, *Musik und Verstehen. Eine Studie zur Musikästhetik Theodor W. Adornos* (Mainz: Matthias-Grünewald-Verlag 1976), especially pp. 226–35. On the development of Bloch's philosophy of music cf. H. Mayer, 'Musik als Luft von anderem Planeten. Ernst Blochs "Philosophie der Musik" und Ferruccio Busonis 'Neue Ästhetik der Tonkunst' in *Materialien zu Ernst Blochs "Prinzip Hoffnung"*, B. Schmidt (ed.) (Frankfurt a. M.: Suhrkamp, 1978) pp. 464–72.
81. *Geist der Utopie, GA*, vol. 16, pp. 225–7, and *Das Prinzip Hoffnung, GA*, vol. 5, ch. 51.

82. *Das Prinzip Hoffnung, GA,* vol. 5, p. 1256.
83. ibid., p. 1258.
84. ibid., pp. 1277-8.
85. ibid., pp. 1279.
86. Cf. *Geist der Utopie* (1918), *GA,* vol. 16, pp. 226-7.
87. See 'Über das mathematische und dialektische Wesen in der Musik' (Ein Versuch, 1925) in *Philosophische Aufsätze, GA,* vol. 10, pp. 501-14. Cf. 'Die Idealbilder Keplers' (1931) and 'Exkurs: Über Zeittechnik' (1928) in *Philosophische Aufsätze, GA,* vol. 10, pp. 514-26 and 567-72.
88. See Ernst Bloch and Hanns Eisler, 'Avantgarde-Kunst und Volksfront' in *Die neue Weltbühne,* 9 December 1937, and 'Die Kunst zu erben' in *Die neue Weltbühne,* 6 January 1938; both reprinted in *Ernst Blochs Wirkung. Ein Arbeitsbuch zum 90. Geburtstag* (Frankfurt a. M.: Suhrkamp, 1975) pp. 188-200. *Tendenz - Latenz -Utopie* op. cit., pp. 158-171.
89. *Geist der Utopie* (1918), *GA,* vol. 16, pp. 67-77.
90. See 'Der Expressionismus, jetzt erblickt' (1937), 'Diskussionen über Expressionismus' (1938) (originally published in *Das Wort,* Moscow, 3, no. 6, pp. 103-12); 'Das Problem des Expressionismus nochmals' (1940) in *Erbschaft dieser Zeit, GA,* vol. 4, pp. 255-78 and *Tendenz - Latenz - Utopie* op. cit., pp. 158-71. In English, see *Aesthetics and Politics,* translation ed. R. Taylor (London: New Left Books, 1977) pp. 9-27.
91. *Erbschaft dieser Zeit, GA,* vol. 4, pp. 265-6.
92. ibid., pp. 268, 255-63.
93. See G. Lukács, 'Realism in the Balance' in *Aesthetics and Politics,* op. cit., p. 34.
94. *Erbschaft dieser Zeit, GA,* vol. 4, pp. 278, 270.
95. ibid., p. 270.
96. ibid., pp. 270-1, 278. Cf. *Das Prinzip Hoffnung, GA,* vol. 5, pp. 256-8.
97. *Erbschaft dieser Zeit, GA,* vol. 4, pp. 268-71.
98. For Bloch's treatment of the problem of montage, see ibid., pp. 218-28.
99. Cf. Bloch's answer to Lukács essay 'Es geht um den Realismus' in *Das Prinzip Hoffnung, GA,* vol. 5, pp. 256-8.
100. *Tübinger Einleitung in die Philosophie, GA,* vol. 13, p. 122.
101. See, for example, 'Mangel an Opernstoffen' (1930) in *Literarische Aufsätze, GA,* vol. 9, pp. 161-5 and 'Zeitecho Stravinskij' in *Erbschaft dieser Zeit, GA,* vol. 4, pp. 232-40.
102. Bloch's views had a major impact on leading East German writers such as Günter Kunert and Peter Huchel, see J. Flores, *Poetry in East Germany* (London: Yale University Press, 1971) pp. 173-7, 291.
103. See, for example, *Das Prinzip Hoffnung, GA,* vol. 5, chs 26, 27, 28, 29, 38, 40, 51.
104. For Bloch's work on cinema see 'Über die Melodie im Kino' (Versuch 1913), 'Nochmals die Melodieschicht im Kino' (Fassung von 1919), and 'Bezeichnender Wandel in Kinofabeln' (1932) in *Literarische Aufsätze, GA,* vol. 9, pp. 75-8, 183-90, 'Der glänzende Filmmensch' in *Erbschaft dieser Zeit, GA,* vol. 4, pp. 35-6, and *Das Prinzip Hoffnung, GA,* vol. 5, pp. 471-8.

105. *Das Prinzip Hoffnung, GA,* vol. 5, pp. 969–77 and ch. 38.
106. ibid., chs 25, 26, 27, 28. 29.
107. Bloch's emphasis on the revolutionary potential of kolportage is unparalleled in Marxist aesthetics, see 'Rettung Wagners durch surrealistische Kolportage' (1929) in *Erbschaft dieser Zeit, GA,* vol. 4, pp. 372–80; ibid., pp. 168–81; *Das Prinzip Hoffnung, GA,* vol. 5, pp. 426–8, and *Literarische Aufsätze, GA,* vol. 9, pp. 131–5.
108. *Das Prinzip Hoffnung, GA,* vol. 5, pp. 1069–73.
109. *Erbschaft dieser Zeit, GA,* vol. 4, pp. 61–75.
110. *Das Materialismusproblem, GA,* vol. 7, pp. 409–25, especially 415.
111. See *Erbschaft dieser Zeit, GA,* vol. 4, pp. 230–2, and 250–5, cf. K. A. Dickson, *Towards Utopia: A Study of Brecht* (Oxford: Clarendon Press, 1978).
112. *Das Prinzip Hoffnung, GA,* vol. 5, ch. 30.
113. Bloch outlined his concept of *Verfremdung* in *Das Prinzip Hoffnung, GA,* vol. 5, pp. 430–5, but he develops it at greater length in his two volume *Verfremdungen* (Frankfurt a. M.: Suhrkamp, 1962 and 1964) reprinted in *Literarische Aufsätze, GA,* vol. 9, pp. 220–548.
114. *Literarische Aufsätze, GA,* vol. 9, pp. 277–84.
115. ibid., pp. 401–548.
116. Cf. G. Figal, *Theodor W. Adorno. Das Naturschöne als spekulative Gedankenfigur* (Bonn: Bouvier Verlag Herbert Grundmann, 1977).
117. For a reassessment of the 'warm stream' in Lenin's views on aesthetics, see V. Shcherbina, *Lenin and Problems of Literature* (English trans.) (Moscow: Progress Publishers, 1974), and for a contrast, Z. Apresyan, *Freedom and the Artist,* trans. B. Meares (Moscow: Progress Publishers, 1968) and A. Zis, *Foundations of Marxist Aesthetics,* trans. K. Judelson (Moscow: Progress Publishers, 1977).
118. *Atheismus im Christentum, GA,* vol. 14, pp. 91–2, and *Das Prinzip Hoffnung, GA,* vol. 5, 307–10.
119. *Atheismus im Christentum, GA,* vol. 14, p. 303.
120. *Das Prinzip Hoffnung, GA,* vol. 5, pp. 1404, 1524.
121. *Experimentum Mundi, GA,* vol. 15, ch. 43.
122. *Das Prinzip Hoffnung, GA,* vol. 5, ch. 53.
123. ibid., p. 1416.
124. *Atheismus im Christentum, GA,* vol. 14, ch. 48.
125. ibid., pp. 316–17.
126. ibid., p. 317.
127. *Das Prinzip Hoffnung, GA,* vol. 5, pp. 1405–17, 1515–24.
128. *Atheismus im Christentum, GA,* vol. 14, p. 282.
129. ibid., p. 284.
130. *Das Prinzip Hoffnung, GA,* vol. 5, pp. 1524–34.
131. ibid., p. 1533.
132. Cf. *Atheismus im Christentum, GA,* vol. 14, frontpiece.
133. *Das Prinzip Hoffnung, GA,* vol. 5, p. 1416.
134. ibid., cf. p. 1550.
135. ibid., p. 1548.
136. *Erbschaft dieser Zeit, GA,* vol. 4, pp. 405–9, and *Naturrecht und menschliche Würde, GA,* vol. 6, pp. 310–14.

137. *Das Prinzip Hoffnung, GA*, vol. 5, pp. 1521-2.
138. *Tübinger Einleitung in die Philosophie, GA*, vol. 13, p. 181.
139. ibid., pp. 184, 357-76.
140. *Das Prinzip Hoffnung, GA*, vol. 5, p. 254.
141. *Atheismus im Christentum, GA*, vol. 14, pp. 98-111, especially p. 111.
142. ibid., pp. 116-27, and *Das Prinzip Hoffnung, GA*, vol. 5, pp. 1450-64.
143. *Das Prinzip Hoffnung, GA*, vol. 5, pp. 1454-5.
144. *Atheismus im Christentum, GA*, vol. 14, pp. 126-48.
145. ibid., pp. 148-66, and 207-12.
146. *Das Prinzip Hoffnung, GA*, vol. 5, pp. 1482-1504, and *Atheismus im Christentum, GA*, vol. 14, pp. 172-83.
147. *Atheismus im Christentum, GA*, vol. 14, pp. 207-31.
148. *Das Prinzip Hoffnung, GA*, vol. 5, p. 1404.
149. *Atheismus im Christentum, GA*, vol. 14, pp. 64-80 and 218-25.
150. ibid., pp. 173-83.
151. ibid., pp. 182-3.
152. ibid., pp. 226-31, and *Das Prinzip Hoffnung, GA*, vol. 5, pp. 1540-50.
153. *Atheismus im Christentum, GA*, vol. 14, pp. 218-25.
154. See Bloch's monograph, *Thomas Münzer als Theologe der Revolution, GA*, vol. 2, in which Bloch breaks with the Engels–Kautsky pattern of Communist interpretation and takes Münzer's theology seriously as political theology and a revival of true Christianity.
155. Cf. ibid., pp. 117-217.
156. *Atheismus im Christentum, GA*, vol. 14, frontpiece.
157. ibid., pp. 350-4.
158. ibid., frontpiece.
159. For Lenin's attack on the 'God-builders', see V. I. Lenin, *Materialism and Empirio-Criticism*, English trans. (Moscow: Progress Publishers, 1970) pp. 333-5.
160. *Das Prinzip Hoffnung, GA*, vol. 5, pp. 1482-93, and *Atheismus im Christentum, GA*, vol. 14, ch. 49, and *Experimentum Mundi, GA*, vol. 15, ch. 45.
161. See J. Moltmann, *A Theology of Hope*, trans. J. W. Leitch (London: S.C.M., 1967) especially pp. 16, 79, 92; and for the ensuing controversy, W-D. Marsch (ed.) *Diskussion über die "Theologie der Hoffnung" von Jürgen Moltmann* (Munich: Kaiser, 1967). For the influence of Bloch on Moltmann's subsequent work, see *Religion, Revolution and the Future*, trans. M. D. Meeks (New York: Charles Scribner's Sons, 1969), *Man. Christian Anthropology in the Conflicts of the Present*, trans. J. Sturdy (London: S.P.C.K. 1974) and *The Experiment Hope* (ed., trans.) with a foreword by M. D. Meeks (Philadelphia: Fortress Press, 1975).
162. W. Pannenberg, *Basic Questions in Theology*, trans. G. H. Kehm (London: S.C.M., 1971) vol. 2, pp. 237-8. Cf. Harvey Cox's foreword to the volume, *Man On His Own*, trans. E. B. Ashton (New York: Herder and Herder, 1970) pp. 7-18.
163. For Bloch's influence on the Catholic theologian Karl Rahner, see K. Rahner, *Theological Investigations*, trans. D. Bourke (London: Darton, Longman and Todd, 1973) vol. X, pp. 242-59.

164. J. Metz, *Theology of the World*, trans. W. Glen-Doepel (London: Burns and Oates, 1969) pp. 87–100. See Metz's 'Gott vor uns' in *Ernst Bloch zu ehren*, op. cit., pp. 227–41.

165. See J. M. Bonino, *Christians and Marxists. The Mutual Challenge to Revolution* (London: Hodder and Stoughton, 1976); G. Gutiérrez, *A Theology of Liberation*, trans. and ed. Sister Caridad Inda and John Eagleson (Maryknoll: Orbis, 1973) especially pp. 216–24; J. Miranda, *Marx and the Bible*, trans. J. Eagleson (Maryknoll: Orbis, 1974); R. Alves, *A Theology of Human Hope* (Washington: Corpus Books, 1969); J. L. Segundo, *The Liberation of Theology*, trans. J. Drury (Dublin: Gill and Macmillan, 1977); cf. D. Winter, *Hope in Captivity. The Prophetic Church in Latin America* (London: Epworth Press, 1977); A. Kee (ed.), *A Reader in Political Theology* (London: S.C.M., 1974).

166. The dialogue was mutual. See H. Gollwitzer *The Christian Faith and the Marxist Criticism of Religion* trans. D. Cairns (Edinburgh: The Saint Andrew Press, 1970); W. Machovec̆, *A Marxist Looks at Jesus*, intro. by P. Hebblethwaite (London: Darton, Longman and Todd, 1976) and V. Gardavsky, *God is Not Yet Dead*, trans. V. Menkes (Harmondsworth: Penguin, 1973). For Bloch's continuing influence on Christian Theology, see E. Jüngel, *Gott als Geheimnis der Welt*, 3rd ed. (Tübingen: J. C. B. Mohr (Paul Siebeck), 1978) pp. 104, 135, 462, 536, and J. Macquarrie, *Christian Hope* (Oxford: Mowbrays, 1978).

167. *Das Materialismusproblem*, GA, vol. 7, p. 308.

168. *Das Prinzip Hoffnung, GA*, vol. 5, pp. 301–2, 332–3.

169. ibid., pp. 299–303.

170. ibid., pp. 301–2.

171. ibid., pp. 295–303.

172. ibid., p. 328.

173. ibid., p. 302.

174. *Das Materialismusproblem*, GA, vol. 7, pp. 382–9.

175. ibid., pp. 384–5.

176. *Experimentum Mundi, GA*, vol. 15, p. 146.

177. See 'Freiheit, ihre Schichtung und ihr Verhältnis zur Wahrheit' (1956) in *Philosophische Aufsätze, GA*, vol. 10, pp. 573–98, especially pp. 592–8, and 'Über Freiheit und objektive Gesetzlichkeit, im Prozess gesehen' (1954) in ibid., pp. 531–67, especially pp. 541–50.

178. ibid., p. 546.

179. ibid., pp. 584–6.

180. *Experimentum Mundi, GA*, vol. 15, ch. 29.

181. ibid., pp. 126–9.

182. *Das Materialismusproblem*, GA, vol. 7, pp. 389–401.

183. ibid., p. 397.

184. ibid., pp. 391–8.

185. ibid., p. 402.

186. ibid., pp. 401–25, 394.

187. See E. Bloch 'Theory-Praxis in the Long Run', trans. W. Hudson, in R. Fitzgerald (ed.), *The Sources of Hope* (London: Pergamon,

1979), pp. 153-7; cf. *Tendenz - Latenz - Utopie*, op. cit., pp. 246-50.

188. *Tübinger Einleitung in die Philosophie*, GA, vol. 13, pp. 124-5, and *Das Prinzip Hoffnung*, GA, vol. 5, pp. 569-75, 582-90.
189. *Tübinger Einleitung in die Philosophie*, GA, vol. 13, pp. 145-6.
190. ibid., ch. 15.
191. ibid., pp. 127-9.
192. K. Popper, *The Poverty of Historicism*, 2nd ed. (London: Routledge and Kegan Paul, 1969).
193. See 'Epikur in der Dissertation von Karl Marx oder ein subjektiver Faktor im Fall der Atome' (1967) in *Philosophische Aufsätze*, GA, vol. 10, pp. 526-31.
194. *Das Materialismusproblem*, GA, vol. 7, p. 307.
195. ibid., pp. 16, 307.
196. ibid., pp. 304-13.
197. ibid., pp. 308-9.
198. ibid., p. 308.
199. ibid., pp. 110-11.
200. ibid., pp. 304, 309.
201. ibid., pp. 309-11.
202. ibid., pp. 309-13, 366, 461-6.
203. ibid., pp. 359-71.
204. ibid., p. 360, cf. *Subjekt-Objekt*, GA, vol. 8, pp. 210-11.
205. *Philosophische Aufsätze*, GA, vol. 10, pp. 348-9, and *Das Materialismusproblem*, GA, vol. 7, ch. 38.
206. *Philosophische Aufsätze*, GA, vol. 10, pp. 34-41, 330-44.
207. *Das Materialismusproblem*, GA, vol. 7, pp. 357-8, and *Das Prinzip Hoffnung*, GA, vol. 5, pp. 767-817.
208. *Das Materialismusproblem*, GA, vol. 7, pp. 342-56.
209. *Erbschaft dieser Zeit*, GA, vol. 4, pp. 289-95, and *Das Materialismusproblem*, GA, vol. 7, pp. 425-38.
210. Cf. R. Bhaskar, *A Realist Theory of Science* (Leeds: Leeds Books, 1975) chs 1 and 4, and David-Hillel Ruben, *Marxism and Materialism A Study in Marxist Theory of Knowledge* (Sussex: The Harvester Press, 1977).
211. *Das Materialismusproblem*, GA, vol. 7, pp. 132-303.
212. ibid., pp. 129-30.
213. ibid., p. 18.
214. ibid., p. 474, and *Experimentum Mundi*, GA, vol. 15, p. 261.
215. *Experimentum Mundi*, GA, vol. 15, p. 79, and *Das Materialismusproblem*, GA, vol. 7, pp. 474-5.
216. ibid., pp. 63-5.
217. Cf. B. Schmidt, 'Vom teleologischen Prinzip in der Materie' in *Ernst Blochs Wirkung. Ein Arbeitsbuch zum 90. Geburtstag* (Frankfurt: a. M.: Suhrkamp, 1975) pp. 362-80.
218. *Das Materialismusproblem*, GA, vol. 7, p. 474.
219. ibid., pp. 461-6.
220. ibid., pp. 472-7.
221. ibid., p. 474.

222. ibid., pp. 476, 20.
223. ibid., p. 252.
224. ibid., pp. 32-131.
225. ibid., pp. 113-20.
226. *Experimentum Mundi, GA,* vol. 15, ch. 35, and *Das Materialismusproblem, GA,* vol. 7, pp. 112-26.
227. *Experimentum Mundi, GA,* vol. 15, pp. 50-4, 59-60.
228. ibid., pp. 112-19.
229. ibid., p. 56.
230. ibid., p. 71.
231. ibid., pp. 119-20.
232. ibid., chs 36-40.
233. ibid., p. 78.
234. ibid., pp. 76-9.
235. *Das Materialismusproblem, GA,* vol. 7, p. 446.
236. cf. *Tübinger Einleitung in die Philosophie, GA,* vol. 13, ch. 21.
237. See A. Münster, *Tagträume,* op. cit., p. 143, and *Tübinger Einleitung in die Philosophie, GA,* vol. 13, pp. 207-9, and see 'Utopische Funktion im Materialismus' (1974), in R. Traub and H. Wieser (ed.), *Gespräche mit Ernst Bloch,* op. cit., pp. 269-91.
238. *Das Materialismusproblem, GA,* vol. 7, ch. 47.
239. *Das Materialismusproblem, GA,* vol. 7, pp. 435-8.
240. *Das Prinzip Hoffnung, GA,* vol. 5, pp. 273-4.
241. See Bloch's monograph, *Avicenna und die Aristotelische Linke* (East Berlin, 1952) reprinted in *Das Materialismusproblem, GA,* vol. 7. pp. 479-546.
242. ibid., pp. 516-21.
243. *Experimentum Mundi, GA,* vol. 15, p. 229.

CHAPTER 6

1. L. Kołakowski, *Main Currents of Marxism,* trans. P. S. Falla (Oxford: Clarendon Press, 1978) vol. III, The Breakdown, ch. XII, 'Ernst Bloch: Marxism As A Futuristic Gnosis'.
2. Cf. V. I. Lenin, 'Marxism and Revisionism' (1908), reprinted in *Against Revisionism, in Defence of Marxism* (Moscow: Progress Publishers 1970) pp. 34-43.
3. Cf. P. Anderson, *Considerations on Western Marxism* (London: New Left Books, 1976).
4. L. Marin 'La pratique-fiction Utopie', in G. Raulet (ed.), *Utopie - Marxisme selon Ernst Bloch,* op. cit. pp. 241-64; J-F. Lyotard, 'Puissance des Traces ou Contribution de Bloch à une histoire païenne' in ibid., pp. 57-67, and *Discours, Figure* (Paris: Éditions Klincksieck, 1971); G. Deleuze, *Différence et répétition* (Paris: Presses universitaires de France, 1968); P. Boutang, *Ontologie du Secret* (Paris: Presses universitaires de France, 1973); J. Derrida, *Of Grammatology* (1967), trans. G. C. Spivak (Baltimore: The Johns Hopkins Uni-

versity Press, 1976) and *Writing and Difference* (1967), trans. A. Bass (London: Routledge and Kegan Paul, 1978); J. Kristeva, 'Sémanalyse et production de sens' in *Essais de sémiotique poétique* ed. A. J. Greimas (Paris: Larousse, 1971) pp. 207–34, and *Semiotikè: Recherches pour une sémanalyse* (Paris: Seuil, 1969).

Select Bibliography

PRIMARY SOURCES

Unpublished Correspondence

Bloch to Lukács

Letters from the years 1910 to 1970 held by the Lukács Archive, Budapest, Hungary.

Bloch to Kracauer

Letters from the 1920s and early 1930s with Kracauer's replies, in the Kracauer Nachlass, the Schiller National Museum, Marbach am Neckar, West Germany.

Bloch's Works

A collected edition of Bloch's works has been published by Suhrkamp Verlag in sixteen volumes:

1. *Spuren*
2. *Thomas Münzer als Theologe der Revolution*
3. *Geist der Utopie* (1923)
4. *Erbschaft dieser Zeit*
5. *Das Prinzip Hoffnung* (in three volumes)
6. *Naturrecht und menschliche Würde*
7. *Das Materialismusproblem — seine Geschichte und Substanz*
8. *Subjekt-Objekt — Erläuterungen zu Hegel*
9. *Literarische Aufsätze*
10. *Philosophische Aufsätze zur objektiven Phantasie*
11. *Politische Messungen — Pestzeit Vormärz*

12. *Zwischenwelten in der Philosophiegeschichte (Aus Leipziger Vorlesungen)*
13. *Tübinger Einleitung in die Philosophie*
14. *Atheismus im Christentum*
15. *Experimentum Mundi — Frage, Kategorien des Herausbringens, Praxis*
16. *Geist der Utopie* (facsimile of 1918 edition)
Additional posthumous volume: *Tendenz — Latenz — Utopie*

Original publication details are as follows:
1918 *Geist der Utopie* (Munich and Leipzig); reworked edition Berlin; further revised Frankfurt a. M., 1964.
1921 *Thomas Münzer als Theologe der Revolution* (Munich); East Berlin, 1960; reworked edition Frankfurt a. M., 1962.
1923 *Durch die Wüste. Kritische Aufsätze* (Berlin); revised edition Frankfurt a. M., 1964.
1930 *Spuren* (Berlin); new enlarged edition Berlin and Frankfurt a. M., 1959.
1935 *Erbschaft dieser Zeit* (Zurich); enlarged edition, Frankfurt a. M., 1962.
1946 *Freiheit und Ordnung. Abriss der Sozialutopien* (New York).
1949 *Subjekt-Objekt. Erläuterungen zu Hegel* (East Berlin); 2nd edition 1952; enlarged edition, Frankfurt a. M., 1962; Mexican edition, *Il pensamiento de Hegel,* Mexico City, 1949.
1952 *Avicenna und die Aristotelische Linke* (East Berlin); enlarged edition, Frankfurt a. M., 1963.
1953 *Christian Thomasius. Ein deutscher Gelehrter ohne Misere* (East Berlin).
1954 *Das Prinzip Hoffnung* (East Berlin). 1954 (vol. I), 1955 (vol. II), 1959 (vol. III); revised edition in two volumes, Frankfurt a. M., 1959.
1956 *Differenzierungen im Begriff Fortschritt* (East Berlin).
1961 *Naturrecht und menschliche Würde* (Frankfurt a. M.).
1961 *Philosophische Grundfragen. Zur Ontologie des Noch-Nicht-Seins* (Frankfurt a. M.).
1962 *Verfremdungen I* (Frankfurt a. M.).
1963 *Tübinger Einleitung in die Philosophie,* vol. I (Frankfurt a. M.).
1964 *Tübinger Einleitung in die Philosophie,* vol. II (Frankfurt a. M.).

1964 *Verfremdungen II* (Frankfurt a. M.).
1965 *Literarische Aufsätze* (Frankfurt a. M.).
1968 *Atheismus im Christentum* (Frankfurt a. M.).
1969 *Philosophische Aufsätze zur objektiven Phantasie* (Frankfurt a. M.).
1970 *Politische Messungen, Pestzeit, Vormärz* (Frankfurt a. M.).
1972 *Das Materialismusproblem, seine Geschichte und Substanz* (Frankfurt a. M.).
1972 *Vorlesungen zur Philosophie der Renaissance* (Frankfurt a. M.).
1975 *Experimentum Mundi. Frage, Kategorien des Herausbringens, Praxis* (Frankfurt a. M.).
1977 *Zwischenwelten in der Philosophiegeschichte* (Frankfurt a. M.).
1978 *Tendenz - Latenz - Utopie* (Frankfurt a. M.).

For complete details of Bloch's essays until 1963, see S. Unseld (ed.), *Ernst Bloch zu ehren (sic)* (Frankfurt a. M.: Suhrkamp, 1965) pp. 397–403.

Useful Collections

Abschied von der Utopie?, ed. Hanna Gekle (Frankfurt a.M.: Suhrkamp, 1980) a posthumous selection.
Das antizipierende Bewusstsein (Frankfurt a. M.: Suhrkamp, 1972).
Ästhetik des Vor-Scheins I, ed. Gert Ueding (Frankfurt a. M.: Suhrkamp, 1974).
Ästhetik des Vor-Scheins II, ed. Gert Ueding (Frankfurt a. M.: Suhrkamp, 1974).
Freiheit und Ordnung. Abriss der Sozialutopien (Reinbek b. Hamburg: Rowohlt, 1969).
Vom Hasard zur Katastrophe. Politische Aufsätze aus den Jahren 1934–1939 (Frankfurt a. M.: Suhrkamp, 1972).
Karl Marx und die Menschlichkeit. Utopische Phantasie und Weltveränderung (Reinbek b. Hamburg: Rowohlt, 1969).
Über Karl Marx (Frankfurt a. M.: Suhrkamp, 1971) 3rd ed.
Die Kunst, Schiller zu sprechen und andere literarische Aufsätze (Frankfurt a. M.: Suhrkamp, 1969).
Über Methode und System bei Hegel (Frankfurt a. M.: Suhrkamp, 1970).

Pädagogica (Frankfurt a. M.: Suhrkamp, 1971).
Politik und Ästhetik (Diskussionen der Thesen von Lukács)
(Frankfurt a. M.: Suhrkamp, 1972).
Recht, Moral, Staat (Pfullingen: Günther Neske, 1971).
Widerstand und Friede. Aufsätze zur Politik (Frankfurt a. M.:
Suhrkamp, 1968).

In addition, see especially:
'Marx als Denker der Revolution', *Praxis*, 1969, pp. 17–19, re-
published in *Marx und die Revolution*, Vorträge von Ernst
Bloch *et al.* (Frankfurt a. M.: Suhrkamp, 1970) pp. 7–11.
'Zur empirischen und philosophischen Cruxbildung im Erken-
nen' in *American Imago*, vol. 35, nos. 1–2 (1978) pp. 208–13.

Interviews

Adorno, T. W. and Bloch, E. *Gespräch über die Utopie* (Die
Waage, Zollikerberg, 1973).
Fetscher, I. *et al.* 'Bloch und Lukács im Gespräch', *Neues
Forum,* vol. 14, no. 167–8, Wien, Nov.–Dec. (1967) pp.
837–43.
Landmann, M. 'Gespräche mit Ernst Bloch', *Neue deutsche
Hefte,* vol. 14, 1967, pp. 23–38.
——, 'Talking with Ernst Bloch: Korčula, 1968', trans. D. Parent,
in *Telos*, no. 25, Fall (1975) pp. 165–85.
Lowy, M. 'Interview with Ernst Bloch', *New German Critique,*
no. 9, Fall (1976) pp. 35–45.
Moltmann, J. *Im Gespräch mit Ernst Bloch* (Munich: Chr.
Kaiser Verlag, 1976).
Münster, A. (ed.) *Tagträume vom aufrechten Gang. Sechs Inter-
views mit Ernst Bloch* (Frankfurt a. M.: Suhrkamp, 1977).
Traub, G. and Wieser, H. (ed.) *Gespräche mit Ernst Bloch*
(Frankfurt a. M.: Suhrkamp, 1975).
Im Christentum steckt die Revolte, Gespräch mit Adelbert Reif
(Zurich: Arche, 1971).

English Translations

Atheism in Christianity (New York: Herder and Herder, 1972).
J. T. Swann's translation of *Atheismus im Christentum*
(Frankfurt a. M.: Suhrkamp, 1968).

'Causality and Finality as Active, Objectifying Categories', an extract from *Experimentum Mundi*, prior to publication, trans. G. Ellard, *Telos*, no. 21, Fall (1974) pp. 96-107.

'Dialectics and Hope', a chapter taken from *Subjekt-Objekt. Erläuterungen zu Hegel*, trans. M. Ritter, *New German Critique*, no. 9, Fall (1976) pp. 3-10.

'A Jubilee for Renegades', taken from *Politische Messungen — Pestzeit, Vormärz* and *Vom Hasard zur Katastrophe*, trans. D. Bathrick and N. V. Shults, *New German Critique*, no. 4. Winter (1975) pp. 17-25.

On Karl Marx (New York: Herder and Herder, 1971). John Maxwell's translation of the anthology *Über Karl Marx* (Frankfurt a. M.: Suhrkamp, 1968).

'Man as Possibility' in *Cross Currents*, XVIII, no. 3, Summer (1968) pp. 273-83, trans. W. R. White. A translation of 'Der Mensch als Möglichkeit' which first appeared in *Forum. Oesterreichische Monatsblätter für Kulturelle Freiheit*, vol. XIII, nos. 140-1 (1965) pp. 357-61.

Man On His Own (New York: Herder and Herder, 1970), E. B. Ashton's translation of the anthology *Religion im Erbe. Eine Auswahl aus seinen religionsphilosophischen Schriften* (Frankfurt a. M.: Suhrkamp, 1961).

'Nonsynchronism and the Obligation to its Dialectics', part of *Erbschaft dieser Zeit*, trans. M. Ritter, *New German Critique*, no. 11, Spring (1977) pp. 22-38.

'Odysseus Did Not Die in Ithaca' from *Das Prinzip Hoffnung*, trans. H. Loewy and G. Steiner, in G. Steiner and R. Fagles (ed.), *Homer — A Collection of Critical Essays* (Englewood Cliffs: Prentice Hall, 1962) pp. 81-5.

'Philosophy as Cabaret' in *New Left Review*, no. 116, July–Aug. 1979, pp. 94-6.

A Philosophy of the Future (New York: Herder and Herder, 1970). John Cumming's translation of *Tübinger Einleitung in die Philosophie*, vol. I (Frankfurt a. M.: Suhrkamp, 1963).

'Theory-Praxis in the Long Run', trans. W. Hudson, in R. Fitzgerald (ed.), in *The Sources of Hope* (London: Pergamon, 1979) pp. 153-7.

'On the Threepenny Opera', essay from *Erbschaft dieser Zeit*, trans. S. Wilkins, in M. Solomon (ed.), *Marxism and Art* (Sussex: Harvester Press, 1979) pp. 576-8.

French Translations

L'athéisme dans le christianisme, trans. É. Kaufholz and G. Raulet (Paris: Gallimard, 1978).

Droit Naturel et Dignité Humaine, trans. D. Authier and J. Lacoste (Paris: Payot, 1976).

L'esprit de l'utopie, trans. A-M. Lang and C. Piron-Audard (Paris: Gallimard, 1977).

Héritage de ce temps, trans. J. Lacoste (Paris: Payot, 1978).

La Philosophie de la Renaissance, trans. P. Kamnitzer (Paris: Payot, 1974).

Le Principe Espérance, trans. F. Wuilmart (Paris: Gallimard, 1976).

Sujet – Objet, trans. M. de Gandillac (Paris: Gallimard, 1977).

Thomas Münzer, théologien de la révolution, trans. M. de Gandillac (Paris: Julliard, 1964).

Traces, trans. P. Quillet and H. Hildenbrand (Paris: Gallimard, 1968).

SECONDARY SOURCES

For a full bibliography of secondary materials on Bloch, see Burghart Schmidt's bibliography appended to *Materialen zu Ernst Blochs 'Prinzip Hoffnung'* (Frankfurt a. M.: Suhrkamp, 1978).

Collections of Essays on Bloch

Bahr, H. (*et al.*) *Ernst Blochs Wirkung. Ein Arbeitsbuch zum 90. Geburtstag* (Frankfurt a. M.: Suhrkamp, 1975).

Bloch, K. and Reif A. (ed.) *'Denken heisst überschreiten': In memoriam Ernst Bloch 1885–1977* (Cologne: Europäische Verlagsanstalt, 1978).

Gropp, R. O. (ed.) *Festschrift Ernst Bloch zum 70. Geburtstag* (Berlin: VEB Deutscher Verlag der Wissenschaften, 1955).

Horn, J. H. (ed.) *Ernst Blochs Revision des Marxismus* (Berlin: VEB Deutscher Verlag der Wissenschaften, 1957).

Horster, D. (*et al.*) *Es muss nicht immer Marmor sein. Ernst Bloch zum 90. Geburtstag* (Berlin: Klaus Wagenbach, 1975).

Raulet, G. (ed.) *Utopie — Marxisme selon Ernst Bloch* (Paris: Payot, 1976).
Schmidt, B. (ed.) *Materialien zu Ernst Blochs 'Prinzip Hoffnung'* (Frankfurt a. M.: Suhrkamp, 1978).
Über Ernst Bloch (Frankfurt a. M.: Suhrkamp, 1971).
Unseld, S. (ed.) *Ernst Bloch zu ehren (sic)* (Frankfurt a. M.: Suhrkamp, 1965).

Issues of Journals

Aut-Aut, no. 125, September–October (1971).
Philosophy Today, no. 4, (1970).
Sozialistische Zeitschrift für Kunst und Gesellschaft, 3-4/ 1977 (double issue) 'Ernst Bloch — Aktualität und konkrete Utopie'.

Books and Articles on Bloch

Adorno, T. W. 'Grosse Blochmusik', in *Neue deutsche Hefte,* no. 69, April (1960) pp. 14 ff.
Asperen, G. M. van 'Hope and History, a Critical Inquiry into the Philosophy of Ernst Bloch', Thesis, Rijksuniversiteit, Utrecht, 1973.
Bahr, E. *Ernst Bloch.* (Köpfe des XX. Jahrhunderts series) (Berlin, Colloquium, 1974).
Baumann, G. 'Die Schlüssel-Gewalt der Erkenntnis, Ernst Blochs philosophische Haltung der "konkreten Utopie"', Licentiate Thesis, Université Catholique de Louvain, 1974.
Breines, P. 'Bloch Magic', *continuum,* vol. 7, no. 4, Winter (1970) pp. 619-24.
Bütow, H. G. *Philosophie und Gesellschaft im Denken Ernst Blochs* (Berlin: Ost-Europa Institut, 1963).
Christen, A. F. *Ernst Blochs Metaphysik der Materie* (Bonn: Bouvier, 1979).
Corral, J. P. del *El Marxismo Calido Ernst Bloch* (Madrid: Mañana Editorial Colección «Herramientas», Volumen 5, 1977).
Damus, R. *Ernst Bloch: Hoffnung als Prinzip — Prinzip ohne Hoffnung* (Meisenheim am Glan: Anton Hain, 1971).

Eggeling, K. 'Die Intelligenz in Philosophie und politischem Denken bei Ernst Bloch', Thesis, Hamburg Universität, 1977.

Enden, H. van den, (ed.) *Marxisme van de hoop – hoop van het Marxisme? Essays over de filosofie van Ernst Bloch* (Bussum: Het Wereldvenster, 1980).

Green, R. M. 'Ernst Bloch's Revision of Atheism', *Journal of Religion*, vol. 49, no. 2 (1969) pp. 128–35.

Gropp, R. O. (ed.) 'Die marxistische dialektische Methode und ihr Gegensatz zur idealistischen Dialektik Hegels', *Deutsche Zeitschrift für Philosophie*, vol. 2, no. 1, (1954) p. 69–112.

Gross, D. 'Ernst Bloch, The Dialectics of Hope' in D. Howard and K. Klare (ed.), *The Unknown Dimension European Marxism Since Lenin* (New York: Basic Books, 1972) ch IV. 'Man on His Own', *continuum*, vol. 7, no. 4, Winter (1970) pp. 625–7.

Hobsbawm, E. J. 'The Principle of Hope' in *The Times Literary Supplement*, leader article, 31 March 1961, reprinted in *Revolutionaries* (London: Weidenfeld and Nicolson, 1973) pp. 136–41.

Holz, H. H. *Logos spermatikos, Ernst Blochs Philosophie der unfertigen Welt* (Darmstadt and Neuwied: Luchterhand, 1975).

Horster, D. *Bloch zur Einführung* (Hannover: SOAK-Verlag, 1977).

Hurbon, L. *Ernst Bloch. Utopie et Espérance* (Paris: Les Éditions du Cerf, 1974).

Ivernel, P. 'Soupçons - D'Ernst Bloch à Walter Benjamin', in G. Raulet (ed.), *Utopie - Marxisme selon Ernst Bloch* (Paris: Payot, 1976) pp. 265–77.

Jäger, A. *Reich ohne Gott. Zur Eschatologie Ernst Blochs* (Zurich: EVZ-Verlag, 1969).

Kellner, D. and O'Hara, H. 'Utopia and Marxism in Ernst Bloch' in *New German Critique*, no 9, Fall (1976) pp. 11–34.

Kimmerle, H. *Die Zukunftsbedeutung der Hoffnung* (Bonn: Bouvier, 1966).

Kränzle, K. *Utopie und Ideologie. Gesellschaftskritik und politisches Engagement im Werk Ernst Blochs* (Bern: Verlag H. Lang und CIE, 1970).

Markun, S. *Ernst Bloch* (Hamburg: Rowohlt, 1977).

Marsch, W-D. *Hoffen worauf? Auseinandersetzung mit Ernst Bloch* (Hamburg: Furche Verlag, 1963).

Negt, O. 'Ernst Bloch — The German Philosopher of the October Revolution', trans. J. Zipes, *New German Critique*, no. 4, Winter (1975) pp. 3-16. 'The Non-Synchronous Heritage and the Problem of Propaganda', *New German Critique*, no. 9, Fall (1976) pp. 46-70.

Piccone, P. 'Bloch's Marxism', *continuum*, vol 7, no. 4, Winter (1970) pp. 627-31.

Plattel, M. *De rode en gouden toekomst, de avontuurlijke wijsbegeerte van Ernst Bloch* (Bilthoven, Ambo, 1976).

Rabinbach, A. 'Ernst Bloch's "Heritage of Our Times" and Fascism' in *New German Critique*, no. 11, Spring (1977) pp. 5-21.

Ratschow, C. H. *Atheismus im Christentum? Eine Auseinandersetzung mit Ernst Bloch* (Gütersloh: Gütersloher Verlagshaus Gerd Mohn, 1971).

Raulet, G. 'Critique of Religion and Religion as Critique: The Secularised Hope of Ernst Bloch', trans. D. Parent, ed. T. Luke, *New German Critique*, no. 9, Fall (1976) pp. 71-85.

Reinicke, H. L. *Materie und Revolution, eine materialistisch-erkenntnistheoretische Untersuchung zur Philosophie von Ernst Bloch* (Kronberg: Scriptor Verlag, 1974).

Roeder von Diersburg, E. *Zur Ontologie und Logik offener Systeme* (Hamburg: Felix Meiner, 1967),

Rühle, J. 'The Philosopher of Hope: Ernst Bloch', in L. Labedz (ed.), *Revisionism. Essays on the History of Marxist Ideas* (London: George Allen and Unwin, 1962) pp. 166-78.

Schelsky, H. *Die Hoffnung. Blochs Kritik der marxistischen Existenzphilosophie eines Jugendbewegten* (Stuttgart: Klett-Cotta, 1979).

Schmidt, B. 'The Political Nature of Epistemological Categories: Introduction to Bloch', trans. G. Ellard, *Telos*, no. 21, Fall (1974) pp. 87-91.

Schubardt, W. 'Kritische Bemerkungen zu dem Buch "Subjekt-Objekt" von Ernst Bloch', *Einheit*, vol. 7, no. 6, (1952) p. 600 ff.

Solomon, M. 'Marx and Bloch: Reflections on Utopia and Art', *Telos*, no. 13, Fall (1972) pp. 68-85.

Sonnemans, H. *Hoffnung ohne Gott? In Konfrontation mit Ernst Bloch* (Freiburg-Basel-Wien: Herder, 1973).

Steinacker-Berghäuser, K-P. 'Das Verhältnis der Philosophie Ernst Blochs zur Mystik', Thesis, Philipps-Universität, Marburg/Lahn, 1973.

Tripp, G. M. *Absurdität und Hoffnung. Zum Werk von Albert Camus und Ernst Bloch* (Berlin: Ernst Reuter Gesellschaft, 1968).

Werckmeister, O. K. 'Ernst Blochs Theorie der Kunst' in *Die neue Rundschau*, vol. 79, no. 2 (1968) pp. 233–50.

Widmer P. *Die Anthropologie Ernst Blochs* (Frankfurt a. M.: Akademische Verlagsgesellschaft, 1974).

Wiegmann, H. *Ernst Blochs ästhetische Kriterien und ihre interpretative Funktion in seinen Literarischen Aufsätzen* (Bonn: Bouvier Verlag Herbert Grundmann, 1976).

Zecchi, S. *Utopia e speranza nel communismo. Un'interpretazione della prospettiva di Ernst Bloch* (Milan: Feltrinelli, 1974).

Works by Marx, Engels and Lenin

K. Marx and F. Engels, *Historisch-kritische Gesamtausgabe* (MEGA), ed. D. Rjazanov and V. Adoratskij (Frankfurt-Berlin-Moscow: Marx-Engels-Archiv Verlagsgesellschaft/Marx-Engels-Verlag, 1927--35).

K. Marx, *Letters to Kugelmann* (London: Martin Lawrence, 1934).

K. Marx and F. Engels, *Über Kunst und Literatur* (Berlin: Verlag Bruno Henschel und Sohn, 1950).

K. Marx, *Early Writings*, trans. and ed. T. Bottomore (London: C. A. Watts, 1963).

Writings of the Young Marx on Philosophy and Society, ed. L. D. Easton and K. H. Guddat (New York: Anchor Books, 1967).

K. Marx and F. Engels, *The German Ideology*, 2nd ed. English trans. (Moscow: Progress Publishers, 1968).

K. Marx, *The Poverty of Philosophy*, 3rd ed. English trans. (New York: International Publishers, 1969).

F. Engels, *Anti-Dühring*, 5th ed. English trans. (London: Lawrence and Wishart, 1969).

K. Marx and F. Engels, *Selected Works*, English trans., 3 vols (Moscow: Progress Publishers, 1969–70).

K. Marx, *Capital*, vol. I, trans. S. Moore and E. Aveling (London: Lawrence and Wishart, 1970).

K. Marx, *Critique of Hegel's Philosophy of Right*, trans. and ed. J. O'Malley (Cambridge University Press, 1970).

K. Marx, *Economic and Philosophic Manuscripts of 1844*, trans.

M. Milligan, ed. D. Struick (London: Lawrence and Wishart, 1970).

F. Engels, *Dialectics of Nature*, 5th ed. trans. C. Dutt (Moscow: Progress Publishers, 1972).

K. Marx, *Grundrisse*, trans. M. Nicolaus (Harmondsworth: Penguin Books, 1973).

K. Marx, *Texts on Method*, trans. and ed. T. Carver (Oxford: Basil Blackwell, 1975).

K. Marx and F. Engels, *Selected Correspondence*, trans. I. Lasker (Moscow: Progress Publishers, 1975).

K. Marx and F. Engels, *The Holy Family*, trans. R. Dixon and C. Dutt (Moscow: Progress Publishers, 1975).

K. Marx and F. Engels, *Collected Works*, var. trans. (London: Lawrence and Wishart, 1975-   ).

V. I. Lenin, *Selected Works*, one vol., English trans. (London: Lawrence and Wishart, 1968) especially 'Marxism and Revisionism', pp. 25–32; 'The State and Revolution', pp. 264–351.

V. I. Lenin, *Against Revisionism, in Defence of Marxism*, English trans. (Moscow: Progress Publishers, 1970).

V. I. Lenin, *Materialism and Empirio-Criticism*, English trans. (Moscow: Progress Publishers, 1970).

V. I. Lenin, *Philosophical Notebooks*, ed. S. Smith, trans. C. Dutt, *Collected Works*, vol. 38 (London: Lawrence and Wishart, 1972).

Other Works

Abbagnano, N. *Critical Existentialism*, ed. and trans. N. Langiulli (New York: Anchor Books, 1969).

Adorno, T. W. *Negative Dialectics*, trans. E. B. Ashton (London: Routledge and Kegan Paul, 1973).

Alexander, S. *Space, Time and Deity*, 2 vols (London: Macmillan, 1920).

Aliotta, A. *The Idealistic Reaction Against Science*, trans. A. McCaskill (London: Macmillan, 1914).

Althusser, L. *Lenin and Philosophy and Other Essays*, trans. B. Brewster (London: New Left Books, 1971).

Althusser, L. and Balibar, É. *Reading Capital*, trans. B. Brewster (London: New Left Books, 1970).

Alves, R. *A Theology of Human Hope* (Washington: Corpus Books, 1969).

Anderson, P. *Considerations on Western Marxism* (London: New Left Books, 1976).

Apel, K-O. *Transformation der Philosophie*, 2 vols (Frankfurt a. M.: Suhrkamp, 1976).

Arato, A. 'The Neo-Idealist Defence of Subjectivity' in *Telos*, no. 21, Fall (1974) pp. 108–61.

Arato, A. and Breines, P. *The Young Lukács and the Origins of Western Marxism* (London: Pluto Press, 1979).

Arvon, H. *Marxist Esthetics*, trans. H. R. Lane (Ithaca: Cornell University Press, 1973).

Attensperger, A. (ed.) *Jakob Frohschammers philosophisches System im Grundriss* (Zweibrücken, 1899).

Avineri, S. *Hegel's Theory of the Modern State*, (Cambridge University Press, 1972).

——, *The Social and Political Thought of Karl Marx,* (Cambridge University Press, 1968).

Axelos, K. *Marx, penseur de la technique. De l'aliénation de l'homme à la conquête du monde* (Paris: Ed. de Minuit, 1963).

Bartig, H-F. *Herbert Marcuses utopische Wirkung* (Hannover: H. Loebel, 1971).

Bauman, Z. *Socialism, the Active Utopia* (London: Allen and Unwin, 1976).

Baumgartner, H. M. (ed.) *Schelling* (Freiburg/Munich: Verlag Karl Alber, 1975).

Baxandall, L. *Marxism and Aesthetics: A Selective Annotated Bibliography* (New York: Humanities Press, 1968).

——, (ed.) *Radical Perspectives in the Arts* (Harmondsworth: Penguin, 1972).

Benjamin, W. *Briefe*, ed. G. Scholem and T. W. Adorno, 2 vols (Frankfurt a. M.: Suhrkamp, 1966).

——, *Gesammelte Schriften*, ed. R. Tiedemann and H. Schweppenhäuser, 4 vols (Frankfurt a. M.: Suhrkamp, 1972–77).

——, *Über Haschisch: Novellistisches, Berichte, Materialen*, ed. T. Rexroth (Frankfurt a. M.: Suhrkamp, 1972).

Bernstein, R. J. *The Restructuring of Social and Political Theory* (Oxford: Basil Blackwell, 1976).

Bhaskar, R. *A Realist Theory of Science* (Leeds: Leeds Books, 1975).

Biesterfeld, W. *Die literarische Utopie* (Stuttgart: J. B. Metzler, 1974).

Blondel, M. *L'Action* (Paris: Félix Alcan, 1893).

Boehmer, H. *Studien zu Thomas Müntzer* (Leipzig, 1922).

Bollnow, O. *Das Verhältnis zur Zeit* (Heidelberg: Quelle und Meyer O. J., 1972).

Bonino, J. M. *Christians and Marxists. The Mutual Challenge to Revolution* (London: Hodder and Stoughton, 1976).

Bossle, L. *Utopie und Wirklichkeit im politischen Denken von Reinhold Schneider* (Mainz: Hase and Koehler Verlag, 1965).

Bracken, J. A. *Freiheit und Kausalität bei Schelling* (Freiburg/ Munich: Verlag Karl Alber, 1972).

Broad, C. D. *Leibniz, An Introduction,* ed. C. Lewy (Cambridge University Press, 1975).

Brown, D., James, R. E. and Reeves, G. (ed.) *Process Philosophy and Christian Thought* (Indianapolis and New York: Bobbs-Merrill, 1971).

Brown, R. F. *The Later Philosophy of Schelling. The Influence of Boehme on the Works of 1809-1815* (London: Associated University Presses, 1977).

Buber, M. *Paths in Utopia*, trans. R. F. C. Hull (London: Routledge and Kegan Paul, 1949).

Bubner, R., Cramer, K. and Wiehl R. (ed.). *Hermeneutik und Dialektik,* 2 vols (Tübingen: J. C. B. Mohr (Paul Siebeck), 1970).

Buck-Morss, S. *The Origin of Negative Dialectics. Theodor W. Adorno, Walter Benjamin and the Frankfurt Institute* (Sussex: Harvester Press, 1977).

Bultmann, D. Rudolf. *History and Eschatology* (Edinburgh: The University Press, 1957).

Calian, C. S. *Berdyaev's Philosophy of Hope* (Leiden: E. J. Brill, 1968).

Čapek, M. *The Philosophical Impact of Contemporary Physics* (Princeton: D. Van Nostrand, 1961).

——, 'Simple Location and Fragmentation of Reality', *The Monist,* vol. 48, no. 2, April (1964) pp. 195-218.

Chiodi, P. *Sartre and Marxism*, trans. K. Soper (Sussex: The Harvester Press, 1976).

Chisholm, R. M. (ed.) *Realism and the Background of Phenomenology* (Illinois: The Free Press of Glencoe, 1960).

Cohen, G. A. *Karl Marx's Theory of History: A Defence* (Oxford: Clarendon Press, 1978).

Cohn, N. *The Pursuit of the Millennium* (London: Secker and Warburg, 1957).

Colletti, L. *Marxism and Hegel*, trans. L. Garner (London: New Left Books, 1973).

Cournand, A. and Lévy, M. (ed.) *Shaping the Future, Gaston Berger and the Concept of Prospective* (London: Gordon and Breach Science Publishers, 1973).

Darnoi, D. N. K. *The Unconscious and Eduard von Hartmann. A Historico-Critical Monograph* (The Hague: Martinus Nijhoff, 1967).

Deák, I. *Weimar Germany's Left-Wing Intellectuals* (Berkeley and Los Angeles: University of California Press, 1968).

De Brabander, R. F. *Religion and Human Autonomy, Henry Duméry's Philosophy of Christianity* (The Hague: Martinus Nijhoff, 1972).

Deeken, A. *Process and Permanence in Ethics: Max Scheler's Moral Philosophy* (New York: Paulist Press, 1974).

Desan, W. *The Marxism of Jean-Paul Sartre* (New York: Anchor 1966).

Dickson, K. A. *Towards Utopia: A Study of Brecht* (Oxford: Clarendon Press, 1978).

Duméry, H. *Le problème de Dieu en philosophie de la religion* (Bruges: Desclée de Brouwer, 1957).

Durfee, H. A. (ed.) *Analytical Philosophy and Phenomenology* (The Hague: Martinus Nijhoff, 1976).

Eagleton, T. *Criticism and Ideology. A Study in Marxist Literary Theory* (London: New Left Books, 1976).

Edmaier, A. *Horizonte der Hoffnung* (Regensburg: Pustet, 1968).

Elliston, F. and McCormick, P. (ed.) *Husserl. Expositions and Appraisals* (London: University of Notre Dame Press, 1977).

Fehér, F. 'The Last Phase of Romantic Anti-Capitalism: Lukács' Response to the War', trans. J. Wikoff, *New German Critique*, no. 10, Winter (1977) pp. 139–54.

Fetscher, I. *Karl Marx und der Marxismus* (Munich: R. Piper Verlag, 1967).

Figal, G. *Theodor W. Adorno. Das Naturschöne als spekulative Gedankenfigur* (Bonn: Bouvier Verlag Herbert Grundmann, 1977).

Findlay, J. N. *Meinong's Theory of Objects* (London: Oxford University Press, 1933).

Fischer, E. *Art Against Ideology*, trans. A. Bostock (London: Allen Lane The Penguin Press, 1969).

Fitzgerald, R. (ed.) *The Sources of Hope* (London: Pergamon, 1979).

Fleischer, H. *Marxism and History*, trans. E. Mosbacher (New York: Harper and Row, 1973).

Flores, J. *Poetry in East Germany* (London: Yale University Press, 1971).

Fougeyrollas, P. *marx, freud et la révolution totale* (Paris: éditions anthropos, 1972).

Frank, M. *Der unendliche Mangel an Sein; Schellings Hegelkritik und die Anfänge der Marxschen Dialektik* (Frankfurt a. M.: Suhrkamp, 1975).

Frank, M. and Kurz, G. (ed.) *Materialen zu Schellings philosophischen Anfängen* (Frankfurt a. M.: Suhrkamp, 1975).

Fraser, J. *An Introduction to the thought of Galvano della Volpe* (London: Lawrence and Wishart, 1977).

Friesen, A. 'Thomas Müntzer in Marxist Thought', *Church History*, vol. XXXIV, no. 3, Sept. (1965) pp. 306–27.

Frohschammer, J. *Die Phantasie als Grundprincip des Weltprocesses (sic)* (Munich: Theodor Achermann, 1877).

Fuhrmans, H. *Schellings letzte Philosophie. Die negative und positive Philosophie im Einsatz des Spätidealismus* (Berlin: Junker und Dünnhaupt Verlag, 1940).

Furter, P. *L'imagination créatrice, la violence et le changement social* (Cuernavaca: CIDOC cuarderno, 14, 1968).

Gale, R. M. (ed.) *The Philosophy of Time* (London: Macmillan, 1968).

Gallas, H. *Marxistische Literaturtheorie* (Neuwied/Berlin: Luchterhand, 1971).

Gardavsky, V. *God is Not Yet Dead*, trans. V. Menkes (Harmondsworth: Penguin, 1973).

Gerhards, H-J. *Utopie als innergeschichtlicher Aspekt der Eschatologie* (Gütersloh: Gütersloher Verlagshaus Gerd Mohn, 1973).

Goldmann, L. *Lukács and Heidegger*, trans. W. Q. Boelhower (London: Routledge and Kegan Paul, 1977).

Goode, P. *Karl Korsch. A Study in Western Marxism* (London: Macmillan, 1979).

Goodwin, B. *Social Science and Utopia* (Sussex: Harvester Press, 1978).

Gould, C. C. *Marx's Social Ontology* (London: The MIT Press, 1978).

Gramer, W. *Musik und Verstehen. Eine Studie zur Musikästhetik Theodor W. Adornos* (Mainz: Matthias-Grünewald-Verlag, 1976).

Gray, D. P. *The One and the Many, Teilhard de Chardin's Vision of Unity* (London: Burns and Oates, 1969).

Gutiérrez, G. *A Theology of Liberation*, trans. and ed. Sister Caridad Inda and John Eagleson (Maryknoll: Orbis, 1973).

Habermas, J. *Theory and Praxis*, trans. J. Viertel (London: Heinemann, 1974).

——, *Zur Rekonstruktion des Historischen Materialismus* (Frankfurt a. M.: Suhrkamp, 1976).

Halfmann, J. and Rexroth, T. *Marxismus als Erkenntniskritik* (Munich/Vienna: Carl Hanser Verlag, 1976).

Haller, R. (ed.) *Jenseits von Sein und Nichtsein. Beiträge zur Meinong-Forschung* (Graz: Akademische Verlagsanstalt, 1972).

Harris, H. S. *Hegel's Development* (Oxford: Clarendon Press, 1972).

Hartmann, E. von. *Geschichte der Metaphysik*, pt. II Ausgewählte Werke, vol. 12 (Leipzig: Hermann Haacke, 1900).

——, *Das Grundproblem der Erkenntnisstheorie (sic)* (Leipzig: Verlag von Wilhelm Friedrich, 1889).

——, *Philosophy of the Unconscious*, trans. W. C. Coupland (London: Kegan Paul, Trench, Trubner, 1931).

——, *Schellings philosophisches System* (Leipzig: Hermann Haacke, 1897).

——, *Schellings positive Philosophie als Einheit von Hegel und Schopenhauer* (Berlin: Otto Loewenstein, 1869).

Hartmann, K. *Die Marxsche Theorie* (Berlin: Walter de Gruyter, 1970).

Hartmann, N. *Möglichkeit und Wirklichkeit* (Berlin: de Gruyter, 1938).

Hayner, P. C. *Reason and Existence, Schelling's Philosophy of History* (Leiden: E. J. Brill, 1967).

Hazard, S. (ed.) *Soviet Legal Philosophy* (Cambridge, Mass.: Harvard University Press, 1951).

Hegel, G. W. F. *Early Theology Writings*, trans. T. M. Knox and fragments trans. and intro. R. Kroner (Chicago: University of Chicago Press, 1948).

——, *Hegel's Philosophy of Right*, trans. with notes by T. M. Knox (Oxford: Clarendon Press, 1973).

——, *The Phenomenology of Spirit*, trans. A. V. Miller (Oxford: Clarendon Press, 1977).

——, *Sämtliche Werke*, ed. J. Hoffmeister (Hamburg: Felix Meiner, 1952-60).

Heidegger, M. *Being and Time*, trans. J. Macquarrie and E. Robinson (Oxford: Basil Blackwell, 1967).

Heller, A. *The Theory of Need in Marx* (London: Allison and Busby, 1974).

Hintikka, J. *Time and Necessity Studies in Aristotle's Theory of Modality* (Oxford: Clarendon Press, 1973).

Horster, D. *Die Subjekt-Objekt-Beziehung im Deutschen Idealismus und in der Marxschen Philosophie* (Frankfurt: Campus Verlag, 1979).

Hörz, H. and Iljin, A. J. (ed.) *Der dialektische Materialismus und seine Kritiker* (Berlin: VEB Deutscher Verlag der Wissenschaften, 1975).

Howard, D. *The Marxian Legacy* (London: Macmillan, 1977).

Howard, D. and Klare K. (ed.) *The Unknown Dimension: European Marxism Since Lenin* (New York: Basic Books, 1972).

Iovchuk, M. *Philosophical Traditions Today* (Moscow: Progress Publishers, 1973).

Jähnig, D. *Schelling. Die Kunst in der Philosophie*, 2 vols (Pfullingen: Neske, 1969).

Jameson, F. *Marxism and Form, Twentieth-Century Dialectical Theories of Literature* (New Jersey: Princeton University Press, 1971).

Jaspers, K. *Philosophical Faith and Revelation*, trans. E. B. Ashton (London: Collins, 1967).

Jay, M. 'The Concept of Totality in Lukács and Adorno', *Telos*, no. 32, Summer (1977) pp. 117-37.

——, *The Dialectical Imagination* (London: Heinemann, 1974).

——, 'The Extraterritorial Life of Siegfried Kracauer', *Salmagundi*, no. 31-32, Fall (1975)-Winter (1976) pp. 49-106.

——, 'The Metapolitics of Utopianism', *Dissent*, XVII, no. 4, July–August (1970), reprinted in G. Fischer (ed.) *The Revival of American Socialism* (New York: Oxford University Press, 1971) pp. 244-56.

Johnson, W. A. *The Search for Transcendence* (New York: Harper and Row, 1974).

Jones, G. S. *et al. Western Marxism A Critical Reader* (London: New Left Books, 1977).

Jordan, Z. A. *The Evolution of Dialectical Materialism* (London: Macmillan, 1967).

Jüngel, E. *Gott als Geheimnis der Welt,* 3rd ed. (Tübingen: J. C. B. Mohr (Paul Siebeck), 1978).

Kaiser, H. H. *Subjekt und Gesellschaft. Studie zum Begriff der Utopie* (Frankfurt a. M.: 1960).

Kamenka, E. *Marxism and Ethics* (London: Macmillan, 1969).

——, *The Philosophy of Ludwig Feuerbach* (London: Routledge and Kegan Paul, 1970).

Kamlah, W. *Utopie, Eschatologie, Geschichtsteleologie* (Mannheim: Bibliogr. Inst., Hochschultaschenbücher-Verlag, 1969).

Kee, A. (ed.) *A Reader in Political Theology* (London: S.C.M., 1974).

Királyfalvi, B. *The Aesthetics of György Lukács* (New Jersey: Princeton University Press, 1975).

Klemperer, K. von *Germany's New Conservatism* (New Jersey: Princeton University Press, 1968).

Kline, G. L. (ed.) *Alfred North Whitehead: Essays on his Philosophy* (Englewood Cliffs, Prentice-Hall, 1963).

Kline, G. L. 'Leszek Kołakowski and the Revision of Marxism', in G. L. Kline (ed.), *European Philosophy Today* (Chicago: Quadrangle Books, 1965) pp. 113-56.

Klum, E. *Natur, Kunst und Liebe in der Philosophie Vladimir Solov'evs* (Dissertation) (Munich: Otto Sagner, 1965).

Koktanek, A. M. *Schellings Seinslehre und Kierkegaard* (Munich: R. Oldenbourg, 1962).

Kołakowski, L. *Husserl and the Search for Certitude* (Newhaven and London: Yale University Press, 1975).

——, *Main Currents of Marxism,* 3 vols. trans. P. S. Falla (Oxford: Clarendon Press, 1978).

Korsch, K. *Marxism and Philosophy*, trans. S. Halliday (London: New Left Books, 1970).

Kosík, K. *Dialectics of the Concrete*, trans. K. Kovanda and J. Schmidt (Dordrecht: D. Reidel, 1976).

Koyré, A. *La philosophie de Jacob Boehme* (Paris: Librairie Philosophique J. Vrin, 1929).

Krieger, E. *Grenzwege. Das Konkrete in Reflexion und Geschichte von Hegel bis Bloch* (Freiburg/Munich: Alber, 1968).

Krysmanski, H. J. *Die utopische Methode* (Cologne and Opladen: Westdeutscher Verlag, 1963).

Kutzbach, K. A. (ed.) *Paul Ernst und Georg Lukács. Dokumente einer Freundschaft* (Düsseldorf: Paul Ernst Gesellschaft, 1973-4).

Labedz, L. (ed.) *Revisionism. Essays on the History of Marxist Ideas* (London: George Allen and Unwin, 1962).

Lasky, M. J. *Utopia and Revolution* (London: Macmillan, 1976).

Leeuwen, A. T. van *Critique of Earth* (London: Lutterworth, 1974).

——, *Critique of Heaven* (London: Lutterworth, 1972).

Lefebvre, H. F. *Marx: sa vie, son oeuvre* (Paris: Presses universitaires de France, 1964).

Lieblich, A. *Between Ideology and Utopia. The Politics and Philosophy of August Cieszkowski* (Dordrecht: D. Reidel, 1978).

Lifschitz, M. *The Philosophy of Art of Karl Marx*, trans. R. B. Winn (London: Pluto Press, 1973).

Lindner, B. (ed.) *Text + Kritik. Walter Benjamin* (Munich: Richard Boerberg, 1971).

Lipps, T. *Vom Fühlen, Wollen und Denken*, 3rd ed. (Leipzig: Johann Ambrosius Barth, 1926).

Lochmann, J. M. *Christus oder Prometheus?* (Hamburg: Furch Verlag, 1972).

Loemker, L. E. 'On Substance and Process in Leibniz', in W. L. Reese and E. Freeman (ed.), *Process and Divinity: The Hartshorne Festschrift* (La Salle: Open Court, 1964) pp. 403-25.

Loer, B. *Das Absolute und die Wirklichkeit in Schellings Philosophie* (Berlin: de Gruyter, 1974).

Löwy, M. *George Lukács: From Romanticism to Bolshevism* (London: New Left Books, 1979),

Lukács, G. 'The Dialectic of Labor. Beyond Causality and Teleology', trans. A. W. Grucinski, *Telos*, no. 6, Fall, (1970) pp. 162-74.

——, *Hegel's False and His Genuine Ontology*, trans. D. Fernbach (London: Merlin Press, 1978).

——, *History and Class Consciousness*, trans. R. Livingstone (London: Merlin Press, 1971).

——, *Marx's Basic Ontological Principles*, trans. D. Fernbach (London: Merlin Press, 1978).

——, *The Meaning of Contemporary Realism*, trans. J. and N. Mander (London: Merlin Press, 1963).

——, *Political Writings, 1919-1929*, ed. R. Livingstone, trans. M. McColgan (London: New Left Books, 1972).

——, *Soul and Form*, trans. A. Bostock (London: Merlin Press, 1974).

——, *The Theory of the Novel*, trans. A. Bostock (London: Merlin Press, 1971).

——, *The Young Hegel*, trans. R. Livingstone (Merlin Press: London, 1975).

Mannheim, K. *Ideology and Utopia*, trans. L. Wirth and E. Shils (London: Routledge & Kegan Paul, 1976).

Manuel, F. E. (ed.), *Utopias and Utopian Thought* (London: Souvenir Press, 1973).

Mao Tse-tung *Mao Tse-tung Unrehearsed*, ed. and intro. S. Schram, trans. J. Chinnery and Tieyun (Harmondsworth: Penguin, 1974).

Marcel, G. *Homo Viator*, trans. E. Craufurd (New York: Harper and Row, 1962).

Marcuse, H. *Five Lectures: Psychoanalysis, Politics and Utopia*, trans. J. J. Shapiro and S. M. Weber (London: Allen Lane The Penguin Press, 1970) ch. 4.

——, *Negations, Essays in Critical Theory*, trans. J. J. Shapiro (London: Allen Lane The Penguin Press, 1968).

——, *Reason and Revolution*, 2nd ed. (London, Routledge and Kegan Paul, 1969).

Marković, M. *The Contemporary Marx — Essays on Humanist Communism* (Nottingham: Spokesman Books, 1974).

Marković, M. and Cohen, R. S. *Yugoslavia: The Rise and Fall of Socialist Humanism* (Nottingham: Spokesman Books, 1975).

McAlister, L. (ed.) *The Philosophy of Brentano* (London: Duckworth, 1976).

McInnis, N. *The Western Marxists* (London: Alcove Press, 1972).

McLellan, D. *Karl Marx: His Life and Thought* (London: Macmillan, 1973).

——, *Marx Before Marxism* (London: Macmillan, 1970).

——, *The Young Hegelians and Karl Marx* (London: Macmillan, 1969).

McNeill, J. J. *The Blondelian Synthesis* (Leiden: E. J. Brill, 1966).

Macquarrie, J. *Christian Hope* (Oxford: Mowbrays, 1978).

——, *Twentieth-Century Religious Thought* (London: S.C.M., 1963).

Meeks, M. D. *Origins of the Theology of Hope* (Philadelphia: Fortress Press, 1974).

Mehta, J. L. *The Philosophy of Martin Heidegger*, revised ed. (New York: Harper and Row, 1971).

Meinong, A. *Über Möglichkeit und Wahrscheinlichkeit* (Leipzig: Johann Ambrosius Barth, 1915).

Merleau-Ponty, M. *Adventures of the Dialectic*, trans. J. Bien (London: Heinemann, 1974).

Mészáros, I. (ed.) *Aspects of History and Class Consciousness* (London: Routledge and Kegan Paul, 1971).

——, *Lukács' Concept of Dialectic* (London: Merlin, 1972).

——, *Marx's Theory of Alienation* (London: Merlin, 1970).

Metz, J. *Theology of the World*, trans. W. Glen-Doepel (London: Burns and Oates, 1969).

Miranda, J. *Marx and the Bible*, trans. J. Eagleson (Maryknoll, N.Y.: Orbis Books, 1974).

Mohler, A. *Die Konservative Revolution in Deutschland 1918-32 (sic)* (Stuttgart: Friedrich Vorwerk Verlag, 1950).

Moltmann, J. *The Experiment Hope*, ed. trans., with a foreword by M. D. Meeks (Philadelphia: Fortress Press, 1975).

——, *Man. Christian Anthropology in the Conflicts of the Present*, trans. J. Sturdy (London: S.P.C.K, 1974).

——, *Religion, Revolution and the Future*, trans. M. D. Meeks (New York: Charles Scribner's Sons, 1969).

——, *A Theology of Hope*, trans. J. W. Leitch (London: S.C.M., 1967).

Mosse, G. L. *Germans and Jews* (New York: Howard Fertig, 1970).

Muck, O. (S. J.) *The Transcendental Method*, trans. W. D. Seidensticker (New York: Herder and Herder, 1968).

Müller, L. *Das religionsphilosophische System Vladimir Solovjevs* (Berlin: Evangelische Verlagsanstalt, 1956).

Münz, B. *Jakob Frohschammer, der Philosoph der Weltphantasie* (Breslau: 1894).

Murray, M. (ed.) *Heidegger and Modern Philosophy* (London: Yale University Press, 1978).

Neusüss, A. (ed.) *Utopie: Begriff und Phänomen des Utopischen* (Neuwied und Berlin: Luchterhand, 1968).

The New Hungarian Quarterly, 'In Memoriam György Lukács (1885-1971)', vol. XIII, no. 47, Autumn (1972).

O'Collins, G. *Man and His New Hopes* (New York, 1969).

Oliver, H. H. 'Hope and Knowledge: The Epistemic Status of Religious Language' in *Cultural Hermeneutics,* 2:1 (May, 1974) pp. 75-88.

Ollman, B. *Alienation: Marx's Conception of Man in Capitalist Society* (Cambridge University Press, 1975).

——, 'Marx's Vision of Communism: A Reconstruction' in *Critique*, no. 8, Summer (1976) pp. 4-41.

O'Neill, J. (ed.) *On Critical Theory* (London: Heinemann, 1977).

Paci, E. *The Function of the Sciences and the Meaning of Man,* trans. P. Piccone and J. E. Hansen (Evanston, Northwestern University Press, 1972).

Pannenberg, W. *Basic Questions in Theology*, vol. 2, trans. G. H. Kehm (London: S.C.M., 1971).

Parkinson, G. H. R. (ed.) *Georg Lukács The Man, his work and his ideas* (London: Weidenfeld and Nicolson, 1970).

——, *Logic and Reality in Leibniz's Metaphysics* (Oxford: Clarendon Press, 1965).

Pelczynski, Z. A. (ed.) *Hegel's Political Philosophy* (Cambridge University Press, 1971).

Philosophy in the USSR, Problems of Dialectical Materialism, trans. R. Daglish (Moscow: Progress Publishers, 1977).

Pieper, J. *Hope and History*, trans. R. and C. Winston (London: Burns and Oates, 1969).

Pinkus, T. (ed.) *Conversations with Lukács* trans. D. Fernbach (London: Merlin Press, 1974).

Plattel, M. G. *Utopian and Critical Thinking* (Pittsburgh: Duquesne University Press, 1972).

Pöggeler, O. *Der Denkweg Martin Heideggers* (Pfullingen: Neske, 1963).

Polak, F. L. *The Image of the Future*, 2 vols, trans. E. Boulding (Leyden: A. W. Sythoff, 1961).

——, *Prognostics* (London: Elsevier, 1971) (trans. of abridged ed. of *Prognostica* (Deventer: A. E. Kluwer, 1969).

Popper, K. *The Open Society and its Enemies*, vol. I (London: Routledge and Kegan Paul, 1962).

Poster, M. *Existential Marxism in Postwar France* (New Jersey: Princeton University Press, 1975).

Raddatz, F-J. (ed.) *Marxismus und Literatur*, vol. II (Reinbek b. Hamburg: Rowohlt, 1969).

Reese, W. L. and Freeman, E. (ed.) *Process and Divinity: The Hartshorne Fetschrift* (La Salle: Open Court, 1964).

Rescher, N. *Conceptual Idealism* (Oxford: Basil Blackwell, 1973).

Richardson, D. B. *Berdyaev's Philosophy of History* (The Hague: Martinus Nijhoff, 1968).

Richardson, W. J. (S. J.) *Heidegger, Through Phenomenology to Thought* (The Hague: Martinus Nijhoff, 1974).

Ricoeur, P. *The Conflict of Interpretations*, ed. Don Ihda (Evanston: Northwestern University Press, 1974).

Rideau, É. *La pensée du Père Teilhard de Chardin* (Paris: Éditions du Seuil, 1965).

Ringer, F. *The Decline of the German Mandarins. The German*

276 *The Marxist Philosophy of Ernst Bloch*

Academic Community 1890-1933 (Cambridge, Mass.: Harvard University Press, 1969).

Rintelen, F-J. von *Contemporary German Philosophy and its Background* (Bonn: Bouvier, 1970).

Roberts, L. *The Achievement of Karl Rahner* (New York: Herder and Herder, 1967).

Romanell, P. *The Making of the Mexican Mind* (Notre Dame: University of Notre Dame Press, 1967).

Rose, G. *The Melancholy Science. An Introduction to the Thought of Theodor W. Adorno* (London: Macmillan, 1978).

Rosen, S. G. W. F. *Hegel* (New Haven: Yale University Press, 1974).

Rotenstreich, N. *From Substance to Subject. Studies in Hegel* (The Hague: Martinus Nijhoff, 1974).

Rubel, M. 'Reflections on Utopia and Revolution', trans. J. Malaquais, in Erich Fromm (ed.), *Socialist Humanism* (London: Allen Lane The Penguin Press, 1967) pp. 192-9.

Ruben, D-H. *Marxism and Materialism. A Study in Marxist Theory of Knowledge* (Sussex: The Harvester Press, 1977).

Ruyer, R. *L'Utopie et les utopies* (Paris: Presses universitaires de France, 1950).

Sander, H-D. *Marxistische Ideologie und allgemeine Kunsttheorie* (Tübingen: J. C. B. Mohr (Paul Siebeck), 1970).

Sartre, J-P. *The Psychology of Imagination*, English trans. (London: Methuen, 1972).

Sauter, G. *Zukunft und Verheissung. Das Problem der Zukunft in der gegenwärtigen theologischen und philosophischen Diskussion* (Zürich/Stuttgart: Zwingli Verlag, 1965).

Schaeffler, R. *Was dürfen wir hoffen* (Darmstadt: Wissenschaftliche Buchgesellschaft, 1979) pt. II.

Schelling, F. W. J. von *The Ages of the World*, trans. and intro. by F. de Wolfe Bolman, Jr (New York: Columbia University Press, 1942).

——, *Initia Philosophiae Universae*, Erlanger Vorlesung WS 1820/21, ed. H. Fuhrmans (Bonn: H. Bouvier, 1969).

——, *Sämmtliche Werke*, 14 vols in two divisions, ed. K. F. A. Schelling (Stuttgart and Augsburg: J. G. Cotta, 1856-61).

Schlant, E. *Die Philosophie Hermann Brochs* (Bern/Munich: Francke Verlag, 1971).

Schmidt, A. *The Concept of Nature in Marx*, trans. B. Fowkes (London: New Left Books, 1971).

——, *Geschichte und Struktur. Fragen einer marxistischen Historik* (Munich: Hanser, 1971).

——, *Die kritische Theorie als Geschichtsphilosophie* (Munich/Wien: Hanser, 1976).

Schmidt, F. W. *Zum Begriff der Negativität bei Schelling und Hegel* (Stuttgart: J. B. Metzler, 1971).

Schmitt, H-J. (ed.) *Die Expressionismusdebatte. Materialien zu einer marxistischen Realismuskonzeption* (Frankfurt a. M.: Suhrkamp, 1976).

Scholem, G. *On Jews and Judaism in Crisis*, ed. W. J. Dannhauser (New York: Schocken Books, 1976).

——, *Walter Benjamin — Die Geschichte einer Freundschaft* (Frankfurt a. M.: Suhrkamp, 1975).

Schroyer, T. *A Critique of Domination: The Origins and Development of Critical Theory* (New York: Braziller, 1973).

Schulz, W. *Die Vollendung des deutschen Idealismus in der Spätphilosophie Schellings* (Pfullingen: Neske, 1975).

Sève, L. *Man in Marxist Theory and the Psychology of Personality*, trans. J. McGreal (Sussex: Harvester, 1978).

Shklar, J. N. *After Utopia* (New Jersey: Princeton University Press, 1957).

Simmel, G. *Brücke und Tür,* ed. M. Landmann (Stuttgart: Koehler, 1957).

——, *Fragmente und Aufsätze*, ed. G. Kantorowicz (Munich: Drei Masken Verlag, 1923).

Slater, P. *Origin and Significance of the Frankfurt School* (London: Routledge and Kegan Paul, 1977).

Sohn-Rethel, A. *Intellectual and Manual Labour, a Critique of Epistemology,* trans. M. Sohn-Rethel (London: Macmillan, 1978).

Steele, J. *Socialism with a German Face. The State that came in from the Cold* (London: Jonathan Cape, 1977).

Stern, F. *The Politics of Cultural Despair. A Study in the Rise of German Ideology* (Berkeley: University of California Press, 1961).

Stiernotte, A. P. 'Process Philosophies and Mysticism', *Int. Phil. Quarterly*, vol. IX, no. 4, Dec. (1969) pp. 560–71.

Suchkov, B. *A History of Realism* (Moscow: Progress Publishers, 1973).

Szabó, I. *et al.. The Socialist Concept of Human Rights*, trans. J. Decsényi and G. Pulay, rev. trans. I. Móra (Budapest: Akadémiai Kiadó, 1966).

Talmon, J. *Political Messianism: The Romantic Phase* (London: Secker and Warburg, 1960).

Taylor, C. *Hegel* (Cambridge University Press, 1975).

Taylor, R. (trans. ed.) *Aesthetics and Politics* (London: New Left Books, 1977).

Therborn, G. 'A Critique of the Frankfurt School', *New Left Review,* no. 63, Sept.–Oct. (1970) pp. 65–96.

Theunissen, M. *Hegels Lehre vom absoluten Geist als theologischpolitischer Traktat* (Berlin: Walter de Gruyter, 1970).

——, *Sein und Schein. Die kritische Funktion der Hegelschen Logik* (Frankfurt a. M.: Suhrkamp, 1978).

Tiedemann, R. *Studien zur Philosophie Walter Benjamins,* Frankfurter Beiträge zur Soziologie, vol. 16 (Frankfurt a. M.: Europäische Verlagsanstalt, 1965).

Tumanov, V. A. *Contemporary Bourgeois Legal Thought,* trans. J. Gibbons (Moscow: Progress Publishers, 1974).

Vásquez, A. S. *Art and Society Essays in Marxist Aesthetics* trans. M. Riofrancos (London: Monthly Review Press, 1973).

Vranicki, P. *Geschichte des Marxismus,* 2 vols (Frankfurt a. M.: Suhrkamp, 1972–74).

Wakeman, F. Jr *History and Will. Philosophical Perspectives of Mao Tse-tung's Thought* (Berkeley: University of California Press, 1973).

Weber, M. *Max Weber: Ein Lebensbild* (Tübingen: J. C. B. Mohr (Paul Siebeck), 1926).

Weingartner, R. H. *Experience and Culture: The Philosophy of George Simmel* (Middletown, Conn.: Wesleyan University Press, 1962).

Wetter, G. *Dialectical Materialism,* trans. P. Heath (London: Routledge and Kegan Paul, 1958).

White, A. R. *Modal Thinking* (Oxford: Basil Blackwell, 1978).

Wild, C. *Reflexion und Erfahrung. Eine Interpretation der Früh- und Spätphilosophie Schellings* (Symposion, 25) (Freiburg/Munich: Verlag Karl Alber, 1968).

Willett, J. *Expressionism* (London: World University Library, 1970).

Wyschogrod, E. *Emmanuel Levinas, The Problem of Ethical Metaphysics* (The Hague: Martinus Nijhoff, 1974).

Index